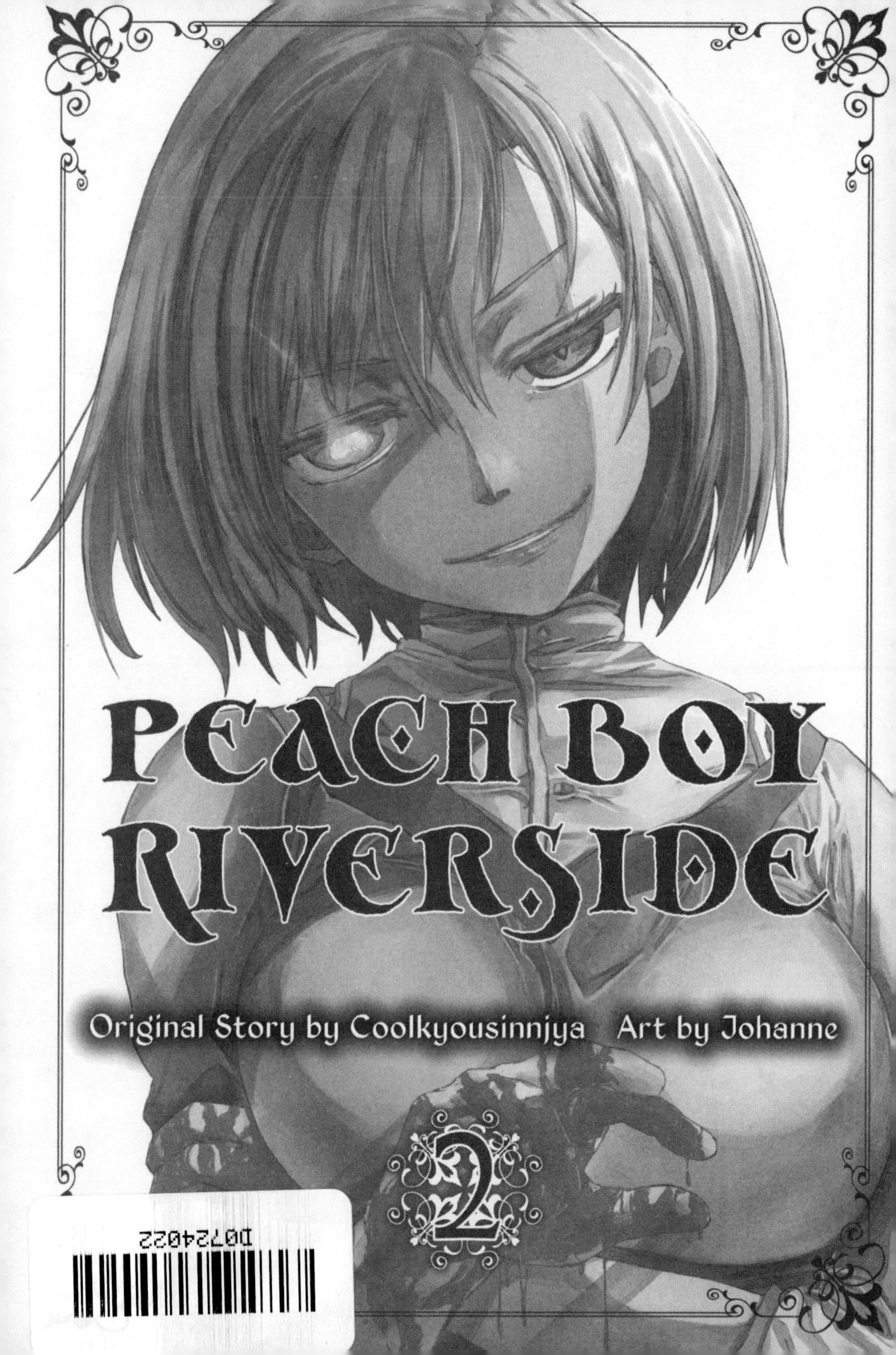

PEACH BOY RIVERSIDE

Original Story by Coolkyousinnjya Art by Johanne

2

CONTENTS

CHAPTER 4:
SMILES AND IMPULSES

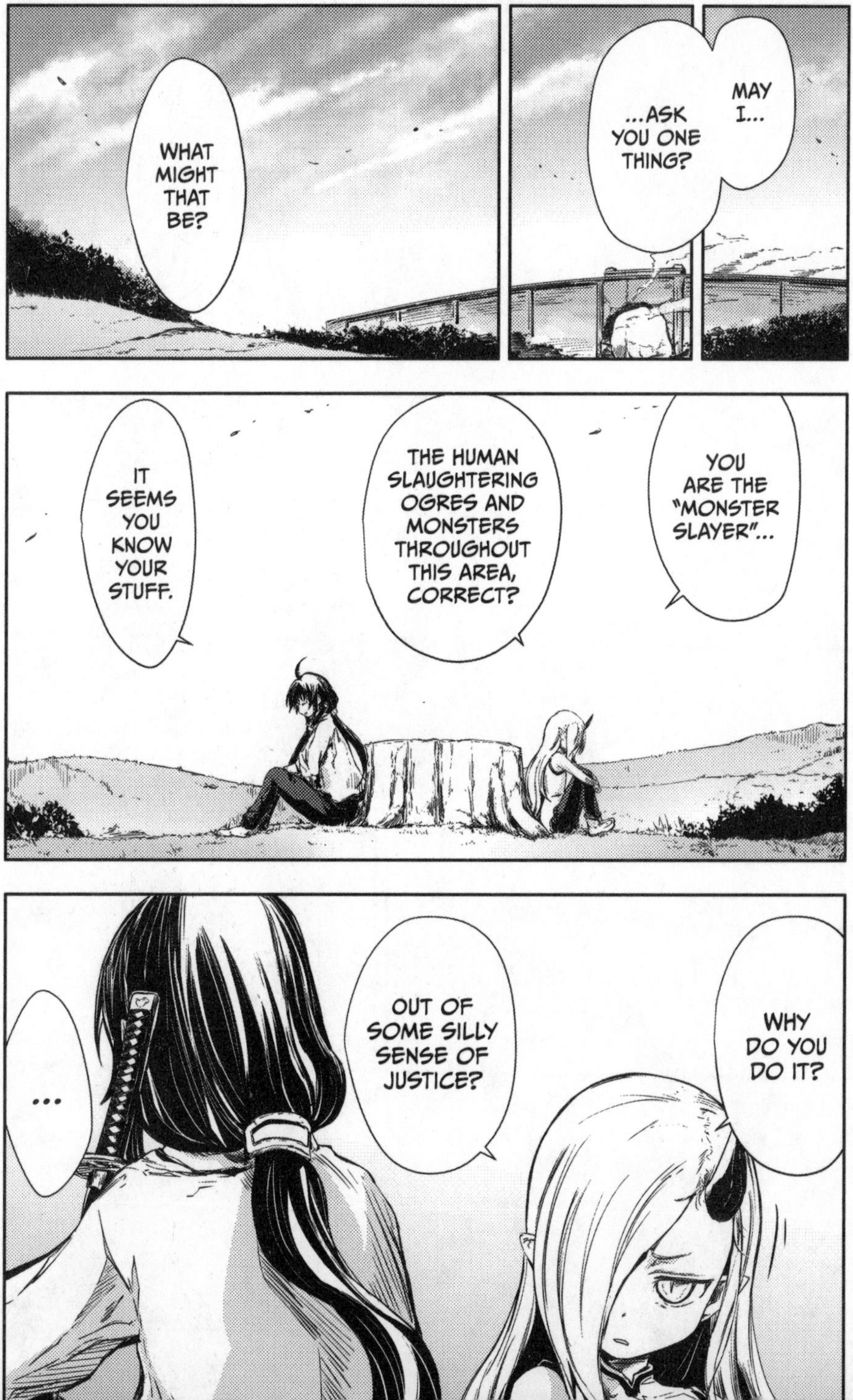
MAY I...
...ASK YOU ONE THING?
WHAT MIGHT THAT BE?
YOU ARE THE "MONSTER SLAYER"...
THE HUMAN SLAUGHTERING OGRES AND MONSTERS THROUGHOUT THIS AREA, CORRECT?
IT SEEMS YOU KNOW YOUR STUFF.
WHY DO YOU DO IT?
OUT OF SOME SILLY SENSE OF JUSTICE?
...

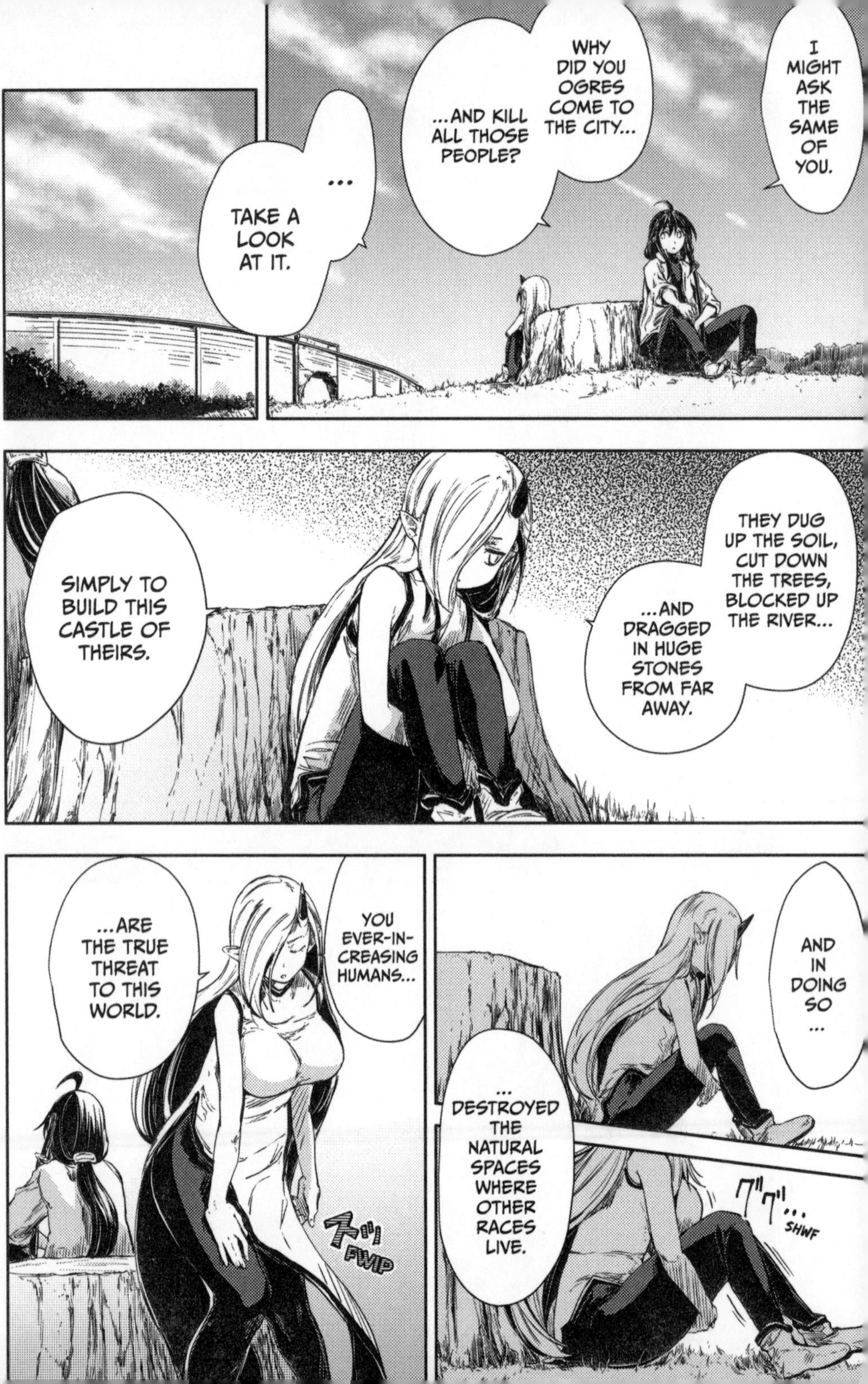

I MIGHT ASK THE SAME OF YOU.
WHY DID YOU OGRES COME TO THE CITY...
...AND KILL ALL THOSE PEOPLE?
...
TAKE A LOOK AT IT.
THEY DUG UP THE SOIL, CUT DOWN THE TREES, BLOCKED UP THE RIVER...
...AND DRAGGED IN HUGE STONES FROM FAR AWAY.
SIMPLY TO BUILD THIS CASTLE OF THEIRS.
AND IN DOING SO ...
... DESTROYED THE NATURAL SPACES WHERE OTHER RACES LIVE.
SHWF
YOU EVER-IN-CREASING HUMANS...
...ARE THE TRUE THREAT TO THIS WORLD.
FWIP

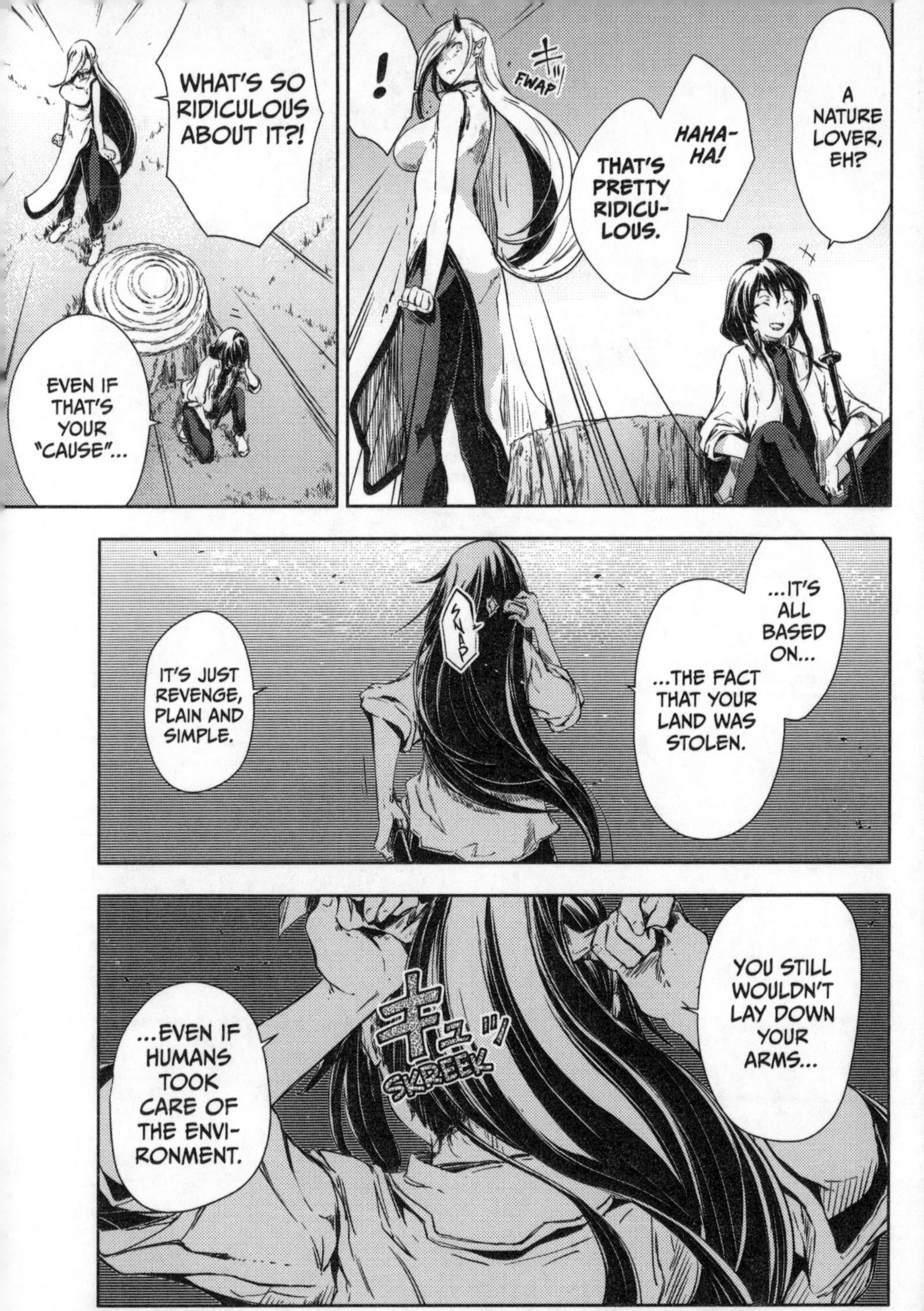
A NATURE LOVER, EH?
HAHA-HA!
THAT'S PRETTY RIDICULOUS.
FWAP
!
WHAT'S SO RIDICULOUS ABOUT IT?!
EVEN IF THAT'S YOUR "CAUSE"...
...IT'S ALL BASED ON...
...THE FACT THAT YOUR LAND WAS STOLEN.
SNAP
IT'S JUST REVENGE, PLAIN AND SIMPLE.
YOU STILL WOULDN'T LAY DOWN YOUR ARMS...
SKREEK
...EVEN IF HUMANS TOOK CARE OF THE ENVIRONMENT.

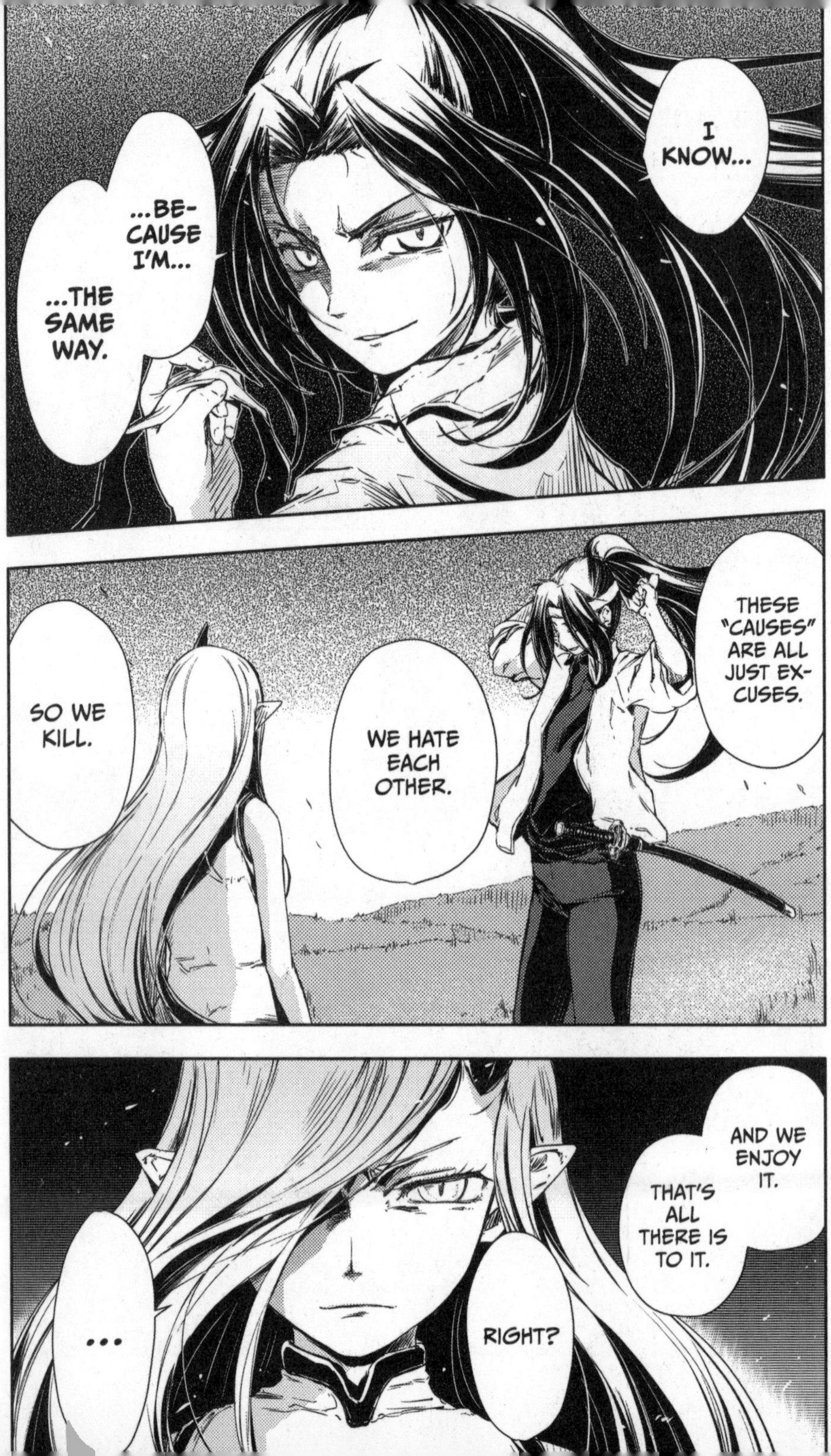
I KNOW...
...BECAUSE I'M...
...THE SAME WAY.
THESE "CAUSES" ARE ALL JUST EXCUSES.
WE HATE EACH OTHER.
SO WE KILL.
AND WE ENJOY IT.
THAT'S ALL THERE IS TO IT.
RIGHT?
...

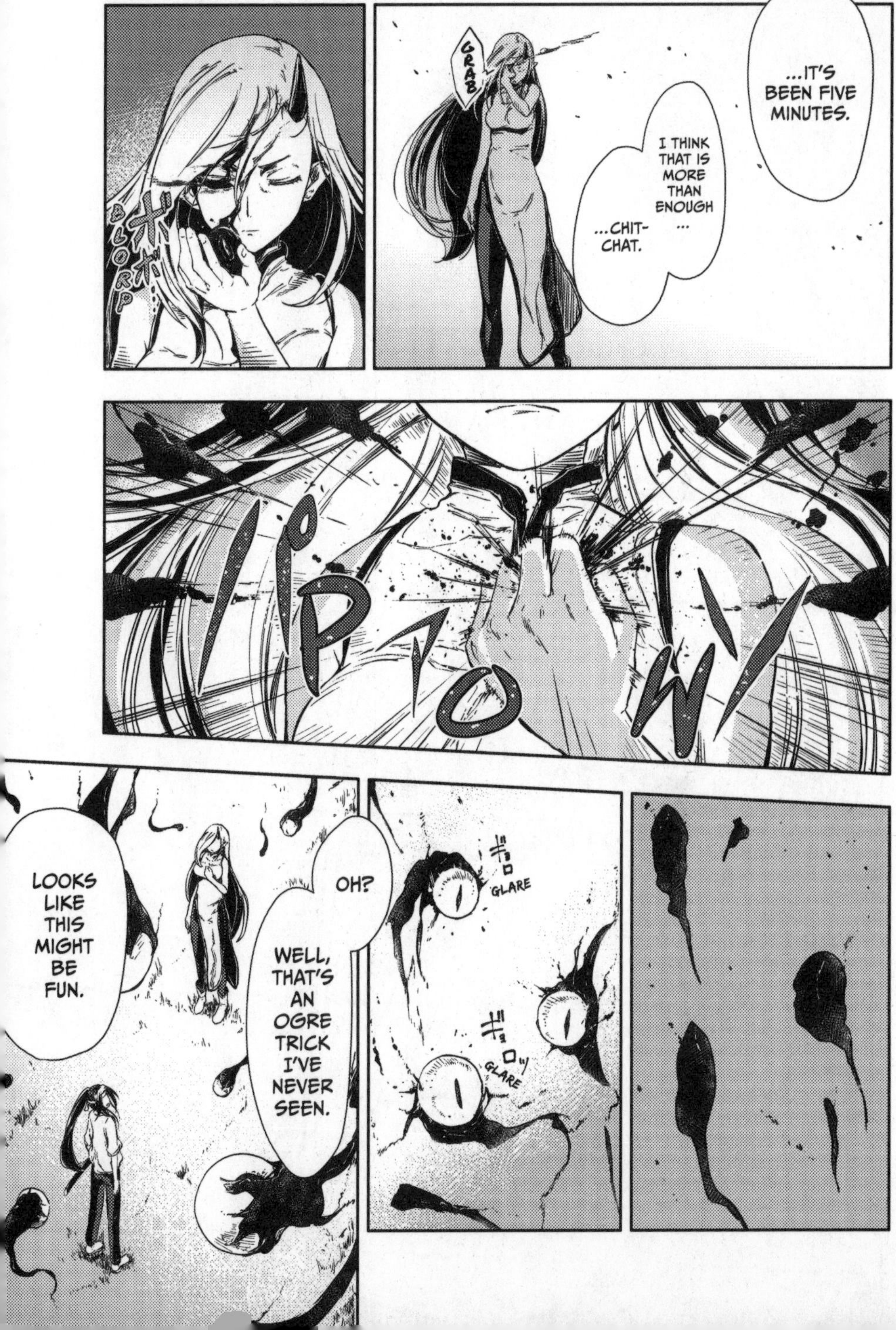
...IT'S BEEN FIVE MINUTES.
I THINK THAT IS MORE THAN ENOUGH ...
...CHIT-CHAT.
GRAB
BLORP
POW
GLARE
GLARE
OH?
WELL, THAT'S AN OGRE TRICK I'VE NEVER SEEN.
LOOKS LIKE THIS MIGHT BE FUN.

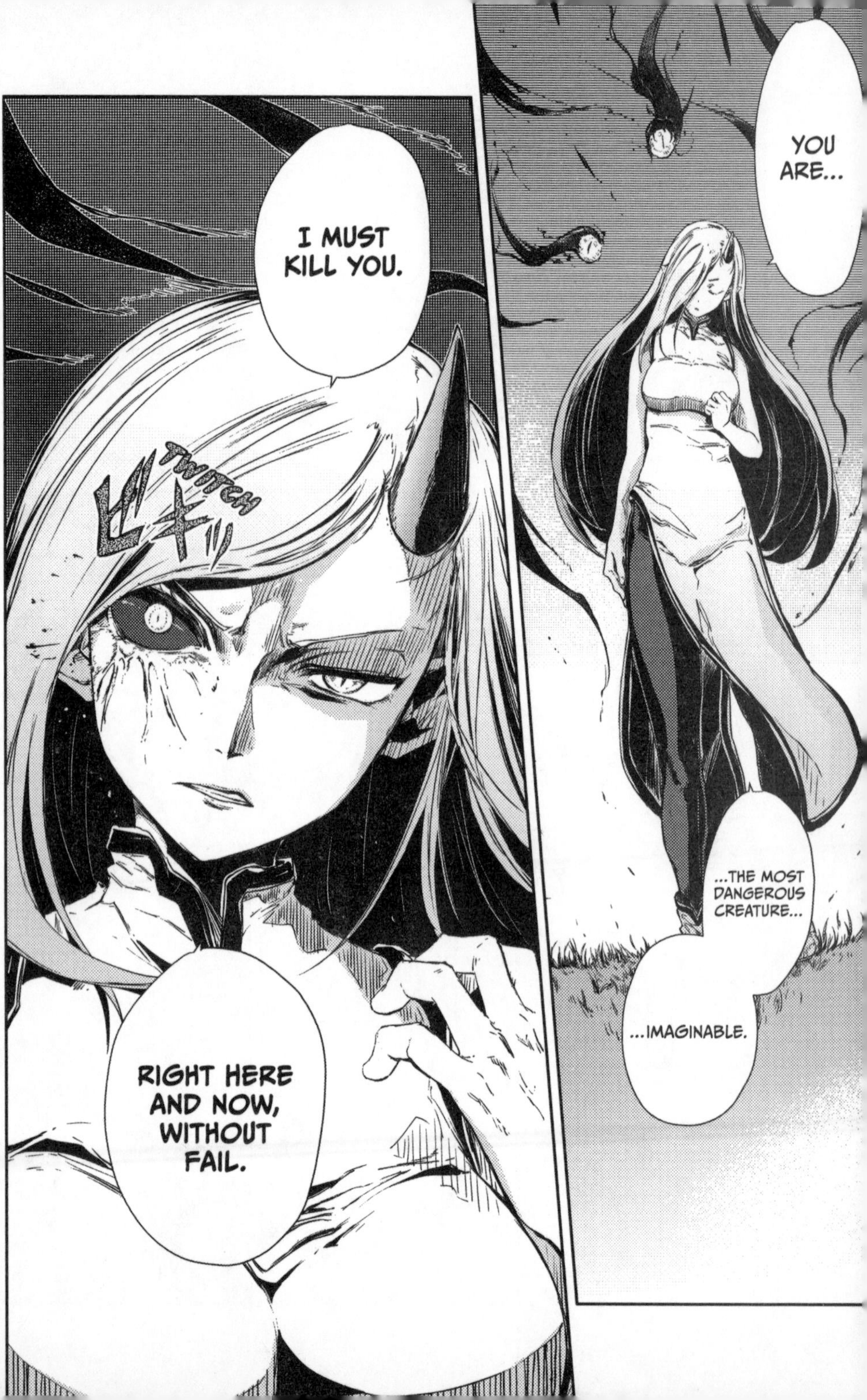
YOU ARE...
...THE MOST DANGEROUS CREATURE...
...IMAGINABLE.
I MUST KILL YOU.
TWITCH
RIGHT HERE AND NOW, WITHOUT FAIL.

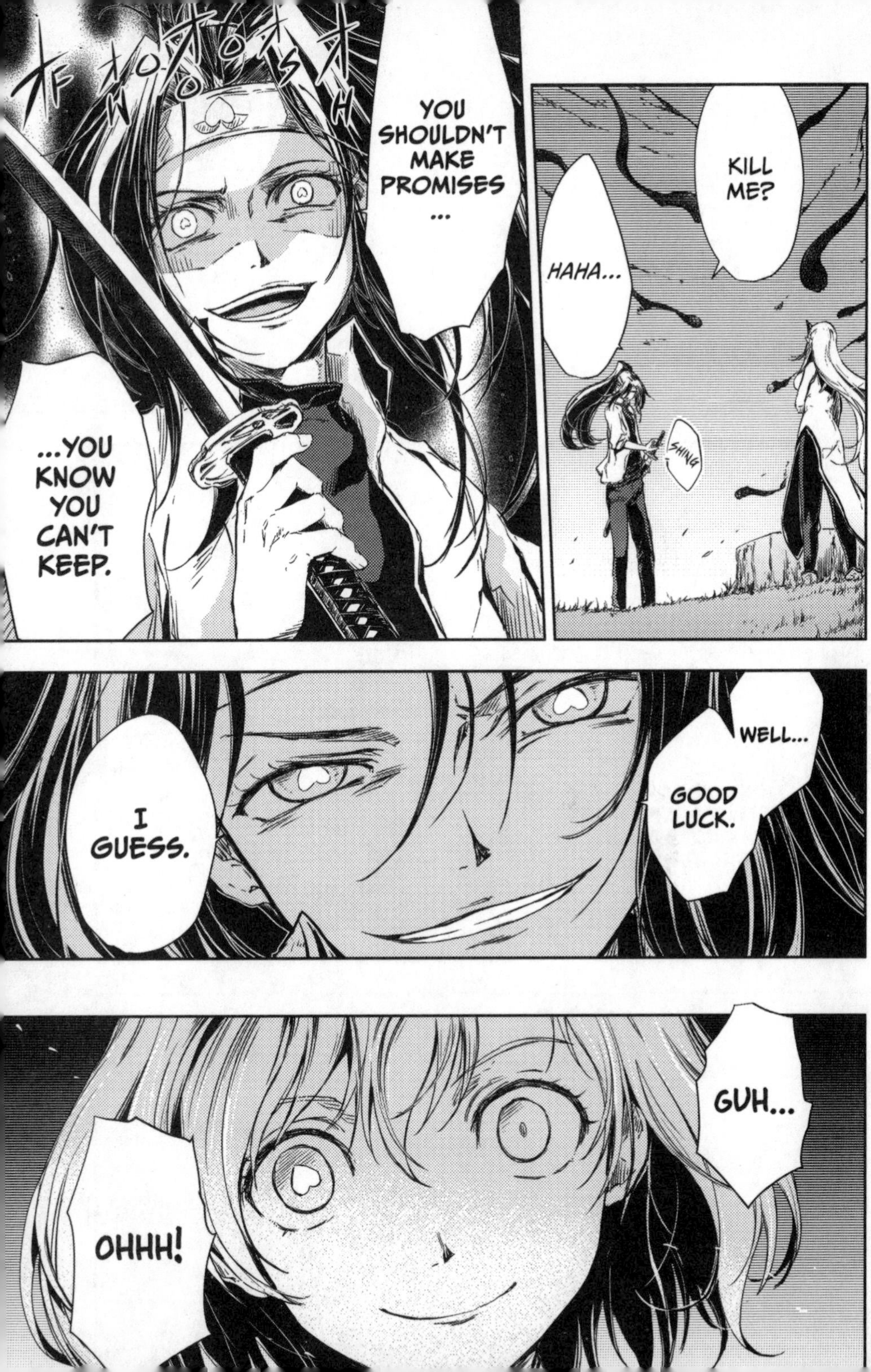
KILL ME?
HAHA...
SHING
YOU SHOULDN'T MAKE PROMISES ...
WHOOSH
...YOU KNOW YOU CAN'T KEEP.
WELL...
GOOD LUCK.
I GUESS.
GUH...
OHHH!

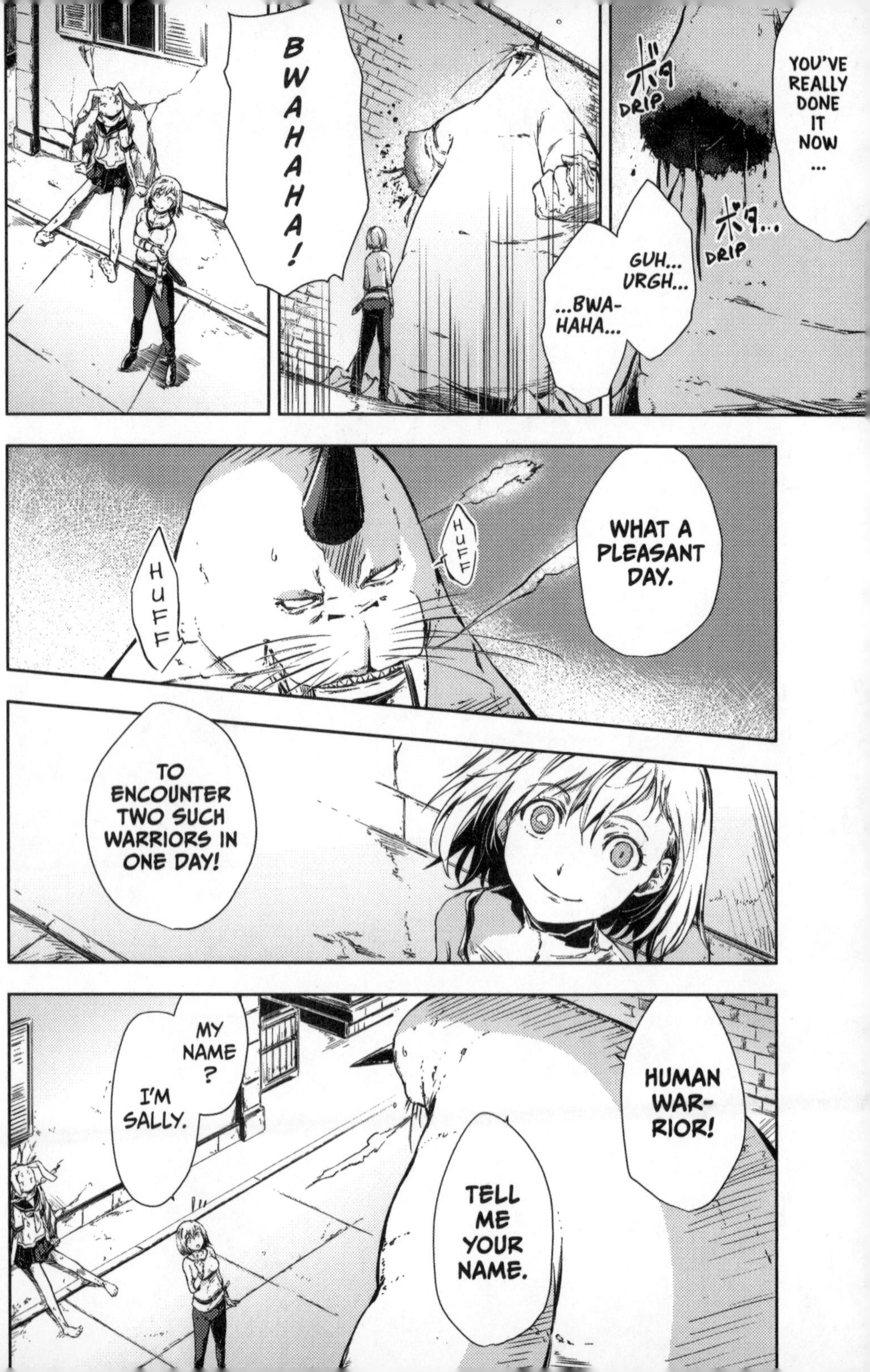
YOU'VE REALLY DONE IT NOW...
ボタ DRIP
ボタ... DRIP
GUH... URGH...
...BWA-HAHA...
BWAHAHAHA!
WHAT A PLEASANT DAY.
HUFF
HUFF
TO ENCOUNTER TWO SUCH WARRIORS IN ONE DAY!
HUMAN WARRIOR!
TELL ME YOUR NAME.
MY NAME?
I'M SALLY.

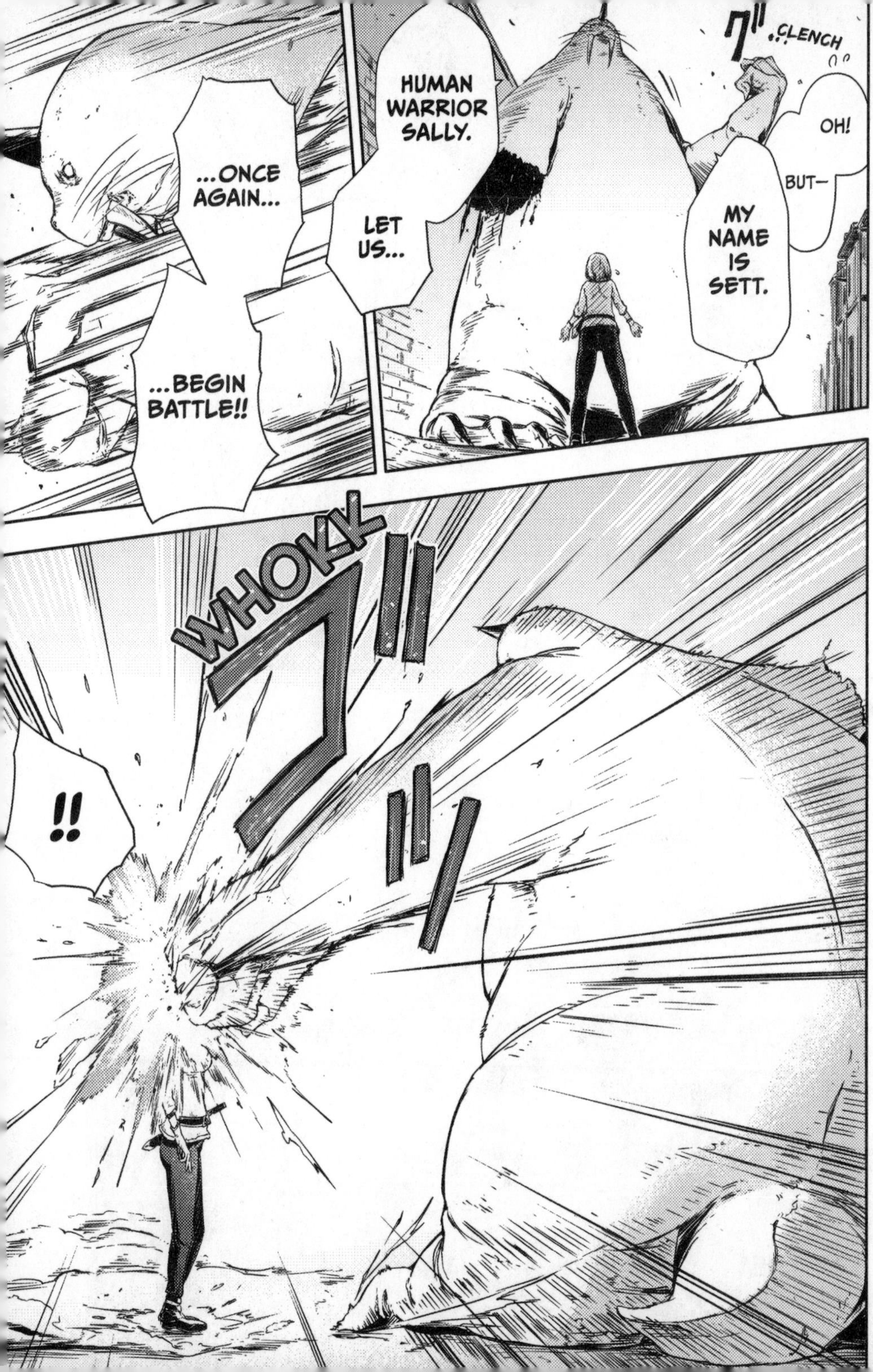
CLENCH
OH!
BUT—
MY NAME IS SETT.
HUMAN WARRIOR SALLY.
LET US...
...ONCE AGAIN...
...BEGIN BATTLE!!
WHOKK
!!

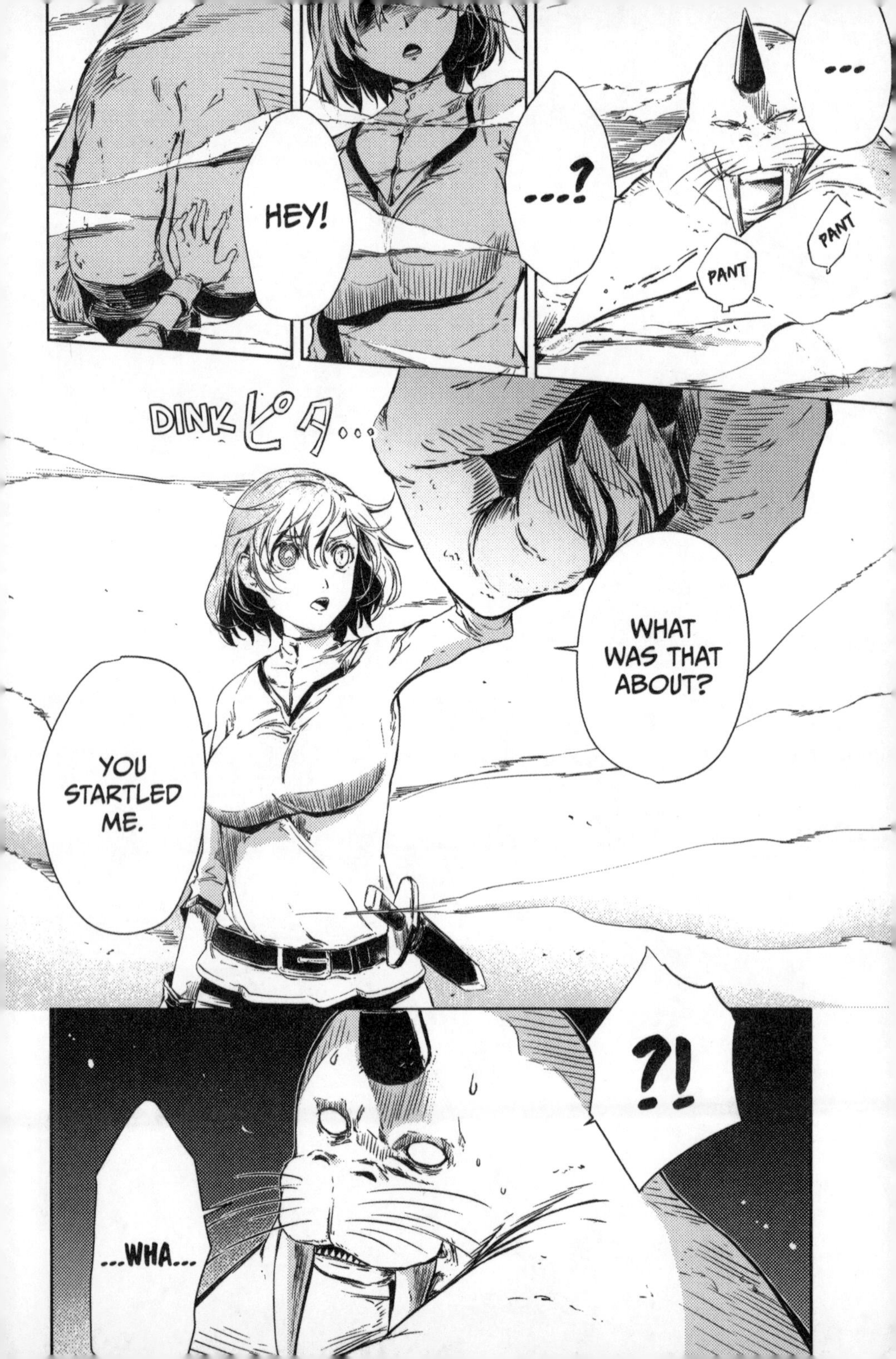
...
PANT
PANT
...?
HEY!
DINK ピタ...
WHAT WAS THAT ABOUT?
YOU STARTLED ME.
?!
...WHA...

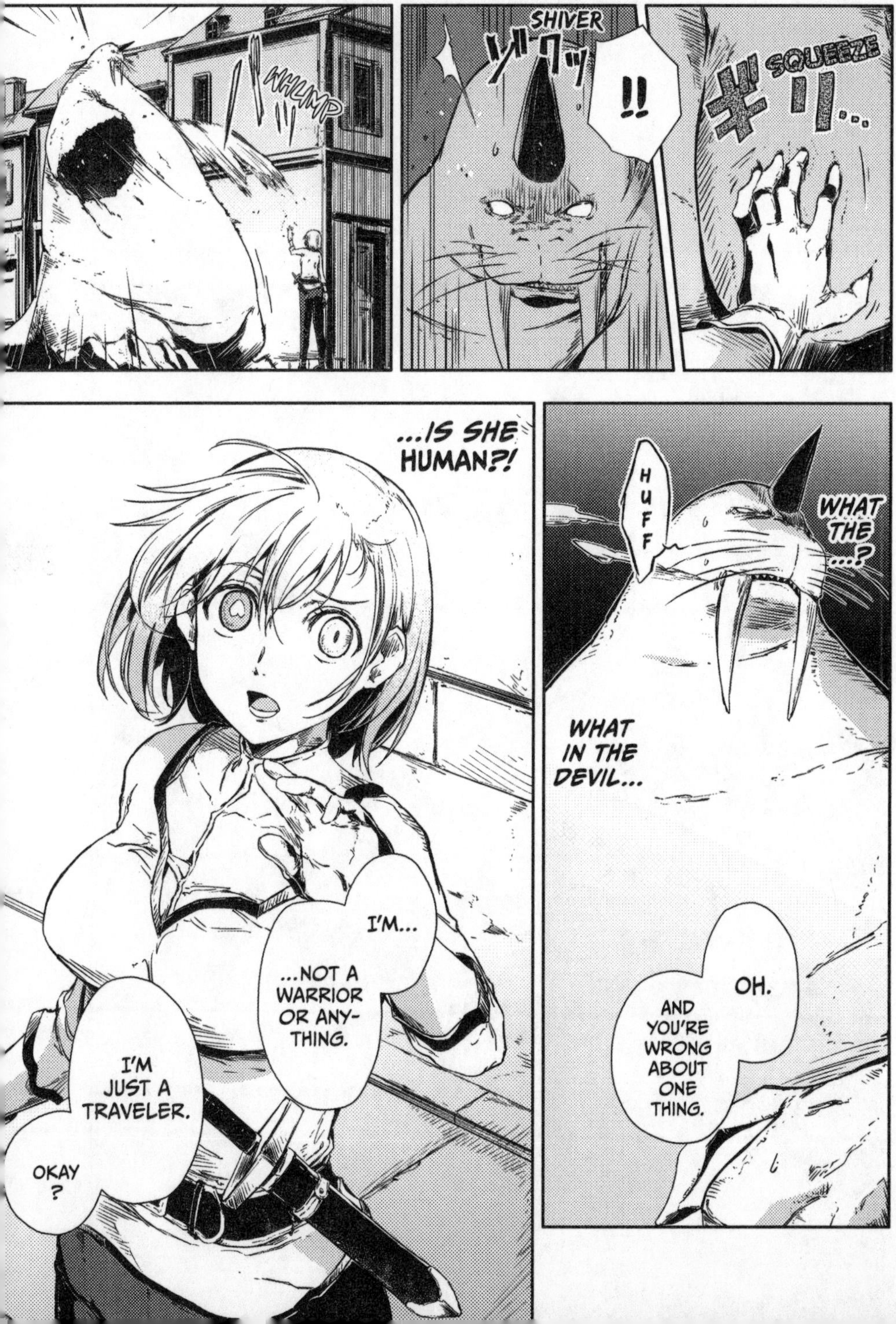
ギリ…
SQUEEZE
ゾワッ
SHIVER
!!
WHLUMP
WHAT THE...?
HUFF
WHAT IN THE DEVIL...
OH.
AND YOU'RE WRONG ABOUT ONE THING.
...IS SHE HUMAN?!
I'M...
...NOT A WARRIOR OR ANY-THING.
I'M JUST A TRAVELER.
OKAY?

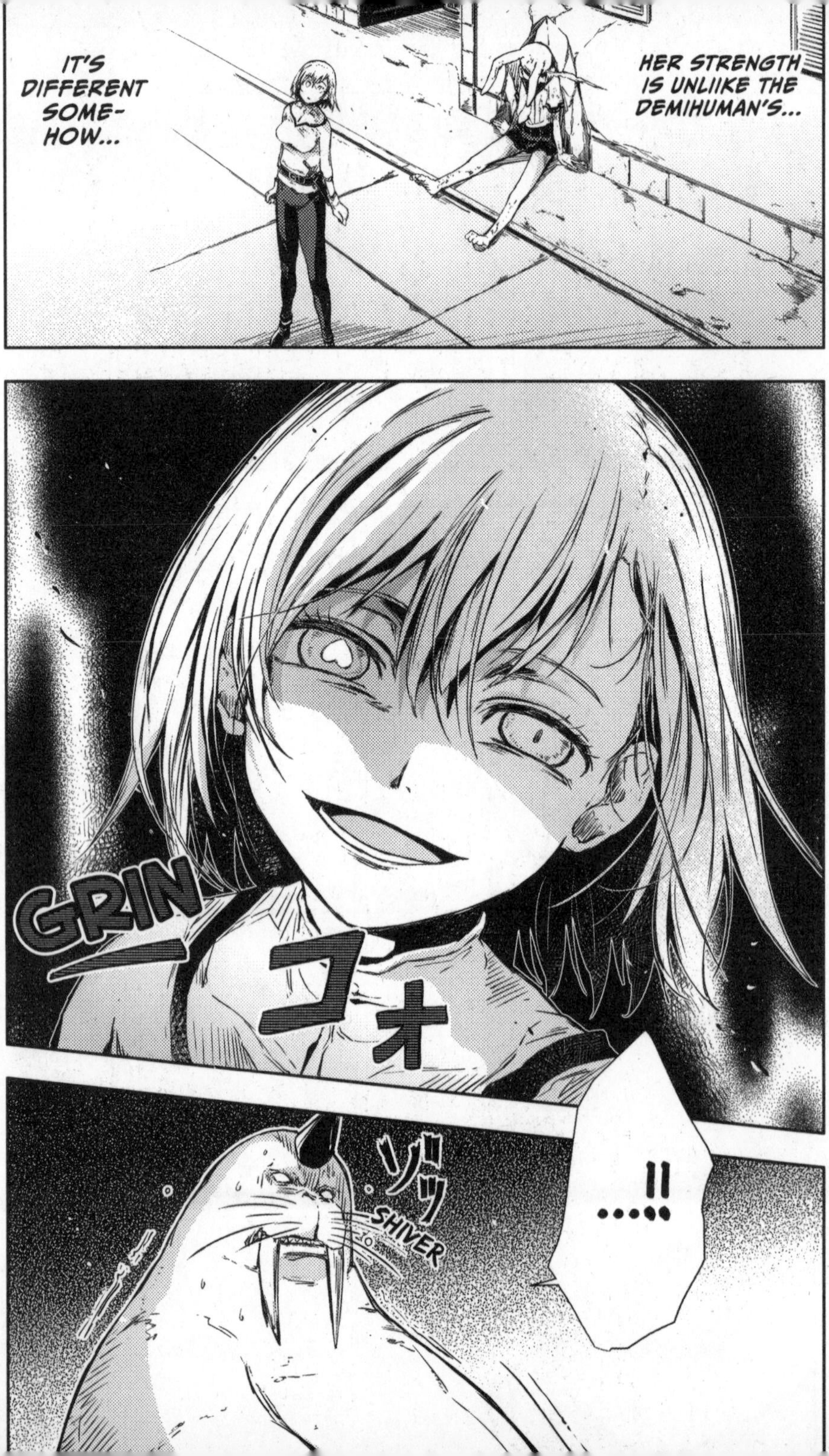
HER STRENGTH IS UNLIIKE THE DEMIHUMAN'S...
IT'S DIFFERENT SOME-HOW...
GRIN
コォ
!!
....!!
ゾッ
SHIVER

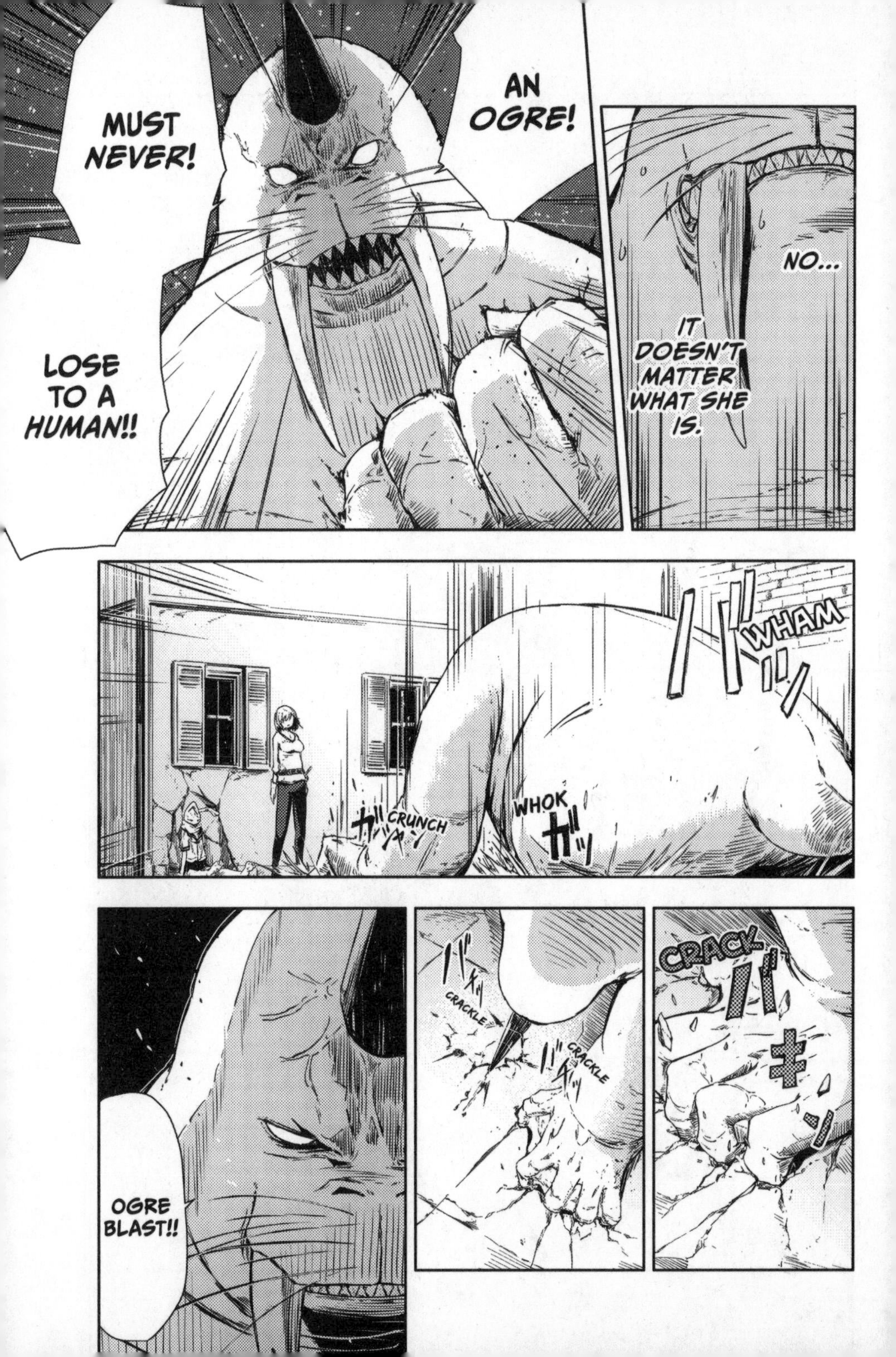
NO...
IT DOESN'T MATTER WHAT SHE IS.
AN OGRE!
MUST NEVER!
LOSE TO A HUMAN!!
WHAM
WHOK
CRUNCH
CRACK
CRACKLE
CRACKLE
OGRE BLAST!!

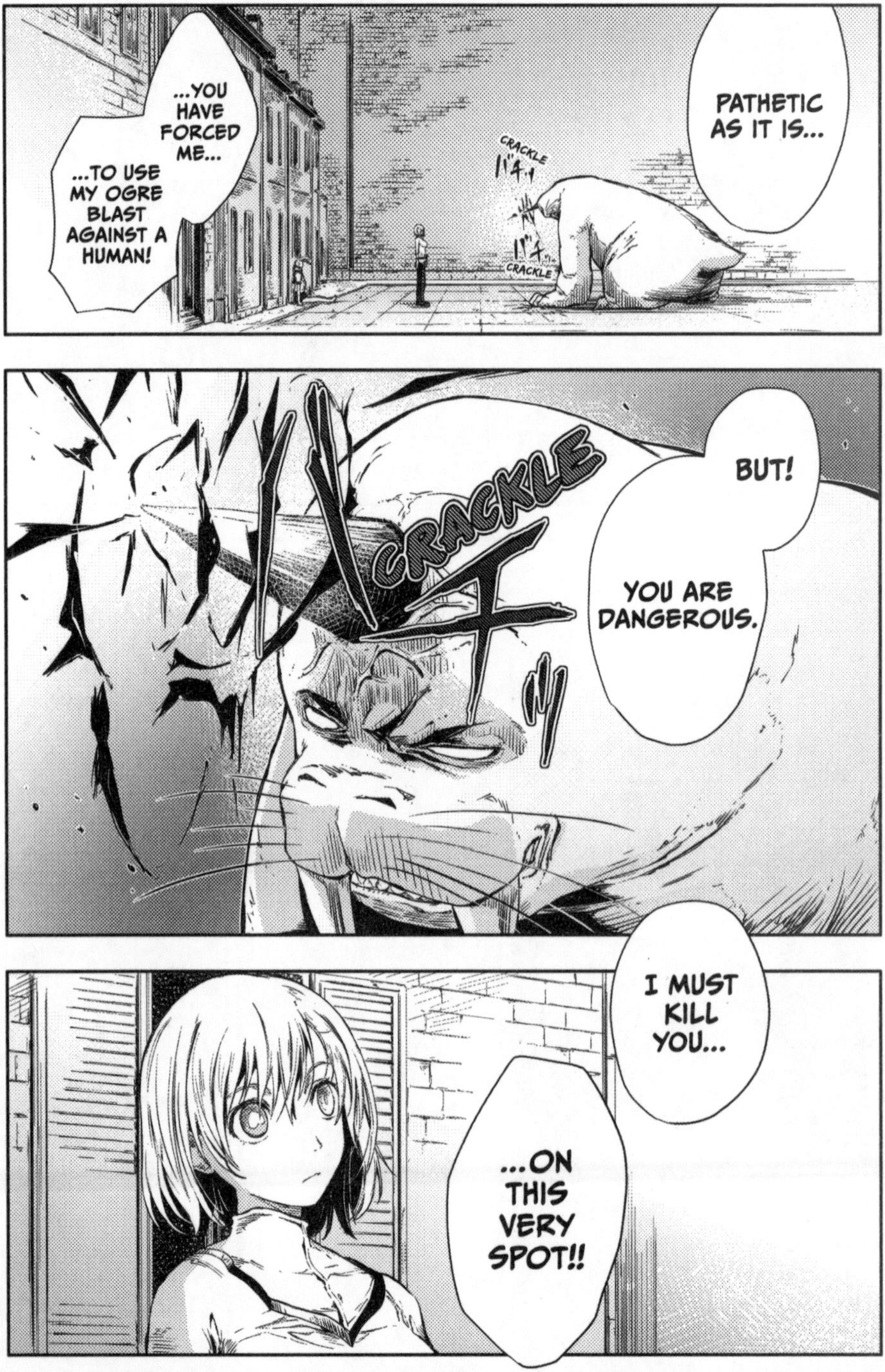
PATHETIC AS IT IS...
CRACKLE
CRACKLE
...YOU HAVE FORCED ME...
...TO USE MY OGRE BLAST AGAINST A HUMAN!
BUT!
YOU ARE DANGEROUS.
CRACKLE
I MUST KILL YOU...
...ON THIS VERY SPOT!!

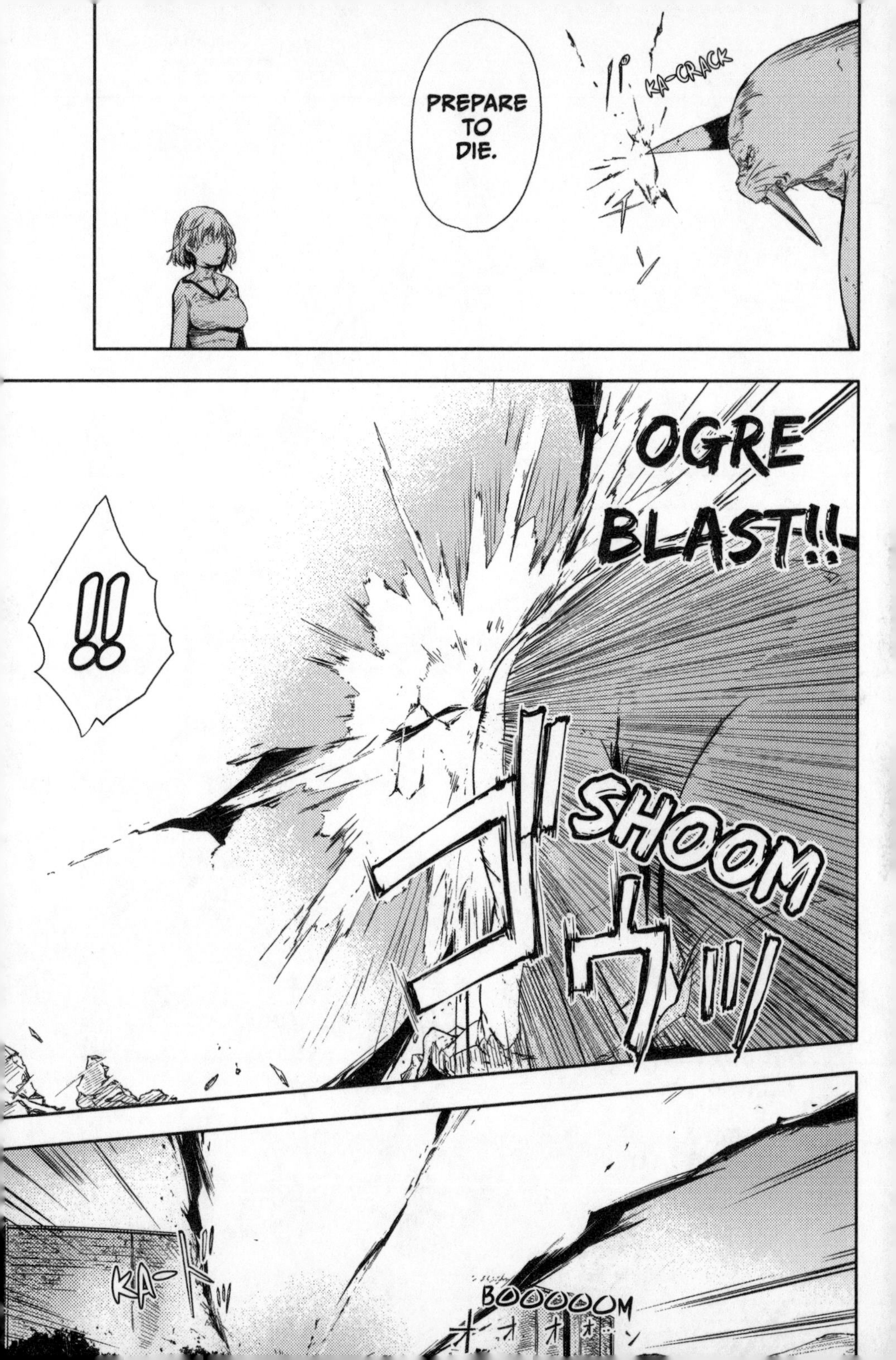
KA-CRACK
PREPARE TO DIE.
OGRE BLAST!!
!!
SHOOM
BOOOOOOM
KA-

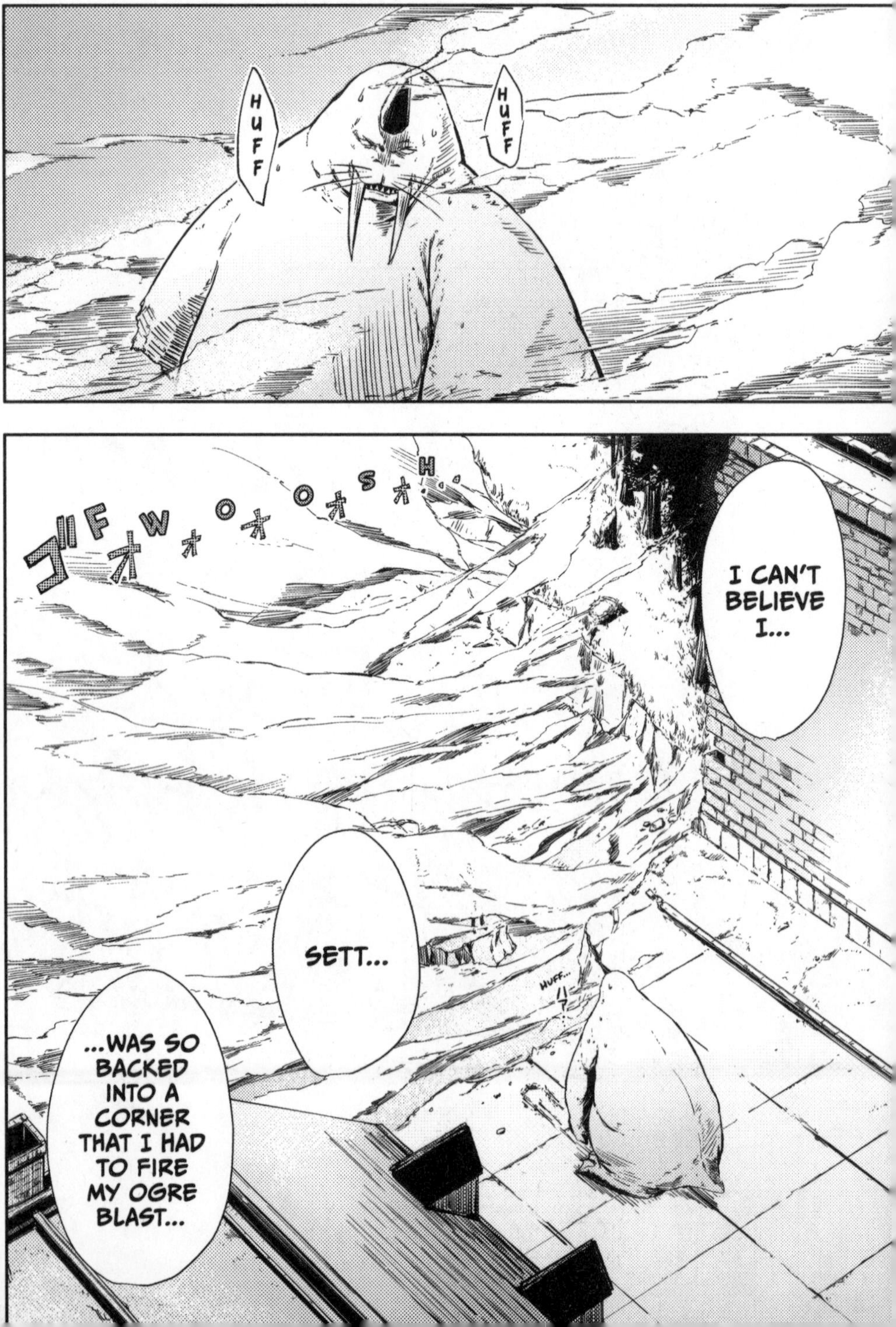
HUFF
HUFF
FWOOSH
I CAN'T BELIEVE I...
SETT...
...WAS SO BACKED INTO A CORNER THAT I HAD TO FIRE MY OGRE BLAST...
HUFF...

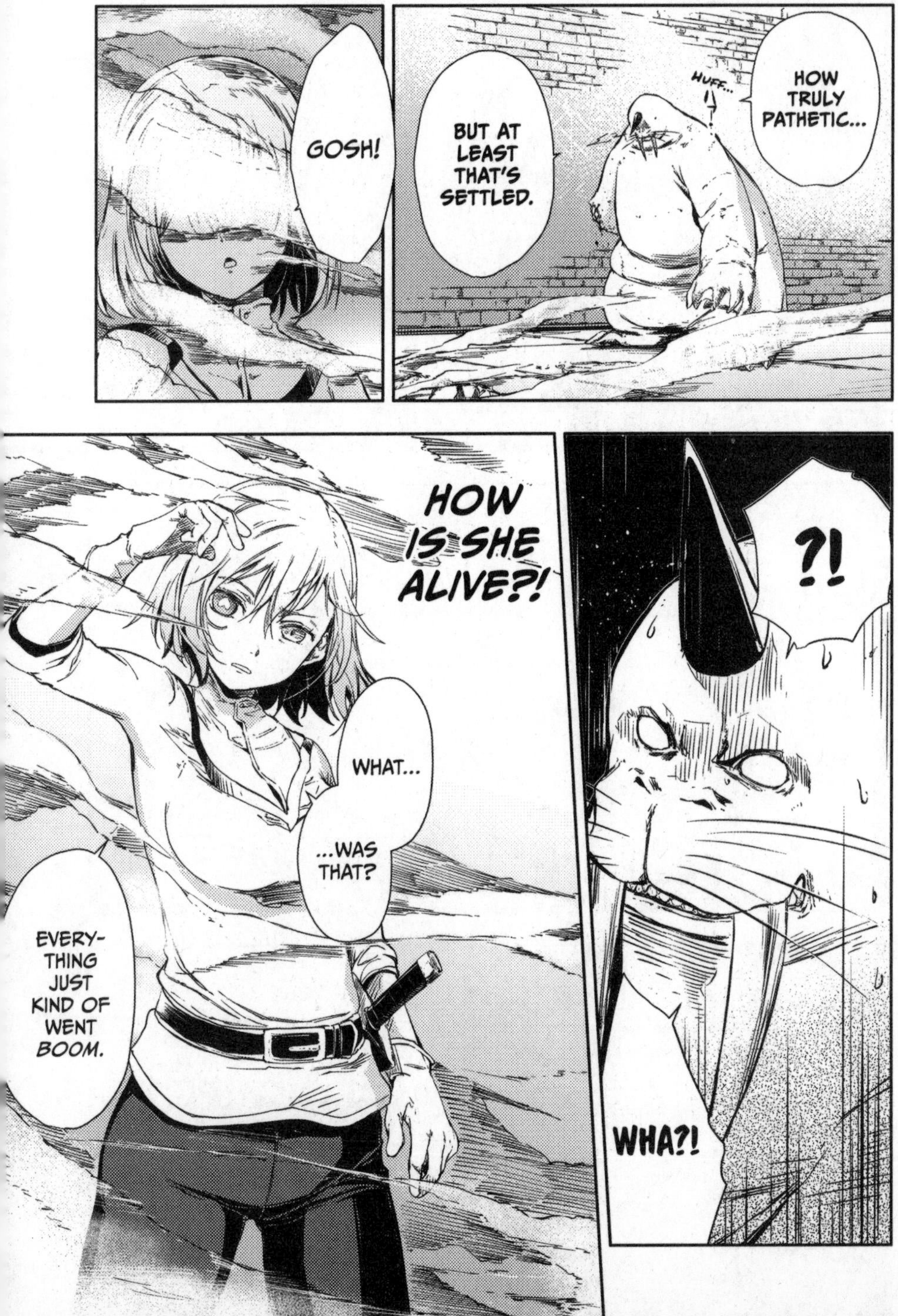
HOW TRULY PATHETIC...
HUFF...
BUT AT LEAST THAT'S SETTLED.
GOSH!
?!
WHA?!
HOW IS SHE ALIVE?!
WHAT...
...WAS THAT?
EVERY-THING JUST KIND OF WENT *BOOM*.

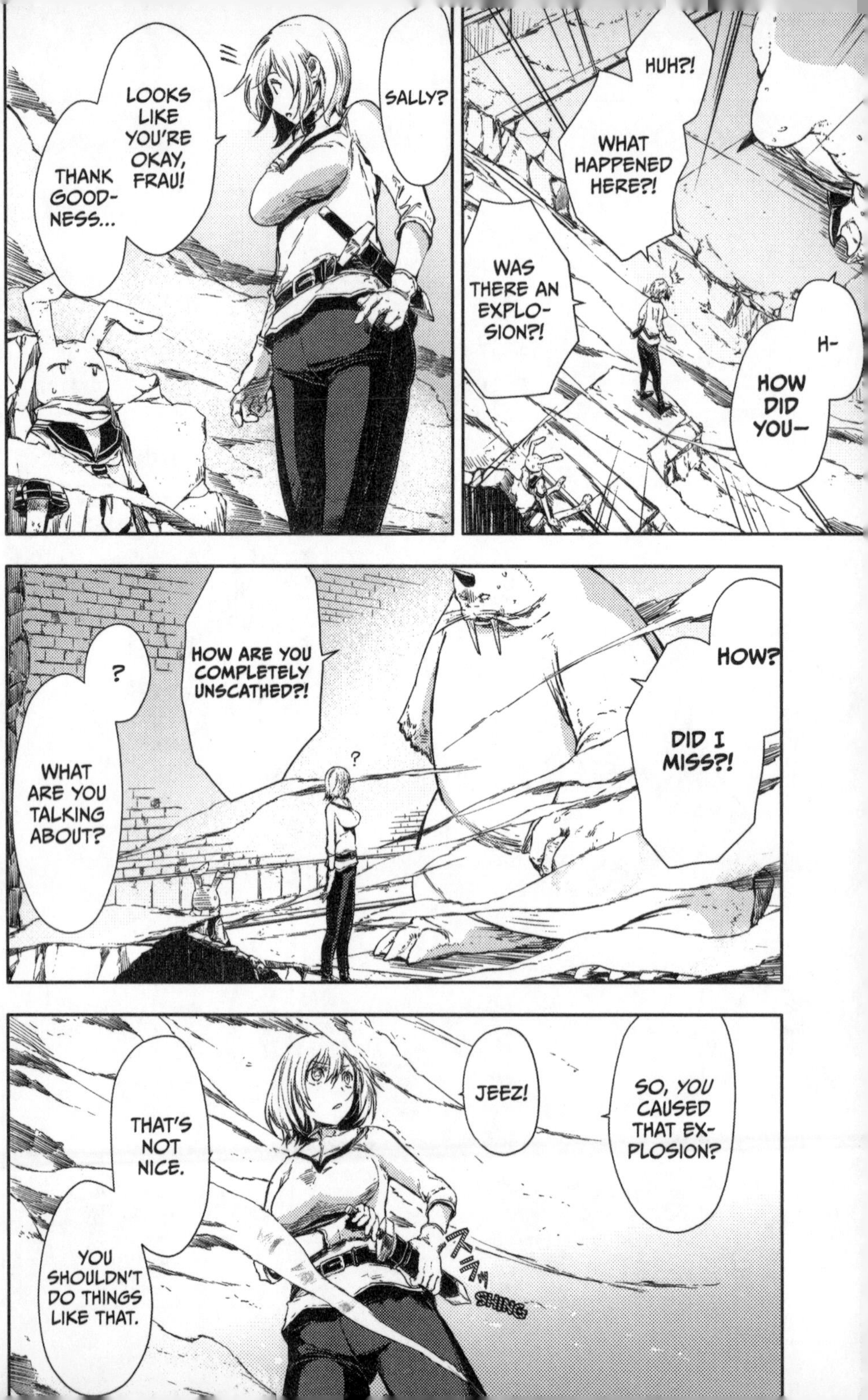
HUH?! WHAT HAPPENED HERE?!
WAS THERE AN EXPLO-SION?!
H- HOW DID YOU—
SALLY?
LOOKS LIKE YOU'RE OKAY, FRAU!
THANK GOOD-NESS...
HOW? DID I MISS?!
HOW ARE YOU COMPLETELY UNSCATHED?!
? WHAT ARE YOU TALKING ABOUT?
?
SO, *YOU* CAUSED THAT EX-PLOSION?
JEEZ!
THAT'S NOT NICE.
YOU SHOULDN'T DO THINGS LIKE THAT.
SHING

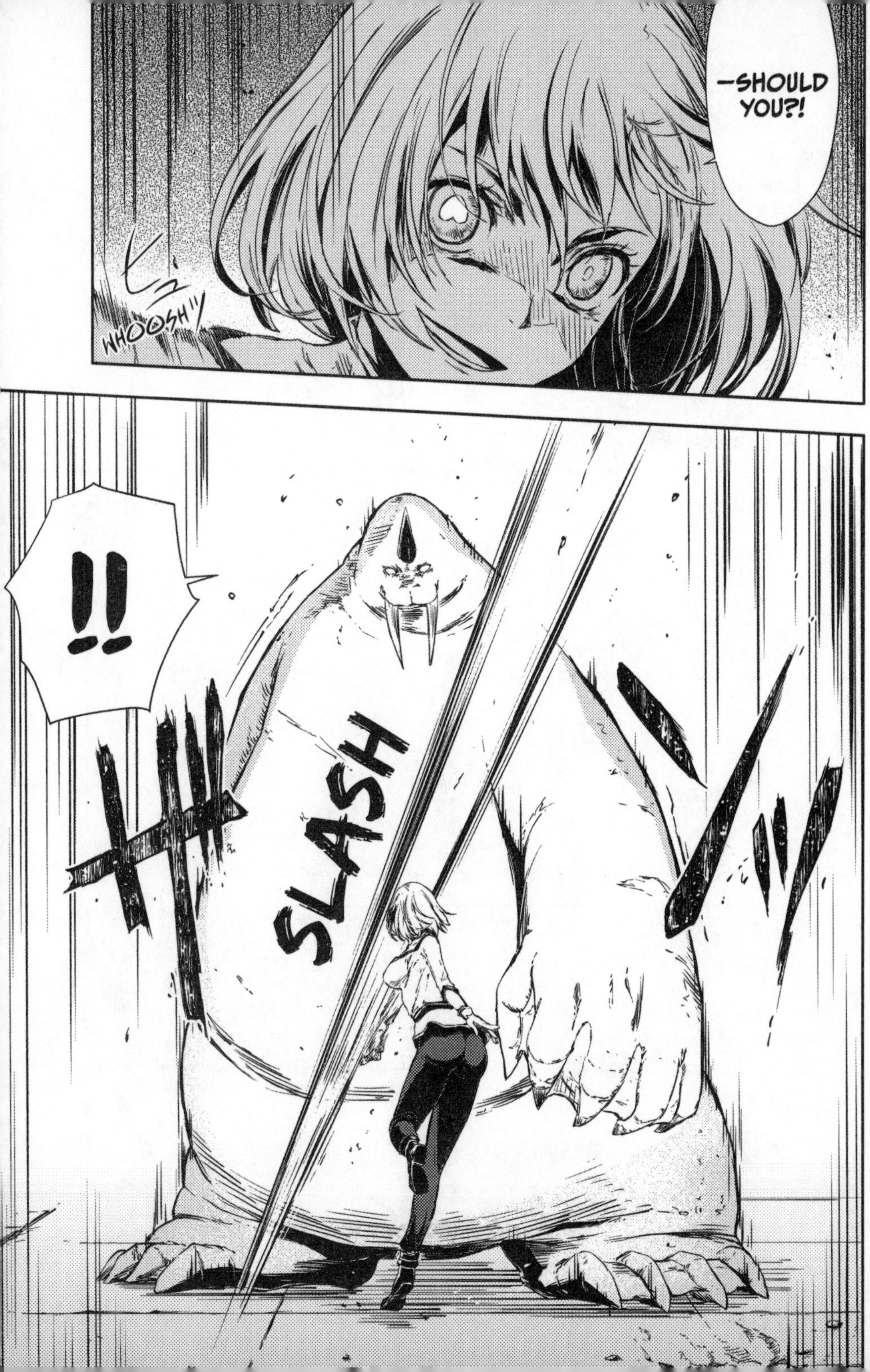
—SHOULD YOU?!
WHOOSH
!!
SLASH

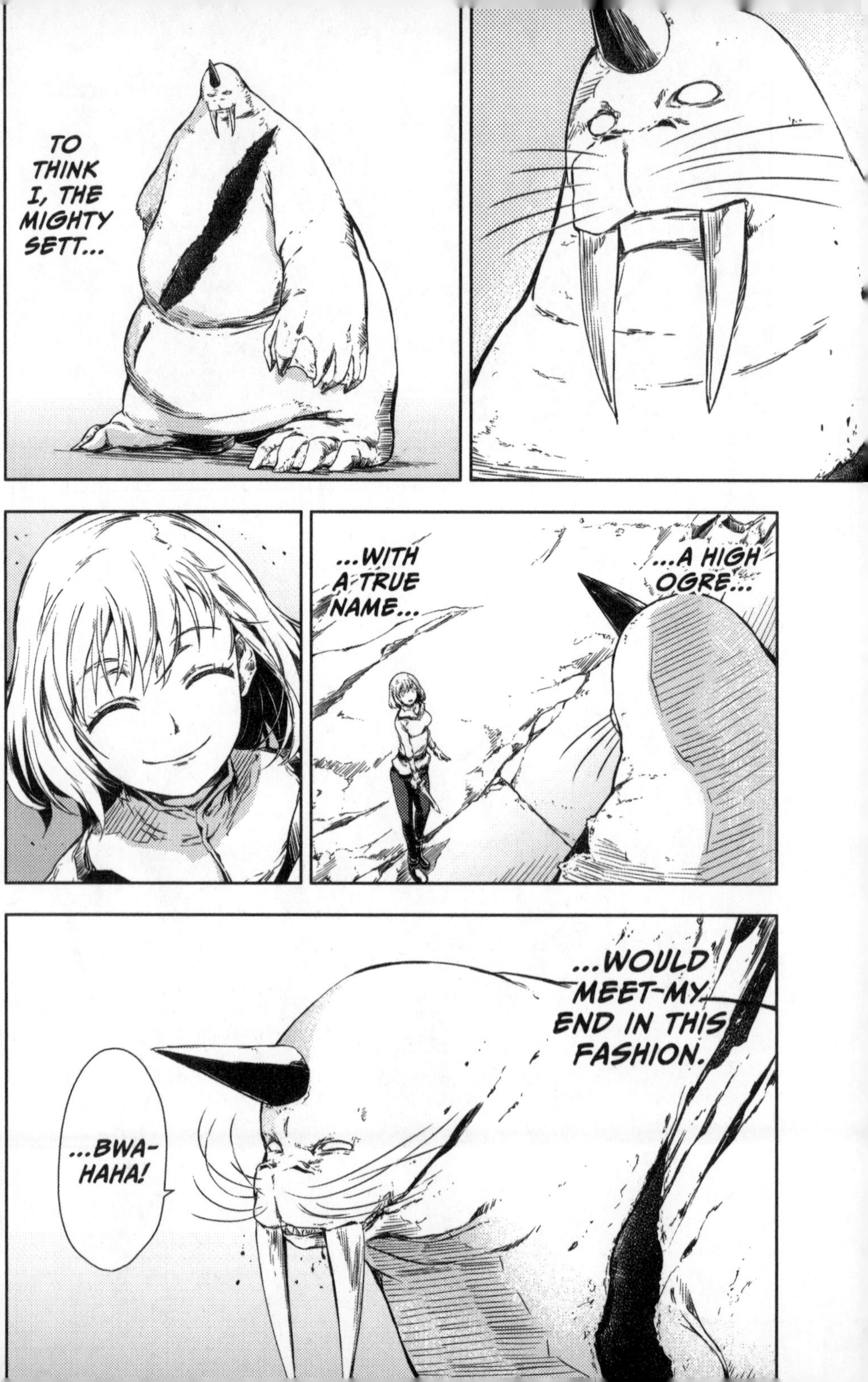
TO THINK I, THE MIGHTY SETT...
...A HIGH OGRE...
...WITH A TRUE NAME...
...WOULD MEET MY END IN THIS FASHION.
...BWA-HAHA!

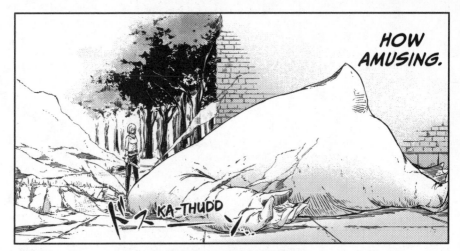

HOW
AMUSING.

KA-THUDD

!

TUMP

FWUMP

CLATTER

SALLY?

SALLY!!

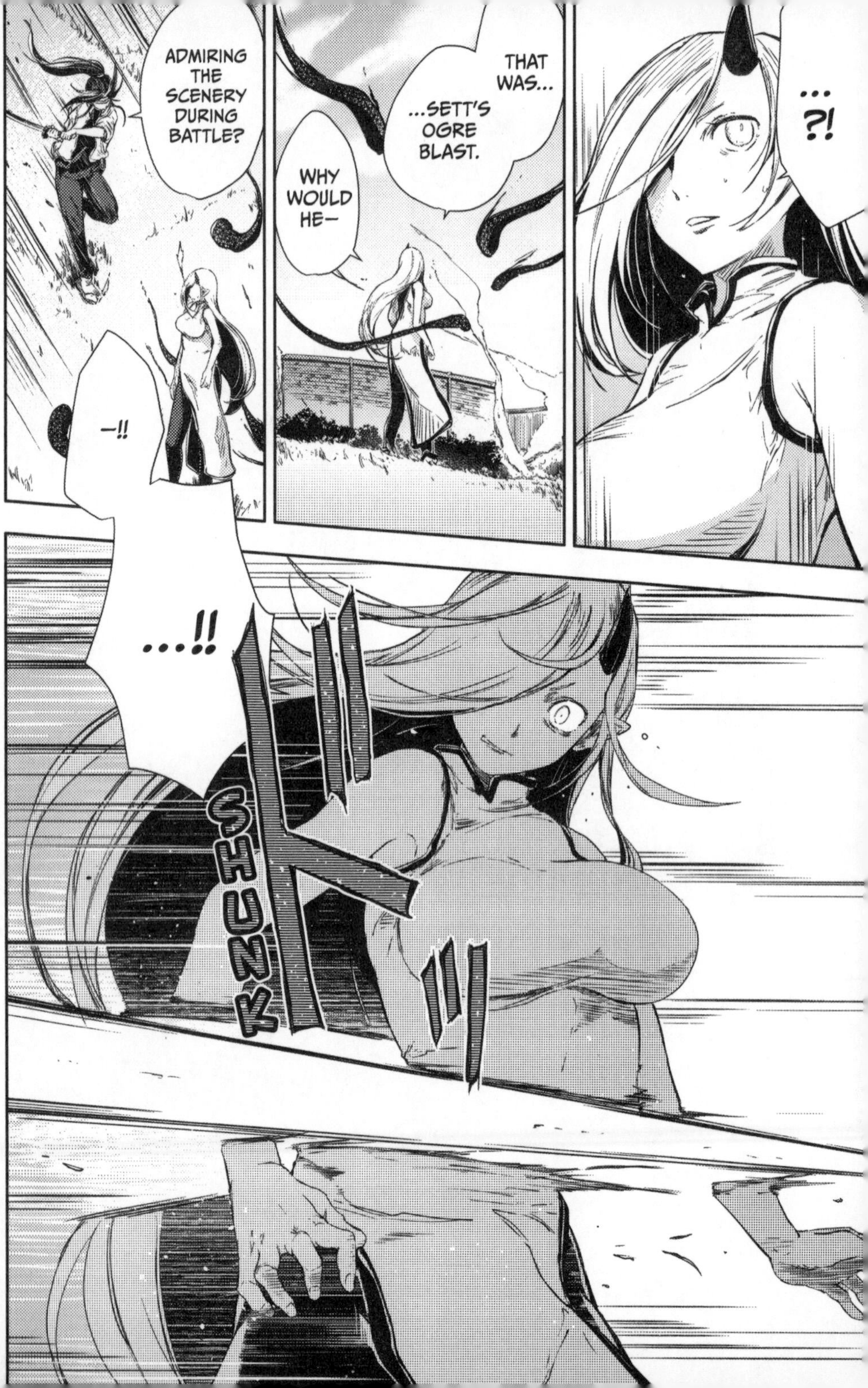
...?!
THAT WAS...
...SETT'S OGRE BLAST.
WHY WOULD HE—
ADMIRING THE SCENERY DURING BATTLE?
—!!
...!!
SHUNK

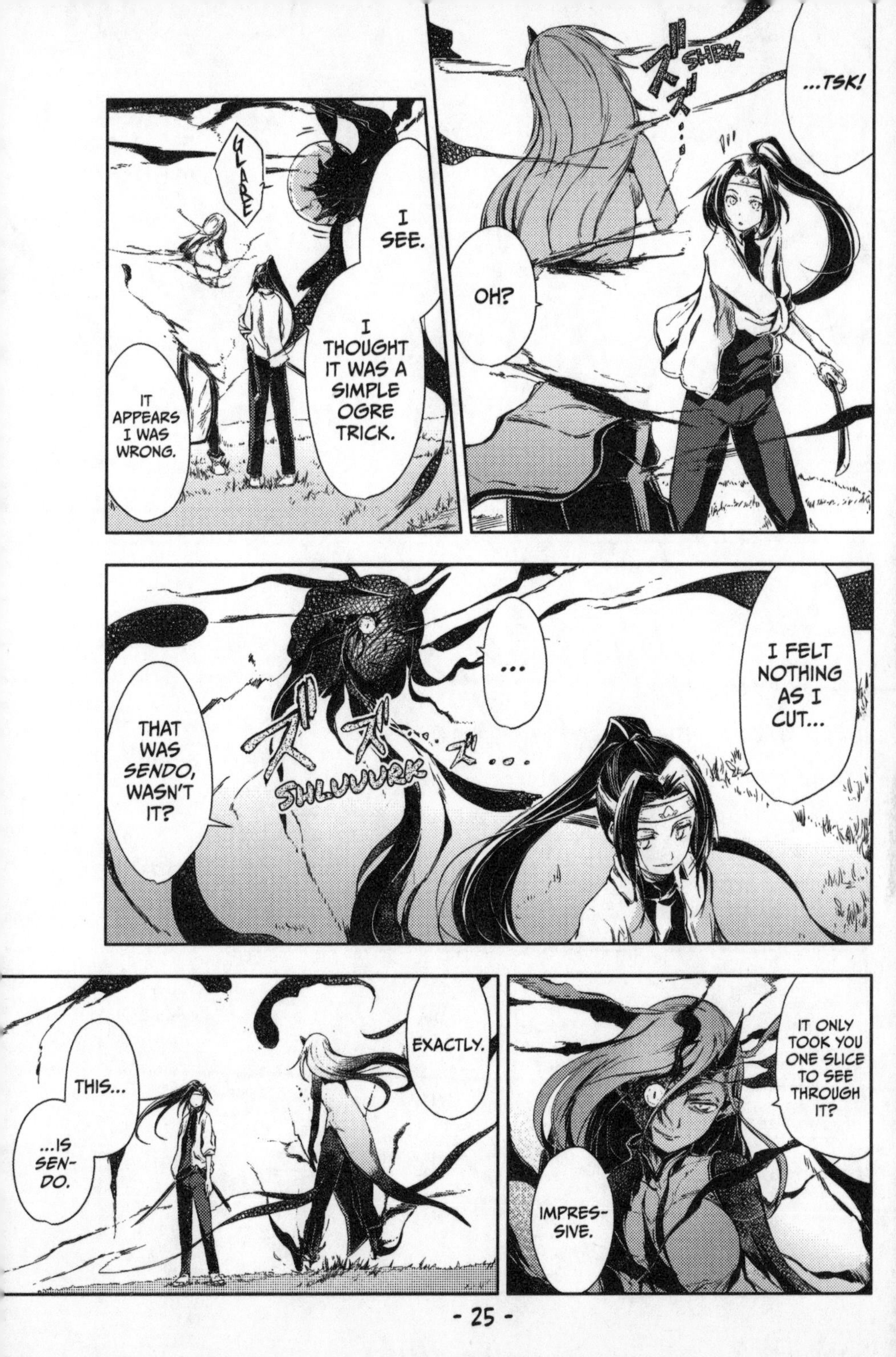

...TSK!
SHRK
OH?
I SEE.
I THOUGHT IT WAS A SIMPLE OGRE TRICK.
GLARE
IT APPEARS I WAS WRONG.
I FELT NOTHING AS I CUT...
...
SHLUUURK
THAT WAS SENDO, WASN'T IT?
IT ONLY TOOK YOU ONE SLICE TO SEE THROUGH IT?
IMPRES-SIVE.
EXACTLY.
THIS...
...IS SEN-DO.

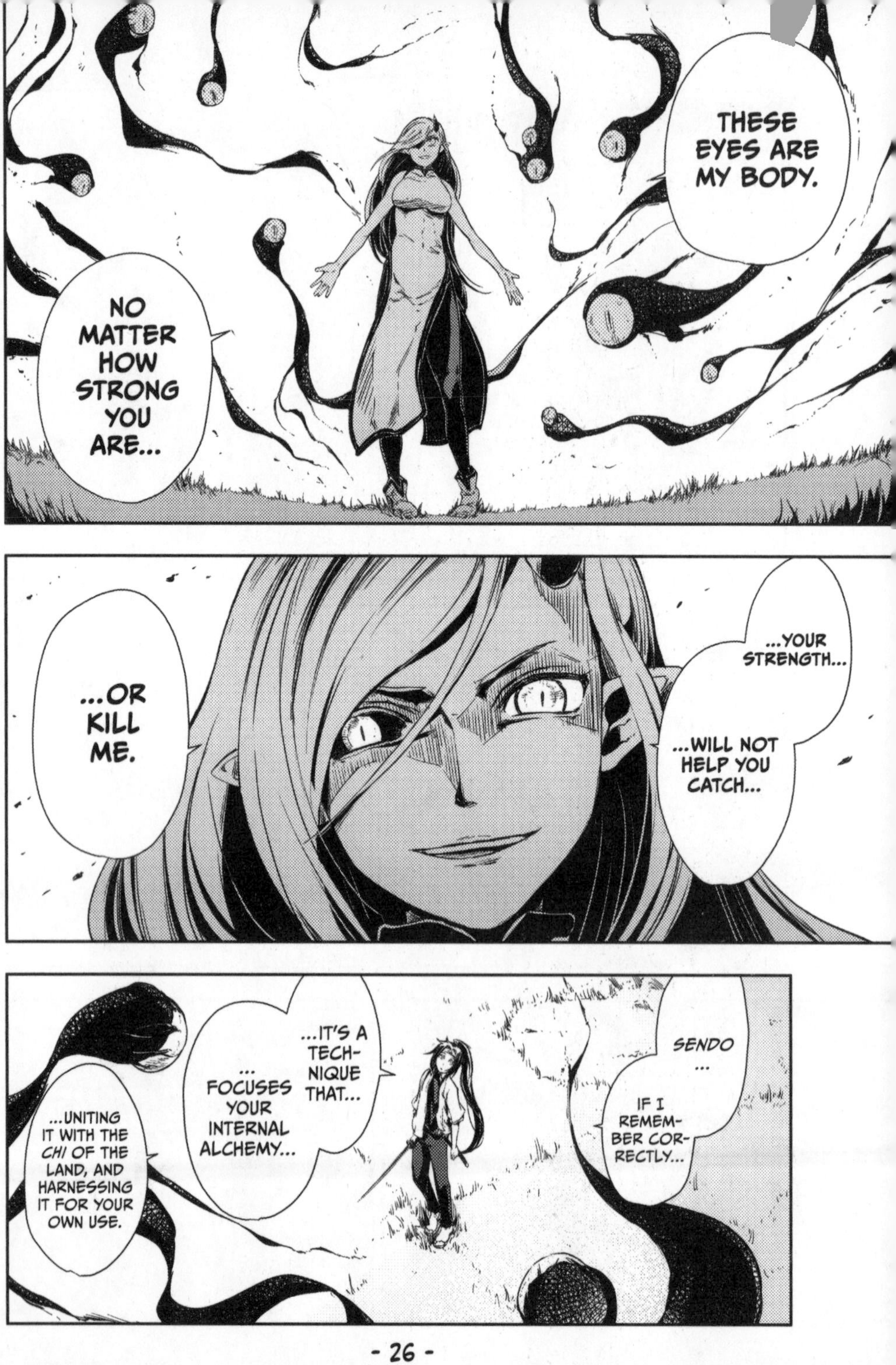
THESE EYES ARE MY BODY.
NO MATTER HOW STRONG YOU ARE...
...YOUR STRENGTH...
...WILL NOT HELP YOU CATCH...
...OR KILL ME.
SENDO ...
IF I REMEMBER CORRECTLY...
...IT'S A TECHNIQUE THAT...
... FOCUSES YOUR INTERNAL ALCHEMY...
...UNITING IT WITH THE *CHI* OF THE LAND, AND HARNESSING IT FOR YOUR OWN USE.

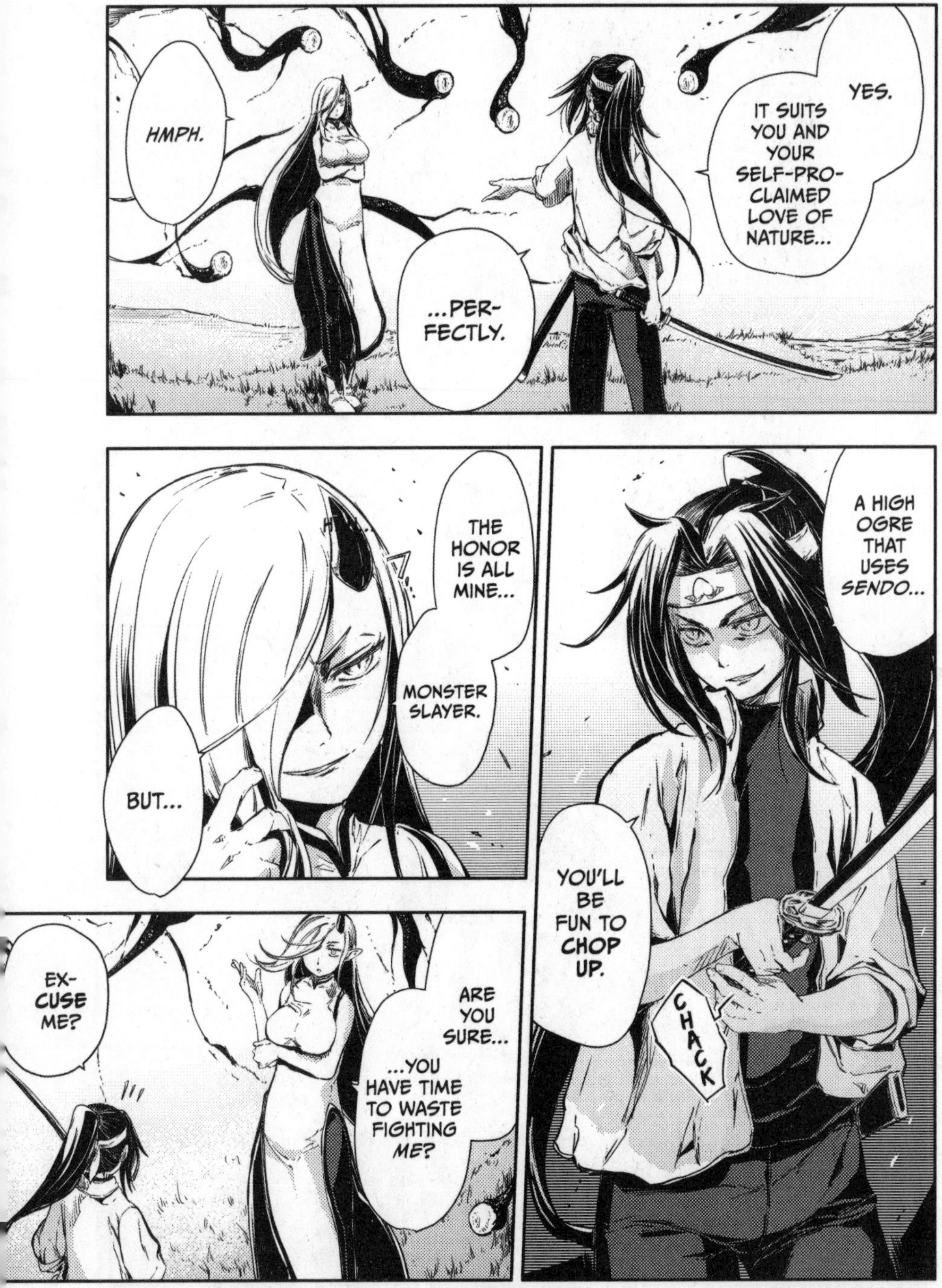
YES. IT SUITS YOU AND YOUR SELF-PROCLAIMED LOVE OF NATURE...
...PERFECTLY.
HMPH.
A HIGH OGRE THAT USES SENDO...
YOU'LL BE FUN TO CHOP UP.
CHACK
THE HONOR IS ALL MINE...
MONSTER SLAYER.
BUT...
ARE YOU SURE...
...YOU HAVE TIME TO WASTE FIGHTING ME?
EXCUSE ME?

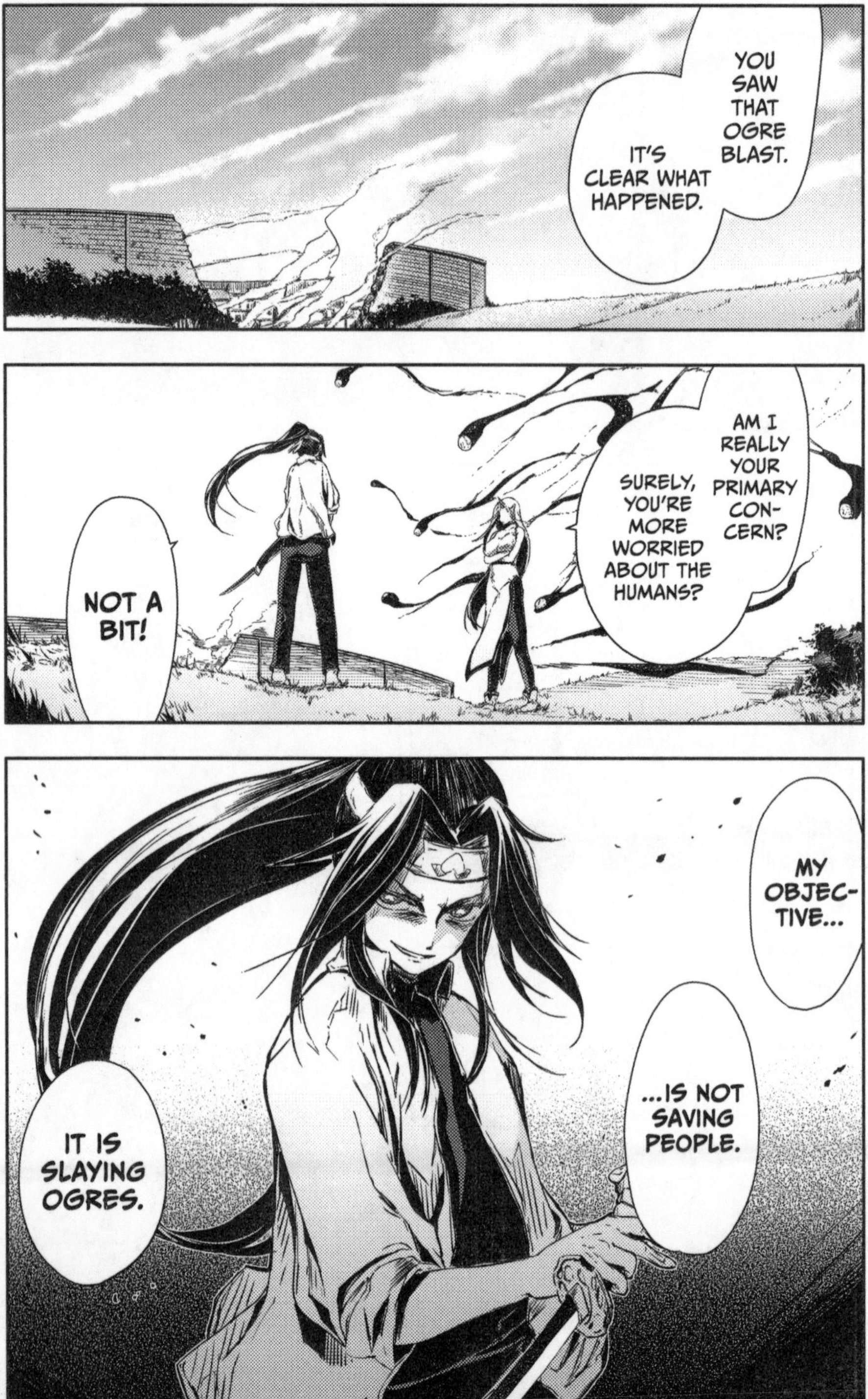
YOU SAW THAT OGRE BLAST.
IT'S CLEAR WHAT HAPPENED.
AM I REALLY YOUR PRIMARY CONCERN?
SURELY, YOU'RE MORE WORRIED ABOUT THE HUMANS?
NOT A BIT!
MY OBJECTIVE...
...IS NOT SAVING PEOPLE.
IT IS SLAYING OGRES.

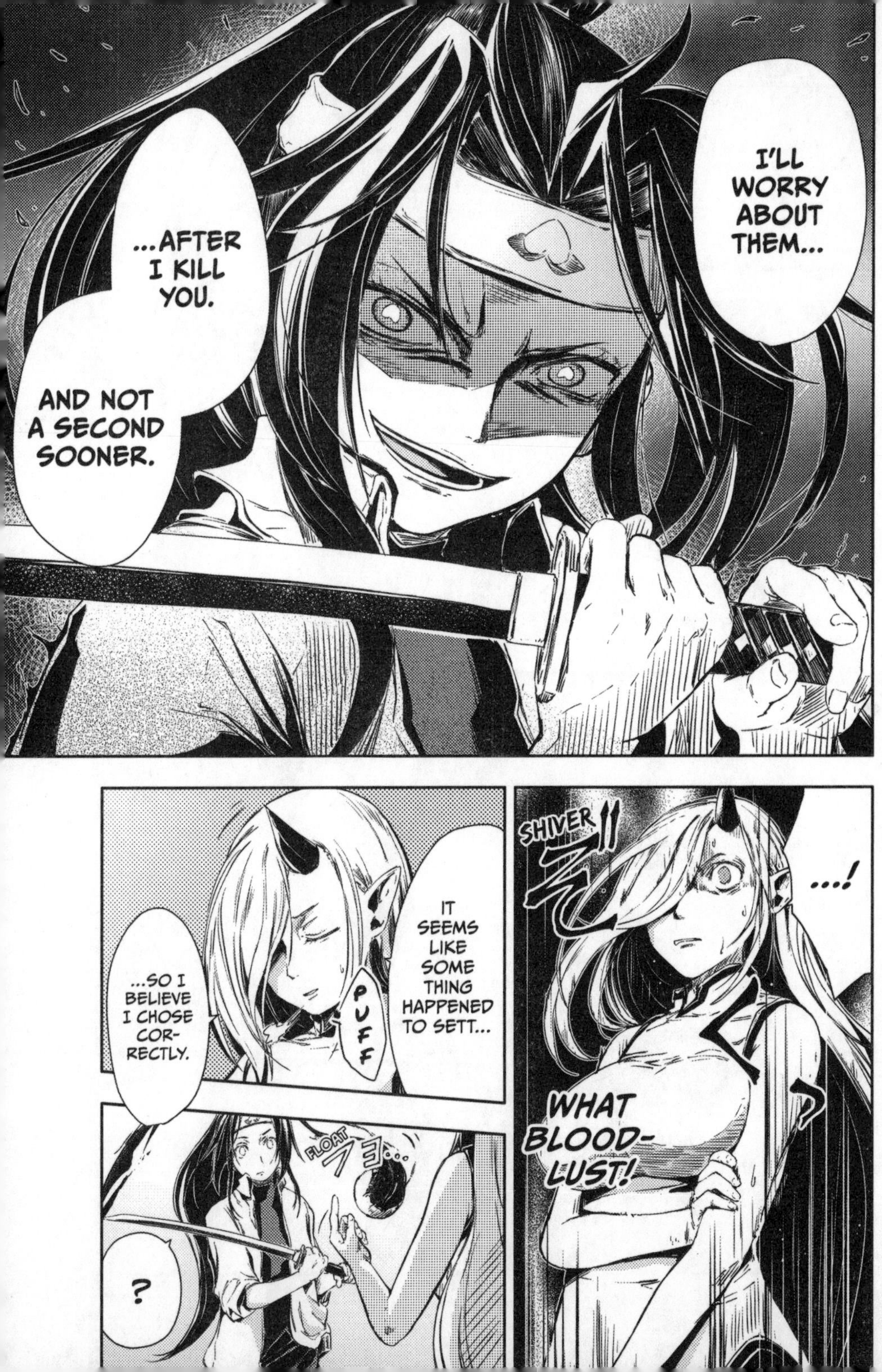
I'LL WORRY ABOUT THEM...
...AFTER I KILL YOU.
AND NOT A SECOND SOONER.
SHIVER
...!
WHAT BLOOD-LUST!
IT SEEMS LIKE SOME THING HAPPENED TO SETT...
PUFF
...SO I BELIEVE I CHOSE COR-RECTLY.
FLOAT
?

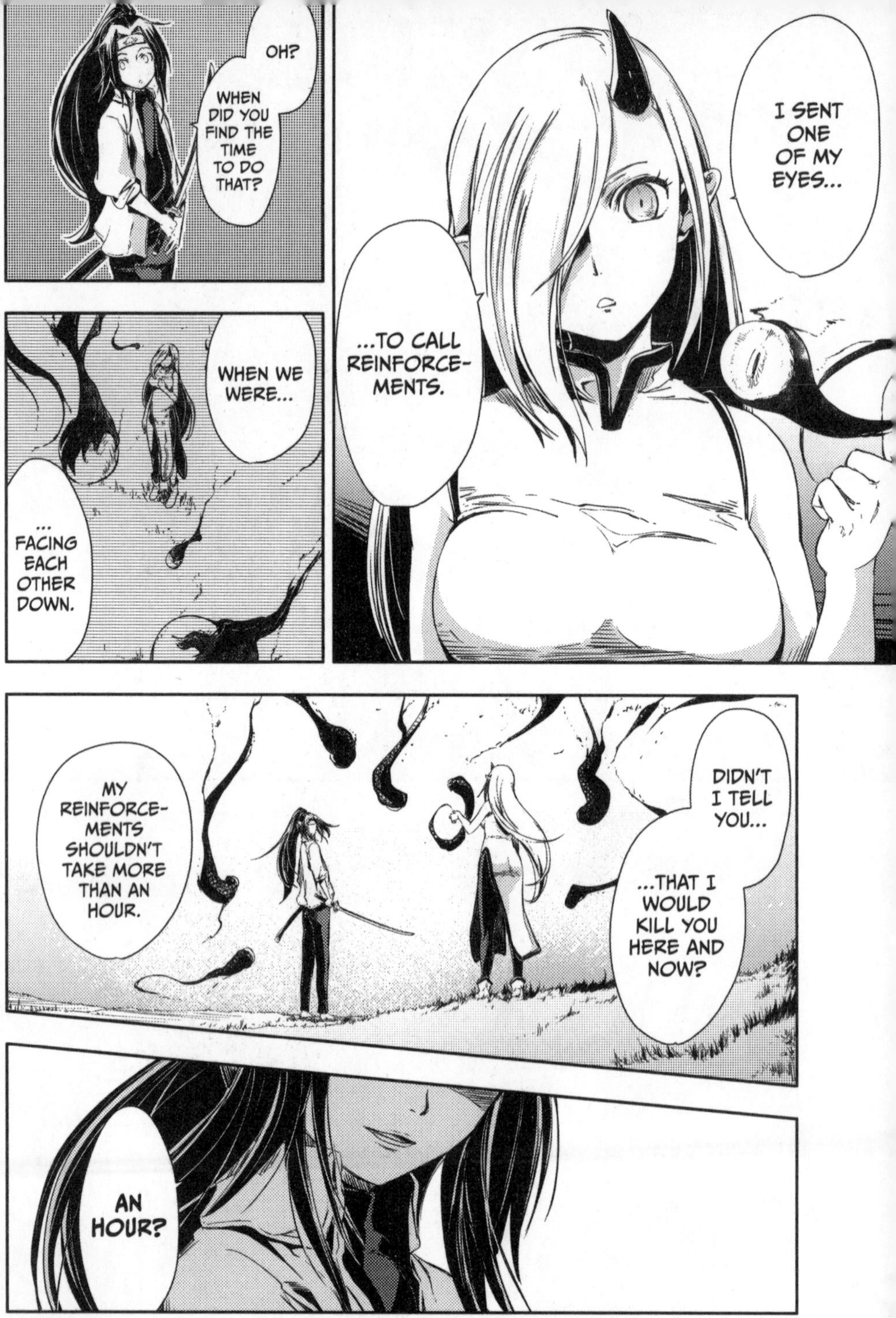
I SENT ONE OF MY EYES...
...TO CALL REINFORCE-MENTS.
OH?
WHEN DID YOU FIND THE TIME TO DO THAT?
WHEN WE WERE...
...FACING EACH OTHER DOWN.
DIDN'T I TELL YOU...
...THAT I WOULD KILL YOU HERE AND NOW?
MY REINFORCE-MENTS SHOULDN'T TAKE MORE THAN AN HOUR.
AN HOUR?

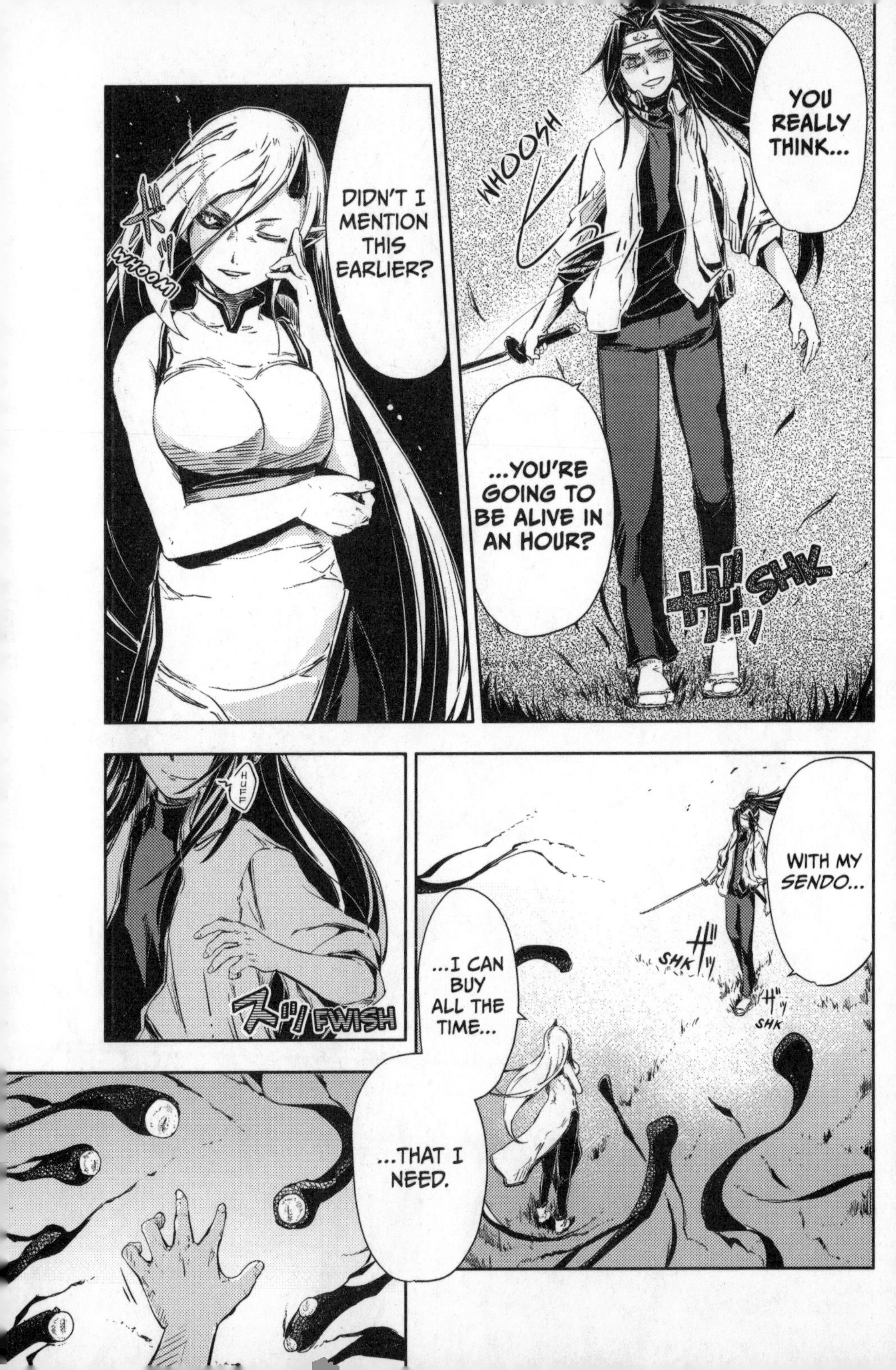
YOU REALLY THINK...
WHOOSH
...YOU'RE GOING TO BE ALIVE IN AN HOUR?
SHK
DIDN'T I MENTION THIS EARLIER?
WHOOM
WITH MY SENDO...
SHK
SHK
...I CAN BUY ALL THE TIME...
...THAT I NEED.
HUFF
FWISH

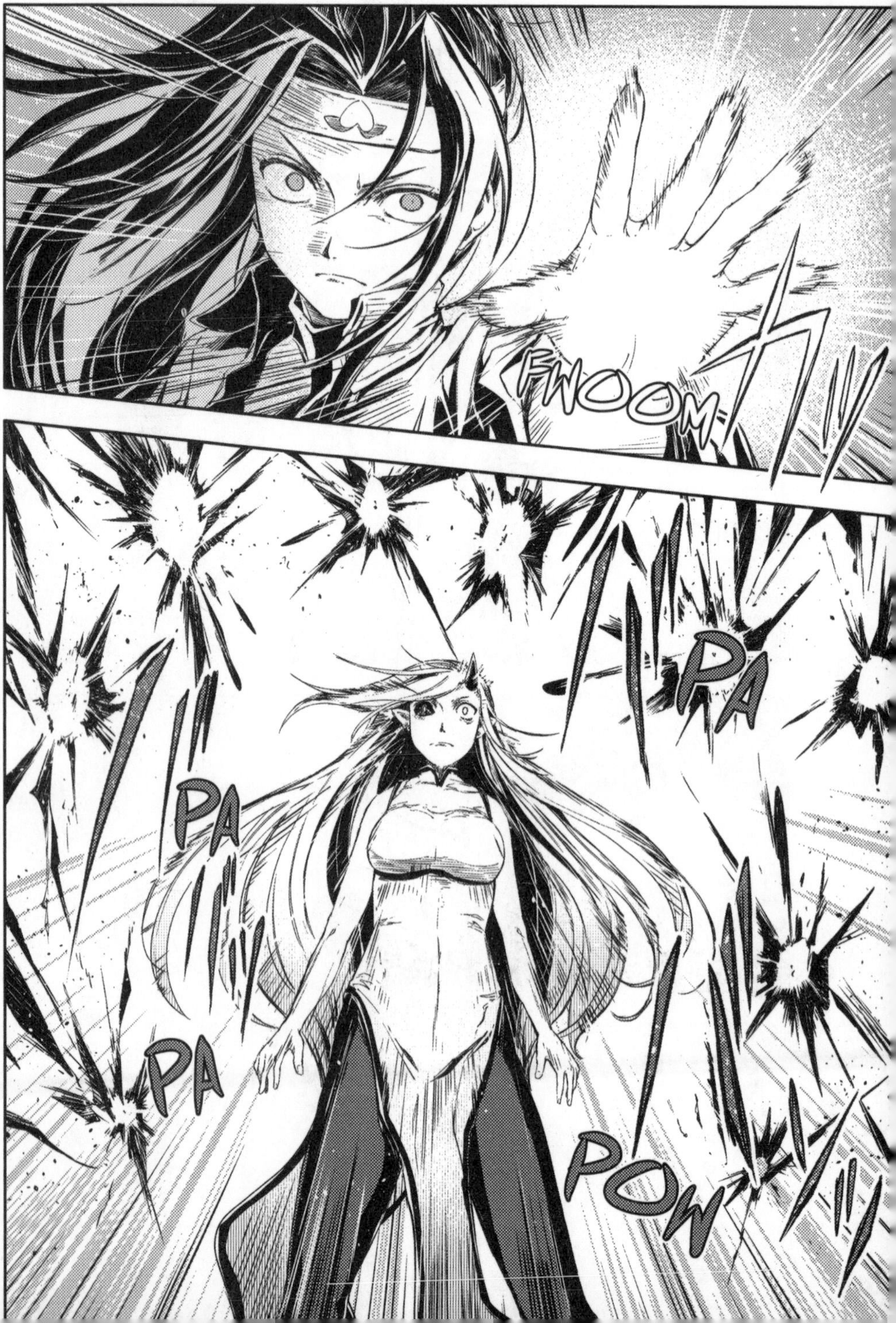
FWOOM
PA
PA
PA
POW

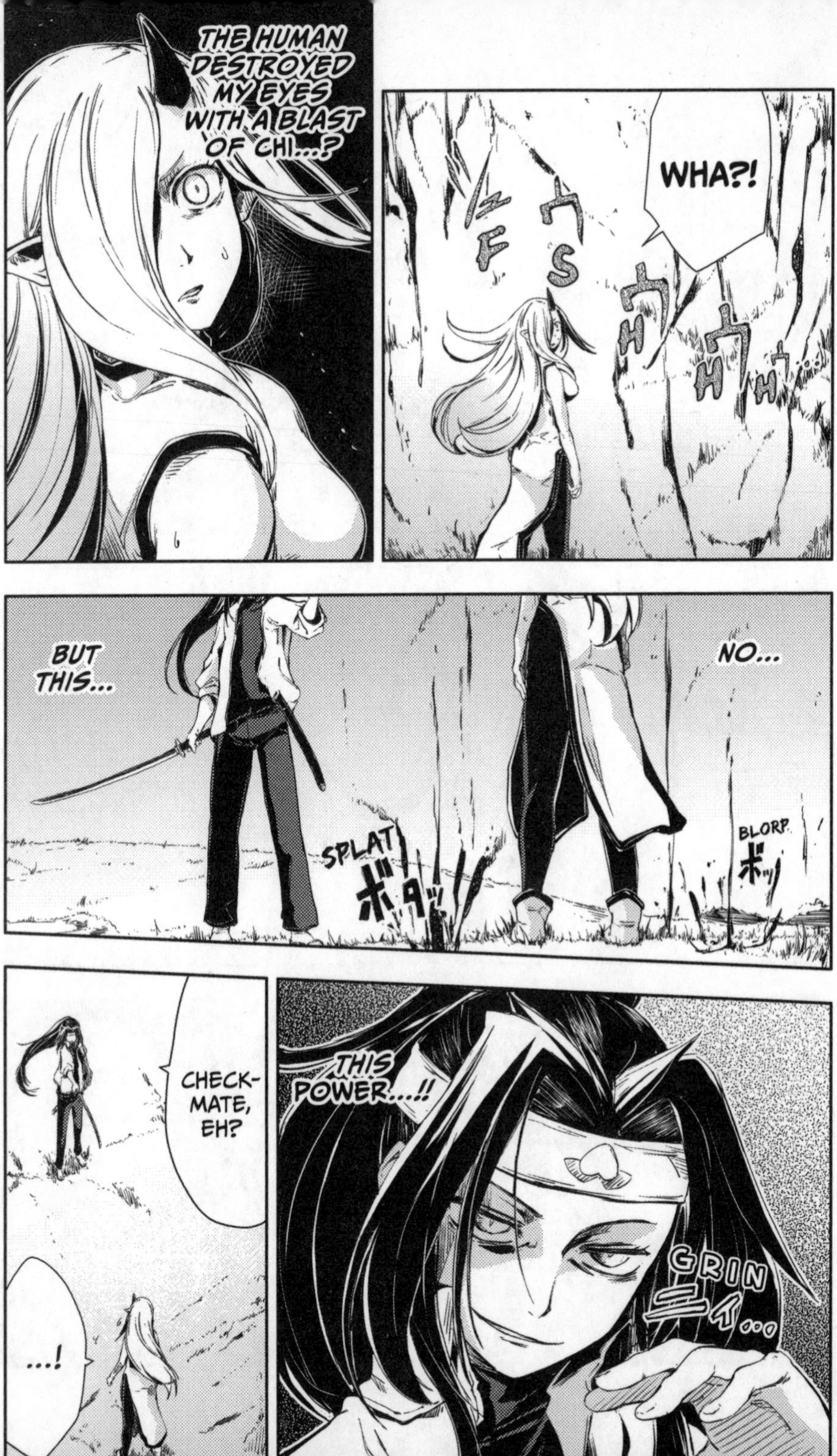
WHA?!
FS
HHH...
THE HUMAN DESTROYED MY EYES WITH A BLAST OF CHI...?
NO...
BLORP
ボッ
SPLAT
ボタッ
BUT THIS...
THIS POWER...!!
GRIN
ニイ...
CHECK-MATE, EH?
...!

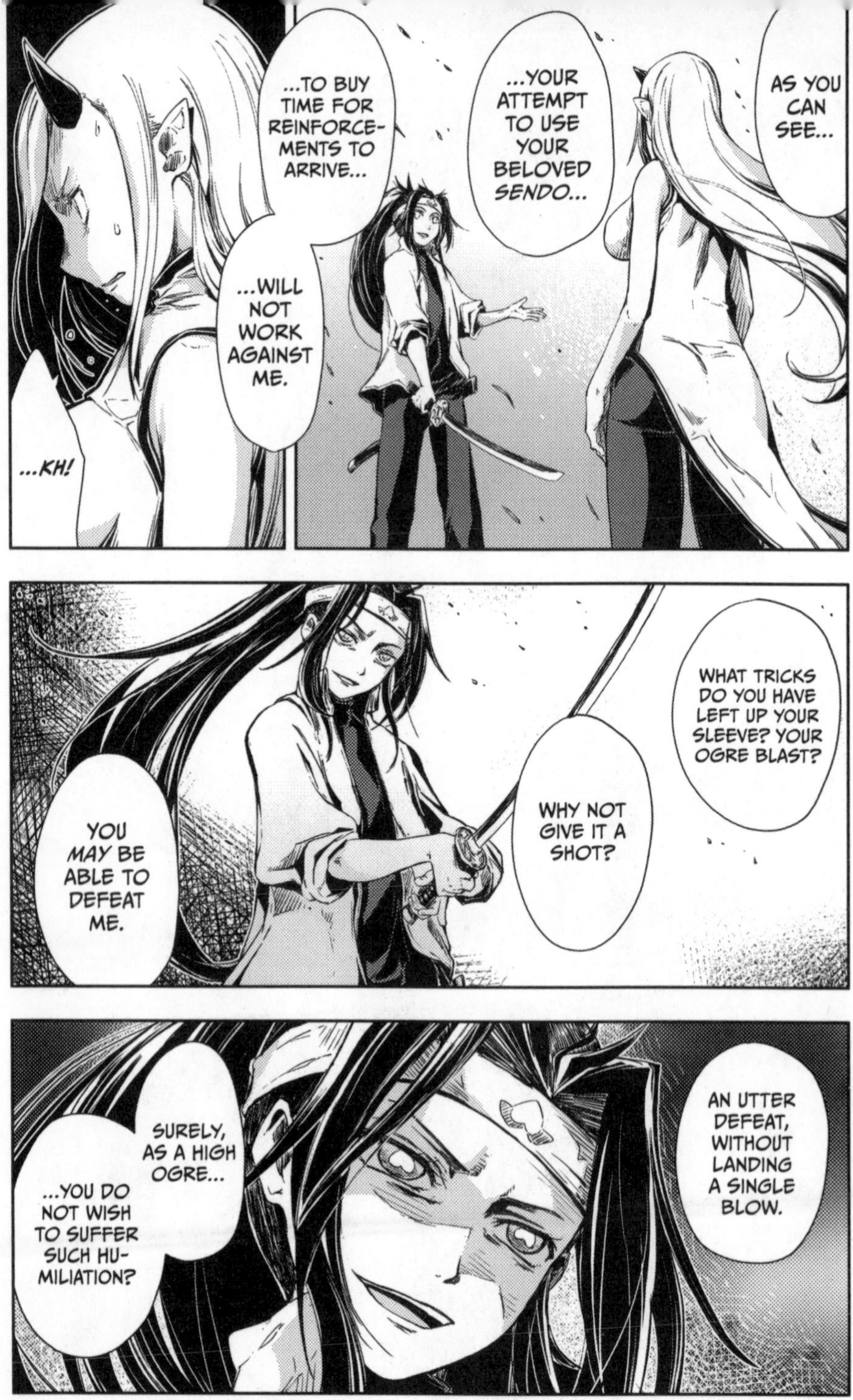
AS YOU CAN SEE...
...YOUR ATTEMPT TO USE YOUR BELOVED SENDO...
...TO BUY TIME FOR REINFORCE-MENTS TO ARRIVE...
...WILL NOT WORK AGAINST ME.
...KH!
WHAT TRICKS DO YOU HAVE LEFT UP YOUR SLEEVE? YOUR OGRE BLAST?
WHY NOT GIVE IT A SHOT?
YOU MAY BE ABLE TO DEFEAT ME.
AN UTTER DEFEAT, WITHOUT LANDING A SINGLE BLOW.
SURELY, AS A HIGH OGRE...
...YOU DO NOT WISH TO SUFFER SUCH HU-MILIATION?

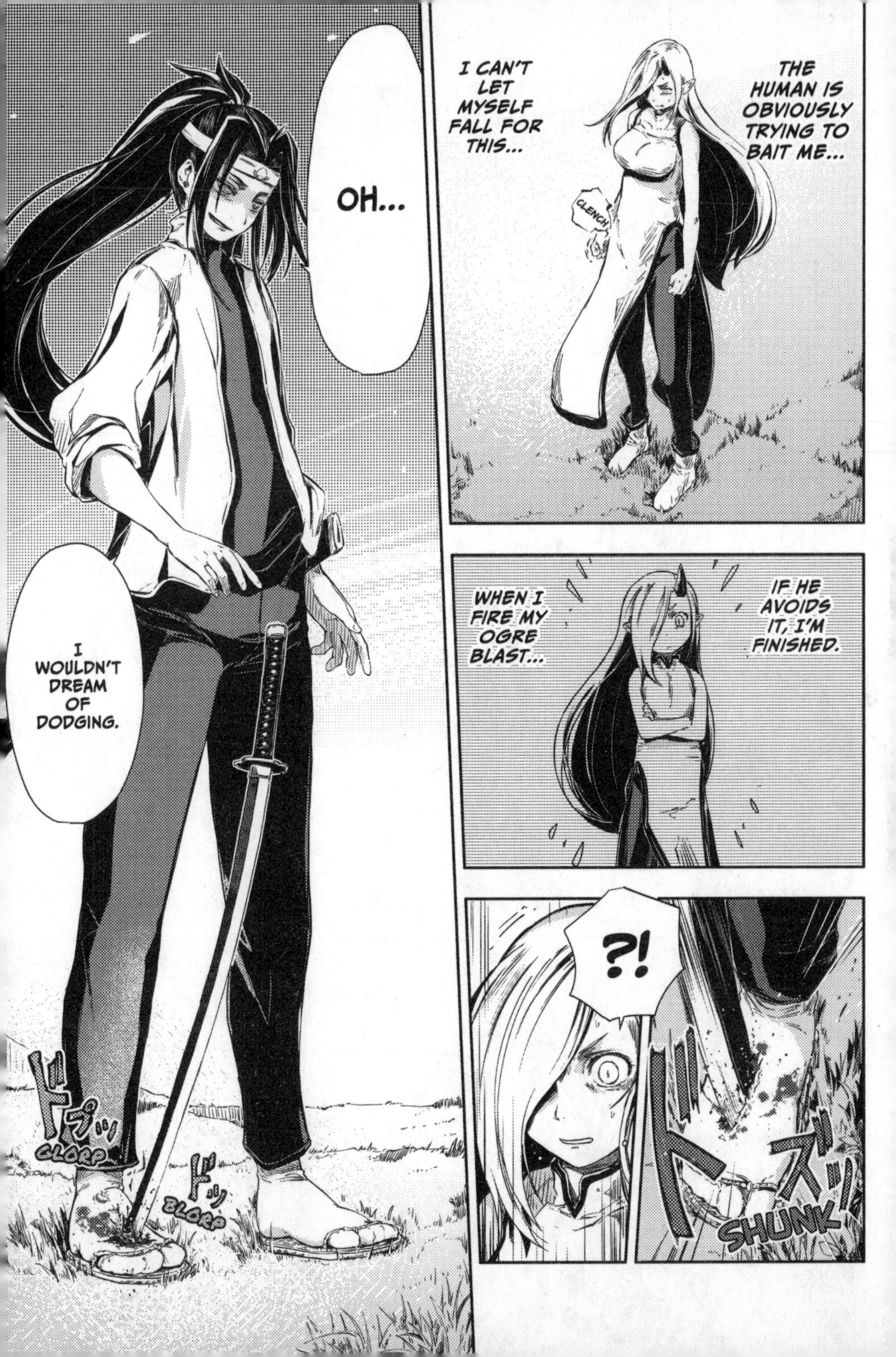
THE HUMAN IS OBVIOUSLY TRYING TO BAIT ME...
I CAN'T LET MYSELF FALL FOR THIS...
CLENCH
WHEN I FIRE MY OGRE BLAST...
IF HE AVOIDS IT, I'M FINISHED.
?!
SHUNK!
OH...
I WOULDN'T DREAM OF DODGING.
GLORP
BLORP

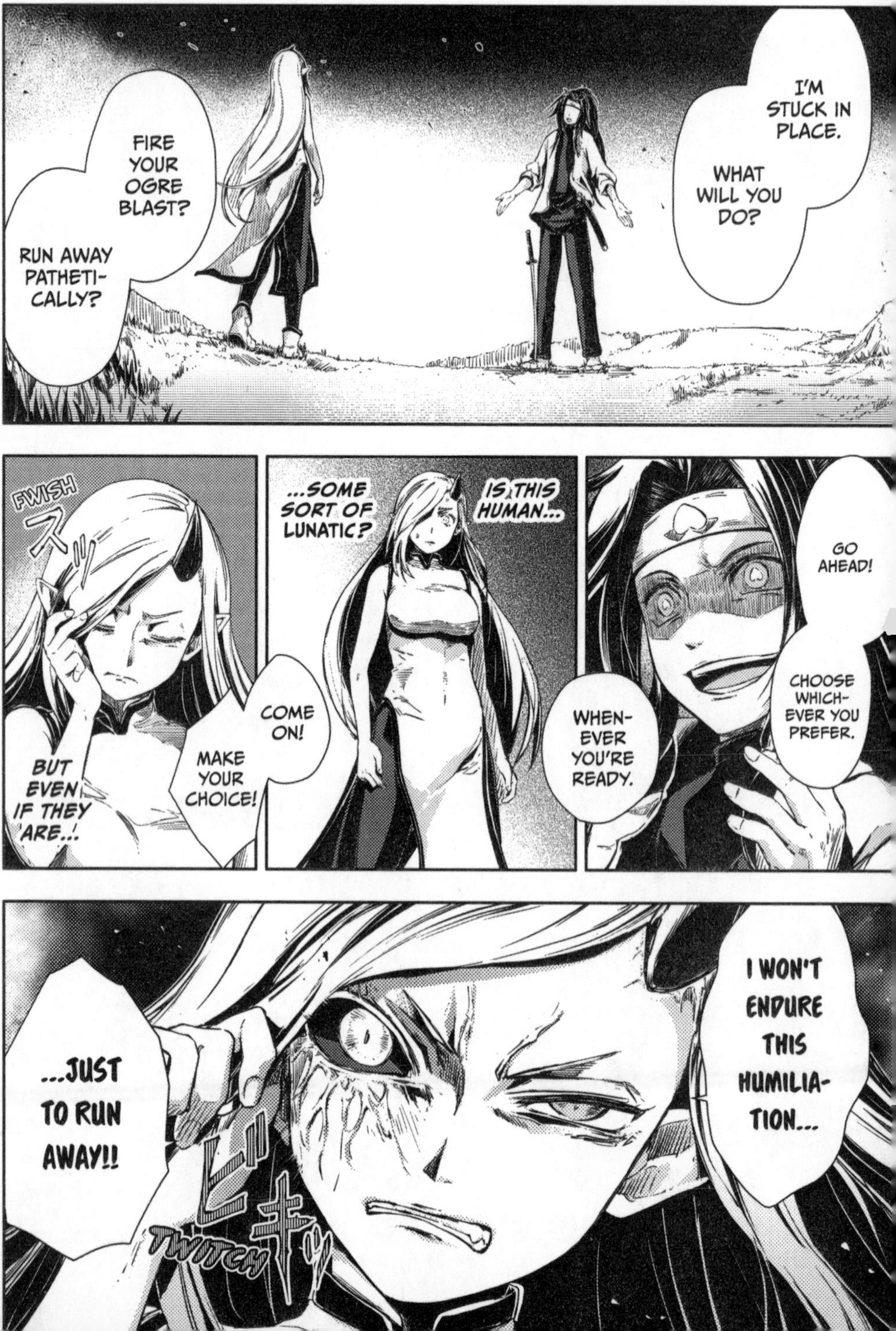

I'M STUCK IN PLACE.
WHAT WILL YOU DO?
FIRE YOUR OGRE BLAST?
RUN AWAY PATHETICALLY?
GO AHEAD!
CHOOSE WHICHEVER YOU PREFER.
WHENEVER YOU'RE READY.
IS THIS HUMAN...
...SOME SORT OF LUNATIC?
COME ON!
MAKE YOUR CHOICE!
FWISH
BUT EVEN IF THEY ARE...!
I WON'T ENDURE THIS HUMILIATION...
...JUST TO RUN AWAY!!
TWITCH

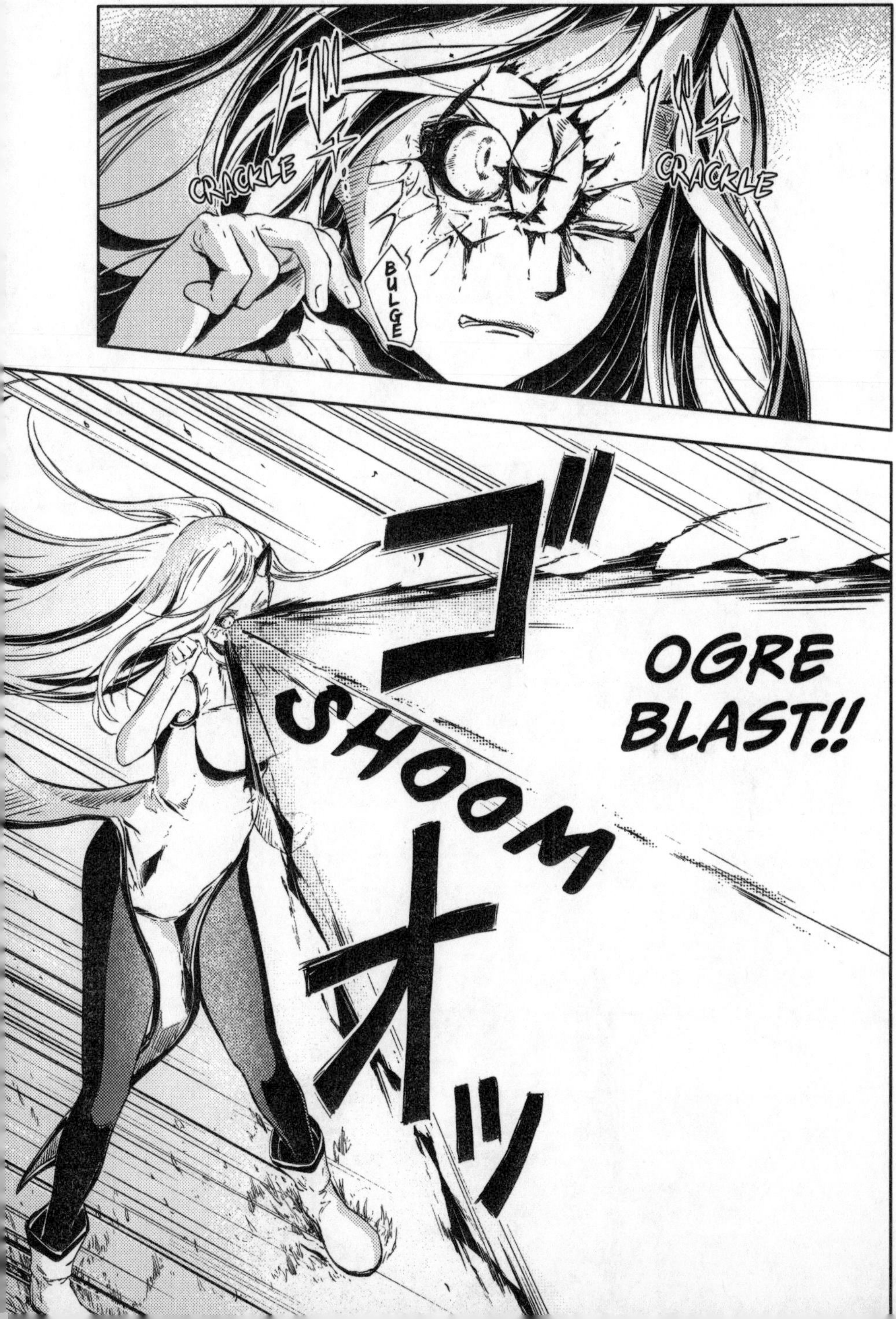
CRACKLE
CRACKLE
BULGE
OGRE BLAST!!
SHOOM
ゴオッ

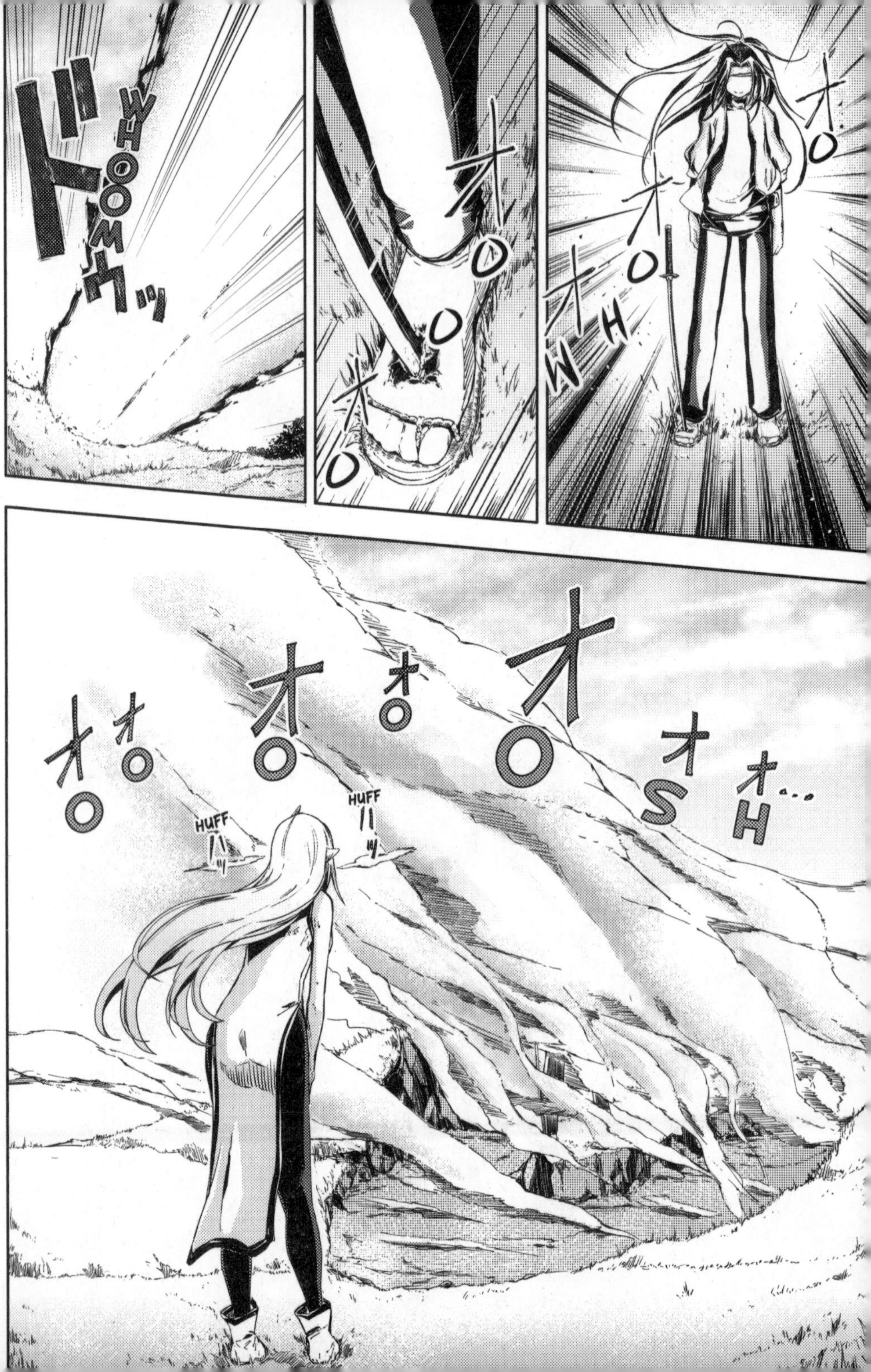
WHOO
オオ
OO
オオ
WHOOMF
ドドッ
オオオオ
OOOOSH...
HUFF
ハッ
HUFF
ハッ

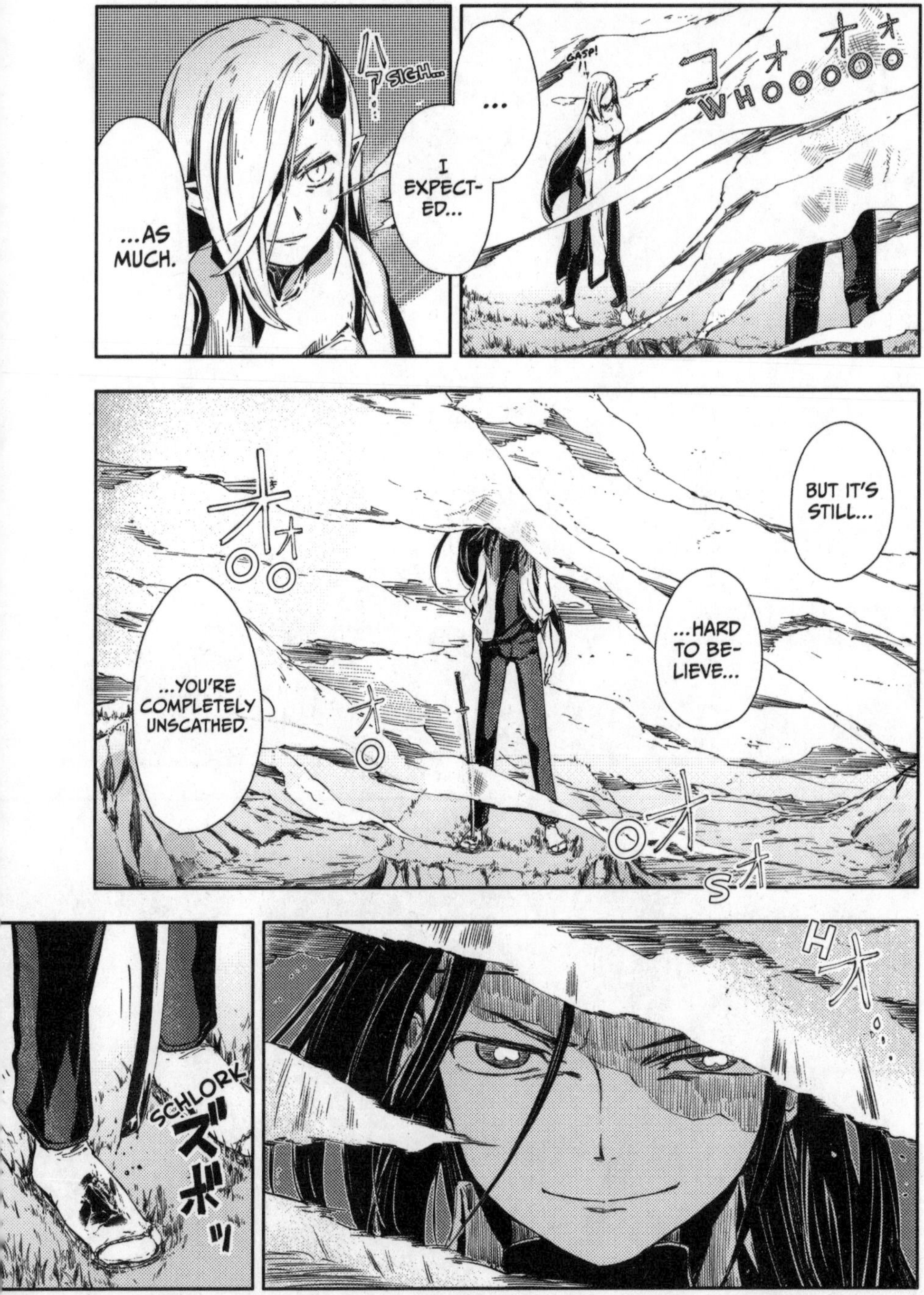
GASP!
WHOOOOOO
...
I EXPECTED...
SIGH...
...AS MUCH.
BUT IT'S STILL...
...HARD TO BELIEVE...
...YOU'RE COMPLETELY UNSCATHED.
SH
SCHLORK

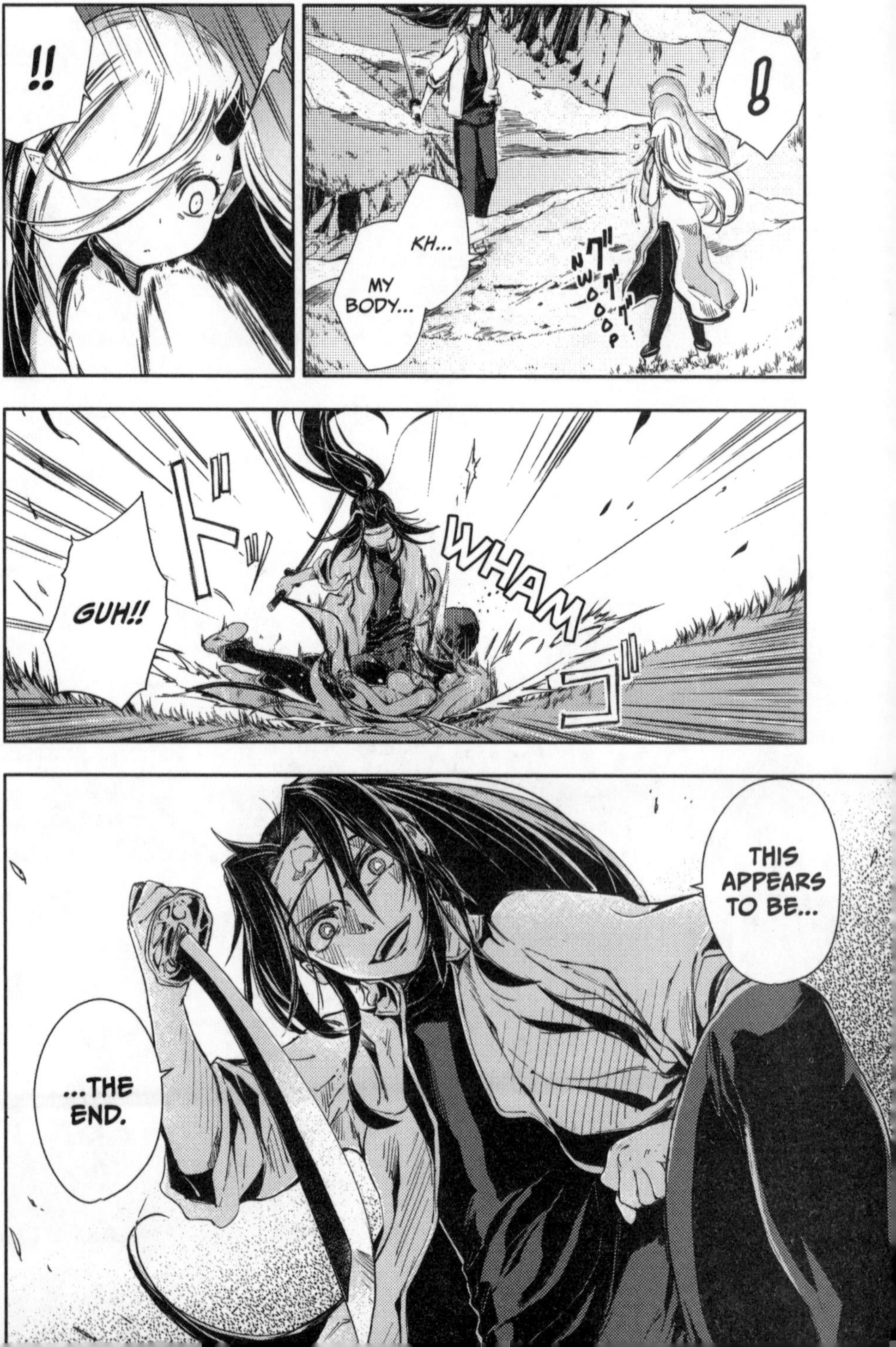
!
KH...
MY BODY...
NWOOOP
!!
GUH!!
ドッ
WHAM
ゴ
THIS APPEARS TO BE...
...THE END.

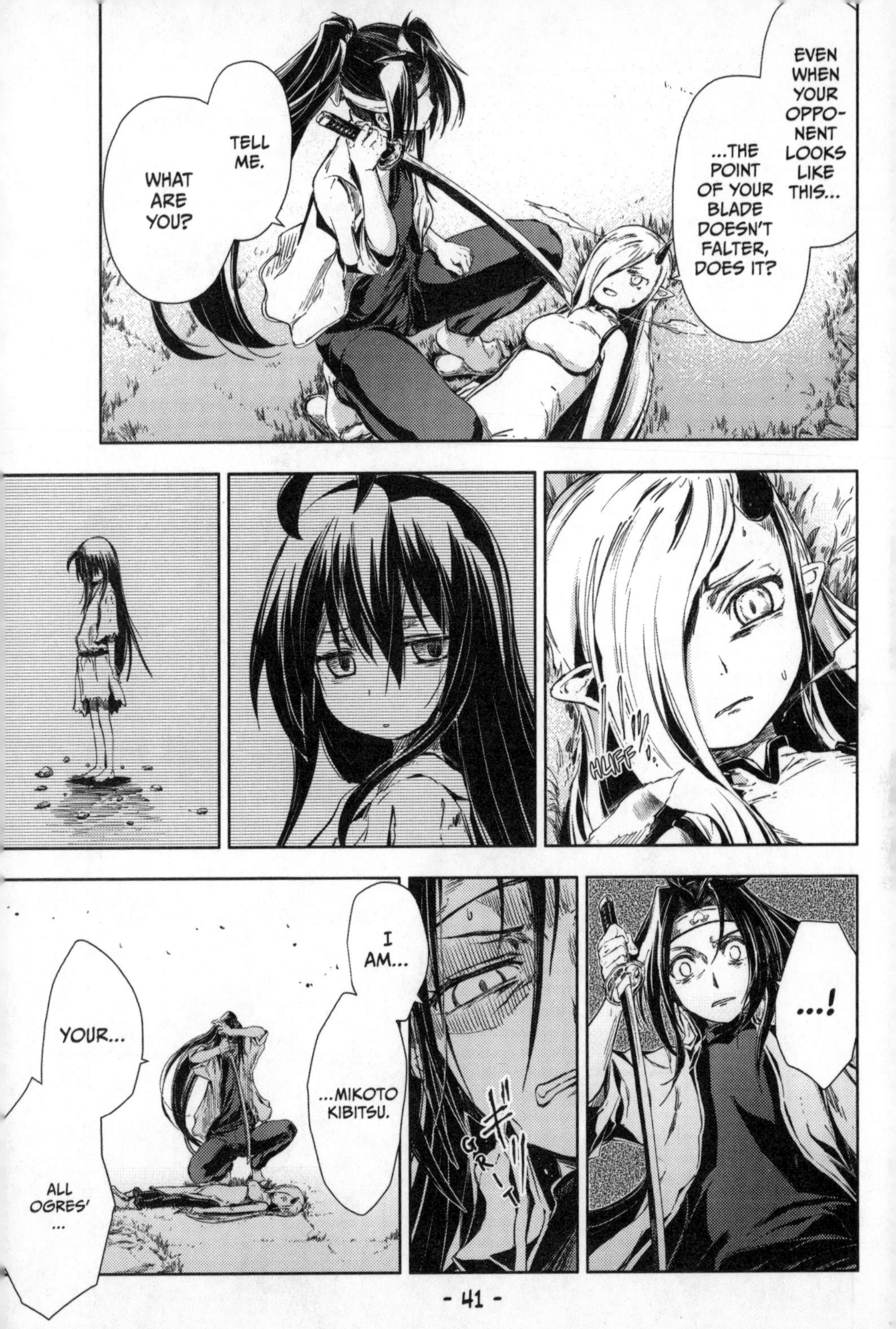
EVEN WHEN YOUR OPPONENT LOOKS LIKE THIS...
...THE POINT OF YOUR BLADE DOESN'T FALTER, DOES IT?
TELL ME.
WHAT ARE YOU?
HUFF
...!
GRIT
I AM...
...MIKOTO KIBITSU.
YOUR...
ALL OGRES' ...

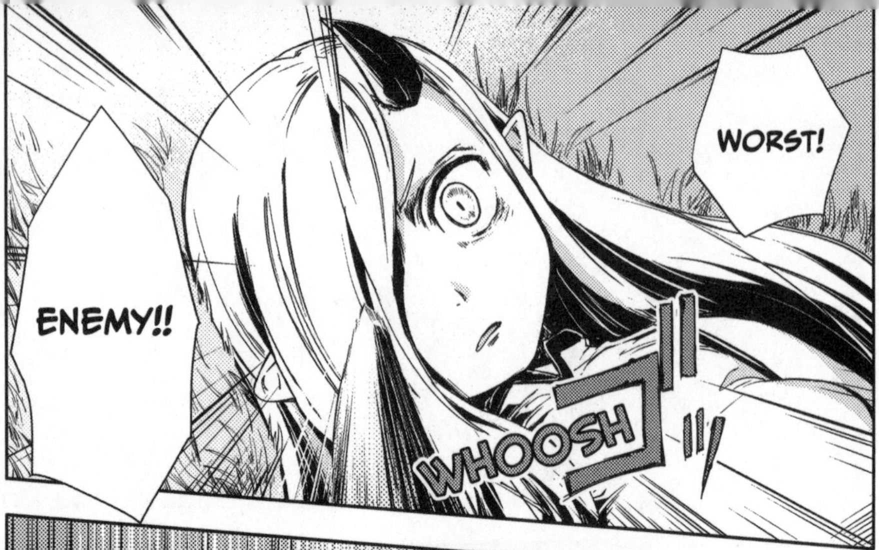
WORST!
ENEMY!!
WHOOSH
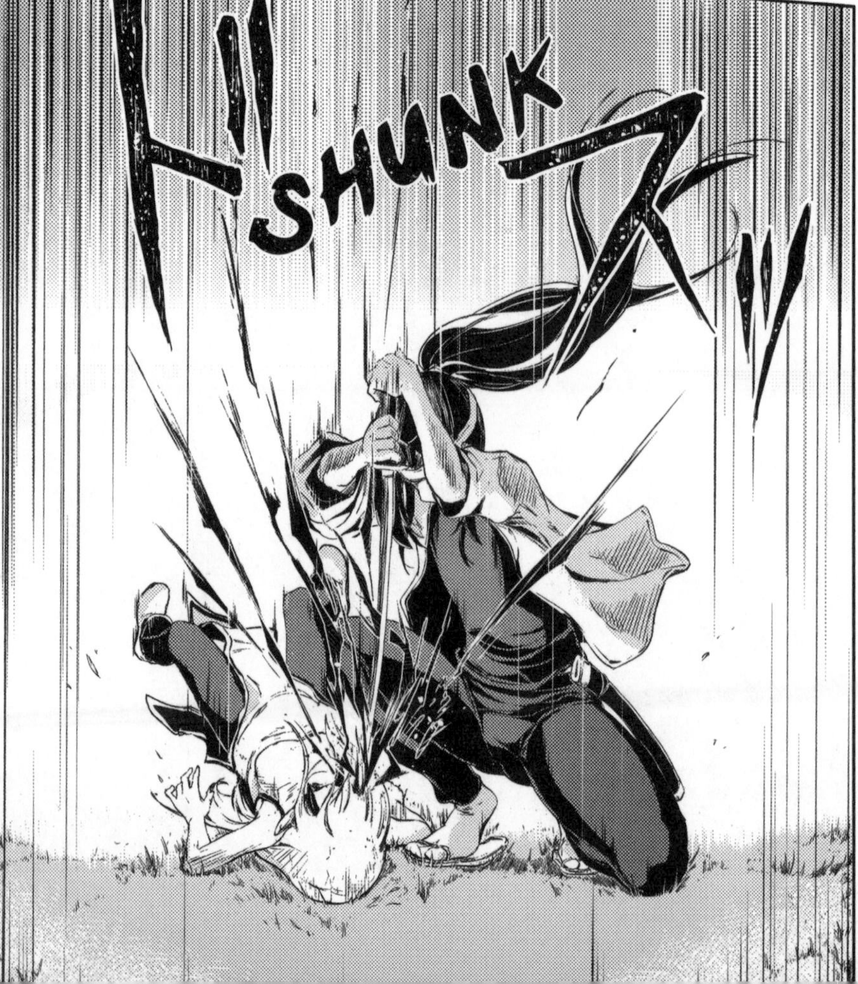
SHUNK

PEACH BOY RIVERSIDE

CHAPTER 5:
OGRES AND HUMANS

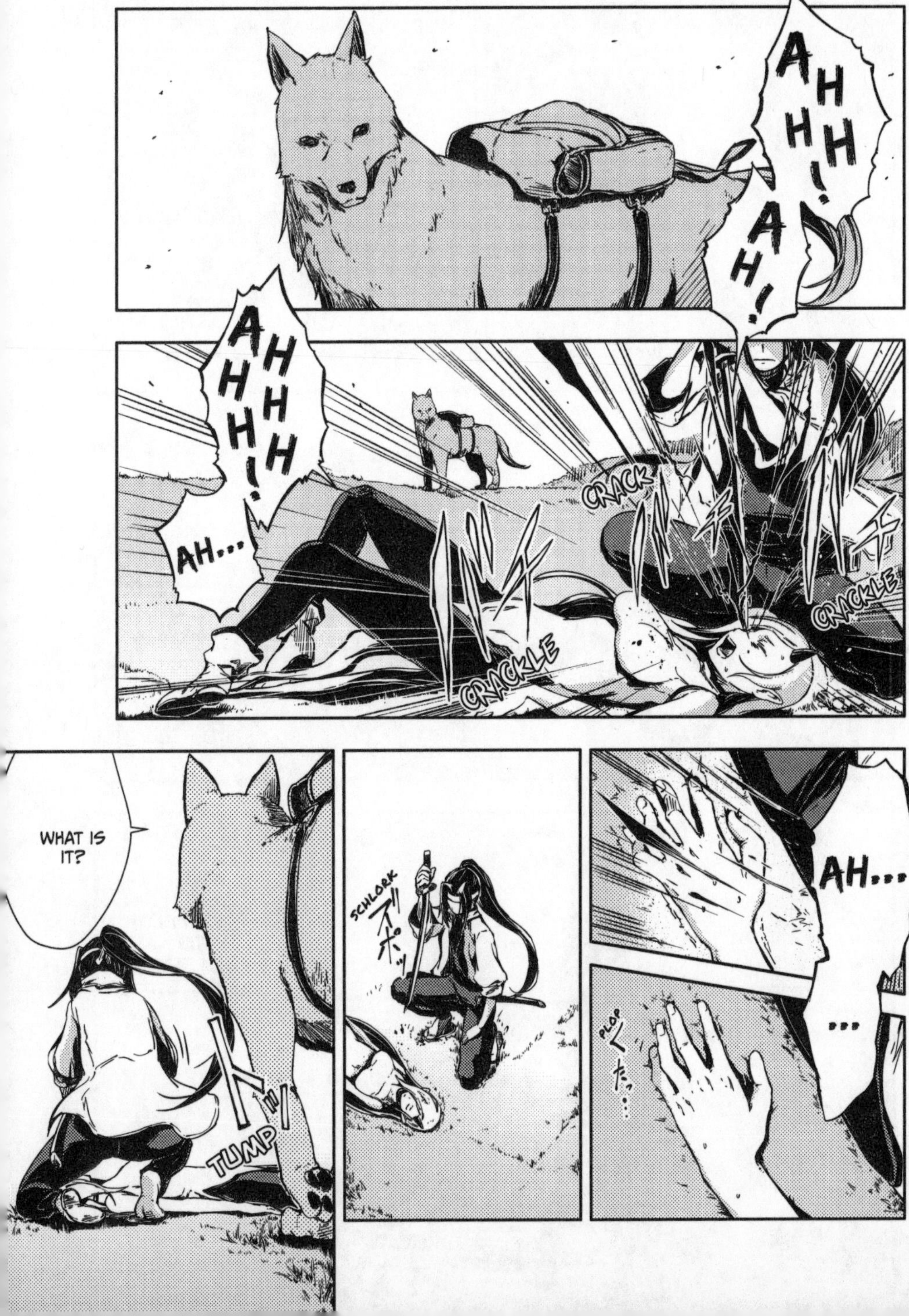
AHHH! AH! AH!
CRACK
CRACKLE
CRACKLE
AHHHHHH!
AH...
AH...
...
PLOP
SCHLORK
WHAT IS IT?
TUMP

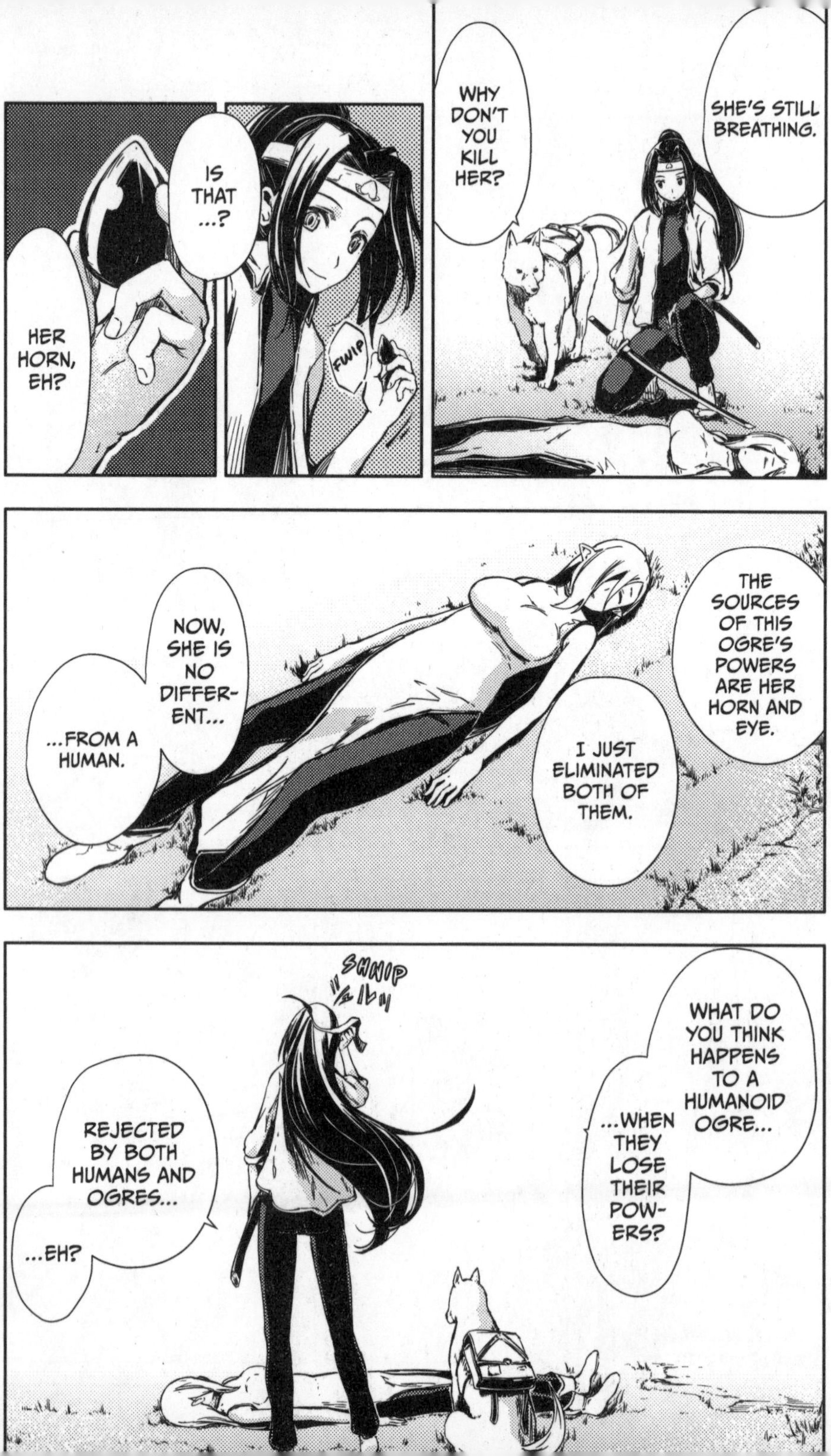
SHE'S STILL BREATHING.
WHY DON'T YOU KILL HER?
IS THAT ...?
FWIP
HER HORN, EH?
THE SOURCES OF THIS OGRE'S POWERS ARE HER HORN AND EYE.
I JUST ELIMINATED BOTH OF THEM.
NOW, SHE IS NO DIFFERENT...
...FROM A HUMAN.
WHAT DO YOU THINK HAPPENS TO A HUMANOID OGRE...
...WHEN THEY LOSE THEIR POWERS?
SHWIP
REJECTED BY BOTH HUMANS AND OGRES...
...EH?

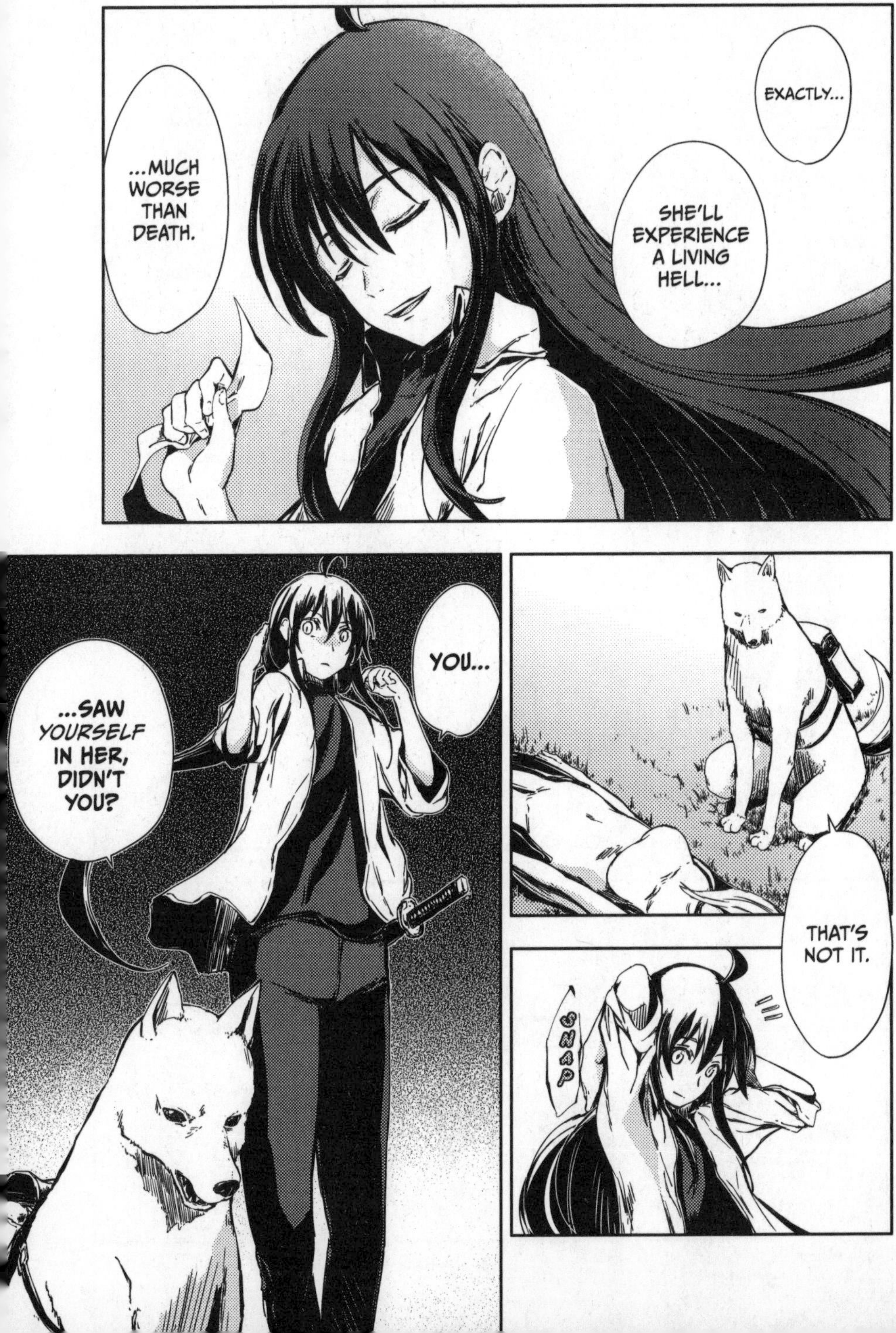
EXACTLY...
SHE'LL EXPERIENCE A LIVING HELL...
...MUCH WORSE THAN DEATH.
THAT'S NOT IT.
SNAP
YOU...
...SAW YOURSELF IN HER, DIDN'T YOU?

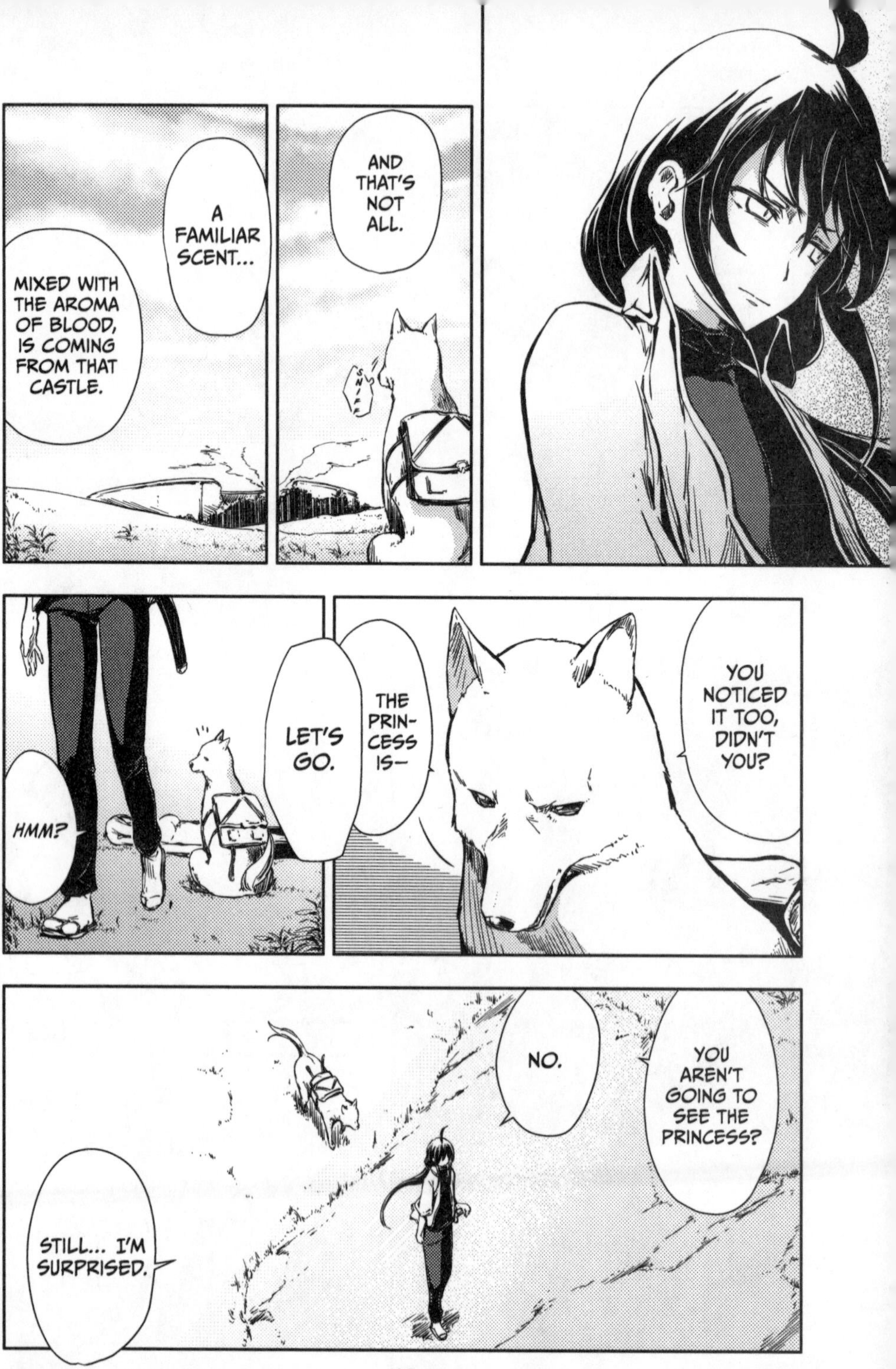
AND THAT'S NOT ALL.
SNIFF
A FAMILIAR SCENT...
MIXED WITH THE AROMA OF BLOOD, IS COMING FROM THAT CASTLE.
YOU NOTICED IT TOO, DIDN'T YOU?
THE PRIN-CESS IS—
LET'S GO.
HMM?
YOU AREN'T GOING TO SEE THE PRINCESS?
NO.
STILL... I'M SURPRISED.

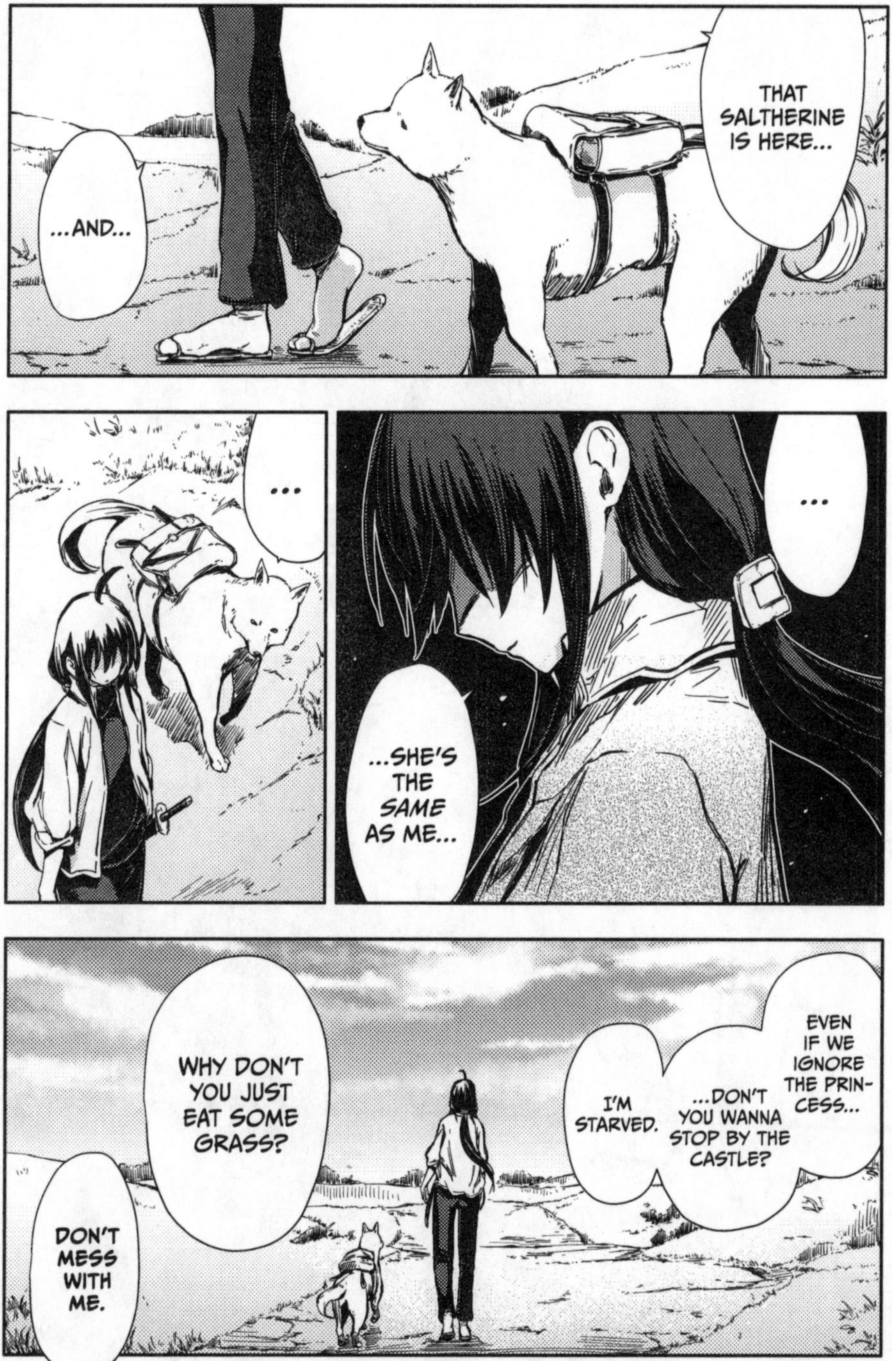
THAT SALTHERINE IS HERE...
...AND...
...
...SHE'S THE *SAME* AS ME...
...
EVEN IF WE IGNORE THE PRIN-CESS...
...DON'T YOU WANNA STOP BY THE CASTLE?
I'M STARVED.
WHY DON'T YOU JUST EAT SOME GRASS?
DON'T MESS WITH ME.

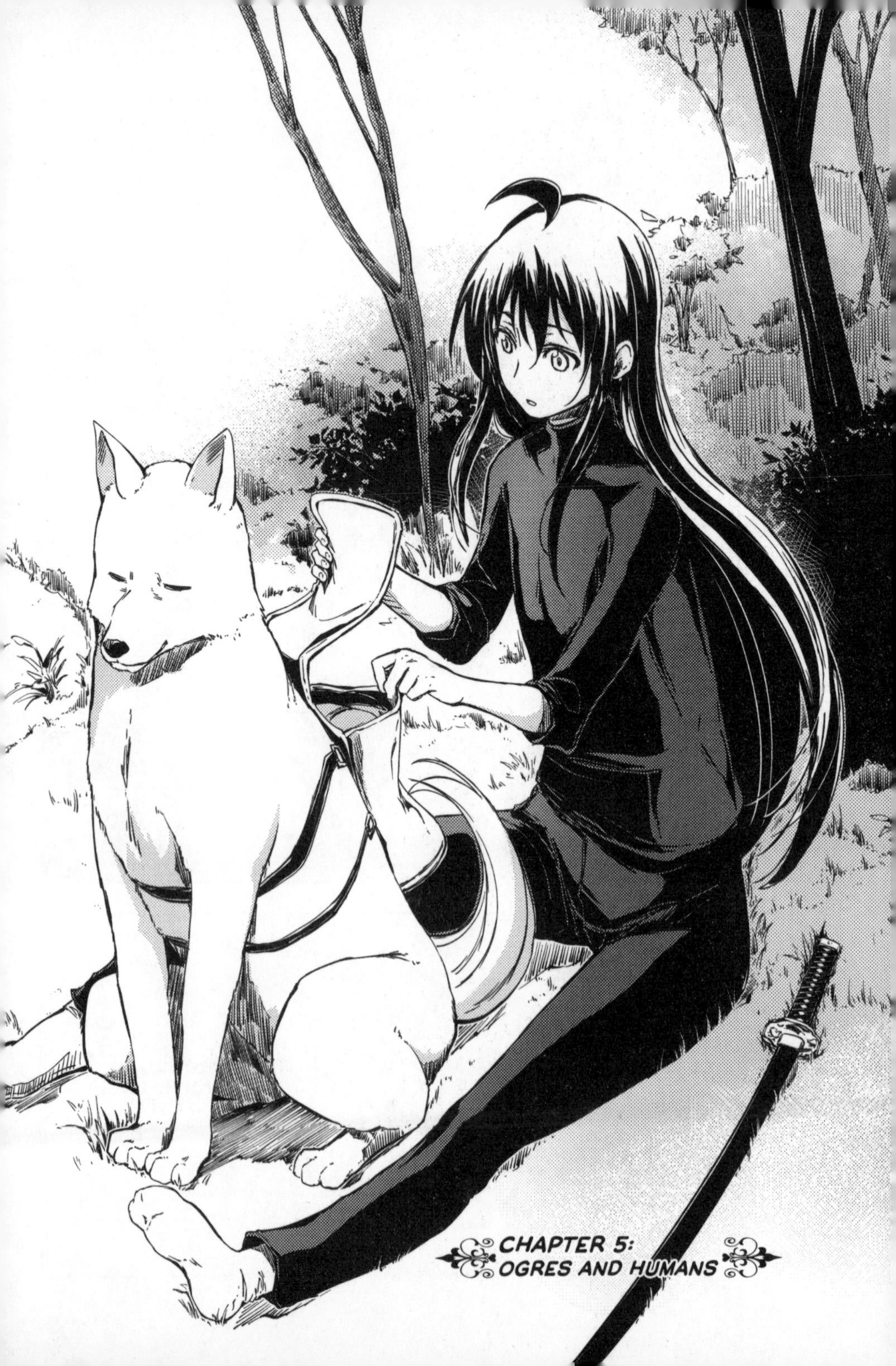
CHAPTER 5:
OGRES AND HUMANS

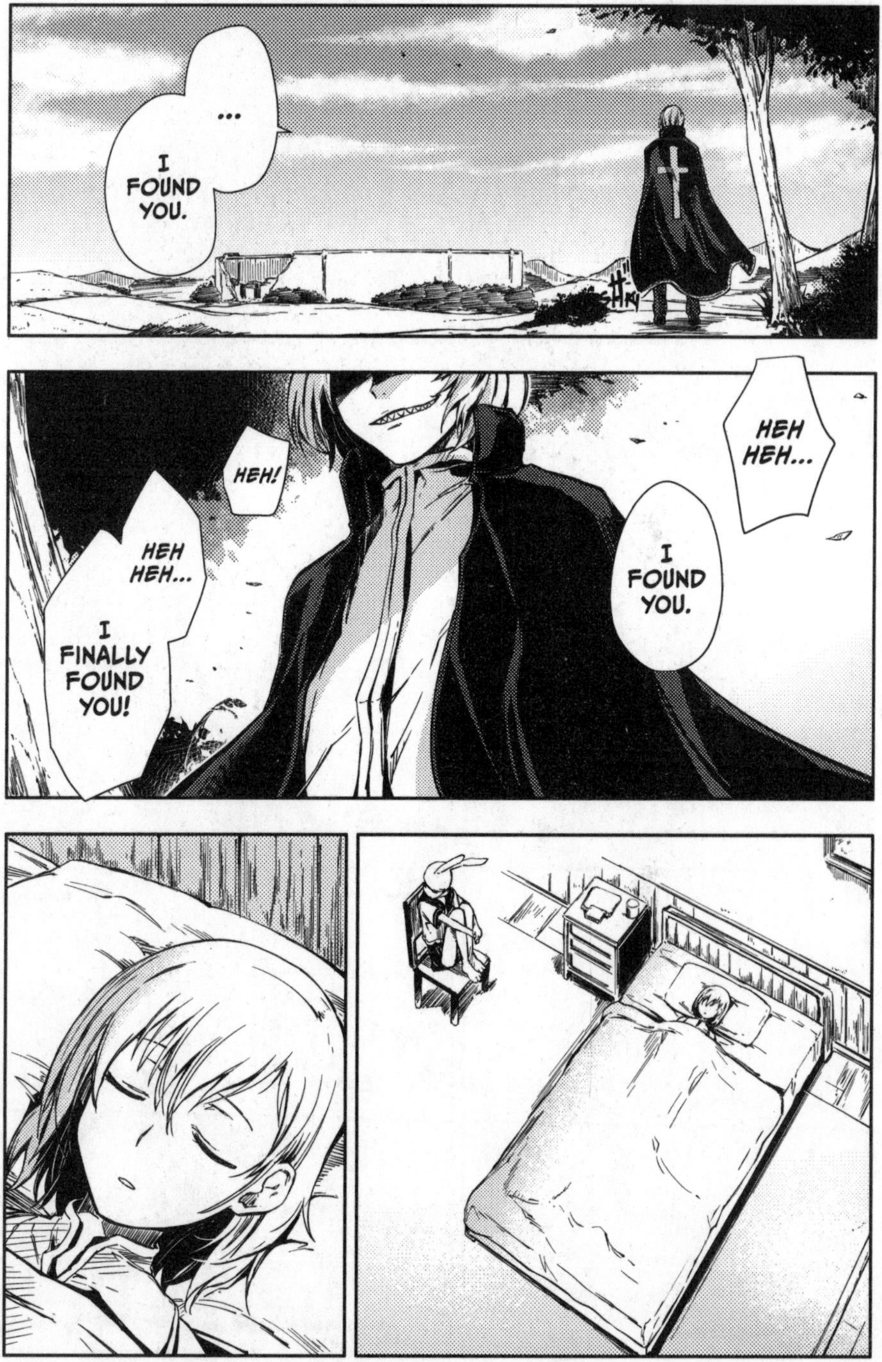
...
I FOUND YOU.
HEH HEH...
I FOUND YOU.
HEH!
HEH HEH...
I FINALLY FOUND YOU!

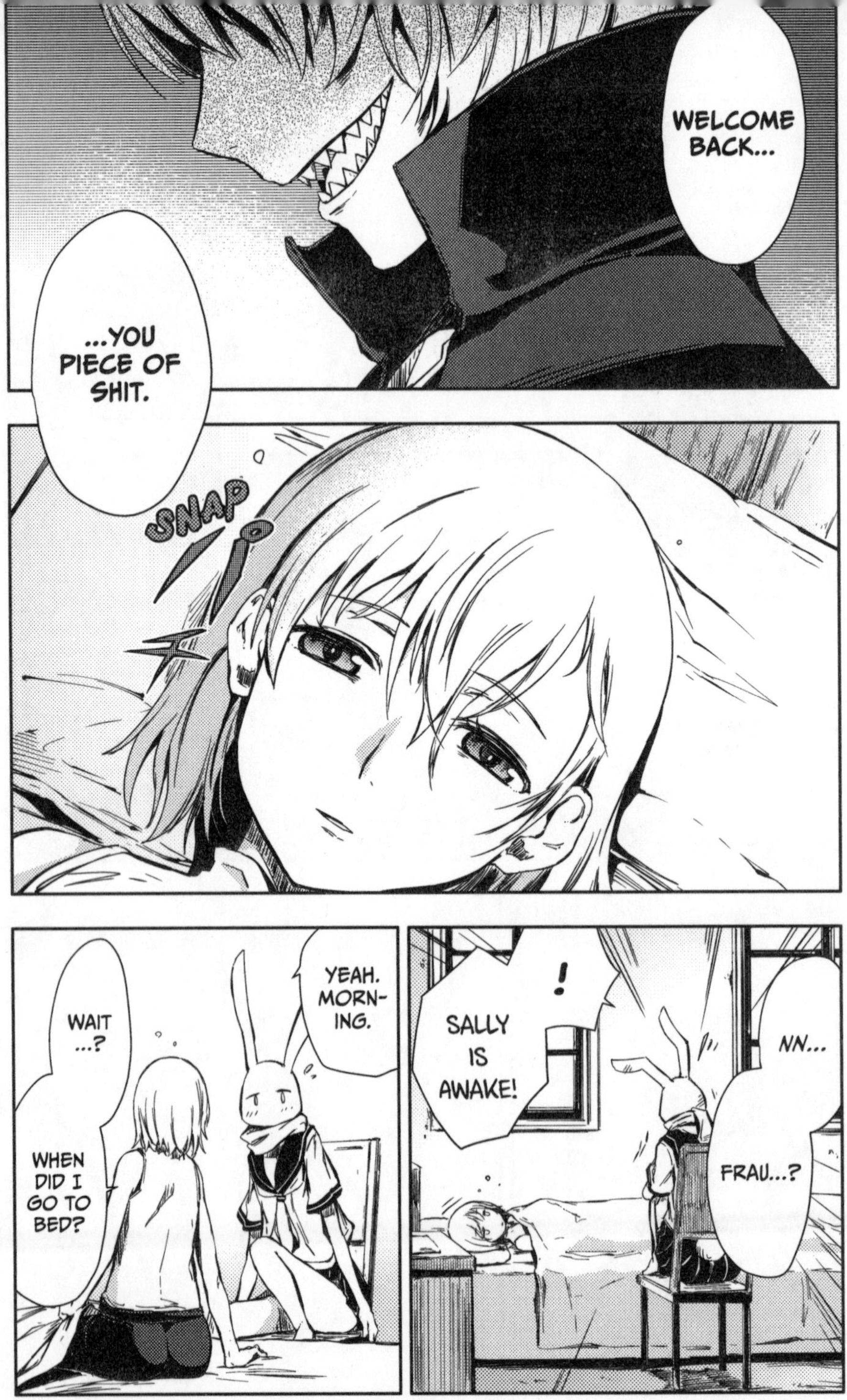
WELCOME BACK...
...YOU PIECE OF SHIT.
SNAP
NN...
FRAU...?
!
SALLY IS AWAKE!
YEAH. MORNING.
WAIT ...?
WHEN DID I GO TO BED?

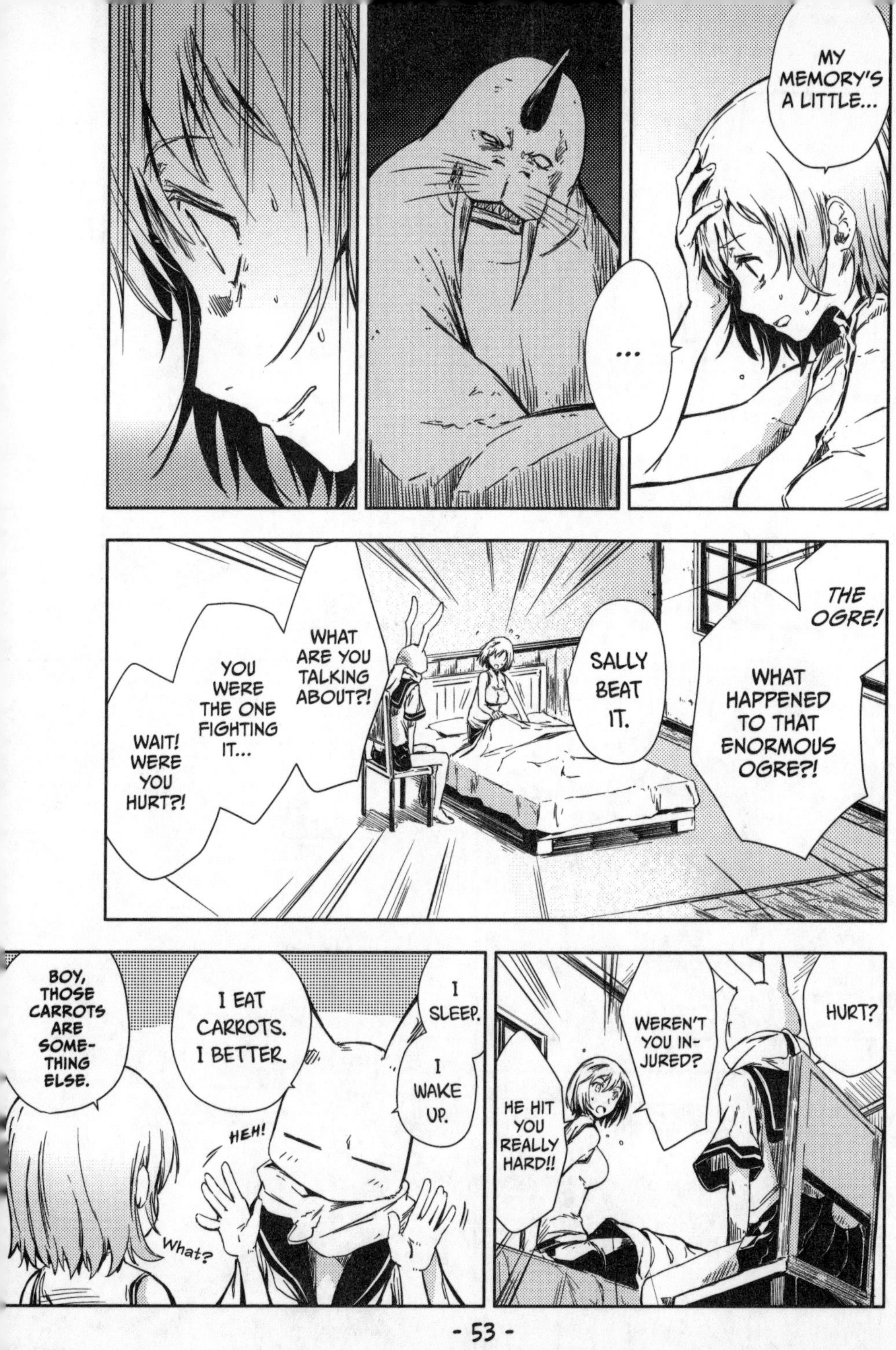
MY MEMORY'S A LITTLE...
...
THE OGRE!
WHAT HAPPENED TO THAT ENORMOUS OGRE?!
SALLY BEAT IT.
WHAT ARE YOU TALKING ABOUT?!
YOU WERE THE ONE FIGHTING IT...
WAIT! WERE YOU HURT?!
HURT?
WEREN'T YOU IN-JURED?
HE HIT YOU REALLY HARD!!
I SLEEP.
I WAKE UP.
I EAT CARROTS. I BETTER.
HEH!
BOY, THOSE CARROTS ARE SOME-THING ELSE.
What?

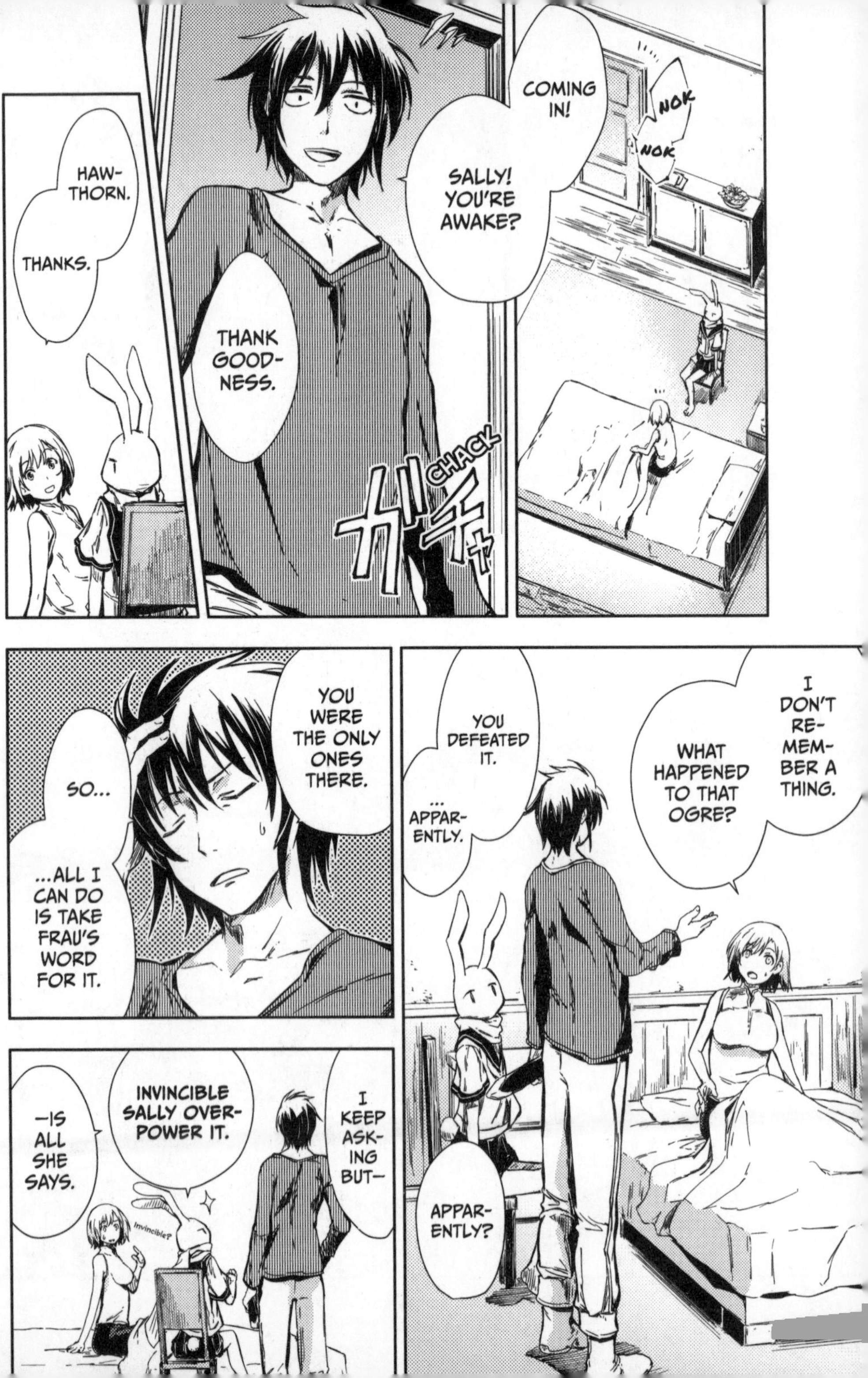
NOK
NOK
COMING IN!
SALLY! YOU'RE AWAKE?
ガチャ CHACK
THANK GOOD-NESS.
HAW-THORN.
THANKS.
I DON'T RE-MEM-BER A THING.
WHAT HAPPENED TO THAT OGRE?
YOU DEFEATED IT.
...APPAR-ENTLY.
APPAR-ENTLY?
YOU WERE THE ONLY ONES THERE.
SO...
...ALL I CAN DO IS TAKE FRAU'S WORD FOR IT.
I KEEP ASK-ING BUT—
INVINCIBLE SALLY OVER-POWER IT.
Invincible?
—IS ALL SHE SAYS.

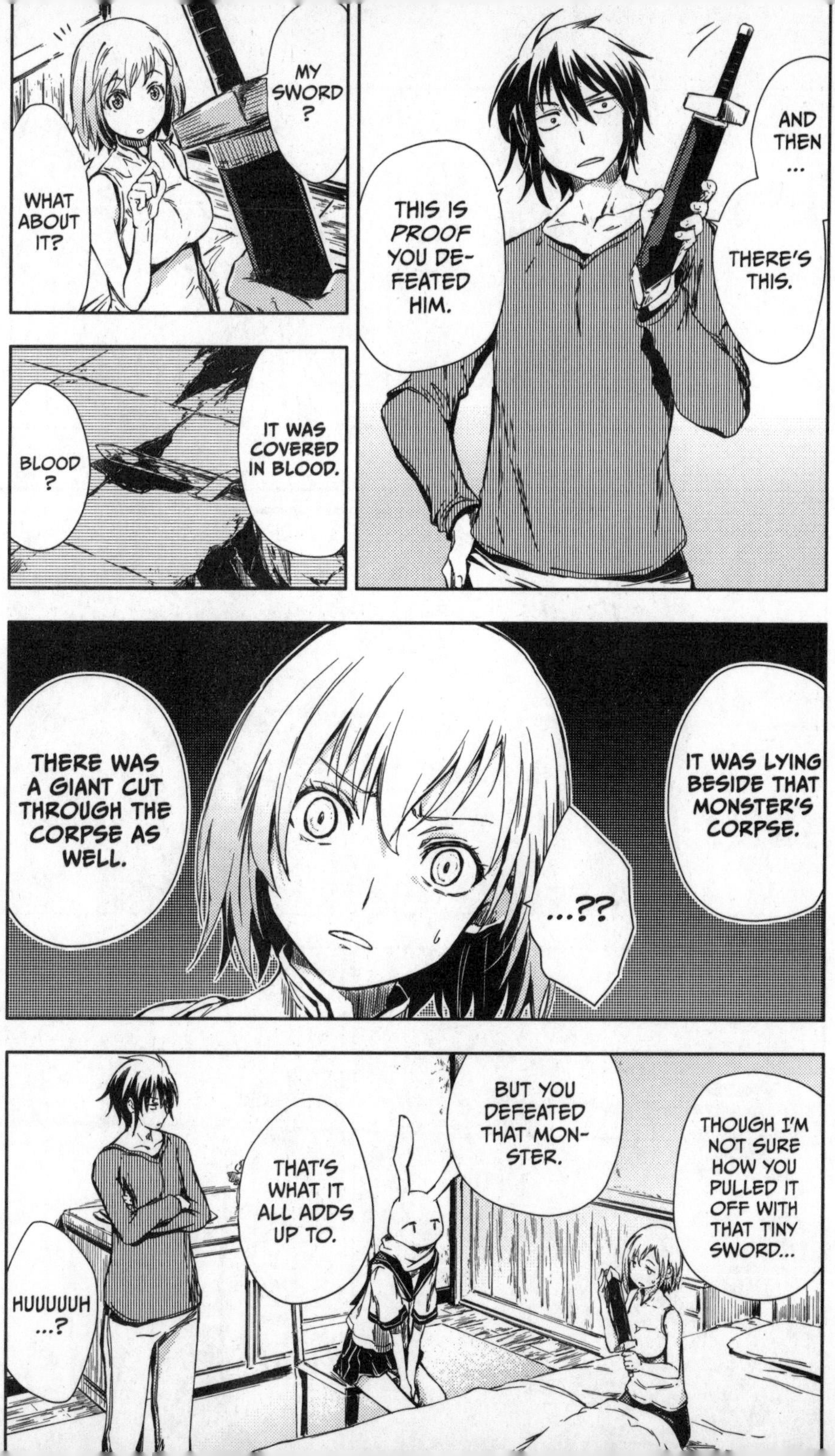
AND THEN ... THERE'S THIS.
THIS IS *PROOF* YOU DE-FEATED HIM.
MY SWORD?
WHAT ABOUT IT?
IT WAS COVERED IN BLOOD.
BLOOD?
IT WAS LYING BESIDE THAT MONSTER'S CORPSE.
...??
THERE WAS A GIANT CUT THROUGH THE CORPSE AS WELL.
THOUGH I'M NOT SURE HOW YOU PULLED IT OFF WITH THAT TINY SWORD...
BUT YOU DEFEATED THAT MON-STER.
THAT'S WHAT IT ALL ADDS UP TO.
HUUUUUH...?

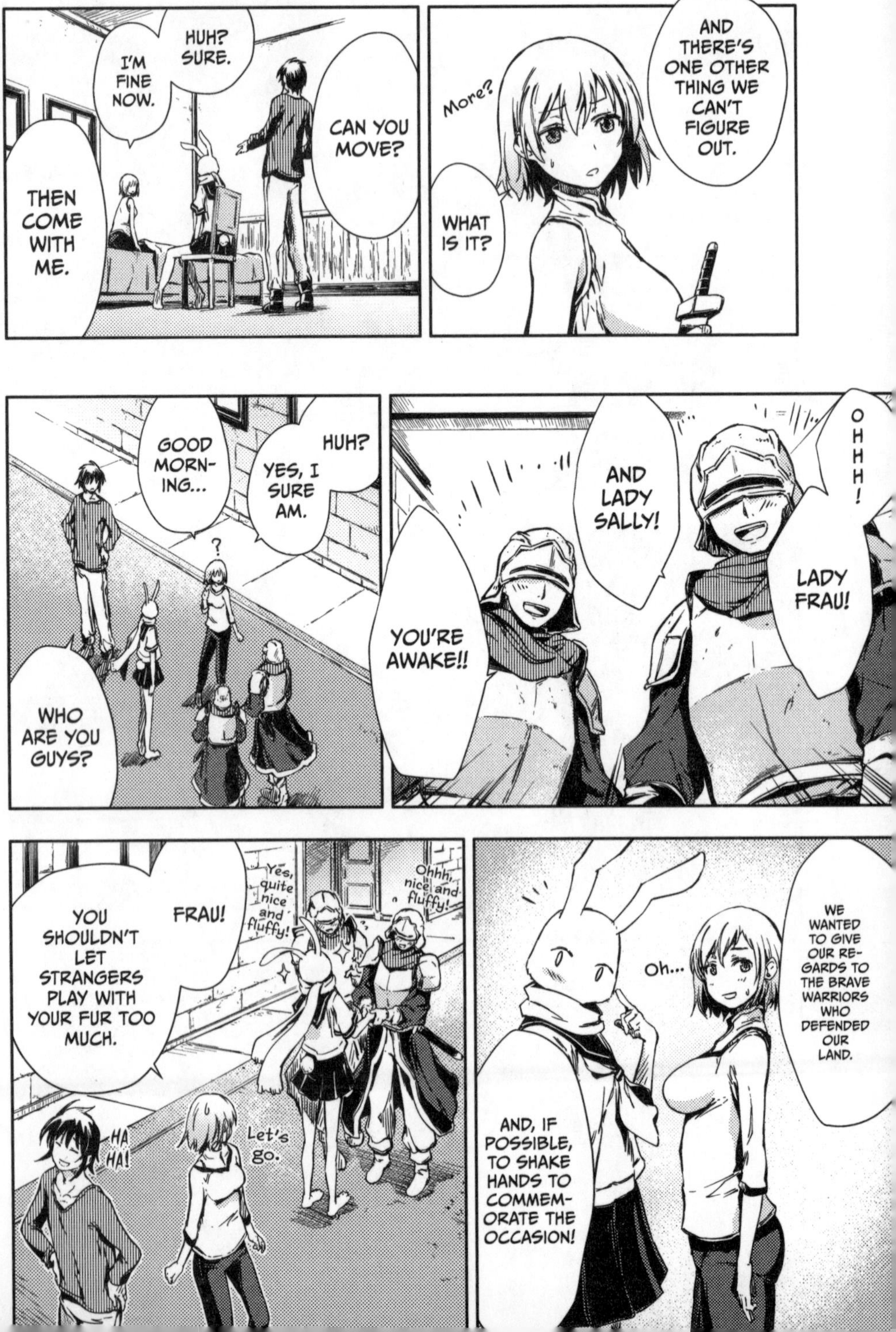
AND THERE'S ONE OTHER THING WE CAN'T FIGURE OUT.
More?
WHAT IS IT?
CAN YOU MOVE?
HUH? SURE.
I'M FINE NOW.
THEN COME WITH ME.
OHHH!
LADY FRAU!
AND LADY SALLY!
YOU'RE AWAKE!!
HUH? YES, I SURE AM.
GOOD MORNING...
WHO ARE YOU GUYS?
WE WANTED TO GIVE OUR REGARDS TO THE BRAVE WARRIORS WHO DEFENDED OUR LAND.
Oh...
AND, IF POSSIBLE, TO SHAKE HANDS TO COMMEMORATE THE OCCASION!
Ohhh, nice and fluffy!
Yes, quite nice and fluffy!
FRAU!
YOU SHOULDN'T LET STRANGERS PLAY WITH YOUR FUR TOO MUCH.
HA HA!
Let's go.

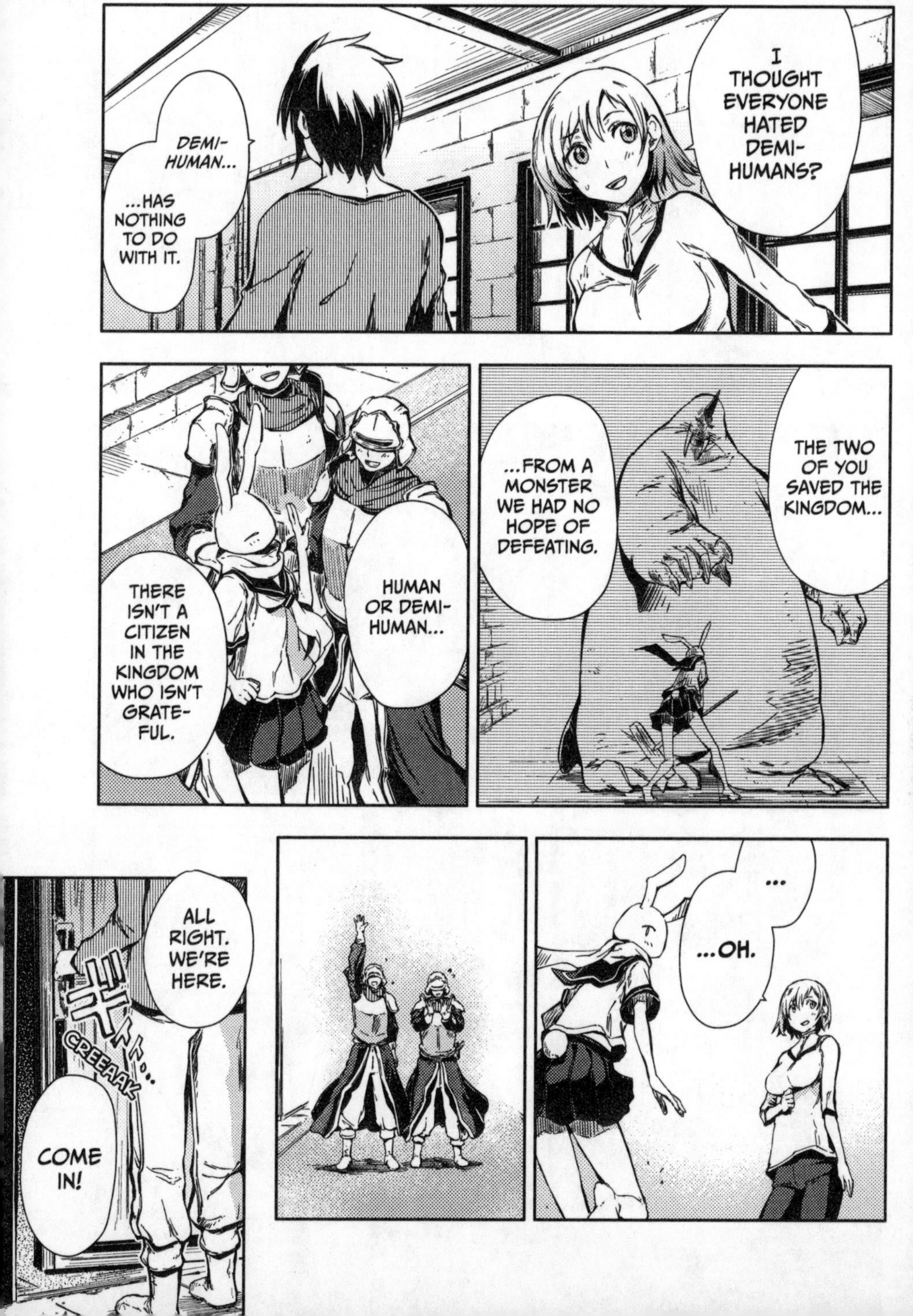
I THOUGHT EVERYONE HATED DEMI-HUMANS?
DEMI-HUMAN...
...HAS NOTHING TO DO WITH IT.
THE TWO OF YOU SAVED THE KINGDOM...
...FROM A MONSTER WE HAD NO HOPE OF DEFEATING.
HUMAN OR DEMI-HUMAN...
THERE ISN'T A CITIZEN IN THE KINGDOM WHO ISN'T GRATE-FUL.
...
...OH.
ALL RIGHT. WE'RE HERE.
CREEAAK
COME IN!

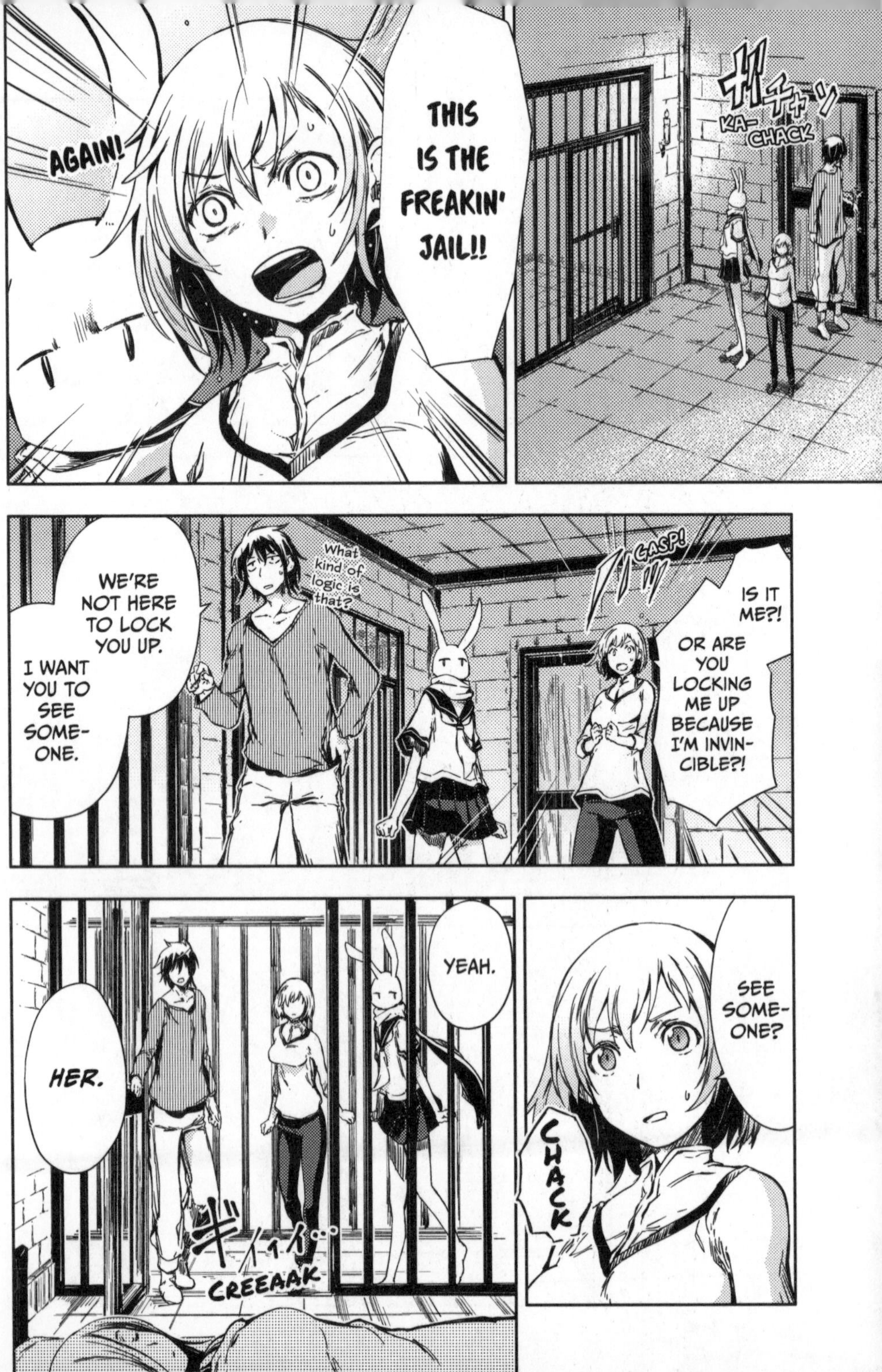
ガチャッ
KA-CHACK
THIS IS THE FREAKIN' JAIL!!
AGAIN!
GASP!
IS IT ME?!
OR ARE YOU LOCKING ME UP BECAUSE I'M INVINCIBLE?!
What kind of logic is that?
WE'RE NOT HERE TO LOCK YOU UP.
I WANT YOU TO SEE SOME-ONE.
SEE SOME-ONE?
CHACK
YEAH.
HER.
ギィィィ…
CREEAAK

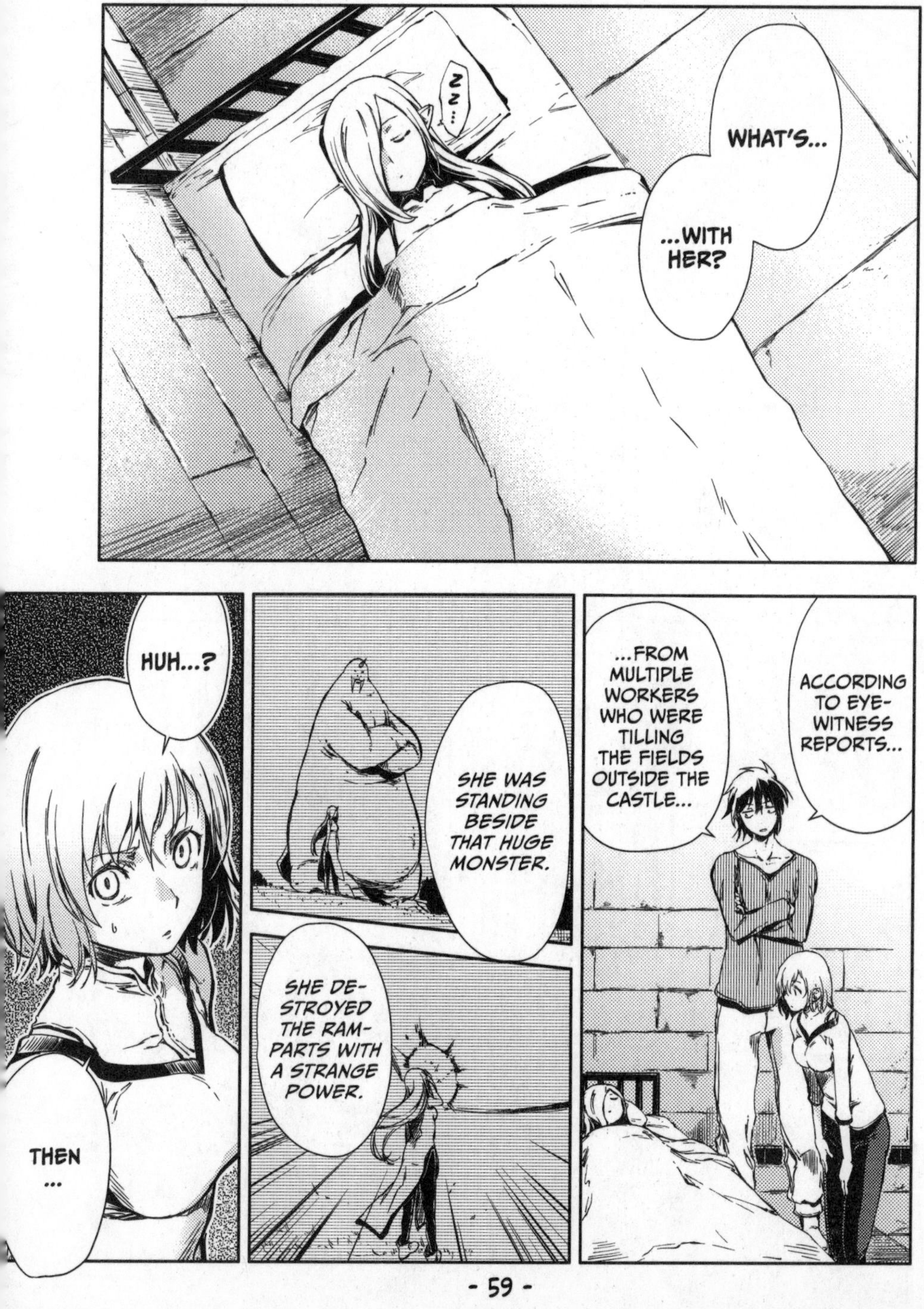
WHAT'S...
...WITH HER?
Z z z...
ACCORDING TO EYE-WITNESS REPORTS...
...FROM MULTIPLE WORKERS WHO WERE TILLING THE FIELDS OUTSIDE THE CASTLE...
SHE WAS STANDING BESIDE THAT HUGE MONSTER.
SHE DE-STROYED THE RAM-PARTS WITH A STRANGE POWER.
HUH...?
THEN ...

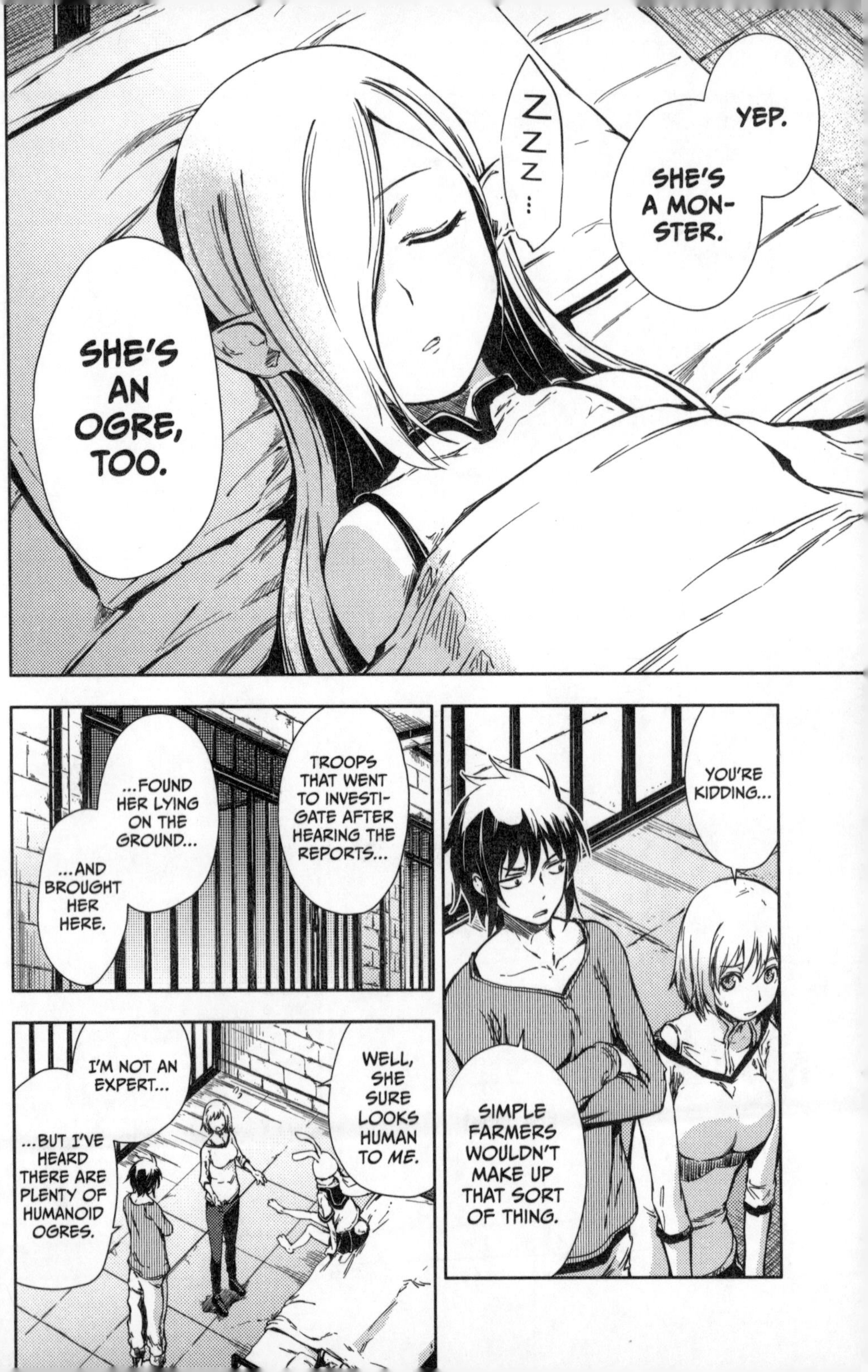
YEP.
SHE'S A MONSTER.
ZZZ...
SHE'S AN OGRE, TOO.
YOU'RE KIDDING...
SIMPLE FARMERS WOULDN'T MAKE UP THAT SORT OF THING.
TROOPS THAT WENT TO INVESTIGATE AFTER HEARING THE REPORTS...
...FOUND HER LYING ON THE GROUND...
...AND BROUGHT HER HERE.
WELL, SHE SURE LOOKS HUMAN TO *ME*.
I'M NOT AN EXPERT...
...BUT I'VE HEARD THERE ARE PLENTY OF HUMANOID OGRES.

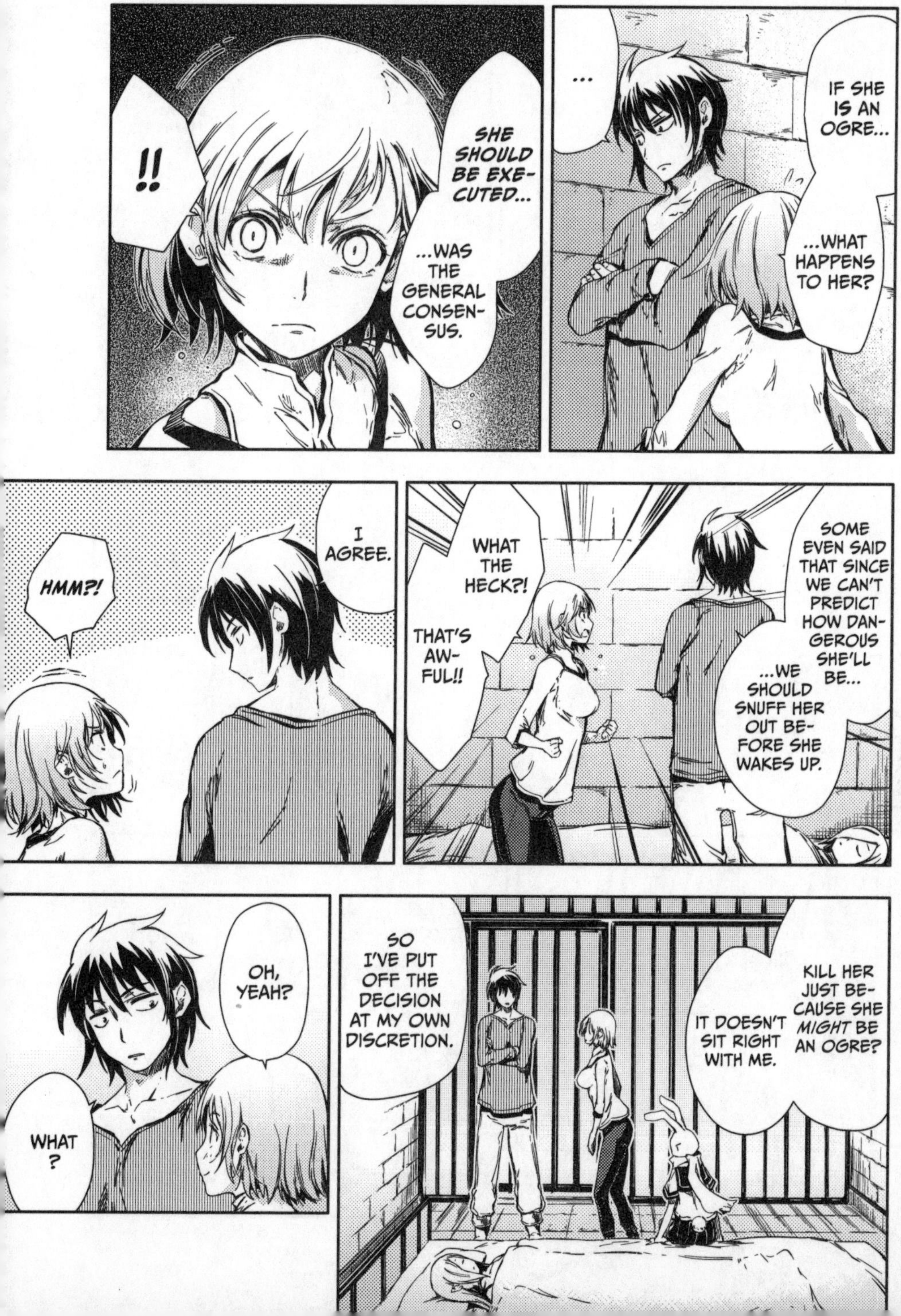
IF SHE IS AN OGRE...
...WHAT HAPPENS TO HER?
...
SHE SHOULD BE EXECUTED...
...WAS THE GENERAL CONSENSUS.
!!
SOME EVEN SAID THAT SINCE WE CAN'T PREDICT HOW DANGEROUS SHE'LL BE...
...WE SHOULD SNUFF HER OUT BEFORE SHE WAKES UP.
WHAT THE HECK?!
THAT'S AWFUL!!
I AGREE.
HMM?!
KILL HER JUST BECAUSE SHE *MIGHT* BE AN OGRE?
IT DOESN'T SIT RIGHT WITH ME.
SO I'VE PUT OFF THE DECISION AT MY OWN DISCRETION.
OH, YEAH?
WHAT?

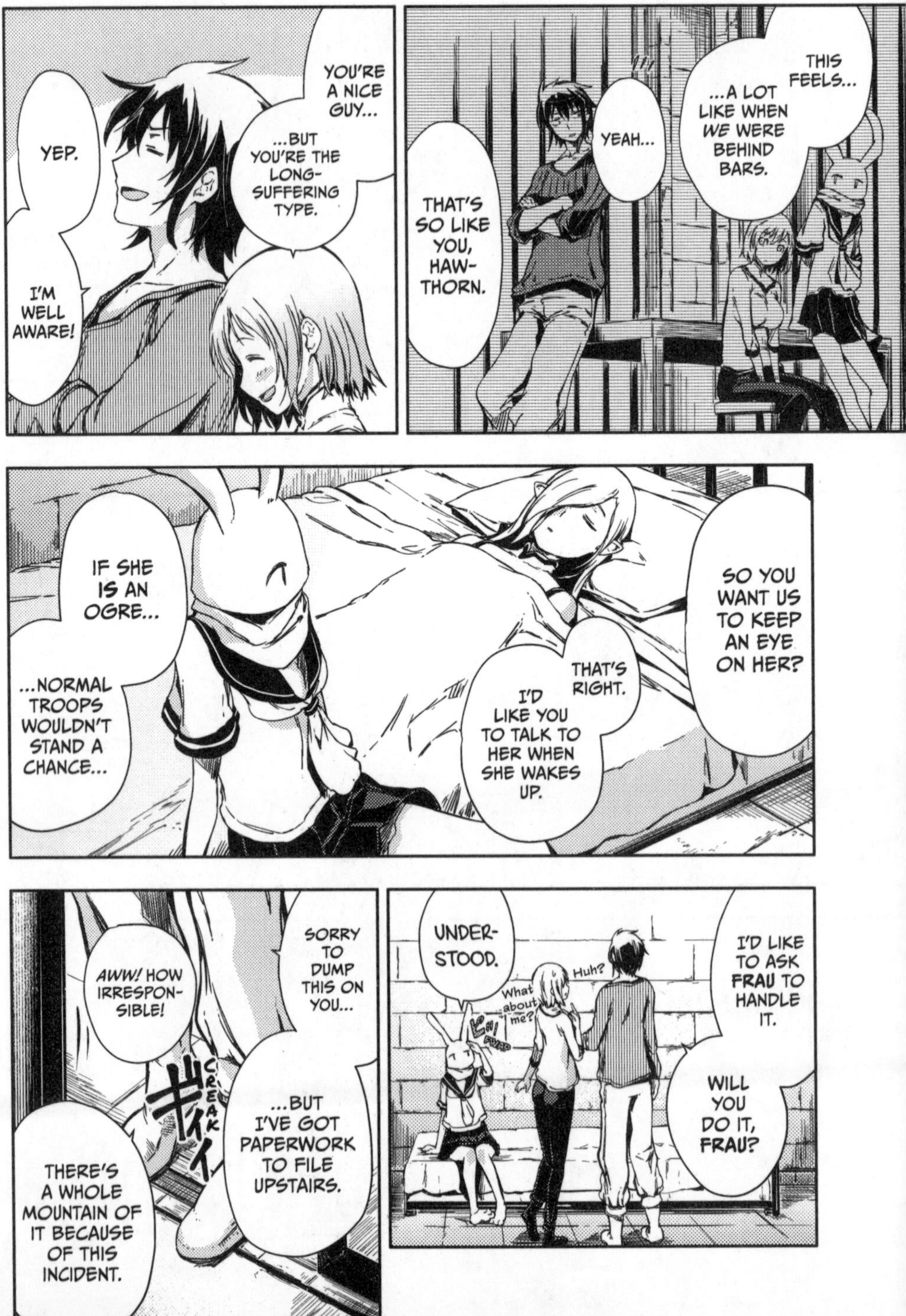
THIS FEELS...
...A LOT LIKE WHEN WE WERE BEHIND BARS.
YEAH...
THAT'S SO LIKE YOU, HAWTHORN.
YOU'RE A NICE GUY...
...BUT YOU'RE THE LONG-SUFFERING TYPE.
YEP.
I'M WELL AWARE!
SO YOU WANT US TO KEEP AN EYE ON HER?
THAT'S RIGHT.
I'D LIKE YOU TO TALK TO HER WHEN SHE WAKES UP.
IF SHE IS AN OGRE...
...NORMAL TROOPS WOULDN'T STAND A CHANCE...
I'D LIKE TO ASK FRAU TO HANDLE IT.
UNDERSTOOD.
Huh?
What about me?
FWAP
WILL YOU DO IT, FRAU?
SORRY TO DUMP THIS ON YOU...
AWW! HOW IRRESPONSIBLE!
...BUT I'VE GOT PAPERWORK TO FILE UPSTAIRS.
CREAK
THERE'S A WHOLE MOUNTAIN OF IT BECAUSE OF THIS INCIDENT.

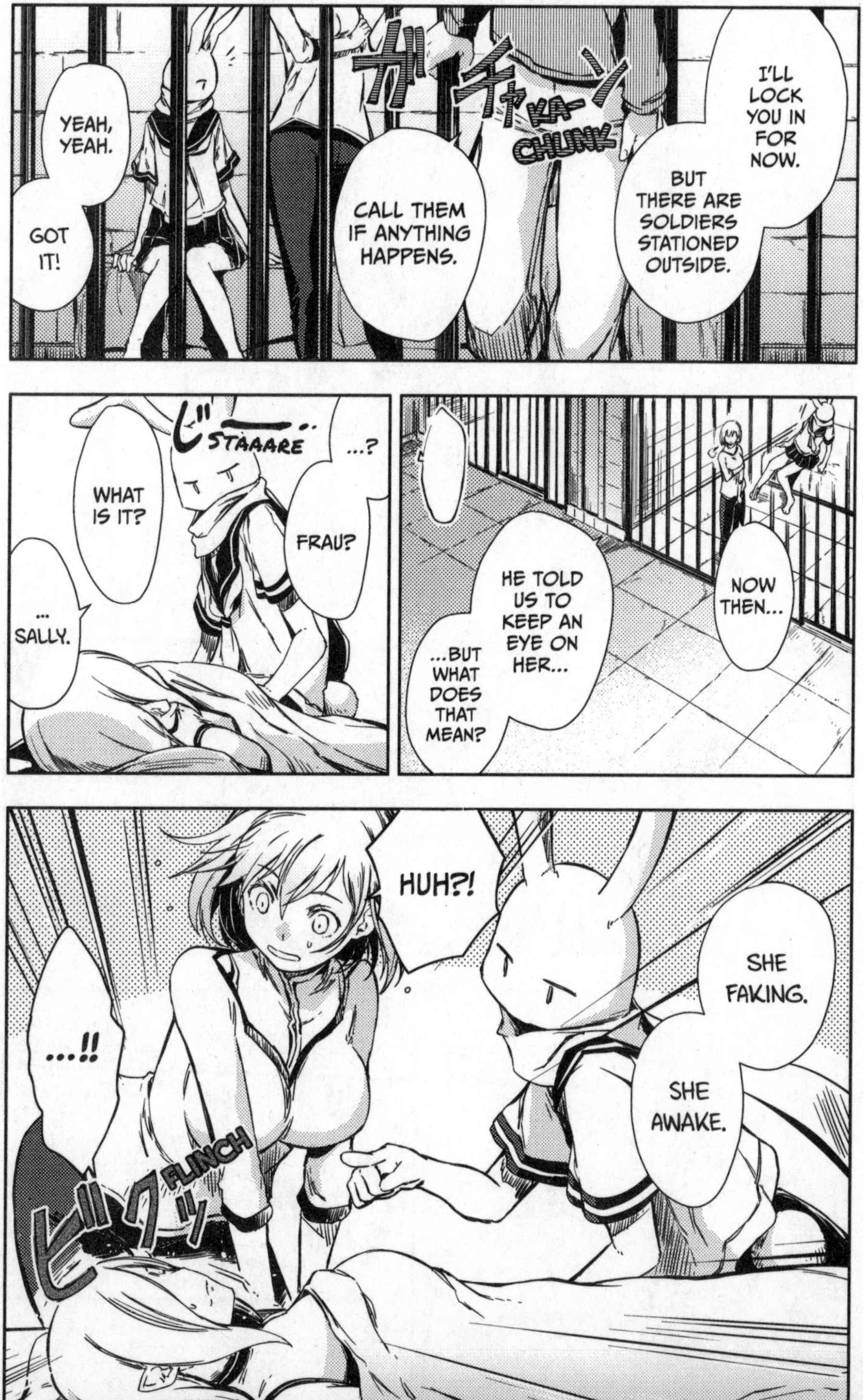
I'LL LOCK YOU IN FOR NOW.
BUT THERE ARE SOLDIERS STATIONED OUTSIDE.
KA-CHUNK
CALL THEM IF ANYTHING HAPPENS.
YEAH, YEAH.
GOT IT!
NOW THEN...
HE TOLD US TO KEEP AN EYE ON HER...
...BUT WHAT DOES THAT MEAN?
...?
FRAU?
STAAARE
WHAT IS IT?
... SALLY.
SHE FAKING.
SHE AWAKE.
HUH?!
...!!
FLINCH

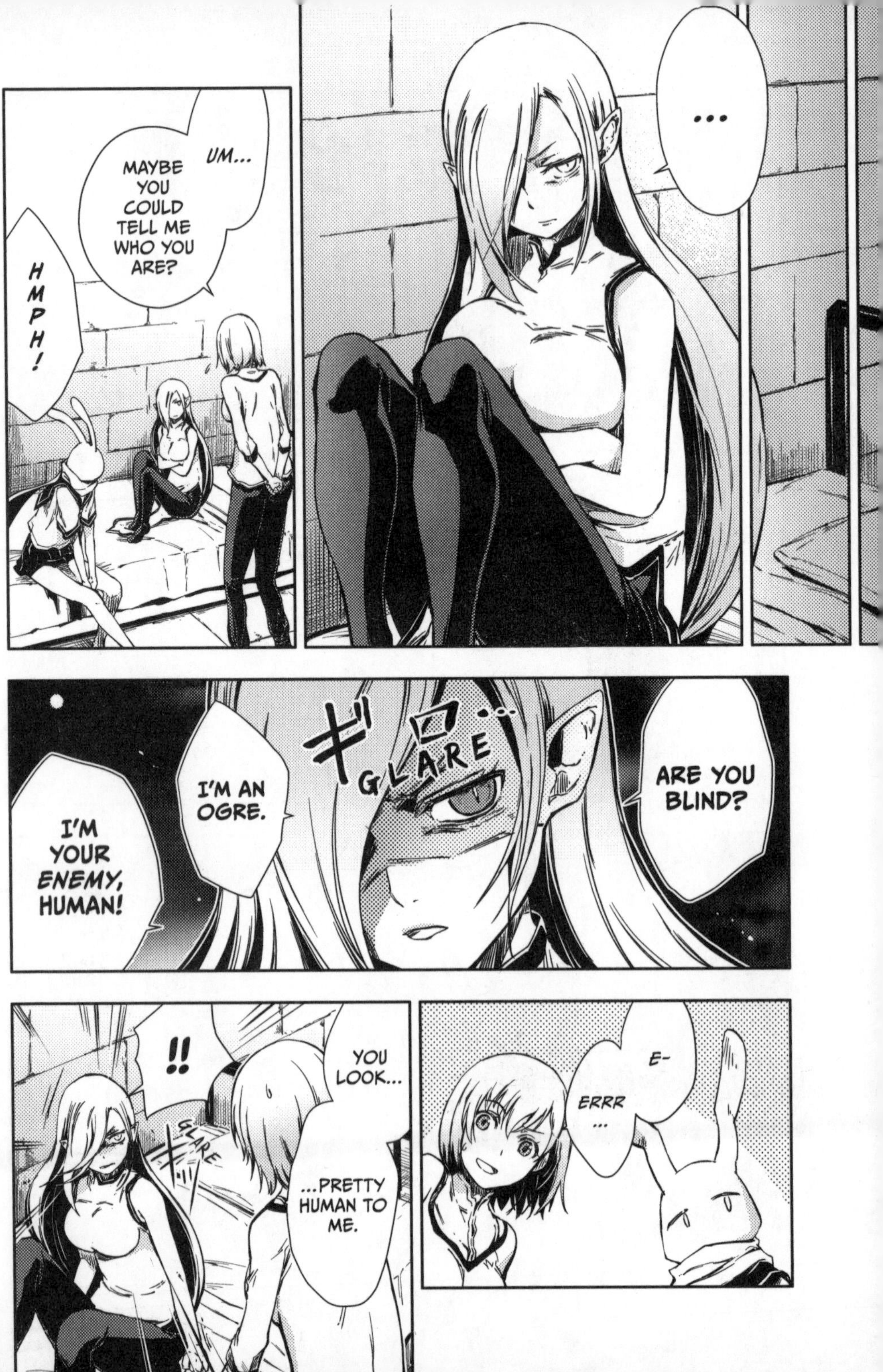
...
UM...
MAYBE YOU COULD TELL ME WHO YOU ARE?
HMPH!
ARE YOU BLIND?
ギロ…
GLARE
I'M AN OGRE.
I'M YOUR ENEMY, HUMAN!
E- ERRR ...
YOU LOOK...
!!
GLARE
...PRETTY HUMAN TO ME.

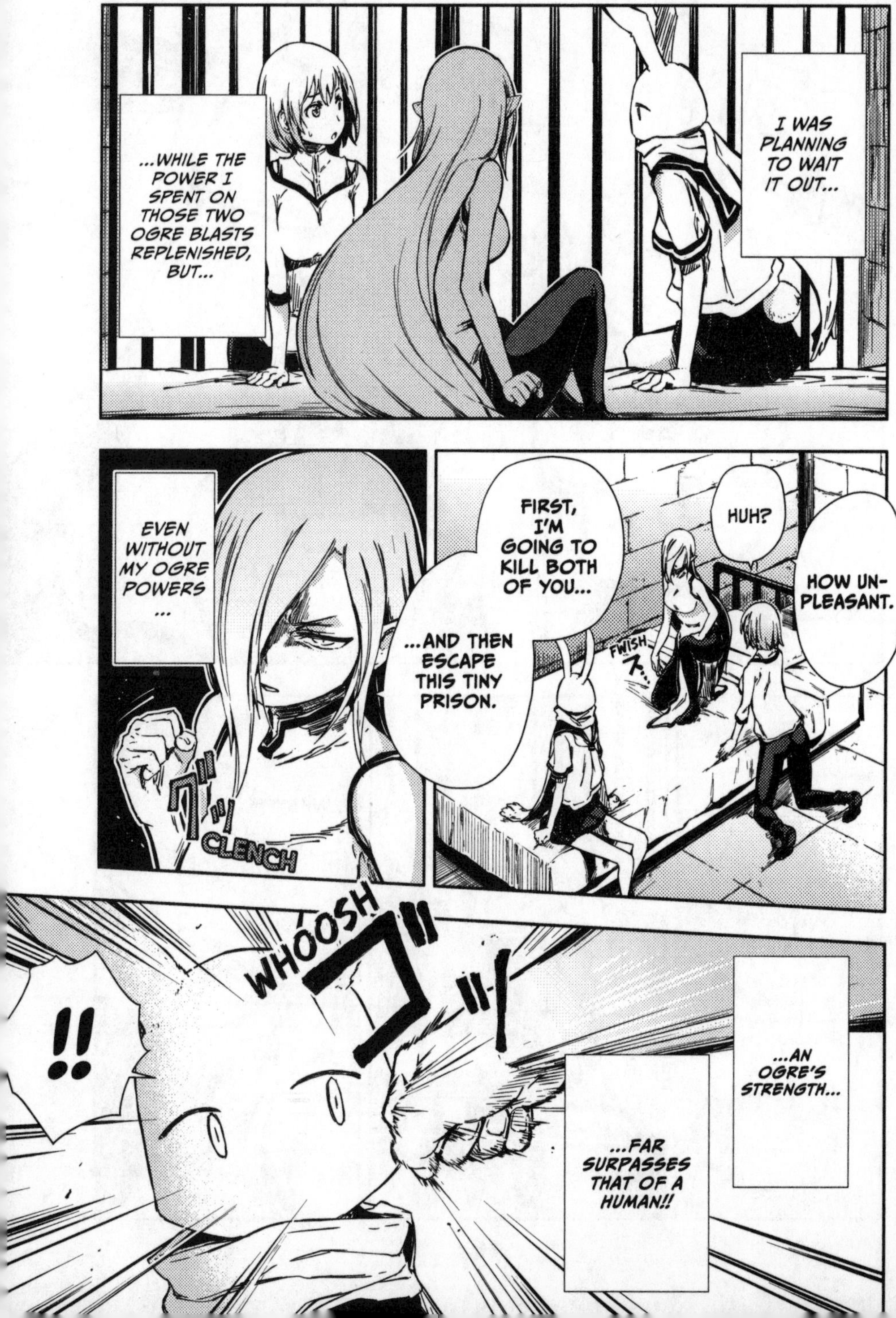
I WAS PLANNING TO WAIT IT OUT...
...WHILE THE POWER I SPENT ON THOSE TWO OGRE BLASTS REPLENISHED, BUT...
HUH?
HOW UN-PLEASANT.
FIRST, I'M GOING TO KILL BOTH OF YOU...
...AND THEN ESCAPE THIS TINY PRISON.
FWISH
EVEN WITHOUT MY OGRE POWERS ...
CLENCH
...AN OGRE'S STRENGTH...
...FAR SURPASSES THAT OF A HUMAN!!
WHOOSH
!!

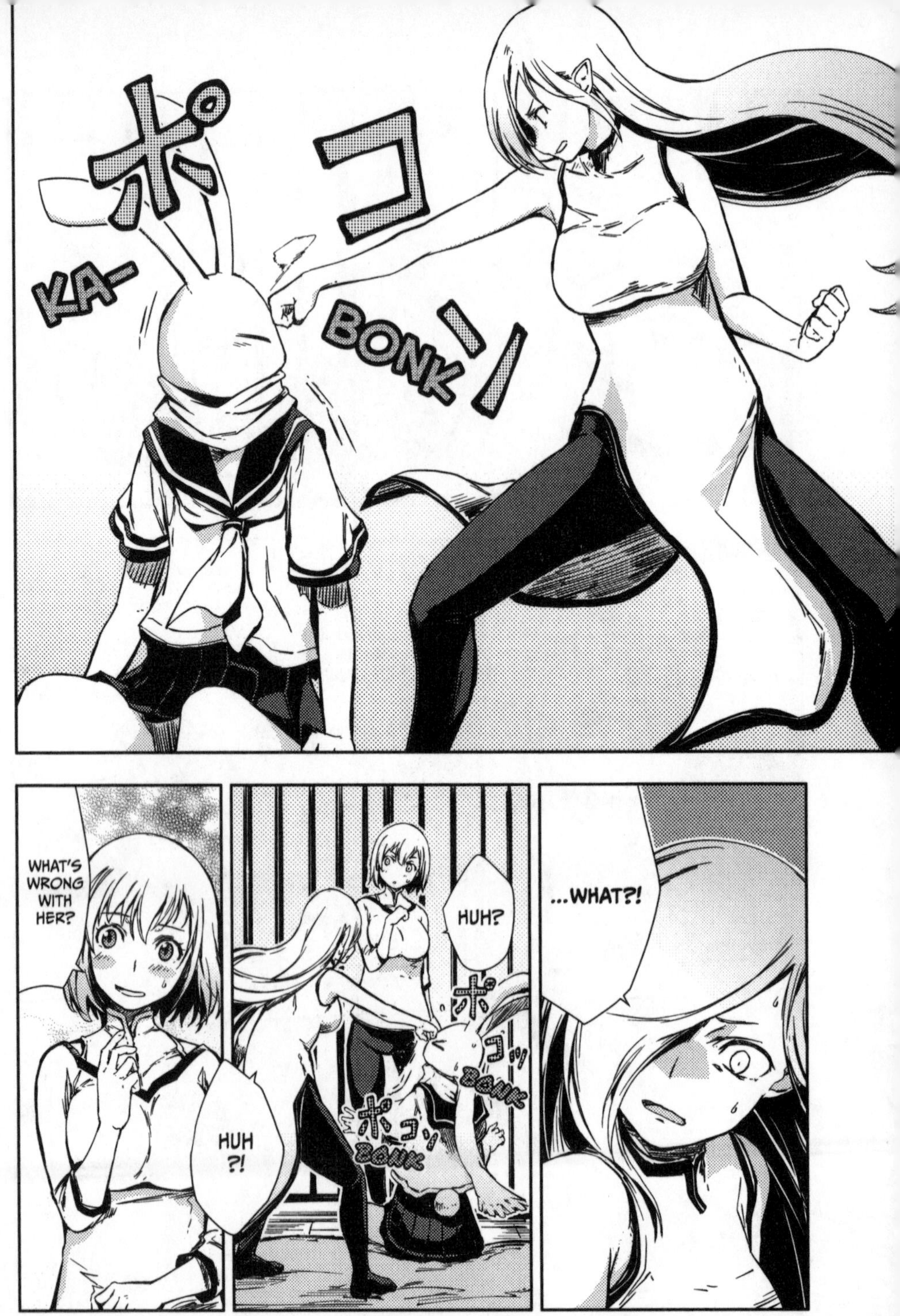
ポコ
KA-
BONK
...WHAT?!
HUH?
ポコッ
BONK
ポコッ
BONK
WHAT'S WRONG WITH HER?
HUH ?!

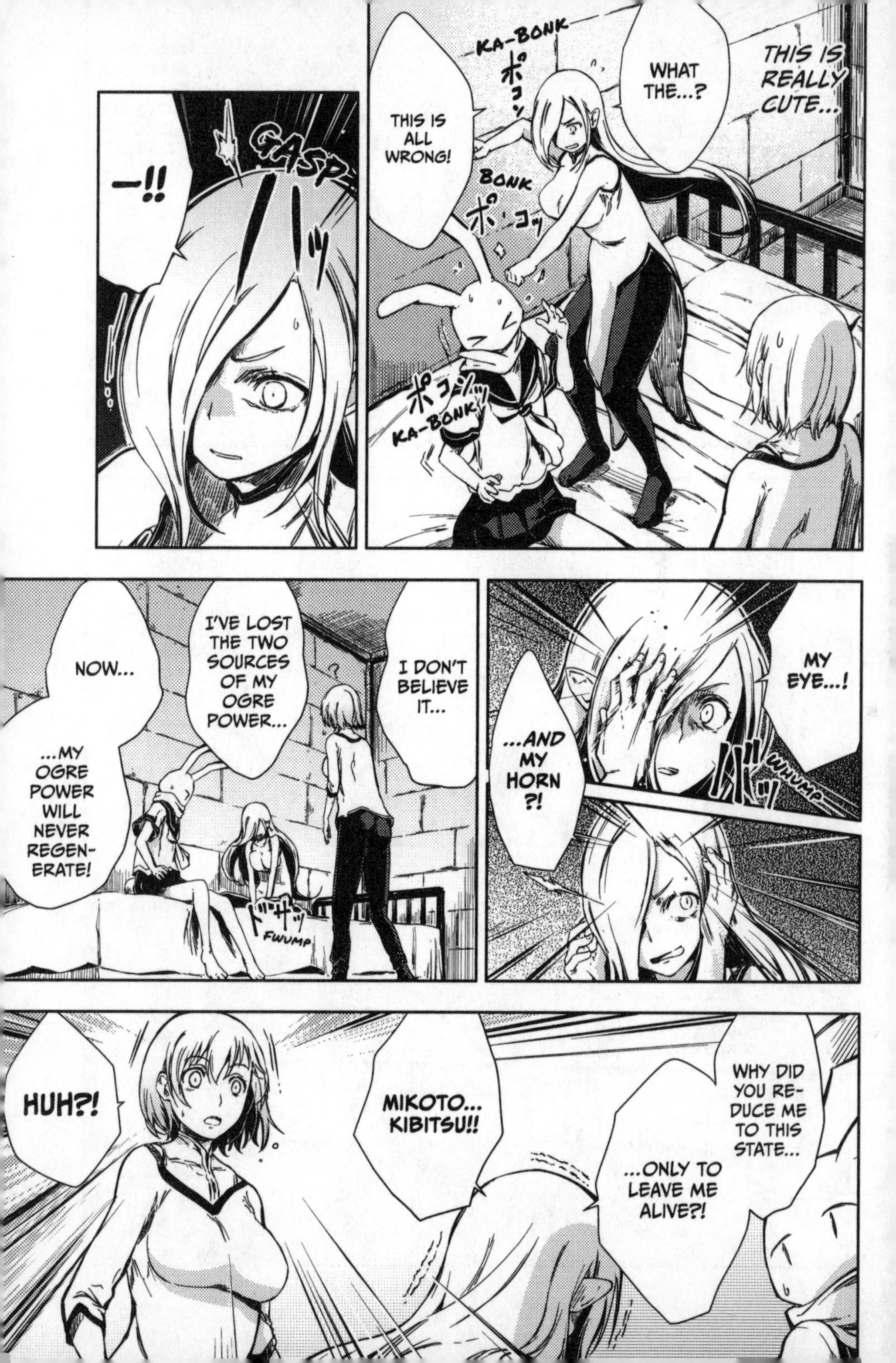
THIS IS REALLY CUTE...
WHAT THE...?
KA-BONK
THIS IS ALL WRONG!
BONK
KA-BONK
GASP
—!!
MY EYE...!
...AND MY HORN?!
WHUMP
I DON'T BELIEVE IT...
I'VE LOST THE TWO SOURCES OF MY OGRE POWER...
NOW...
...MY OGRE POWER WILL NEVER REGENERATE!
FWUMP
WHY DID YOU REDUCE ME TO THIS STATE...
...ONLY TO LEAVE ME ALIVE?!
MIKOTO... KIBITSU!!
HUH?!

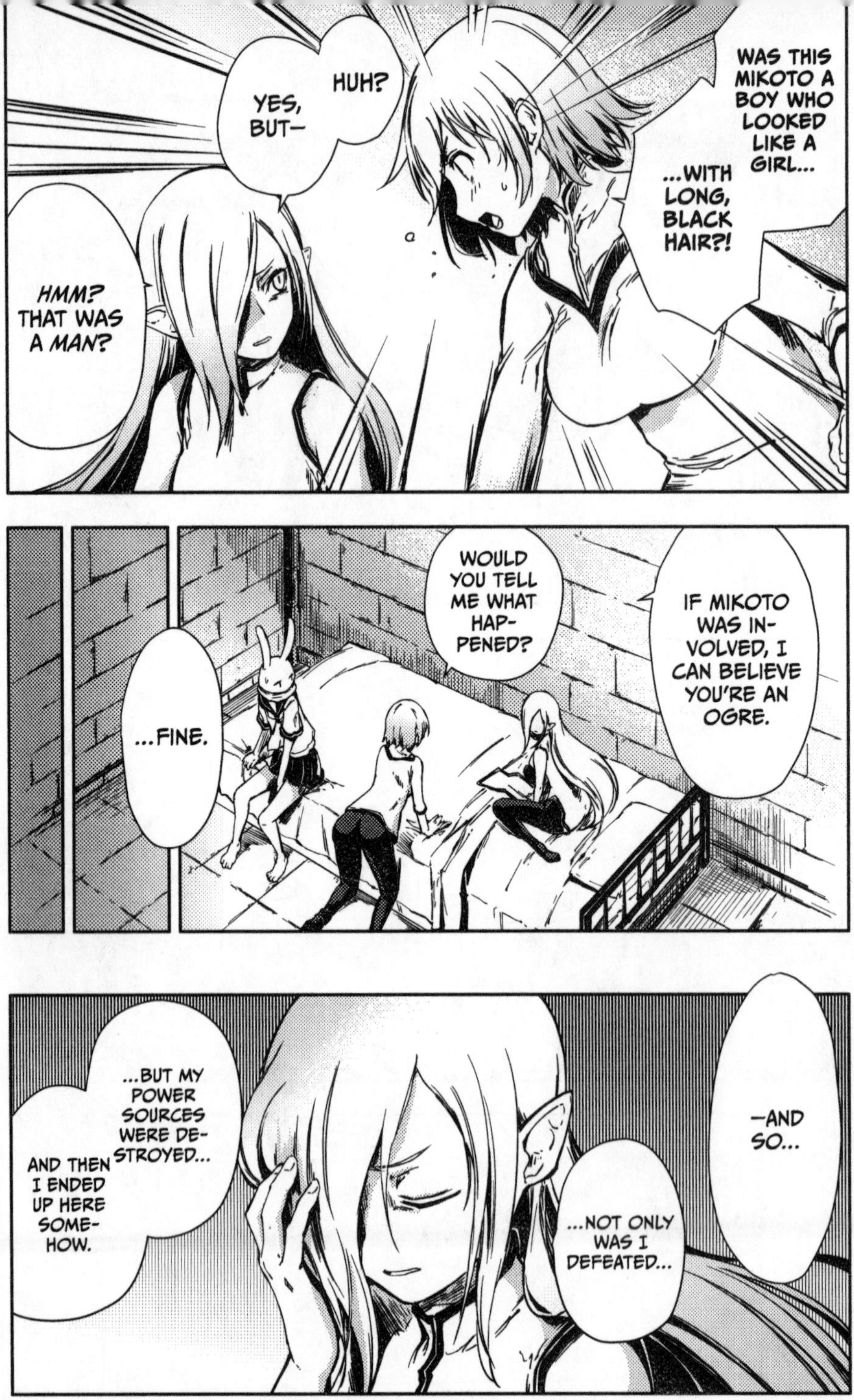
WAS THIS MIKOTO A BOY WHO LOOKED LIKE A GIRL...
...WITH LONG, BLACK HAIR?!
HUH?
YES, BUT—
HMM? THAT WAS A *MAN?*
IF MIKOTO WAS IN- VOLVED, I CAN BELIEVE YOU'RE AN OGRE.
WOULD YOU TELL ME WHAT HAP- PENED?
...FINE.
—AND SO...
...NOT ONLY WAS I DEFEATED...
...BUT MY POWER SOURCES WERE DE- STROYED...
AND THEN I ENDED UP HERE SOME- HOW.

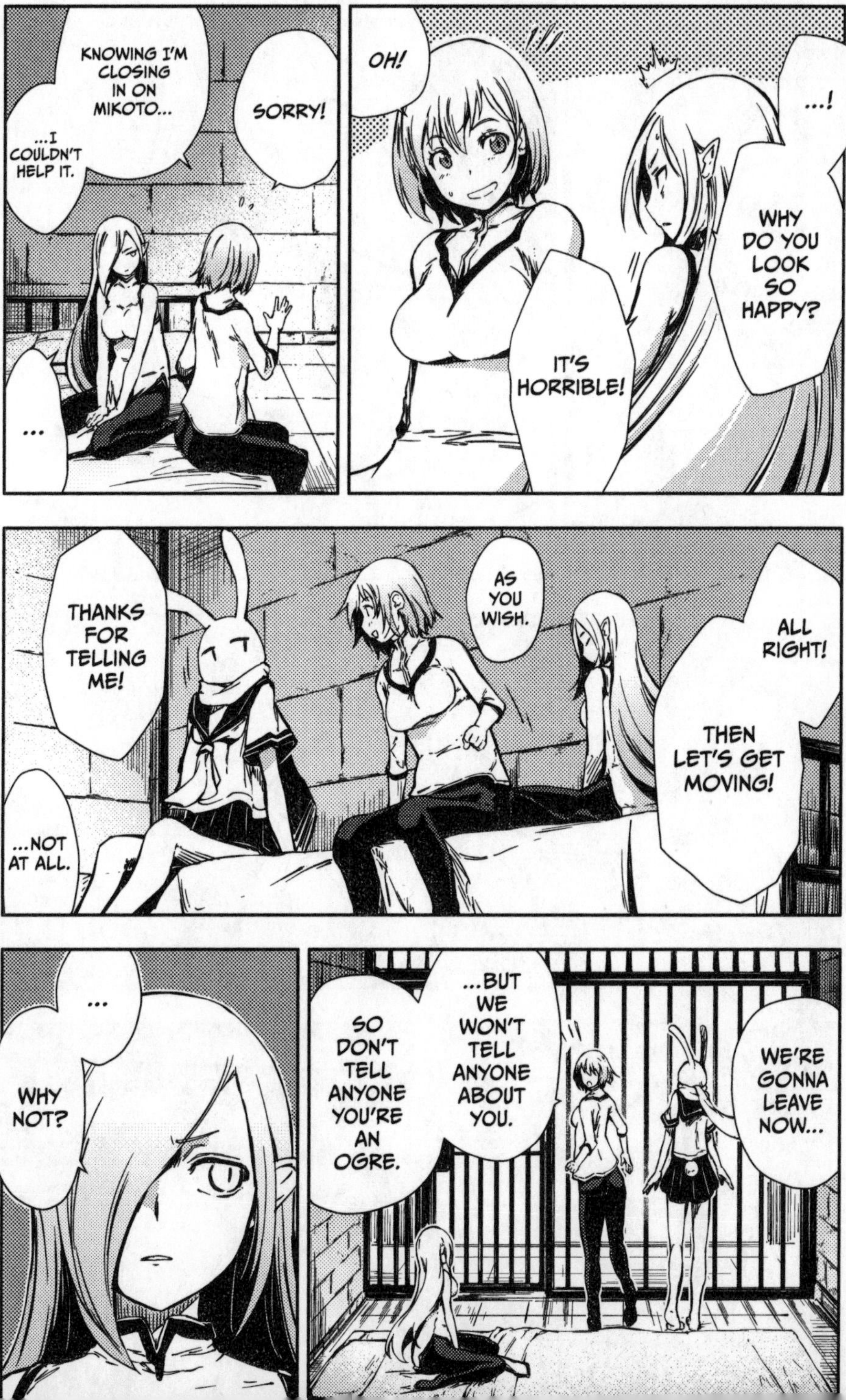
OH!
...!
WHY DO YOU LOOK SO HAPPY?
IT'S HORRIBLE!
SORRY!
KNOWING I'M CLOSING IN ON MIKOTO...
...I COULDN'T HELP IT.
...
ALL RIGHT!
THEN LET'S GET MOVING!
AS YOU WISH.
THANKS FOR TELLING ME!
...NOT AT ALL.
WE'RE GONNA LEAVE NOW...
...BUT WE WON'T TELL ANYONE ABOUT YOU.
SO DON'T TELL ANYONE YOU'RE AN OGRE.
...
WHY NOT?

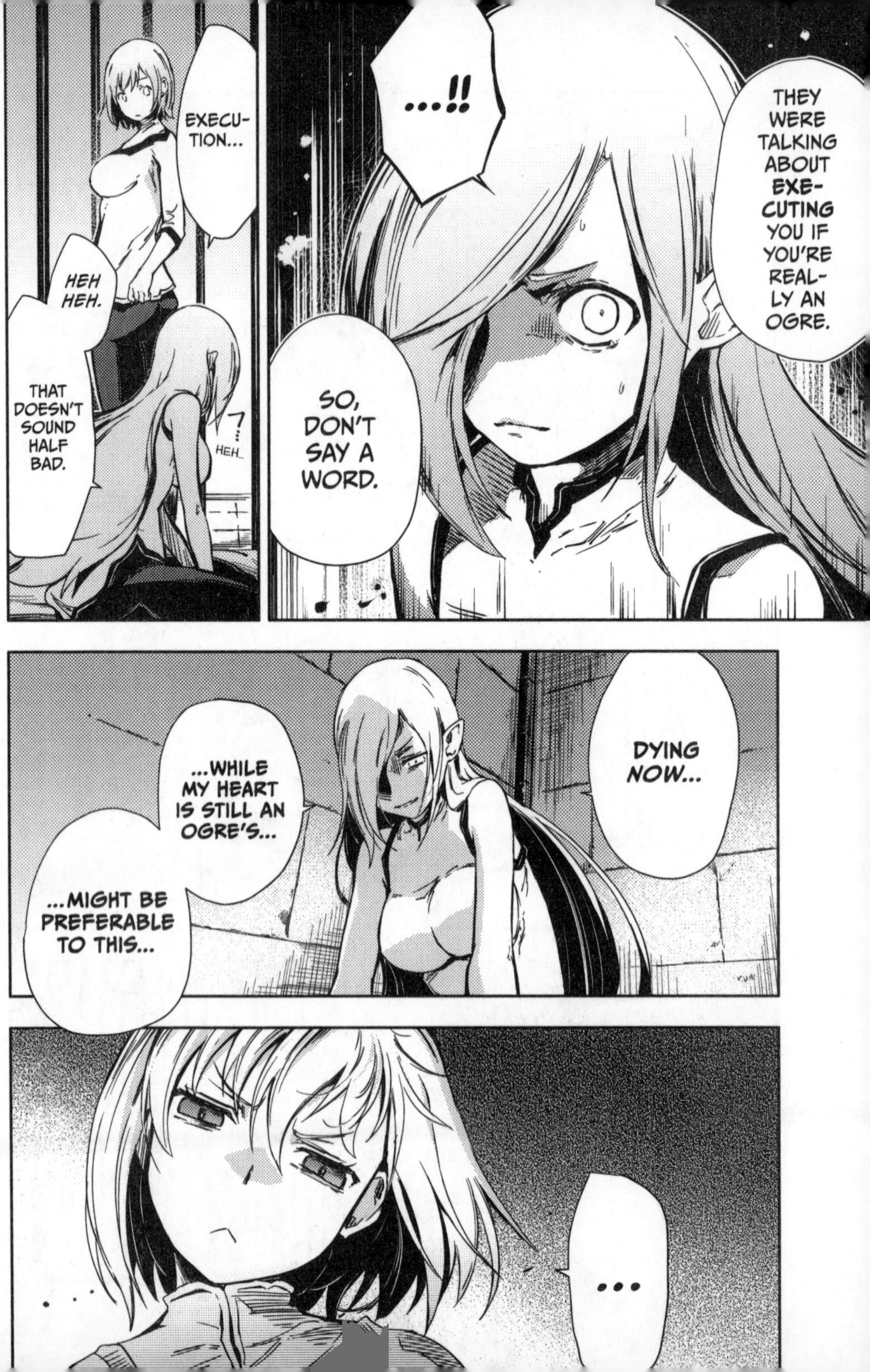
THEY WERE TALKING ABOUT EXECUTING YOU IF YOU'RE REALLY AN OGRE.
...!!
SO, DON'T SAY A WORD.
EXECUTION...
HEH HEH.
THAT DOESN'T SOUND HALF BAD.
HEH...
DYING NOW...
...WHILE MY HEART IS STILL AN OGRE'S...
...MIGHT BE PREFERABLE TO THIS...
...

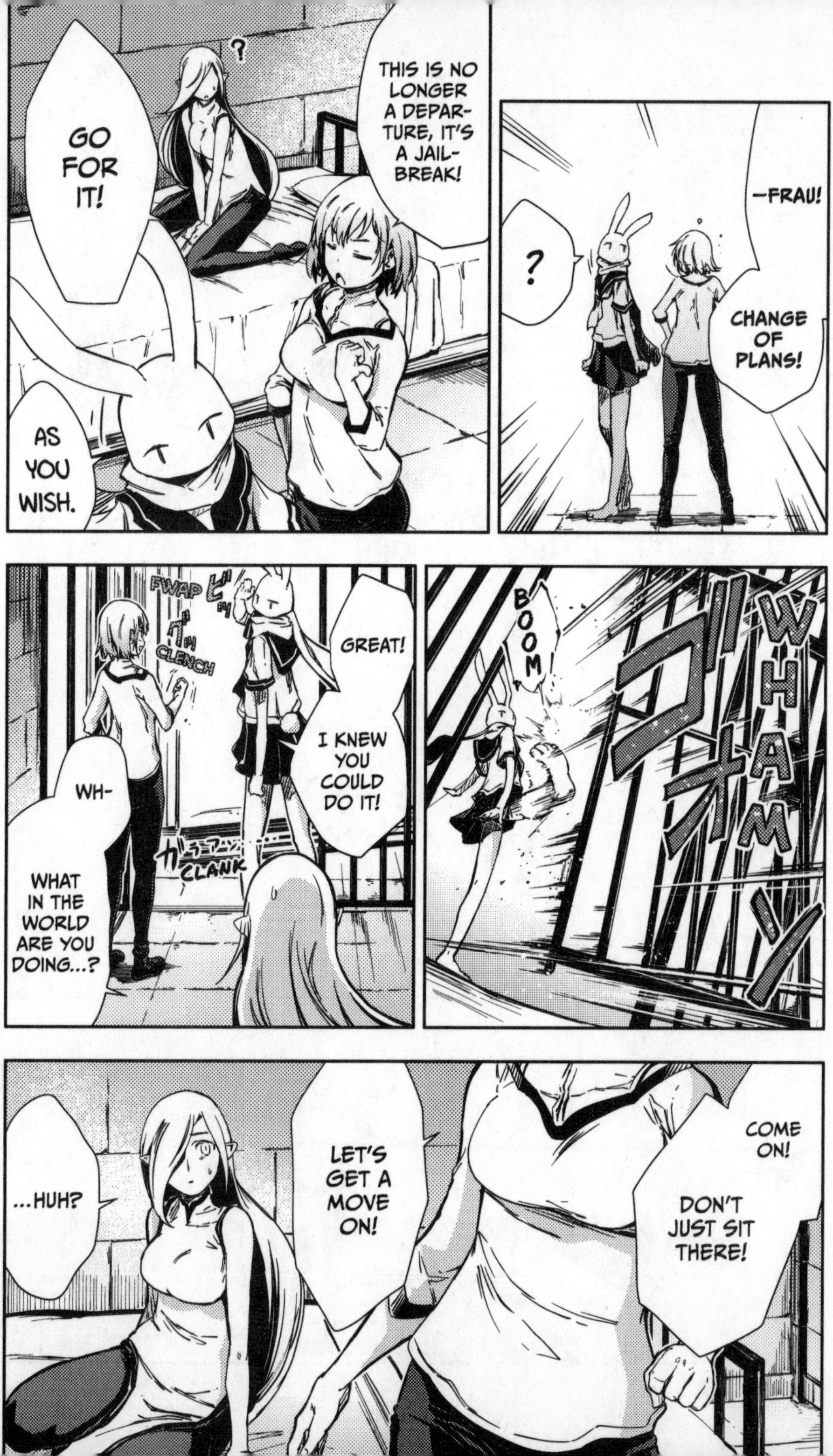
—FRAU!
?
CHANGE OF PLANS!
THIS IS NO LONGER A DEPARTURE, IT'S A JAILBREAK!
?
GO FOR IT!
AS YOU WISH.
WHAM
BOOM
GREAT!
I KNEW YOU COULD DO IT!
FWAP
CLENCH
CLANK
WH-
WHAT IN THE WORLD ARE YOU DOING...?
COME ON!
DON'T JUST SIT THERE!
LET'S GET A MOVE ON!
...HUH?

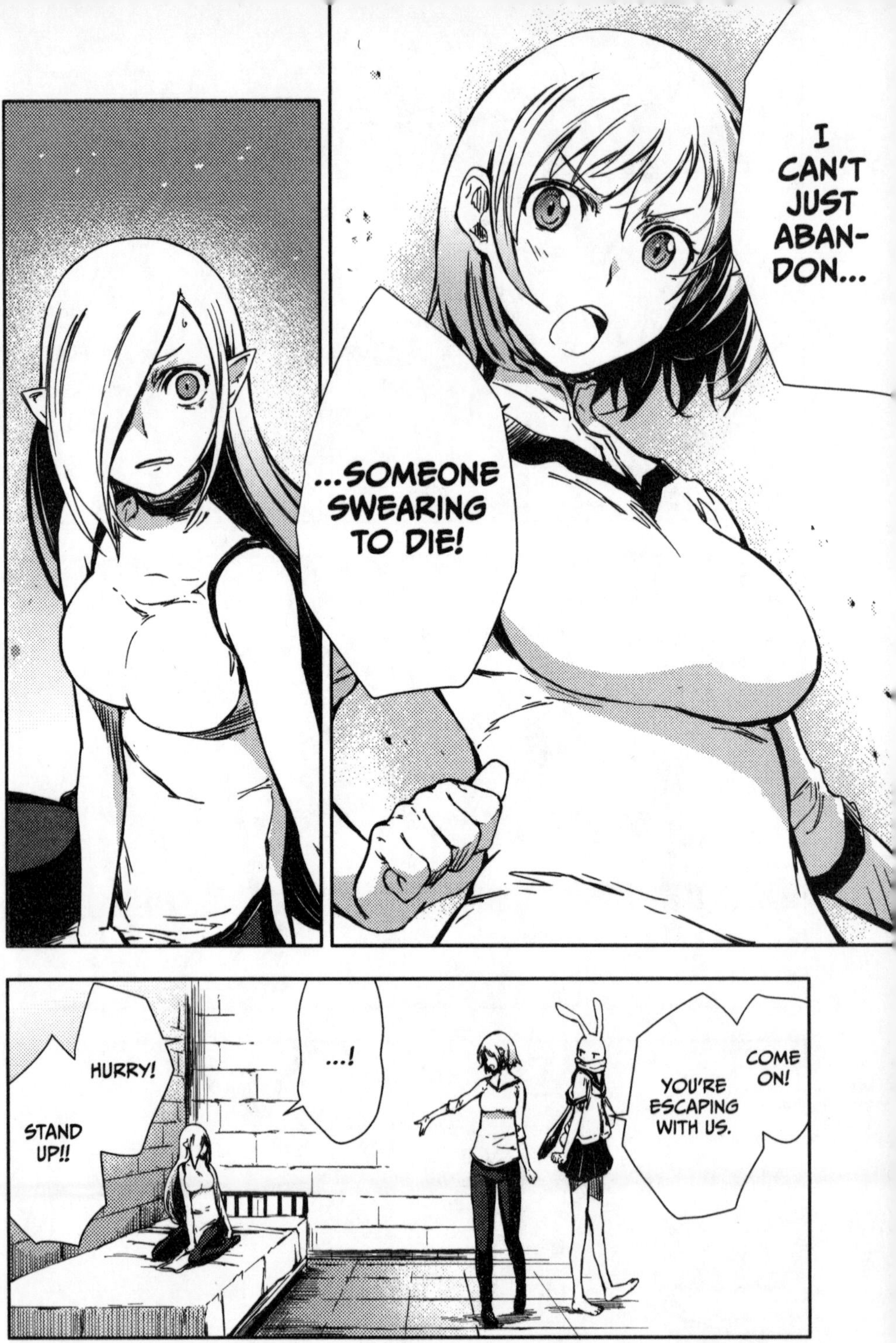
I CAN'T JUST ABANDON...
...SOMEONE SWEARING TO DIE!
COME ON!
YOU'RE ESCAPING WITH US.
...!
HURRY!
STAND UP!!

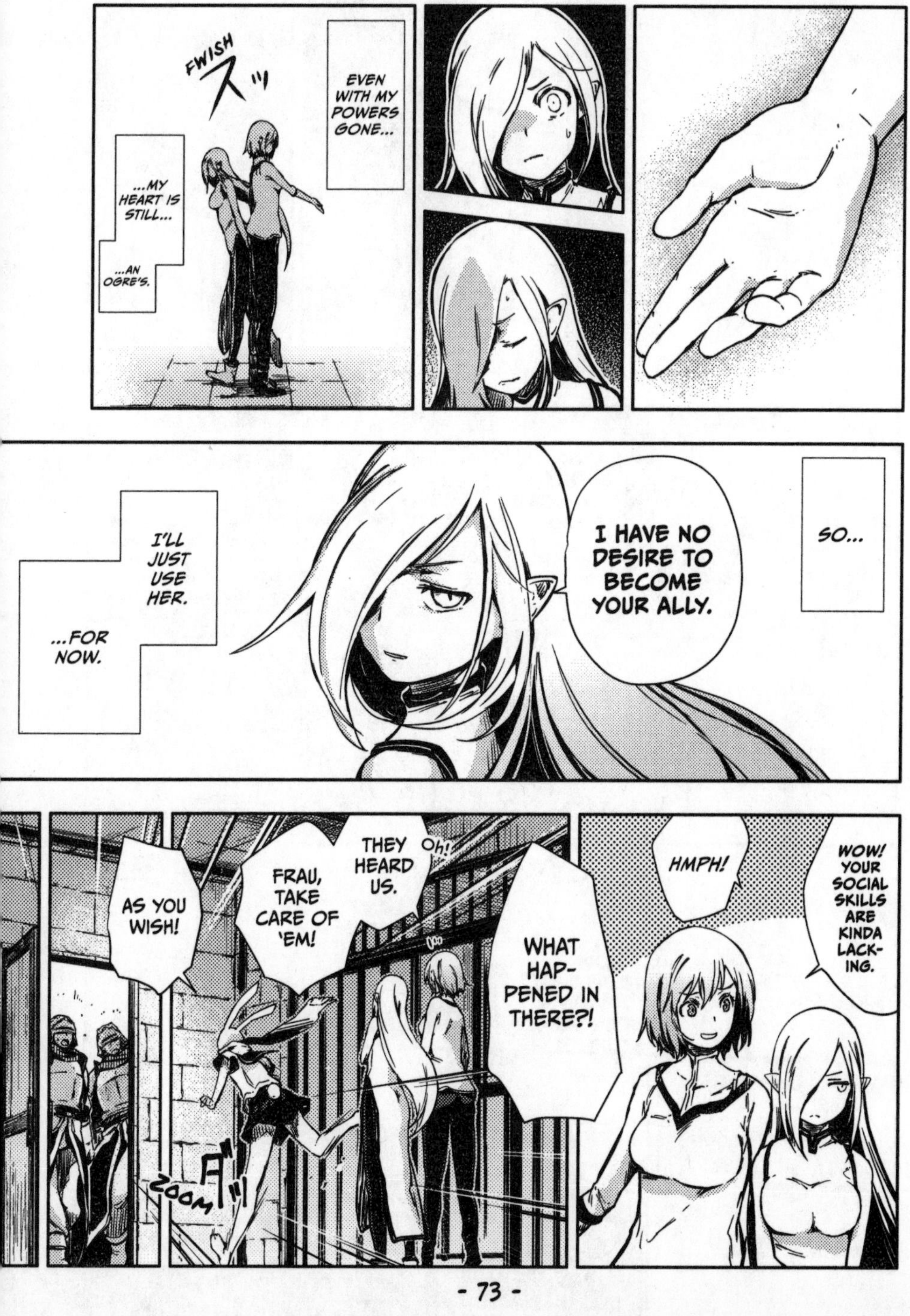
EVEN WITH MY POWERS GONE...
FWISH
スッ
...MY HEART IS STILL...
...AN OGRE'S.
SO...
I HAVE NO DESIRE TO BECOME YOUR ALLY.
I'LL JUST USE HER.
...FOR NOW.
WOW! YOUR SOCIAL SKILLS ARE KINDA LACKING.
HMPH!
WHAT HAP-PENED IN THERE?!
Oh!
THEY HEARD US.
FRAU, TAKE CARE OF 'EM!
AS YOU WISH!
ZOOM

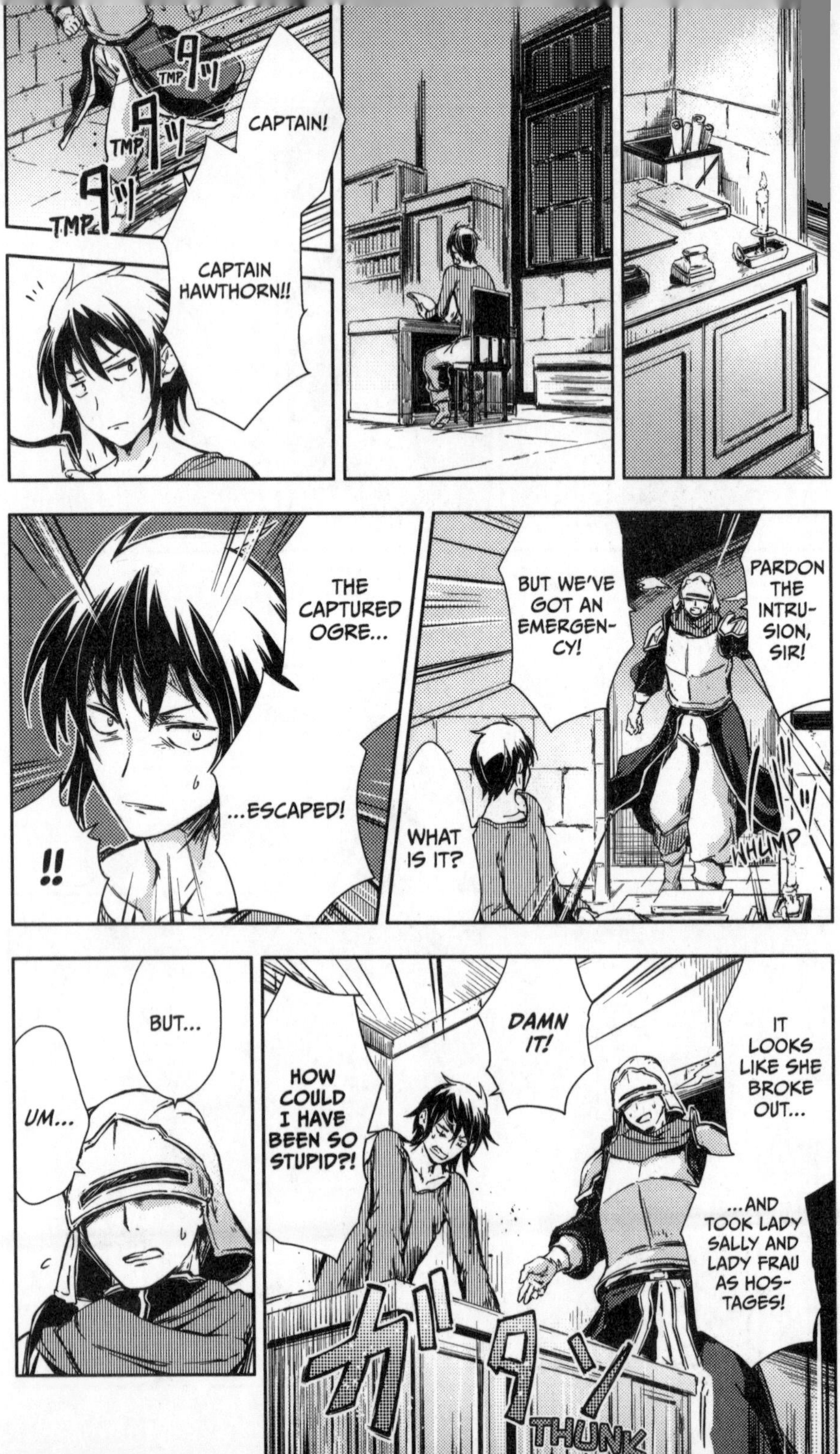
TMP
TMP
TMP
CAPTAIN!
CAPTAIN HAWTHORN!!
PARDON THE INTRU-SION, SIR!
BUT WE'VE GOT AN EMERGEN-CY!
WHUMP
WHAT IS IT?
THE CAPTURED OGRE...
...ESCAPED!
!!
IT LOOKS LIKE SHE BROKE OUT...
...AND TOOK LADY SALLY AND LADY FRAU AS HOS-TAGES!
DAMN IT!
HOW COULD I HAVE BEEN SO STUPID?!
THUNK
BUT...
UM...

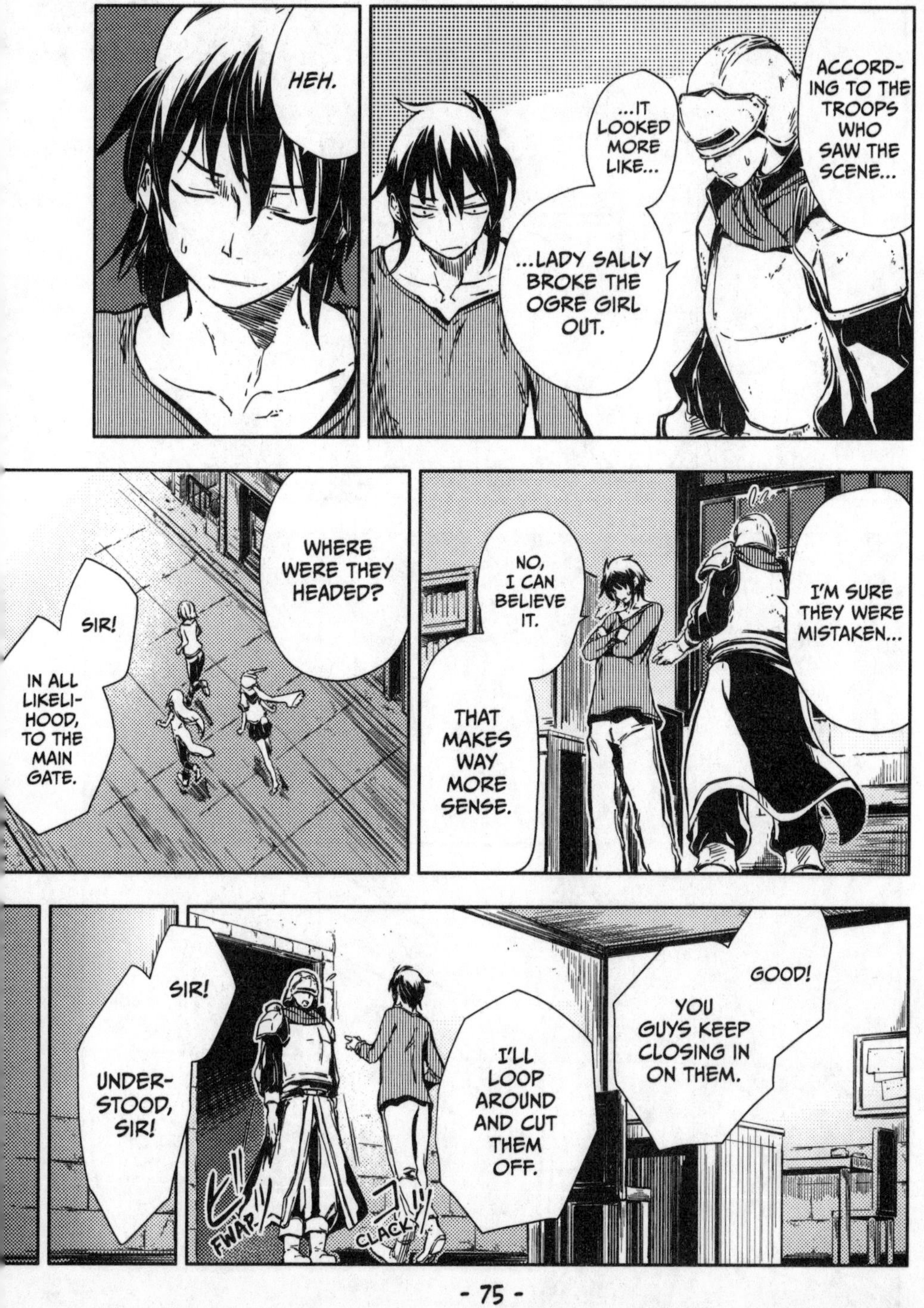
ACCORDING TO THE TROOPS WHO SAW THE SCENE...
...IT LOOKED MORE LIKE...
...LADY SALLY BROKE THE OGRE GIRL OUT.
HEH.
I'M SURE THEY WERE MISTAKEN...
NO, I CAN BELIEVE IT.
THAT MAKES WAY MORE SENSE.
WHERE WERE THEY HEADED?
SIR!
IN ALL LIKELIHOOD, TO THE MAIN GATE.
GOOD!
YOU GUYS KEEP CLOSING IN ON THEM.
I'LL LOOP AROUND AND CUT THEM OFF.
SIR!
UNDERSTOOD, SIR!
CLACK
FWAP!

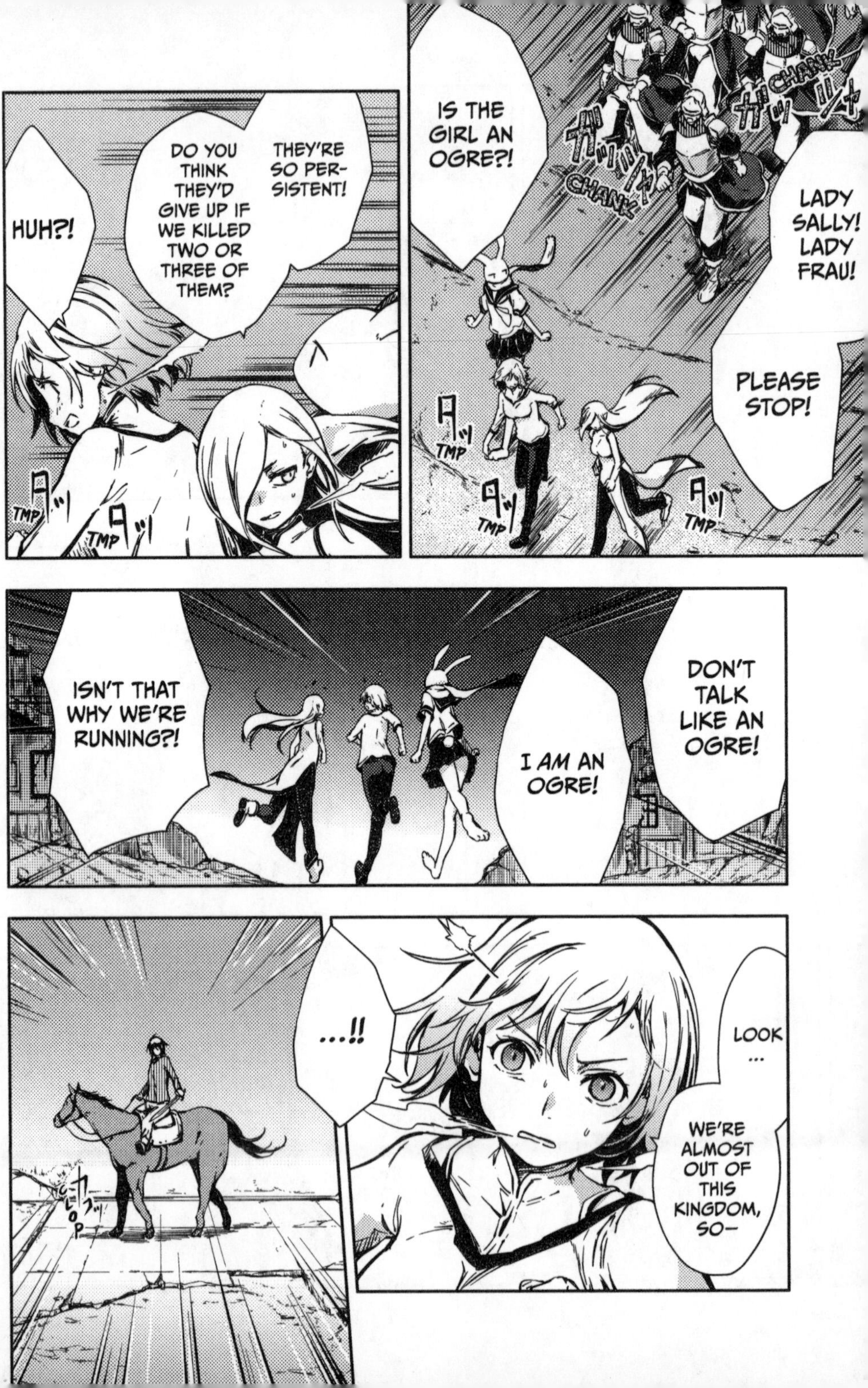
CHANK
CHANK
LADY SALLY! LADY FRAU!
PLEASE STOP!
IS THE GIRL AN OGRE?!
TMP
TMP
TMP
THEY'RE SO PERSISTENT!
DO YOU THINK THEY'D GIVE UP IF WE KILLED TWO OR THREE OF THEM?
HUH?!
TMP
TMP
DON'T TALK LIKE AN OGRE!
I AM AN OGRE!
ISN'T THAT WHY WE'RE RUNNING?!
LOOK...
WE'RE ALMOST OUT OF THIS KINGDOM, SO—
...!!
CLOP

STOP RIGHT THERE...

SALLY.

HAW-THORN!

カツ
CLOP

HUH?

SORRY, HAW-THORN!

I KNOW WHAT YOU'RE THINKING.

AS YOU WISH!

GET 'IM, FRAU!!

BUT AS A WARRIOR...

SHING

HUH?!

ZOOM

...I CAN'T ALLOW YOU TO PASS.

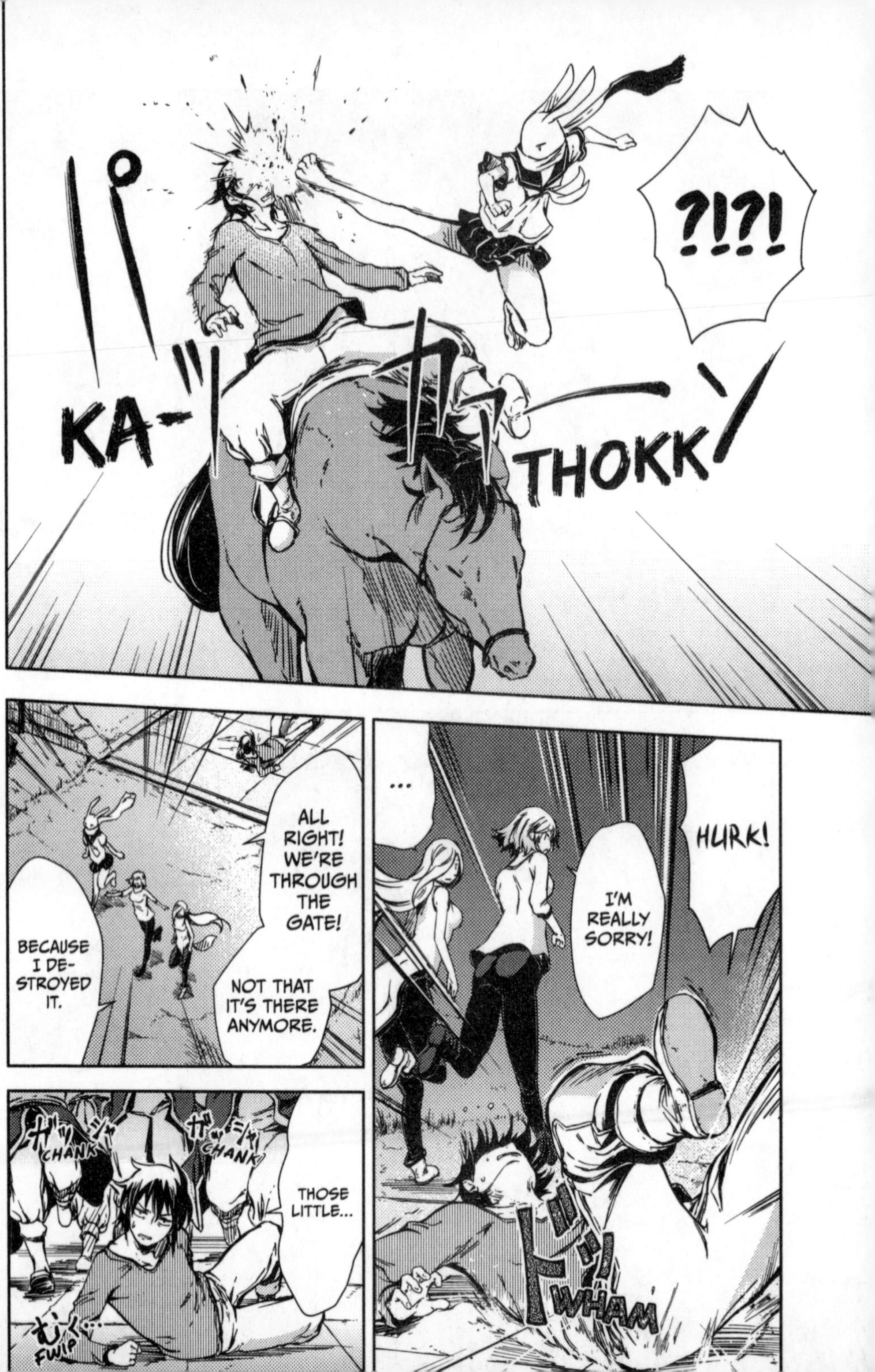
?!?!
KA-THOKK
HURK!
...
I'M REALLY SORRY!
WHAM
ALL RIGHT! WE'RE THROUGH THE GATE!
NOT THAT IT'S THERE ANYMORE.
BECAUSE I DE-STROYED IT.
CHANK
CHANK
THOSE LITTLE...
FWIP

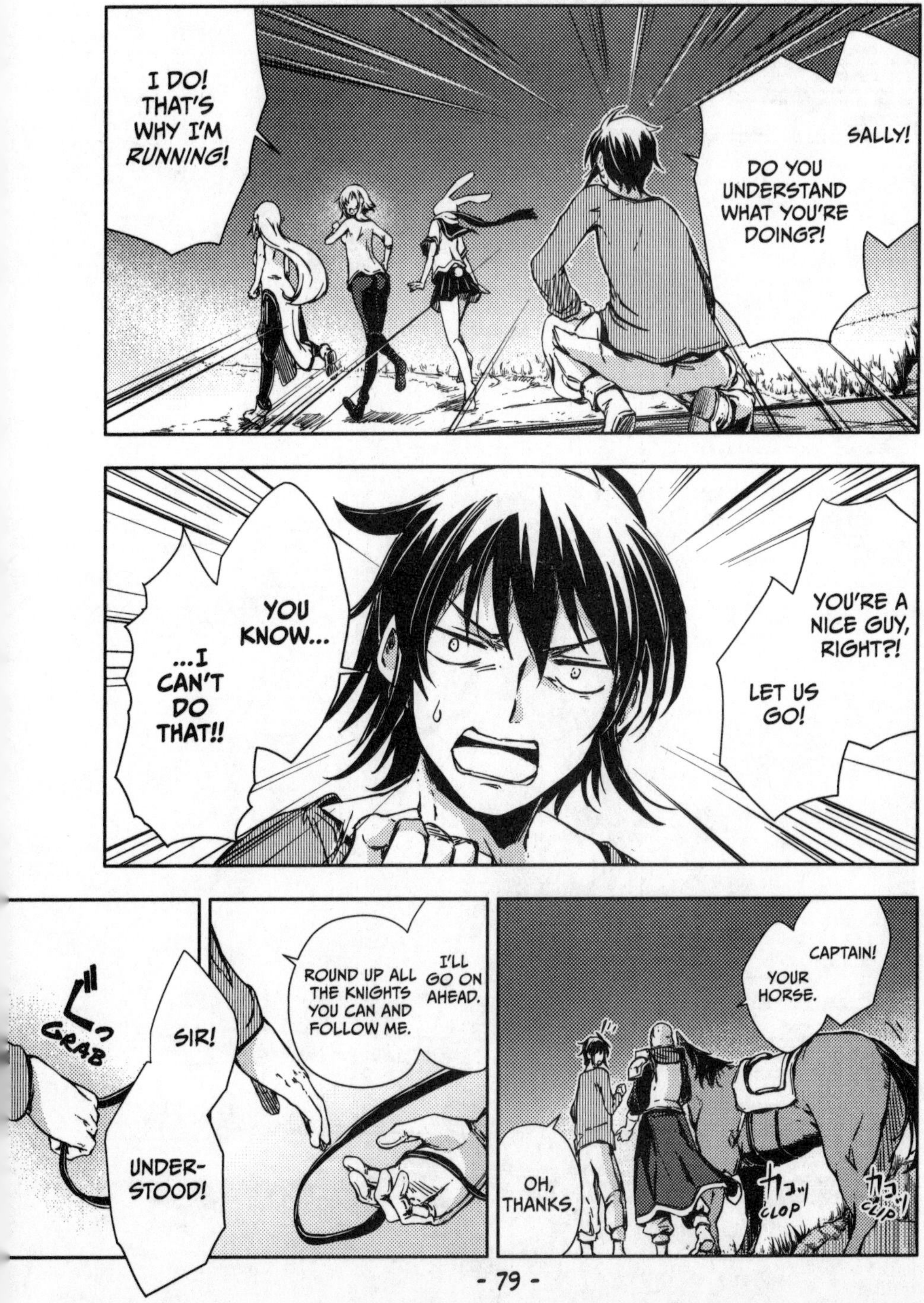
SALLY!
DO YOU UNDERSTAND WHAT YOU'RE DOING?!
I DO! THAT'S WHY I'M *RUNNING*!
YOU'RE A NICE GUY, RIGHT?!
LET US GO!
YOU KNOW...
...I CAN'T DO THAT!!
CAPTAIN!
YOUR HORSE.
CLIP
CLOP
OH, THANKS.
I'LL GO ON AHEAD.
ROUND UP ALL THE KNIGHTS YOU CAN AND FOLLOW ME.
SIR!
UNDER-STOOD!
GRAB

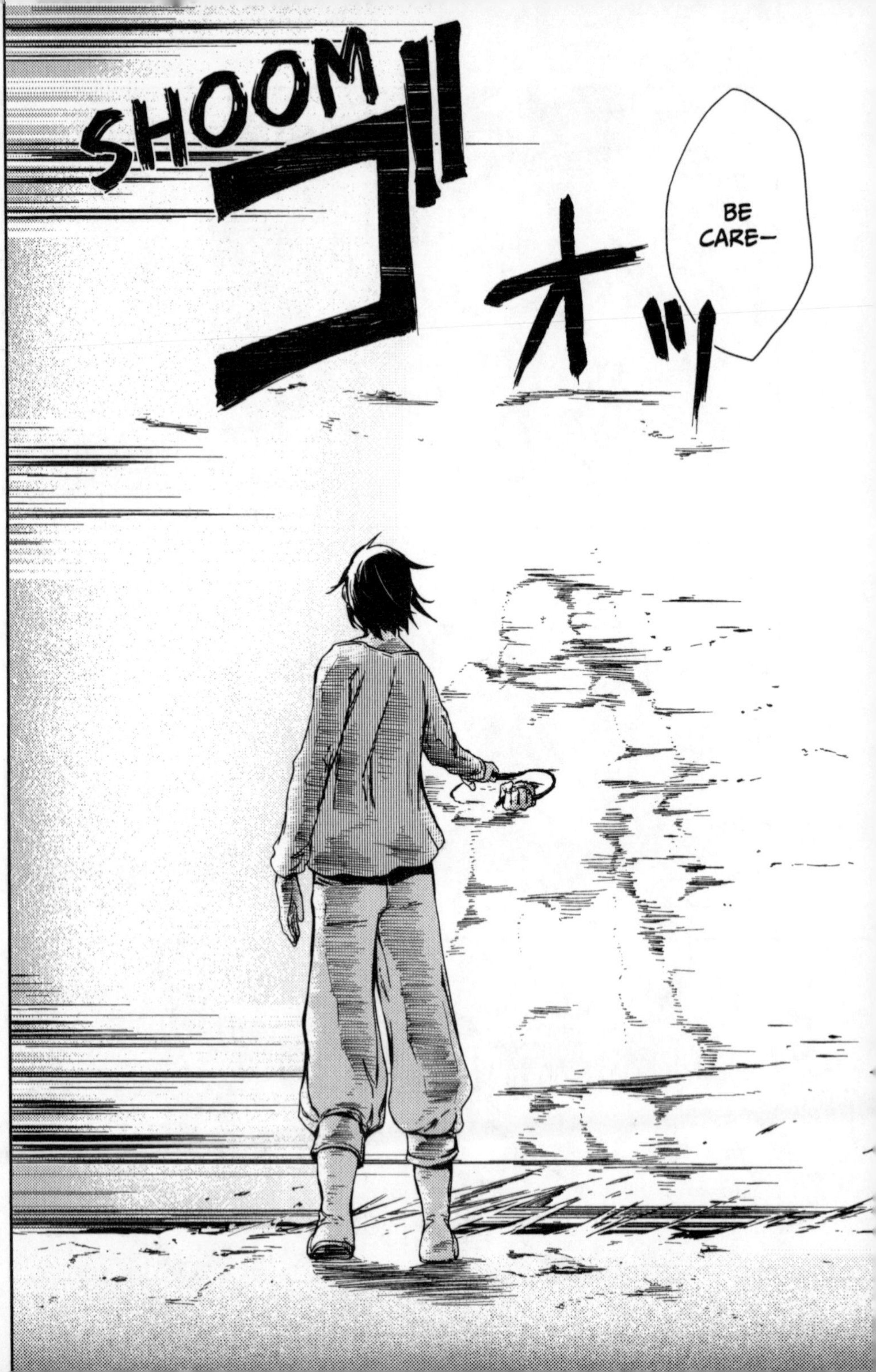
BE CARE—
SHOOM
ゴオッ

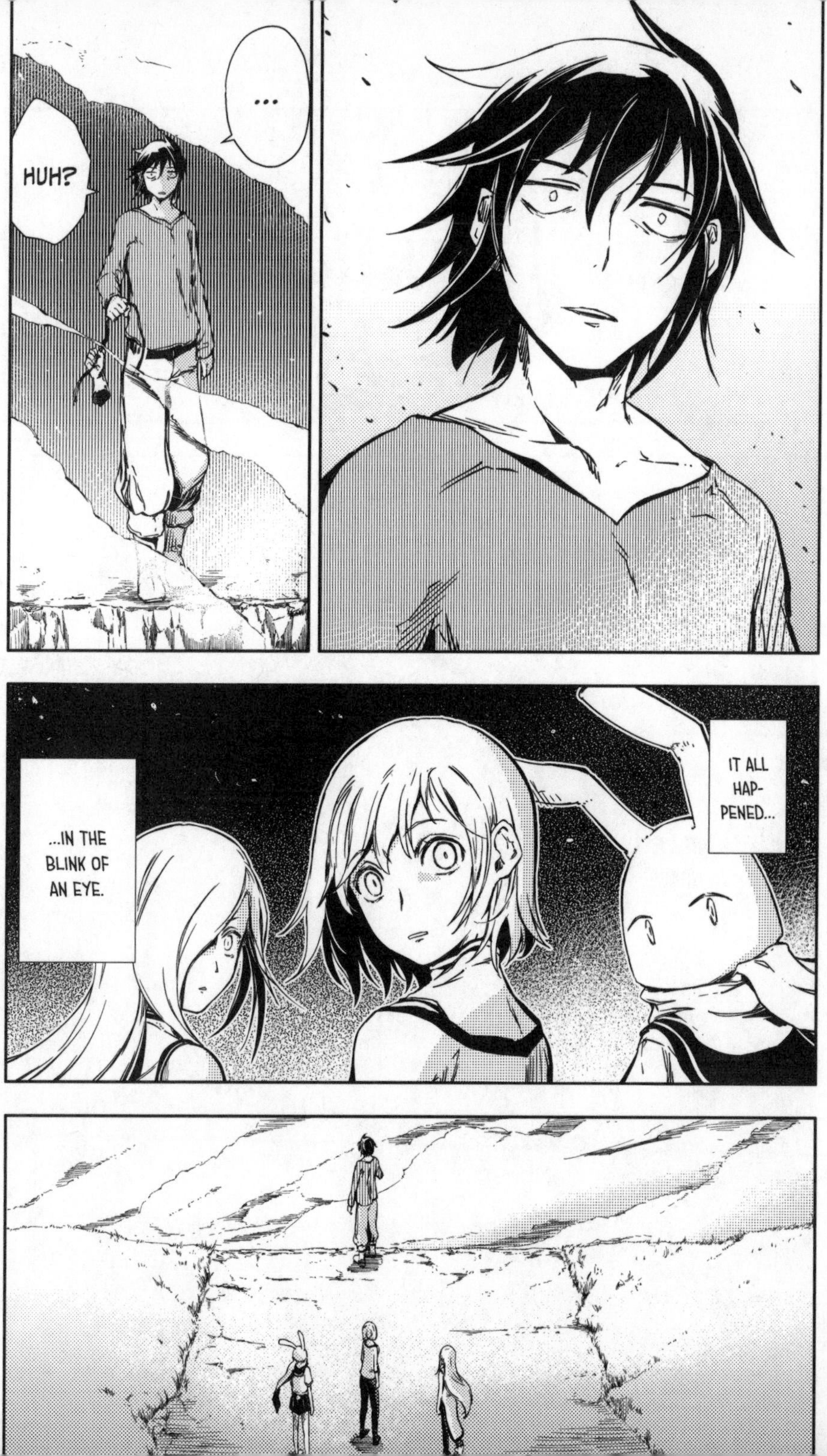
...
HUH?
IT ALL HAP-PENED...
...IN THE BLINK OF AN EYE.

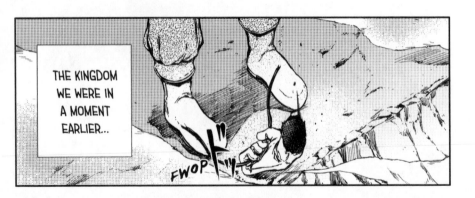

THE KINGDOM
WE WERE IN
A MOMENT
EARLIER...

FWOP"

FWOOOOOOSH...

...VANISHED...

...WITHOUT
A TRACE.

PEACH BOY RIVERSIDE

CHAPTER 6:
RACES AND PLACES

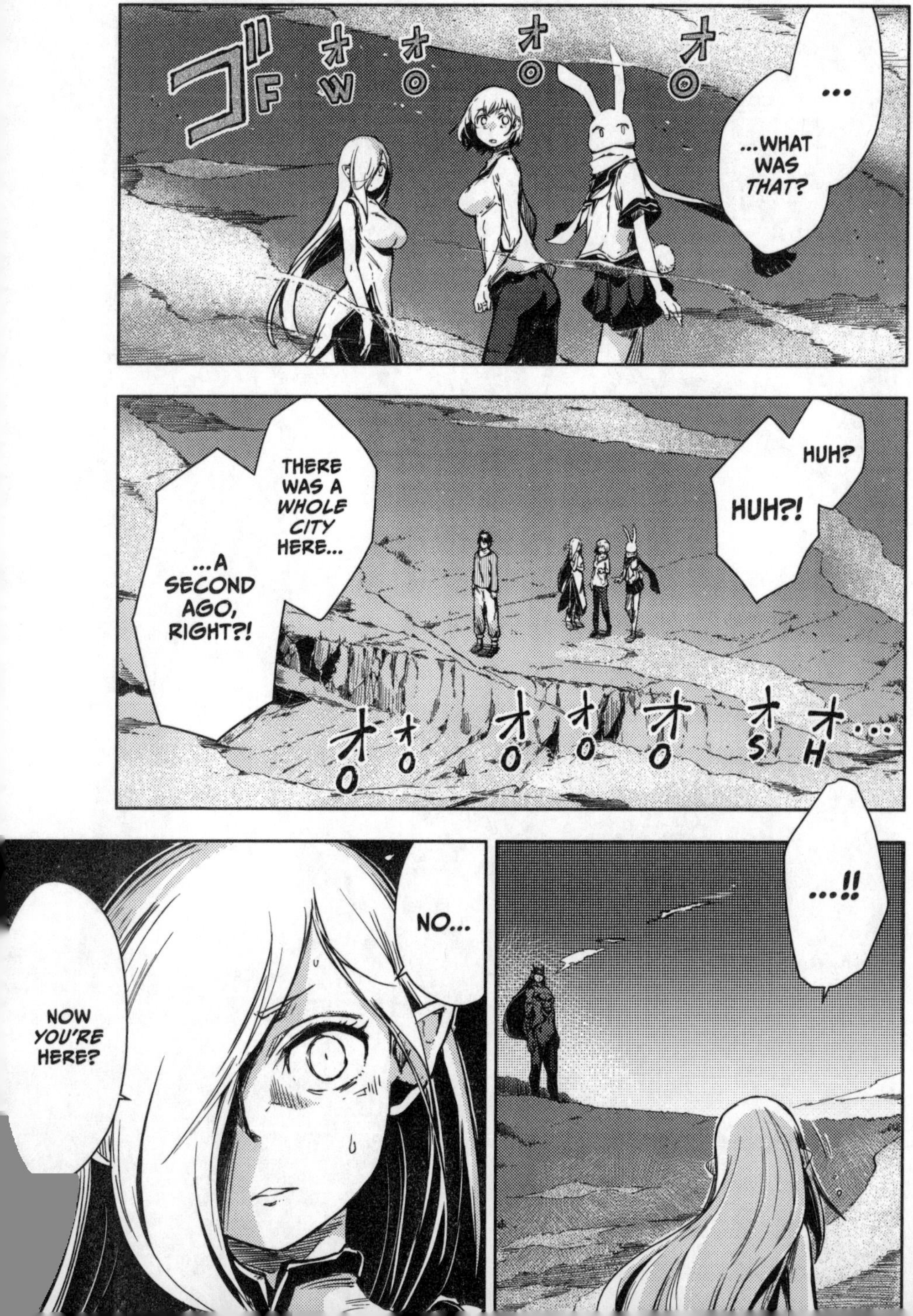
FWOOO
...
...WHAT WAS THAT?
HUH?
HUH?!
THERE WAS A WHOLE CITY HERE...
...A SECOND AGO, RIGHT?!
OOOOOSH...
...!!
NO...
NOW YOU'RE HERE?

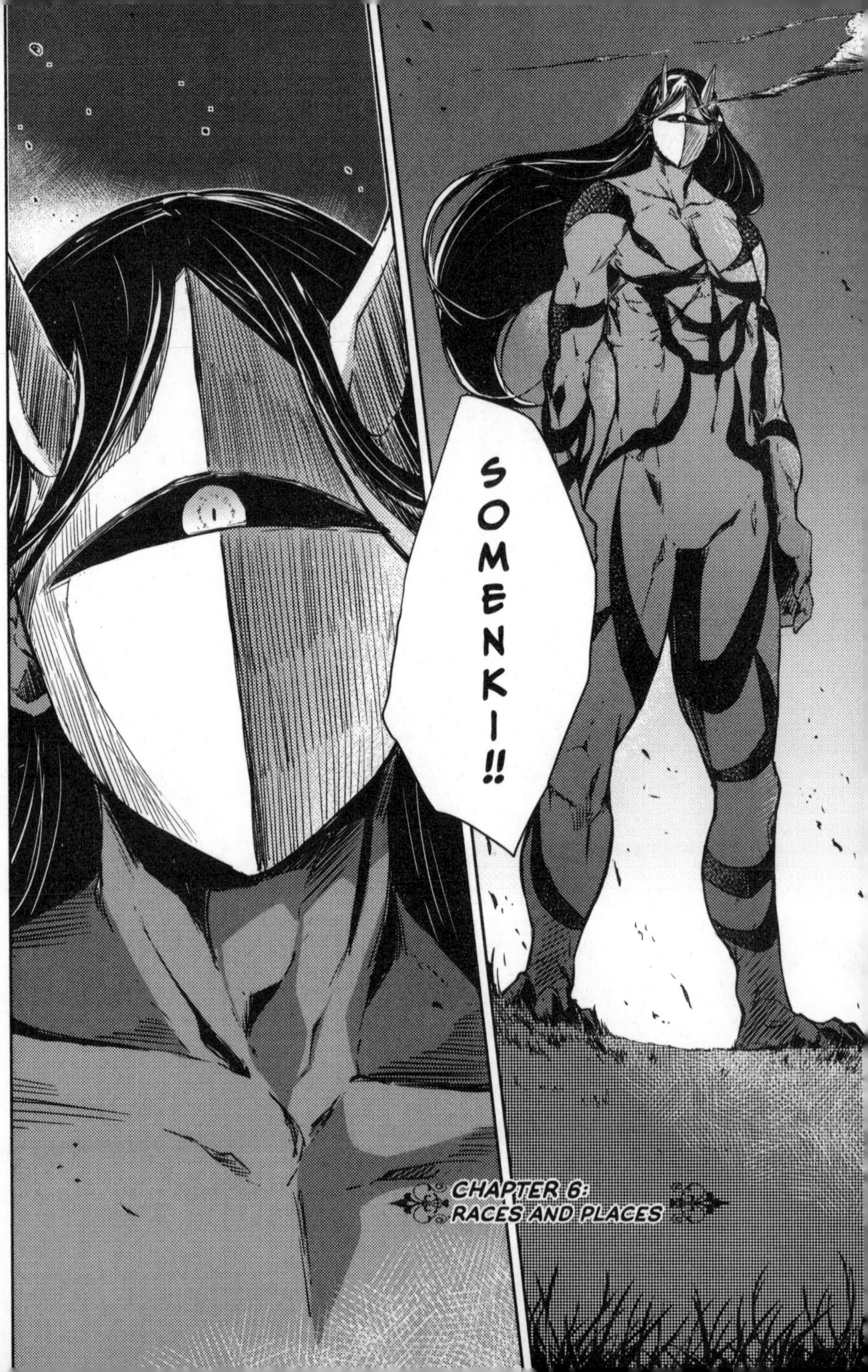
SOMENKI!!
CHAPTER 6:
RACES AND PLACES

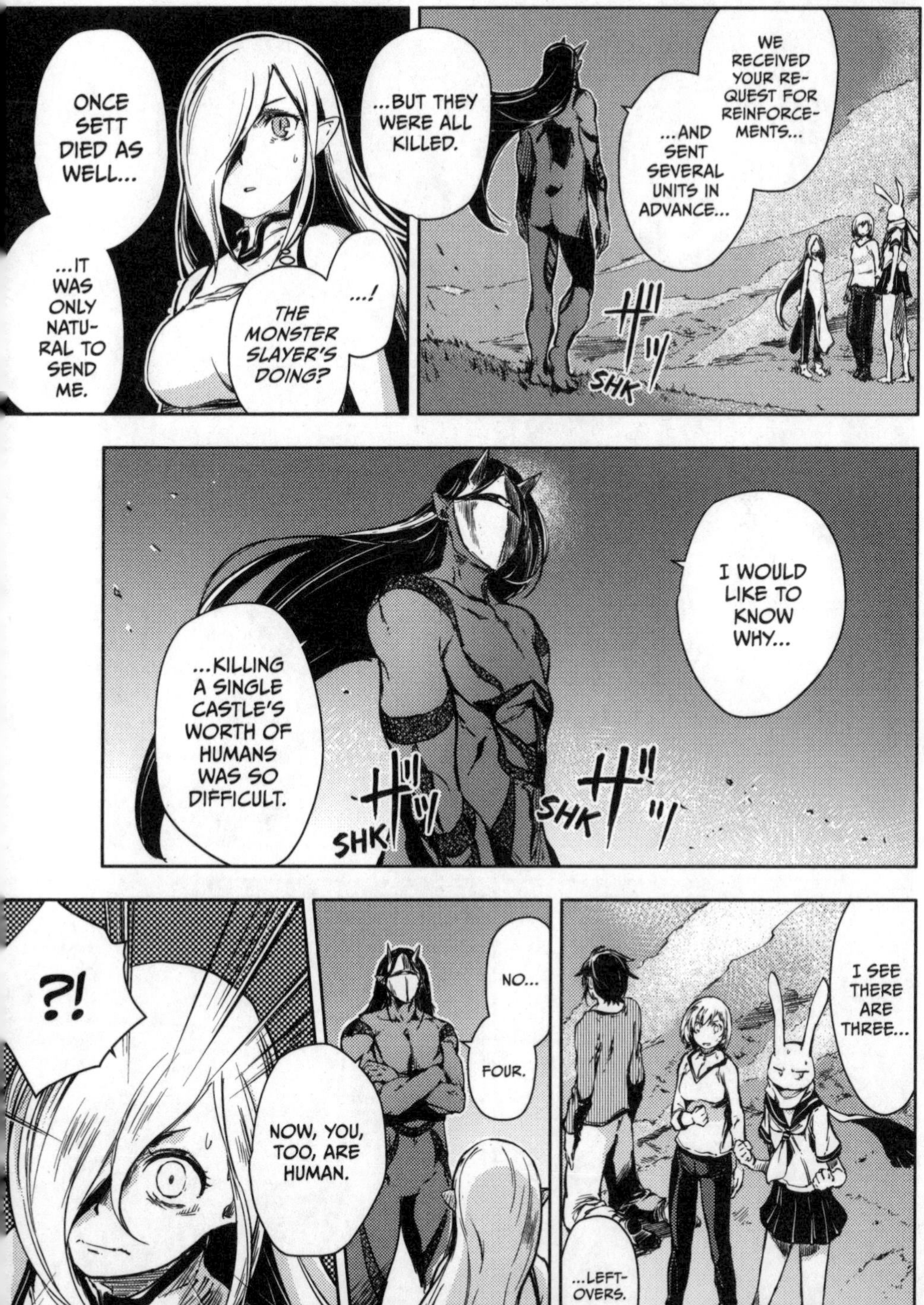
WE RECEIVED YOUR REQUEST FOR REINFORCEMENTS...
...AND SENT SEVERAL UNITS IN ADVANCE...
SHK
...BUT THEY WERE ALL KILLED.
ONCE SETT DIED AS WELL...
...!
THE MONSTER SLAYER'S DOING?
...IT WAS ONLY NATURAL TO SEND ME.
I WOULD LIKE TO KNOW WHY...
SHK
...KILLING A SINGLE CASTLE'S WORTH OF HUMANS WAS SO DIFFICULT.
SHK
I SEE THERE ARE THREE...
...LEFT-OVERS.
NO...
FOUR.
NOW, YOU, TOO, ARE HUMAN.
?!

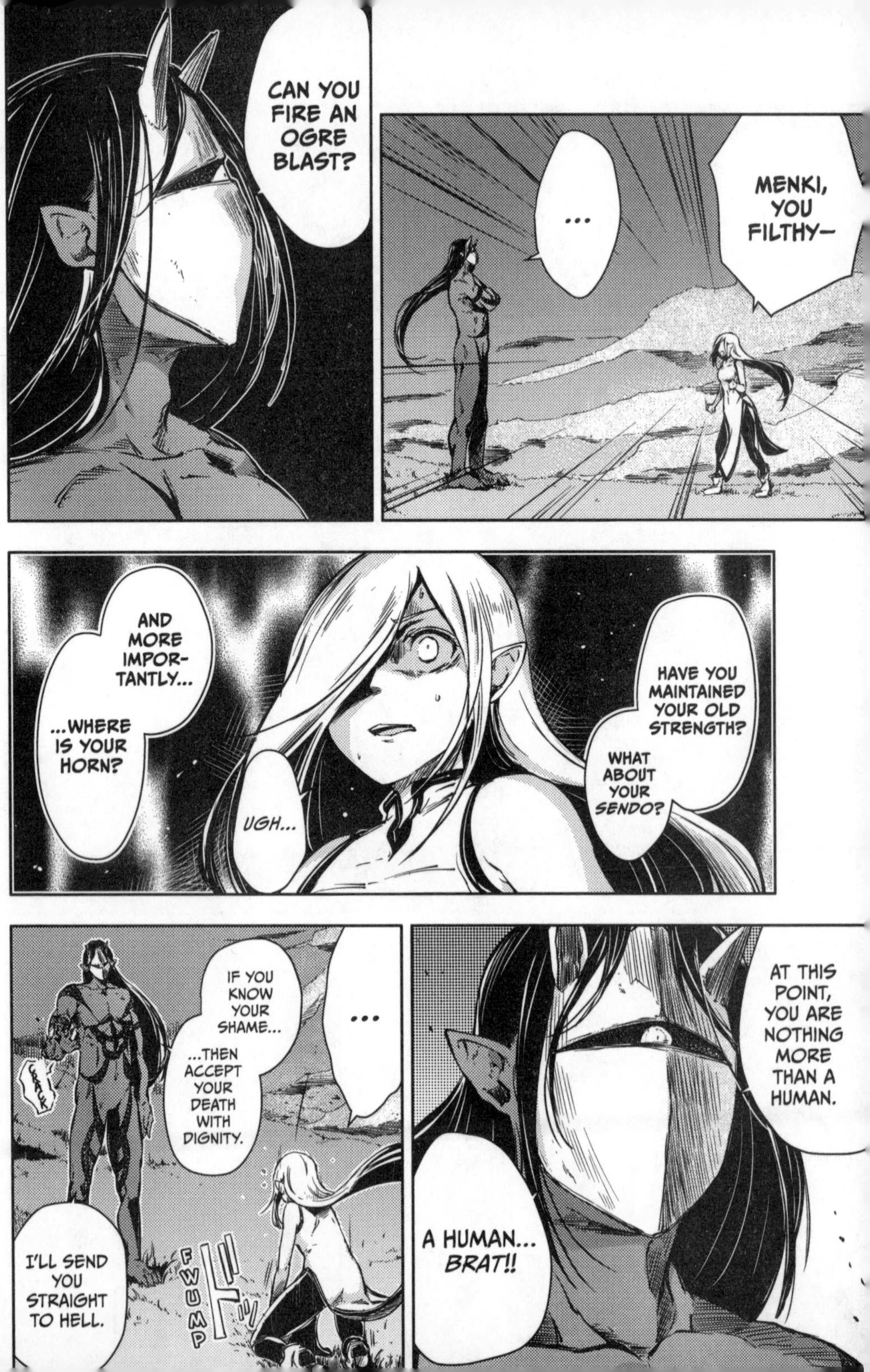
MENKI, YOU FILTHY—
...
CAN YOU FIRE AN OGRE BLAST?
HAVE YOU MAINTAINED YOUR OLD STRENGTH?
WHAT ABOUT YOUR SENDO?
UGH...
AND MORE IMPORTANTLY...
...WHERE IS YOUR HORN?
AT THIS POINT, YOU ARE NOTHING MORE THAN A HUMAN.
A HUMAN... BRAT!!
...
IF YOU KNOW YOUR SHAME...
...THEN ACCEPT YOUR DEATH WITH DIGNITY.
CRACK
FWUMP
I'LL SEND YOU STRAIGHT TO HELL.

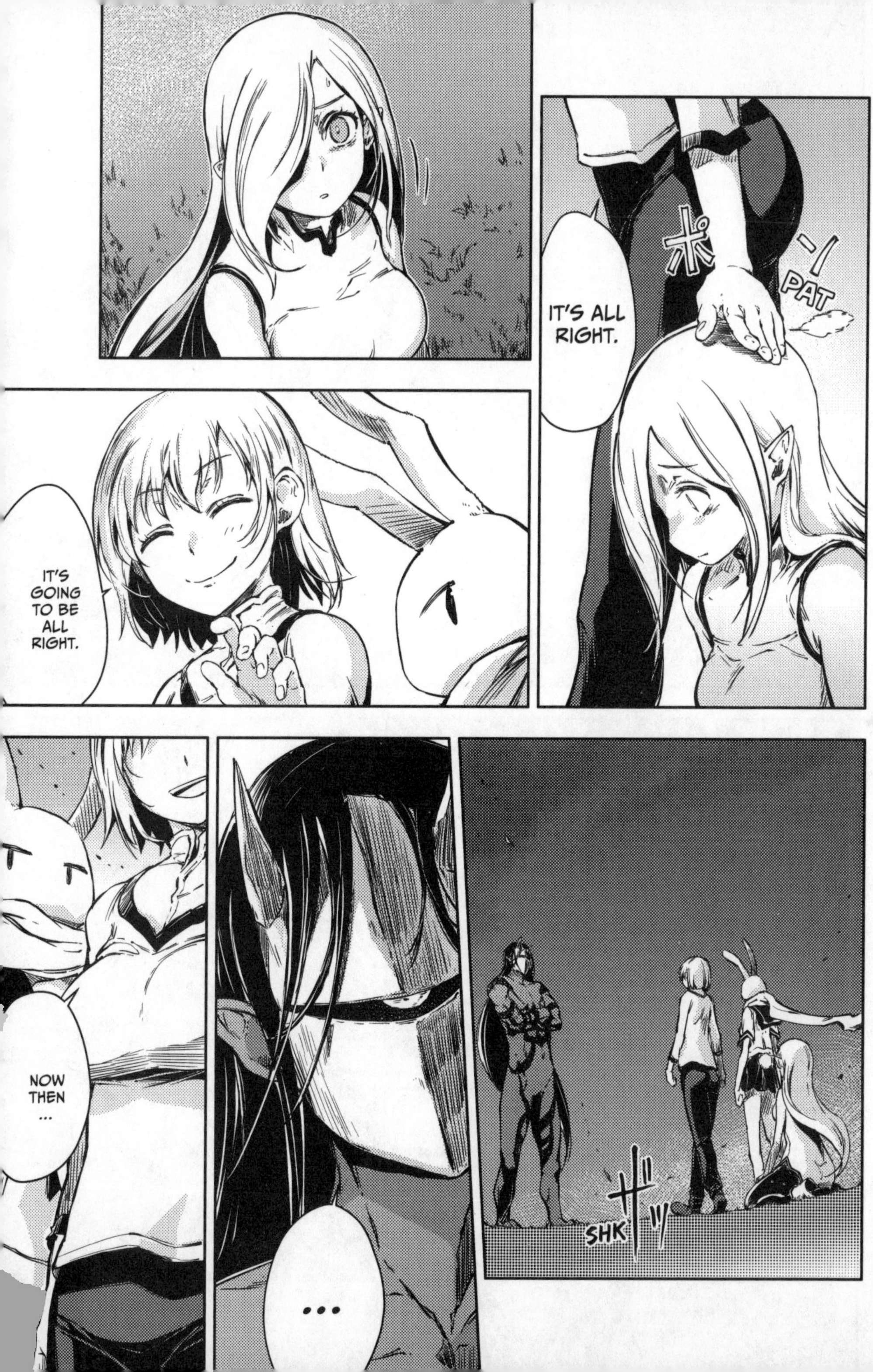
ポン
PAT
IT'S ALL RIGHT.
IT'S GOING TO BE ALL RIGHT.
ザッ
SHK
...
NOW THEN ...

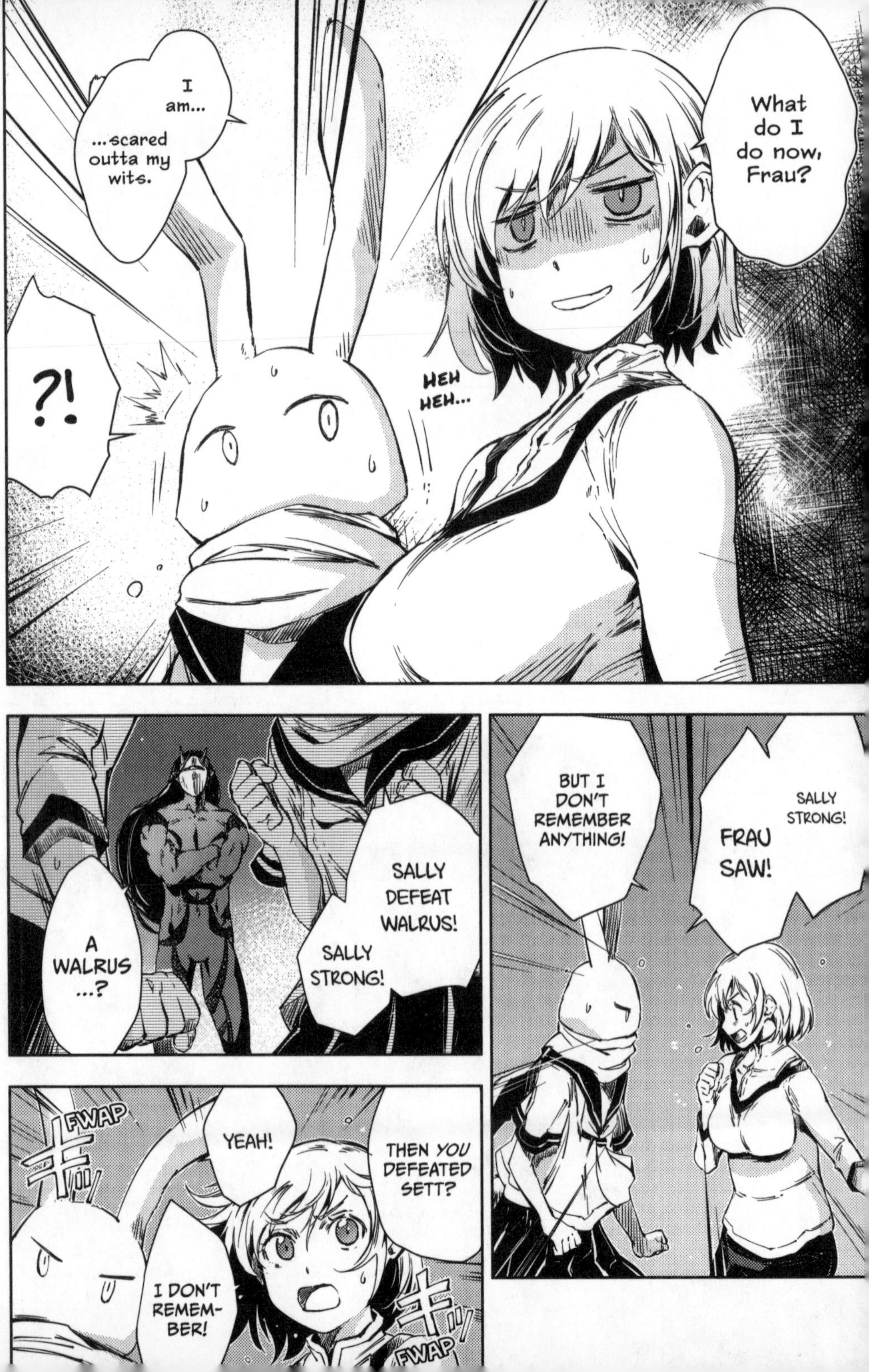
What do I do now, Frau?
HEH HEH...
I am... ...scared outta my wits.
?!
SALLY STRONG!
FRAU SAW!
BUT I DON'T REMEMBER ANYTHING!
SALLY DEFEAT WALRUS!
SALLY STRONG!
A WALRUS ...?
THEN *YOU* DEFEATED SETT?
YEAH!
FWAP
I DON'T REMEMBER!
FWAP

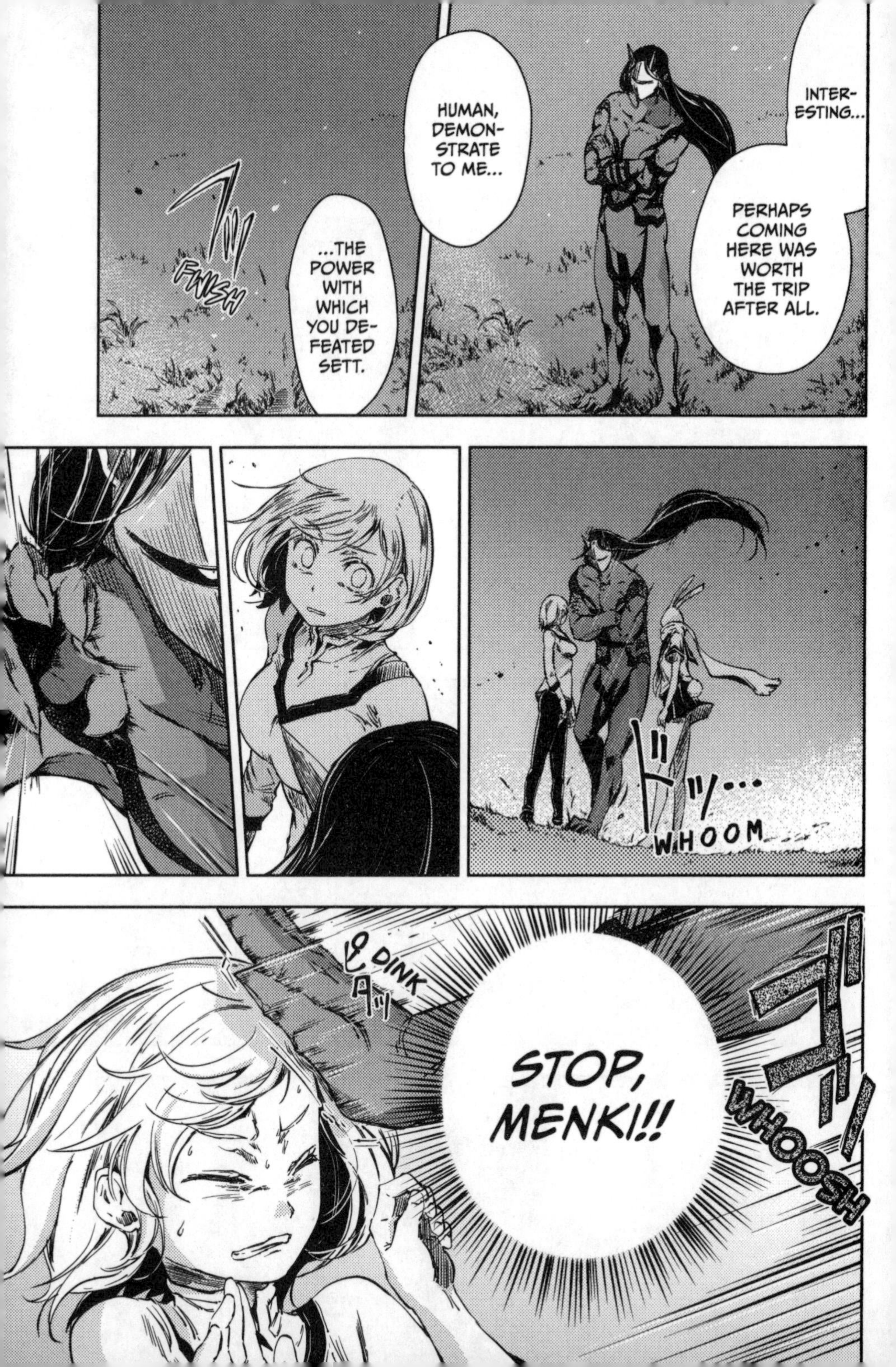
INTERESTING...
PERHAPS COMING HERE WAS WORTH THE TRIP AFTER ALL.
HUMAN, DEMONSTRATE TO ME...
...THE POWER WITH WHICH YOU DEFEATED SETT.
FWISH
WHOOM
WHOOSH
STOP, MENKI!!
DINK

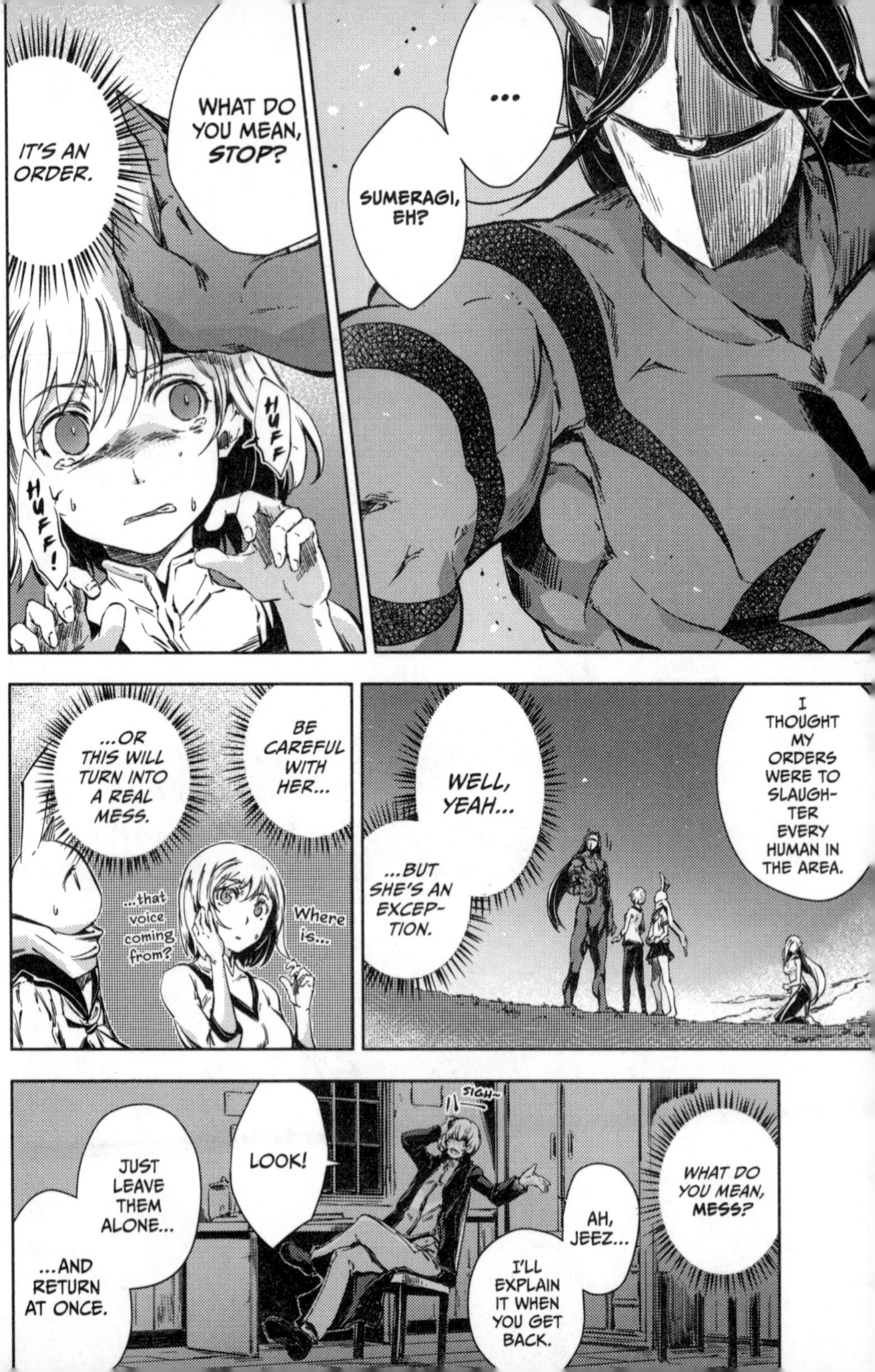
...
SUMERAGI, EH?
WHAT DO YOU MEAN, STOP?
IT'S AN ORDER.
HUFF
HUFF HUFF!
I THOUGHT MY ORDERS WERE TO SLAUGHTER EVERY HUMAN IN THE AREA.
WELL, YEAH...
...BUT SHE'S AN EXCEPTION.
BE CAREFUL WITH HER...
...OR THIS WILL TURN INTO A REAL MESS.
Where is...
...that voice coming from?
WHAT DO YOU MEAN, MESS?
SIGH~
AH, JEEZ...
I'LL EXPLAIN IT WHEN YOU GET BACK.
LOOK!
JUST LEAVE THEM ALONE...
...AND RETURN AT ONCE.

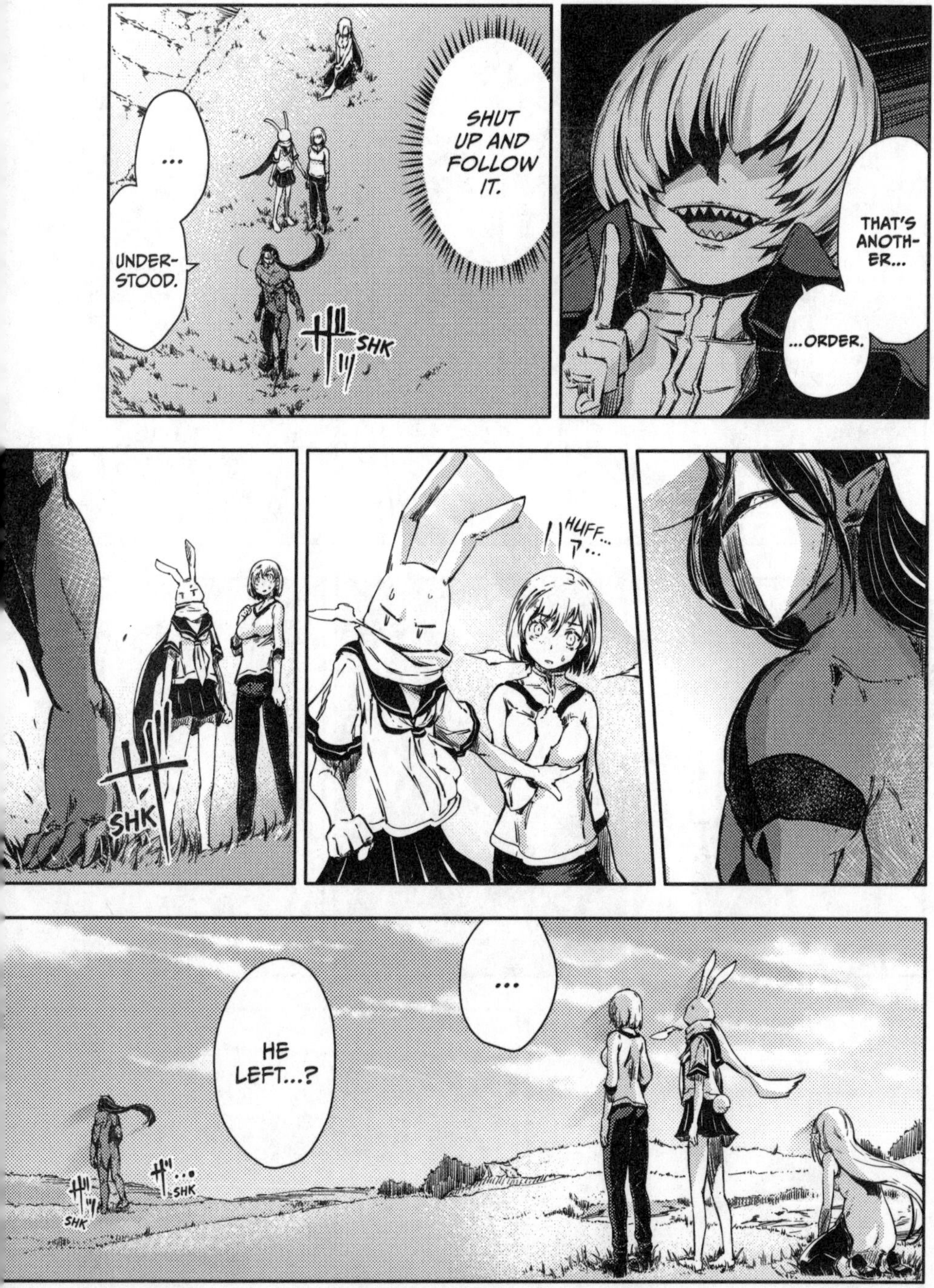
THAT'S ANOTH-ER...
...ORDER.
SHUT UP AND FOLLOW IT.
...
UNDER-STOOD.
SHK
HUFF...
SHK
...
HE LEFT...?
SHK
SHK

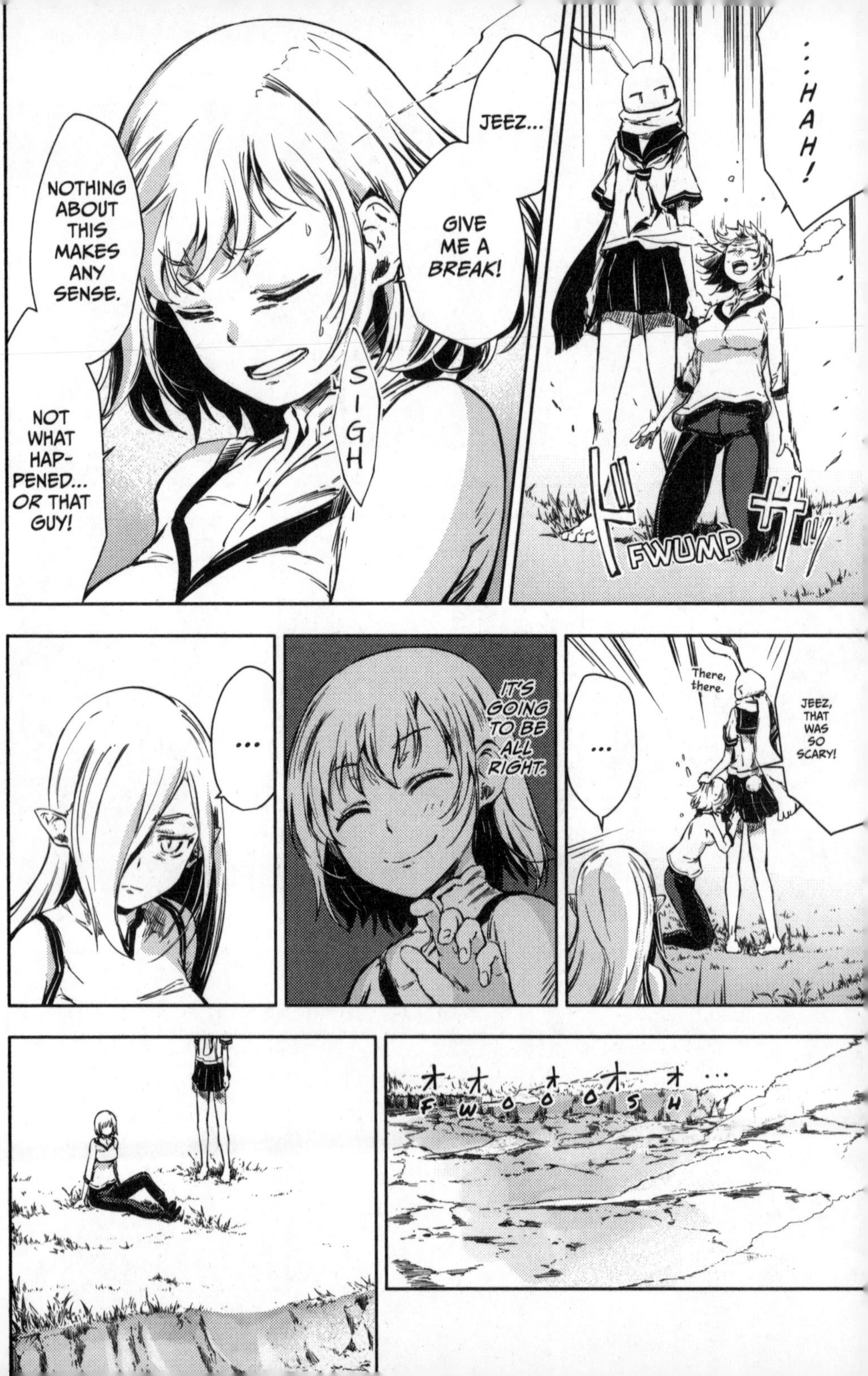
...HAH!
FWUMP
JEEZ...
GIVE ME A BREAK!
SIGH
NOTHING ABOUT THIS MAKES ANY SENSE.
NOT WHAT HAPPENED... OR THAT GUY!
There, there.
JEEZ, THAT WAS SO SCARY!
...
IT'S GOING TO BE ALL RIGHT.
...
FWOOOSH...

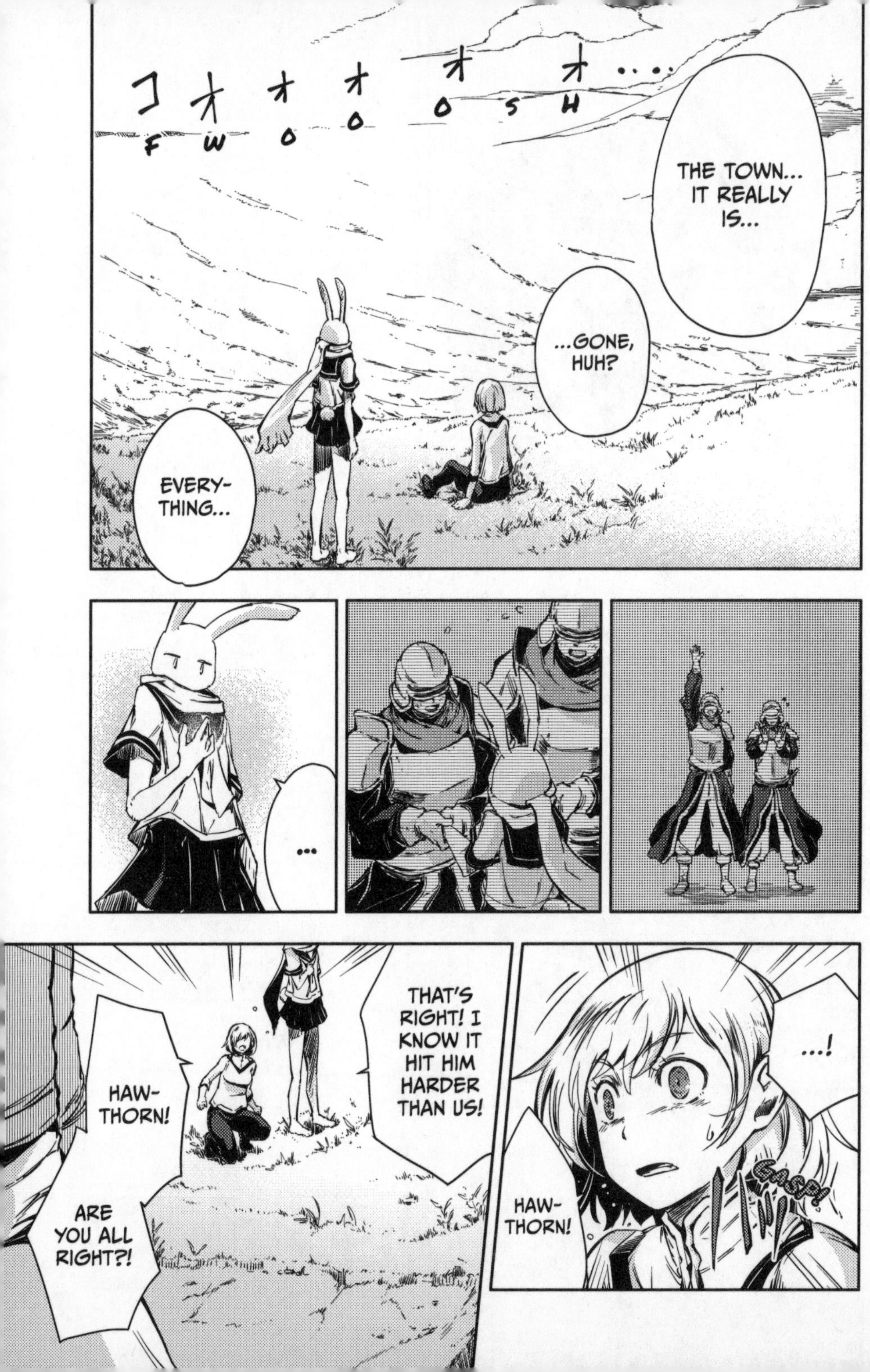
コオオオオオ…
FWOOOSH
THE TOWN... IT REALLY IS...
...GONE, HUH?
EVERY-THING...
...
...!
HAW-THORN!
GASP!
THAT'S RIGHT! I KNOW IT HIT HIM HARDER THAN US!
HAW-THORN!
ARE YOU ALL RIGHT?!

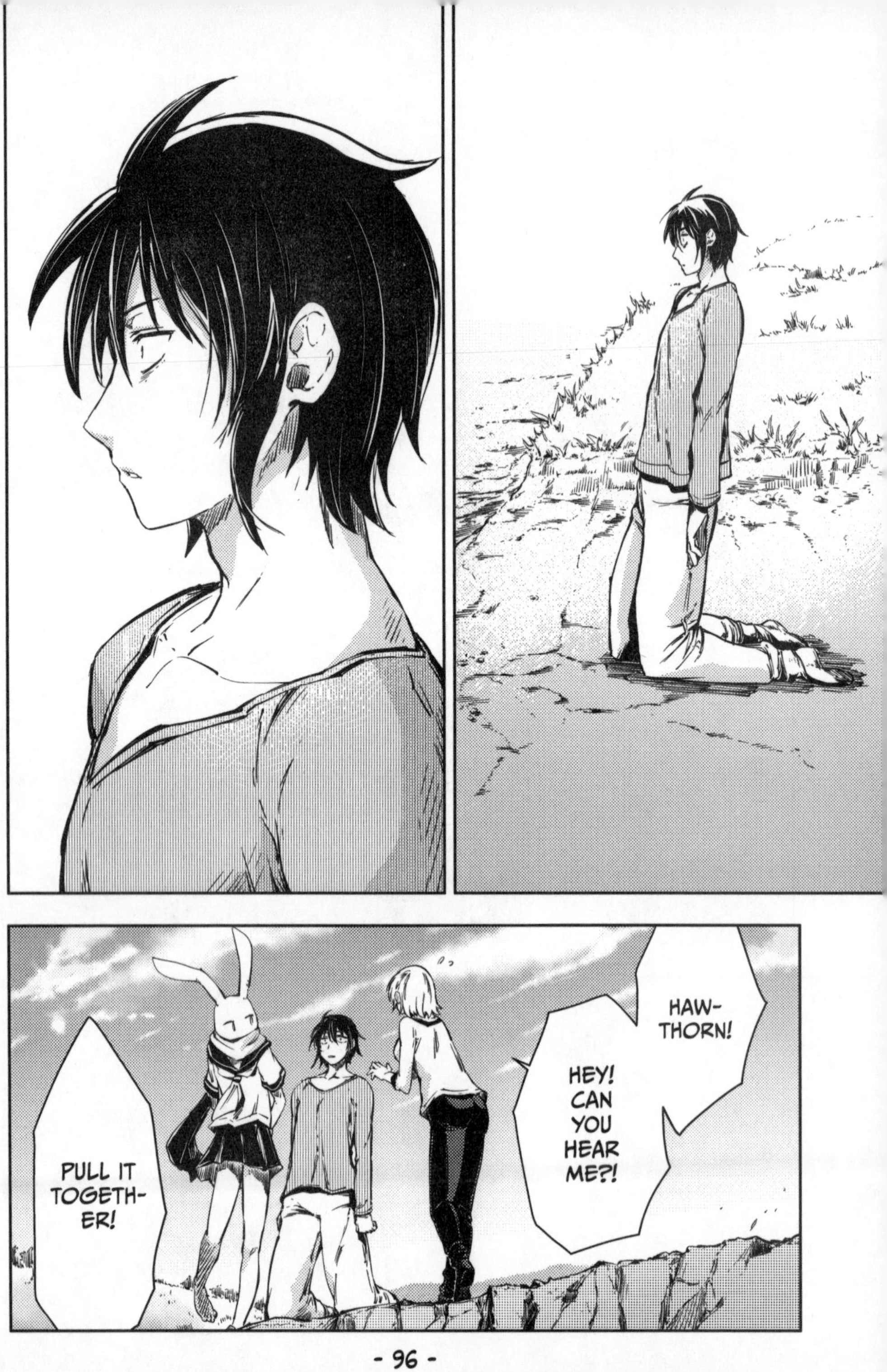
HAW-THORN!
HEY! CAN YOU HEAR ME?!
PULL IT TOGETH-ER!

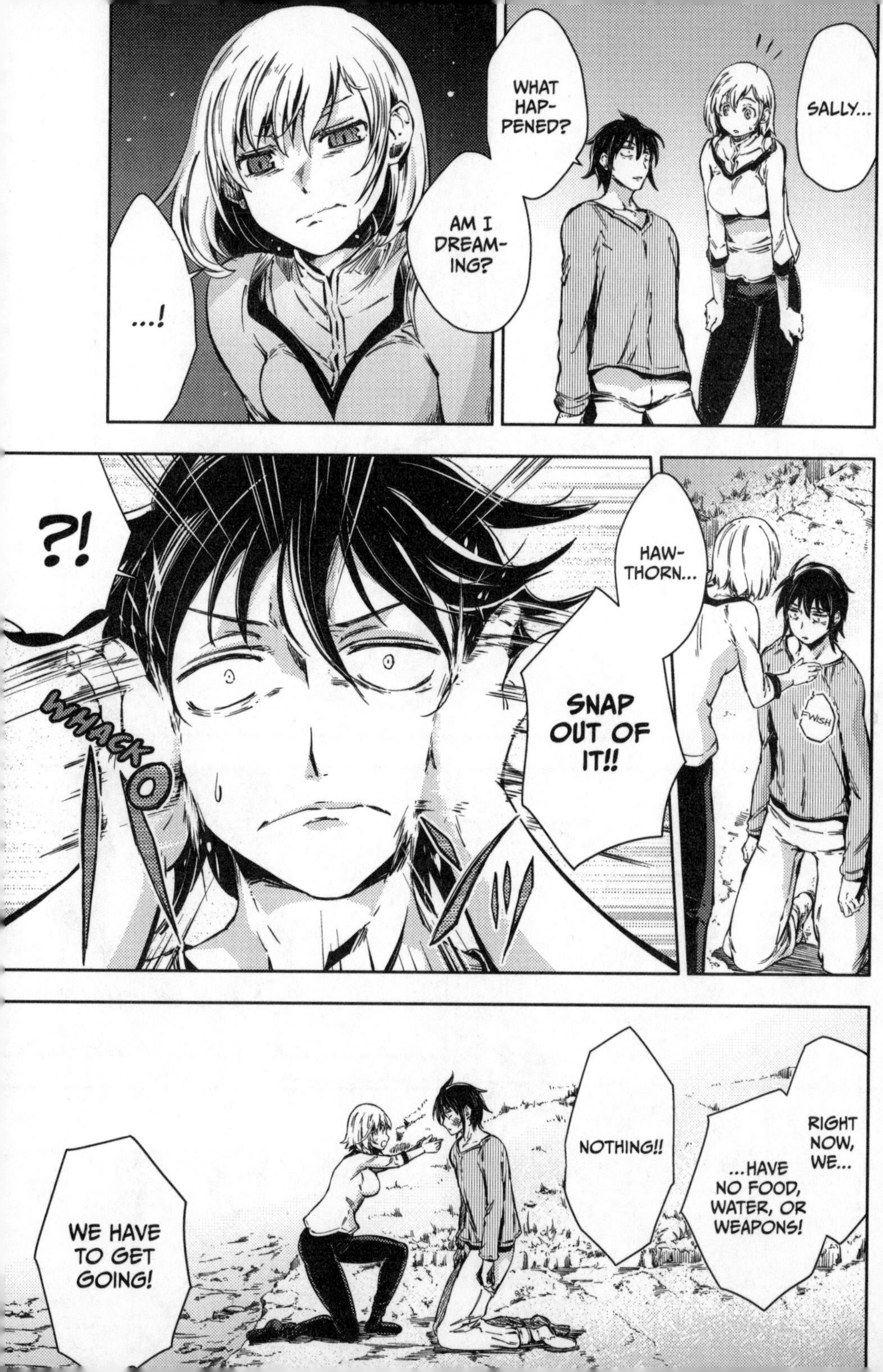
SALLY...
WHAT HAP-PENED?
AM I DREAM-ING?
...!
HAW-THORN...
SNAP OUT OF IT!!
FWISH
?!
WHACK
RIGHT NOW, WE...
...HAVE NO FOOD, WATER, OR WEAPONS!
NOTHING!!
WE HAVE TO GET GOING!

I CAN UNDER-STAND...

YOU'RE THE ONLY ONE WE CAN COUNT ON!

...YOU BEING SHOCKED AND CON-FUSED!

SO GET IT TOGETH-ER!!

BUT!!

YOU'VE GOT A POINT...

RIGHT.

R...

THROB

SORRY, MY BRAIN'S STILL NOT FUNC-TIONING...

WE'D BETTER HEAD TO A NEARBY TOWN.

THAT'S FINE.

I'LL WAIT.

UHHH... WHERE IS IT?

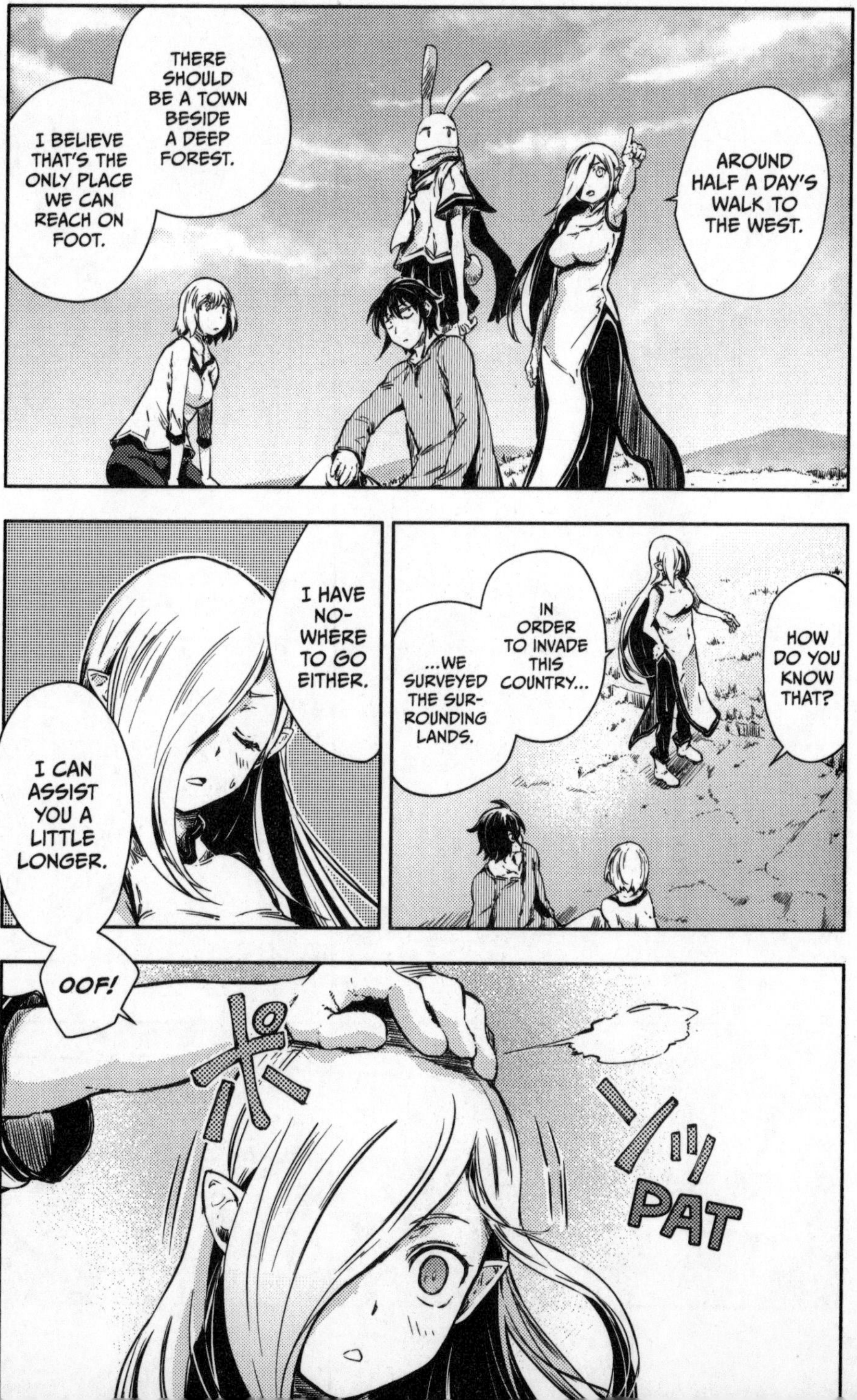
AROUND HALF A DAY'S WALK TO THE WEST.
THERE SHOULD BE A TOWN BESIDE A DEEP FOREST.
I BELIEVE THAT'S THE ONLY PLACE WE CAN REACH ON FOOT.
HOW DO YOU KNOW THAT?
IN ORDER TO INVADE THIS COUNTRY...
...WE SURVEYED THE SUR-ROUNDING LANDS.
I HAVE NO-WHERE TO GO EITHER.
I CAN ASSIST YOU A LITTLE LONGER.
OOF!
PAT

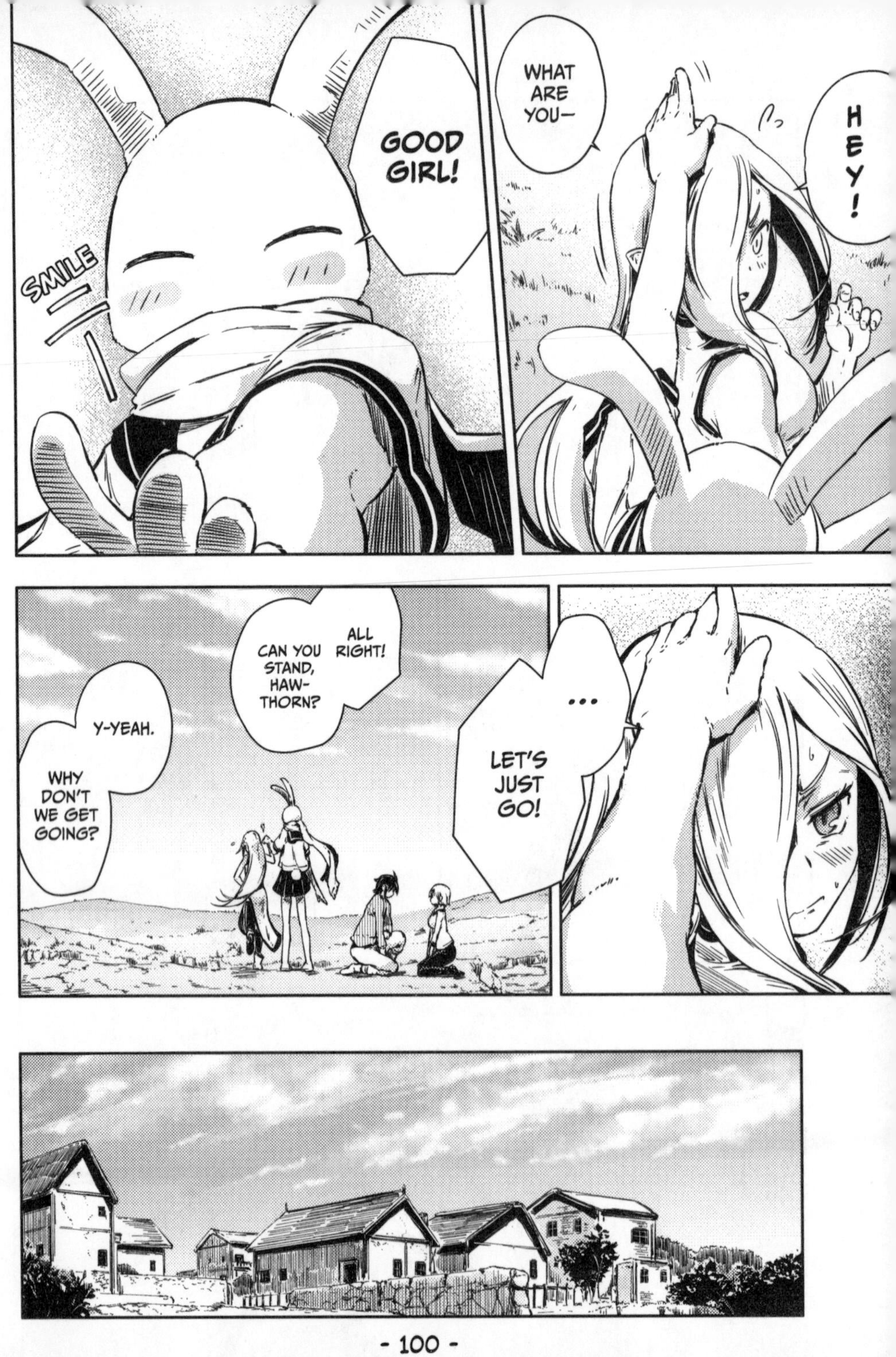
HEY!
WHAT ARE YOU—
GOOD GIRL!
SMILE
...
LET'S JUST GO!
ALL RIGHT!
CAN YOU STAND, HAWTHORN?
Y-YEAH.
WHY DON'T WE GET GOING?

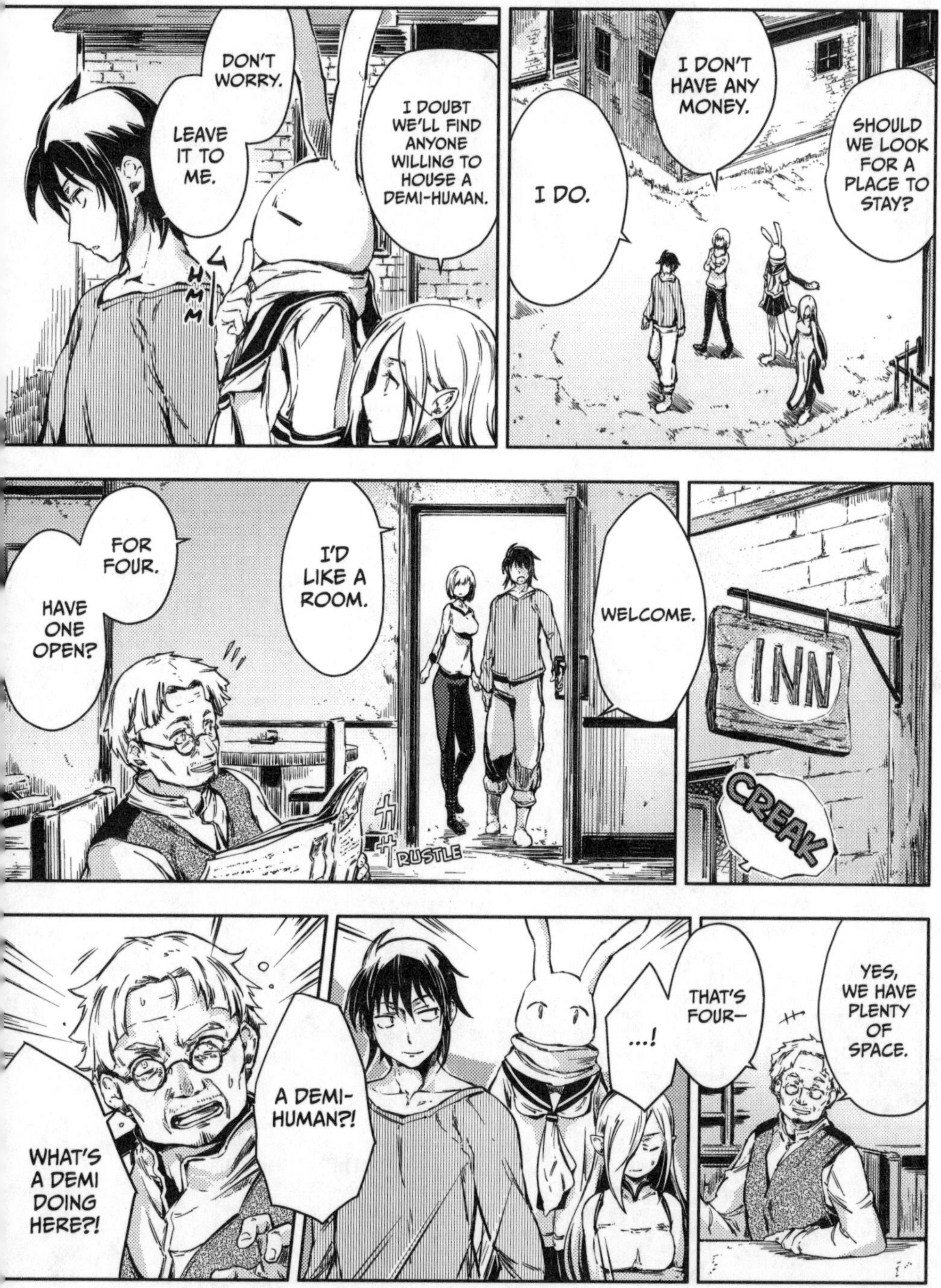
SHOULD WE LOOK FOR A PLACE TO STAY?
I DON'T HAVE ANY MONEY.
I DO.
I DOUBT WE'LL FIND ANYONE WILLING TO HOUSE A DEMI-HUMAN.
DON'T WORRY.
LEAVE IT TO ME.
HMMM
CREAK
INN
WELCOME.
I'D LIKE A ROOM.
FOR FOUR.
HAVE ONE OPEN?
RUSTLE
YES, WE HAVE PLENTY OF SPACE.
THAT'S FOUR—
...!
A DEMI-HUMAN?!
WHAT'S A DEMI DOING HERE?!

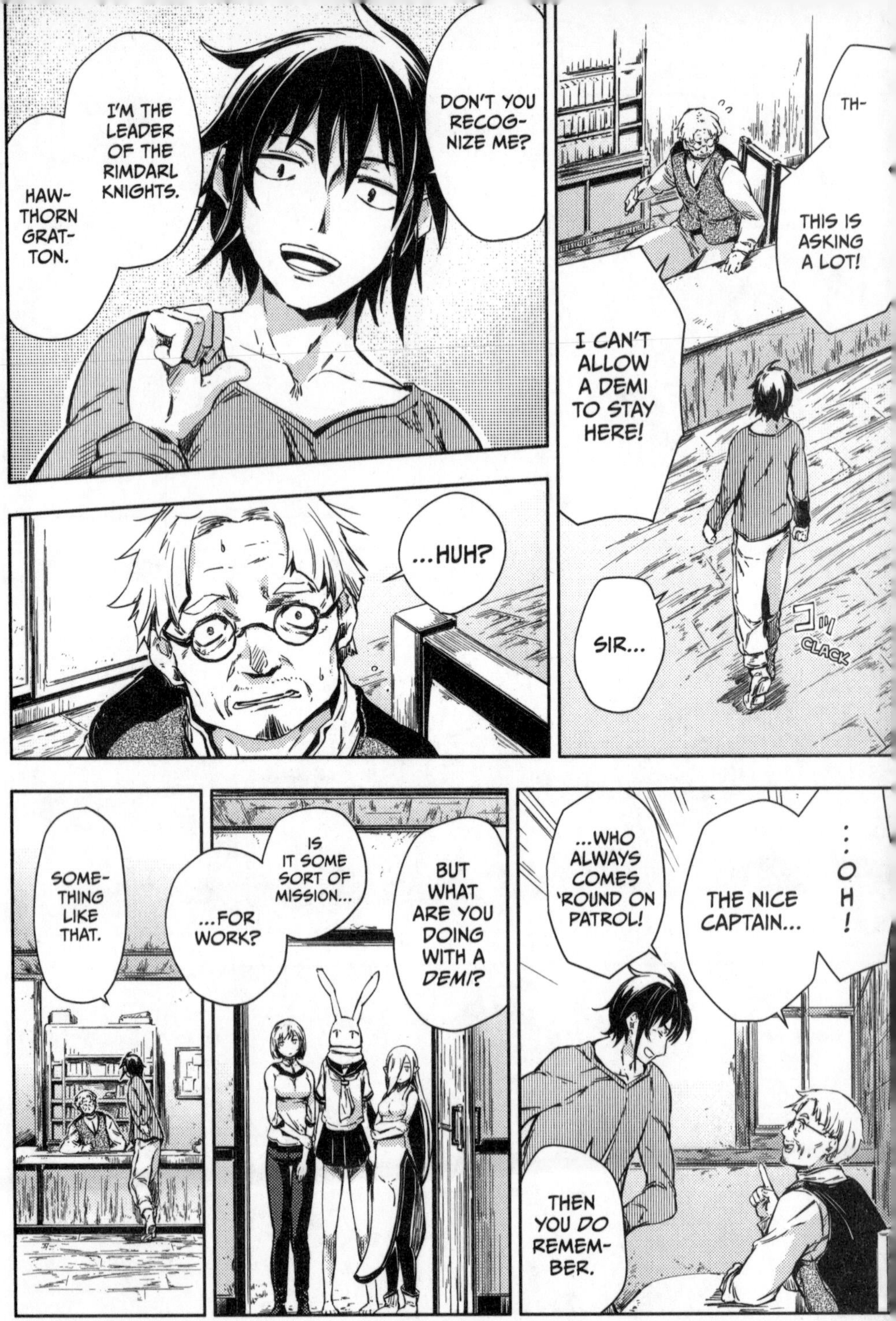
TH-
THIS IS ASKING A LOT!
I CAN'T ALLOW A DEMI TO STAY HERE!
SIR...
コツ
CLACK
DON'T YOU RECOGNIZE ME?
I'M THE LEADER OF THE RIMDARL KNIGHTS.
HAWTHORN GRATTON.
...HUH?
...OH!
THE NICE CAPTAIN...
...WHO ALWAYS COMES 'ROUND ON PATROL!
THEN YOU *DO* REMEMBER.
BUT WHAT ARE YOU DOING WITH A *DEMI*?
IS IT SOME SORT OF MISSION...
...FOR WORK?
SOMETHING LIKE THAT.

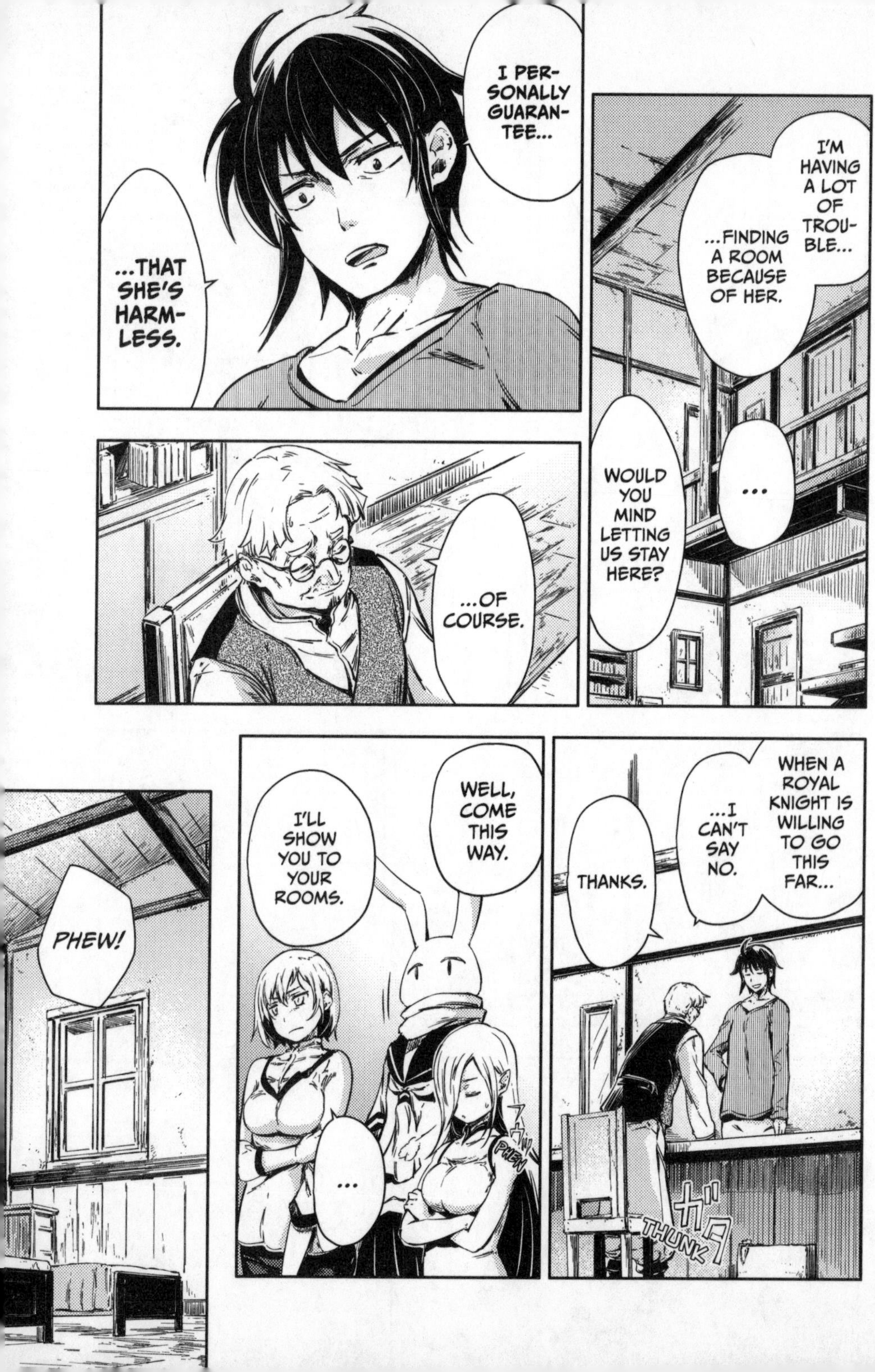
I'M HAVING A LOT OF TROUBLE...
...FINDING A ROOM BECAUSE OF HER.
...
WOULD YOU MIND LETTING US STAY HERE?
I PERSONALLY GUARANTEE...
...THAT SHE'S HARMLESS.
...OF COURSE.
WHEN A ROYAL KNIGHT IS WILLING TO GO THIS FAR...
...I CAN'T SAY NO.
THANKS.
THUNK
WELL, COME THIS WAY.
I'LL SHOW YOU TO YOUR ROOMS.
PHEW
...
PHEW!

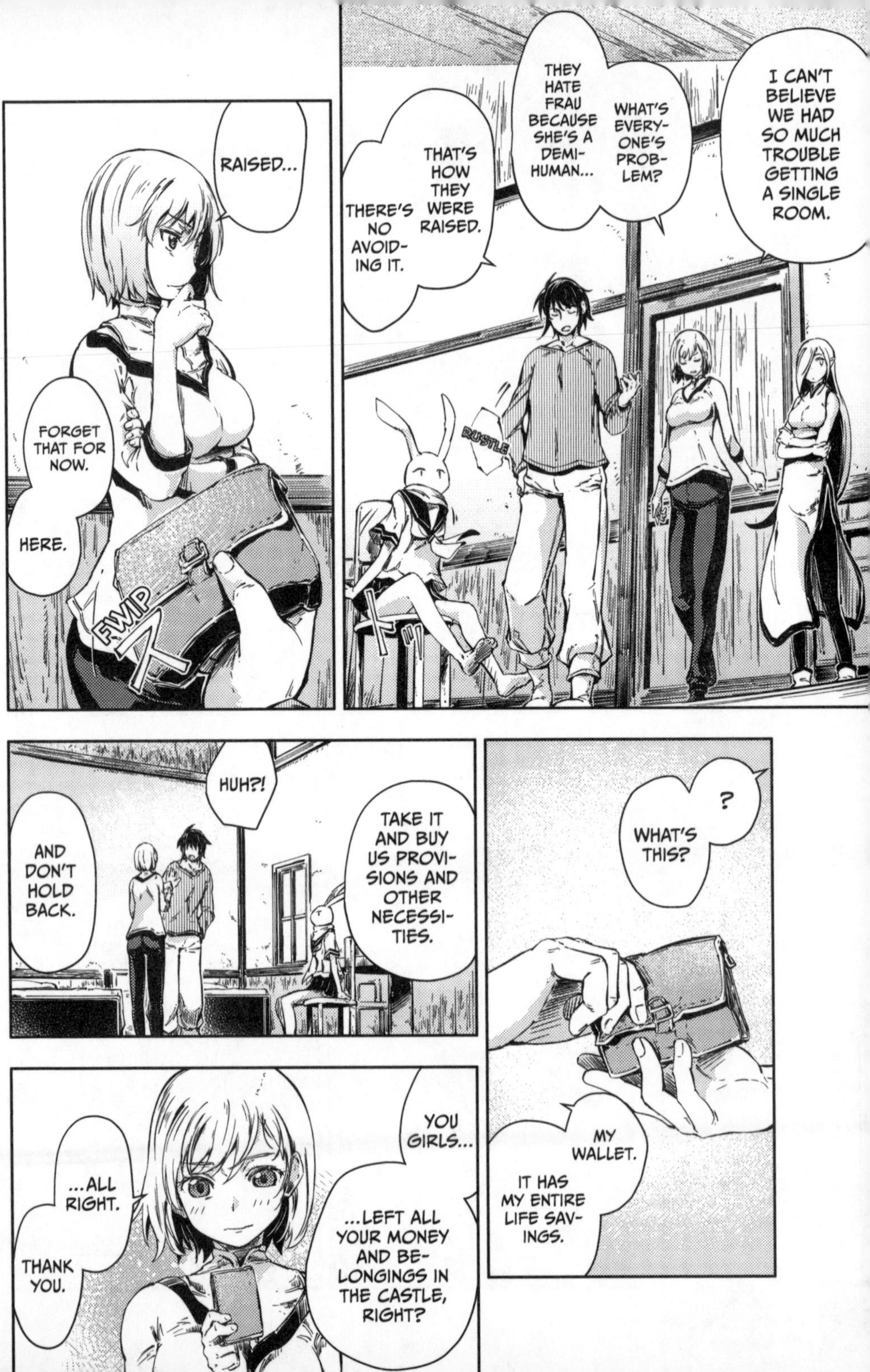
I CAN'T BELIEVE WE HAD SO MUCH TROUBLE GETTING A SINGLE ROOM.
WHAT'S EVERYONE'S PROBLEM?
THEY HATE FRAU BECAUSE SHE'S A DEMI-HUMAN...
THAT'S HOW THEY WERE RAISED.
THERE'S NO AVOIDING IT.
RUSTLE
RAISED...
FORGET THAT FOR NOW.
HERE.
FWIP
?
WHAT'S THIS?
MY WALLET.
IT HAS MY ENTIRE LIFE SAVINGS.
HUH?!
TAKE IT AND BUY US PROVISIONS AND OTHER NECESSITIES.
AND DON'T HOLD BACK.
YOU GIRLS...
...LEFT ALL YOUR MONEY AND BELONGINGS IN THE CASTLE, RIGHT?
...ALL RIGHT.
THANK YOU.

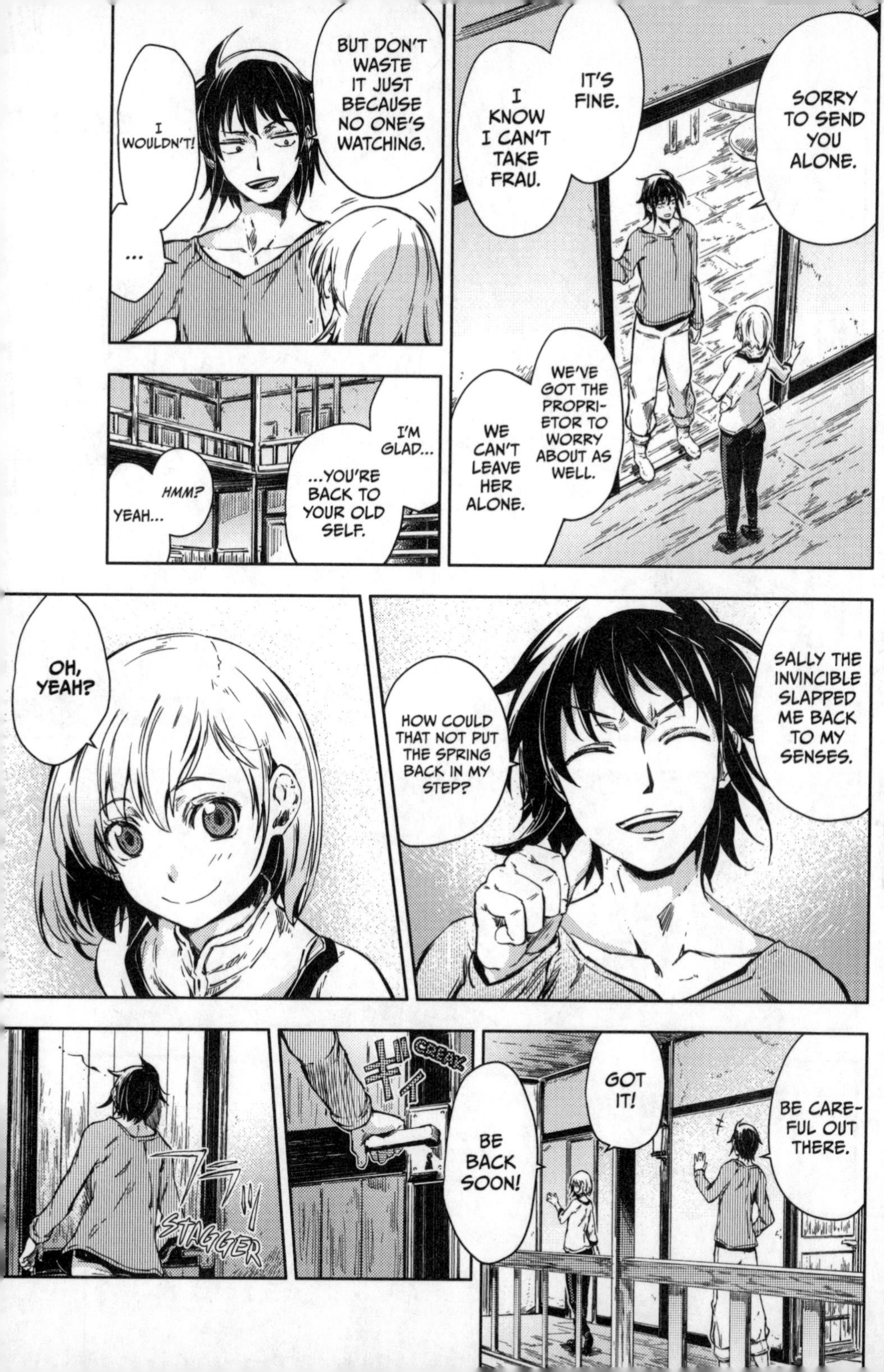
SORRY TO SEND YOU ALONE.
IT'S FINE.
I KNOW I CAN'T TAKE FRAU.
WE'VE GOT THE PROPRI-ETOR TO WORRY ABOUT AS WELL.
WE CAN'T LEAVE HER ALONE.
BUT DON'T WASTE IT JUST BECAUSE NO ONE'S WATCHING.
I WOULDN'T!
...
I'M GLAD...
...YOU'RE BACK TO YOUR OLD SELF.
HMM? YEAH...
SALLY THE INVINCIBLE SLAPPED ME BACK TO MY SENSES.
HOW COULD THAT NOT PUT THE SPRING BACK IN MY STEP?
OH, YEAH?
BE CARE-FUL OUT THERE.
GOT IT!
BE BACK SOON!
キイ
CREAK
STAGGER

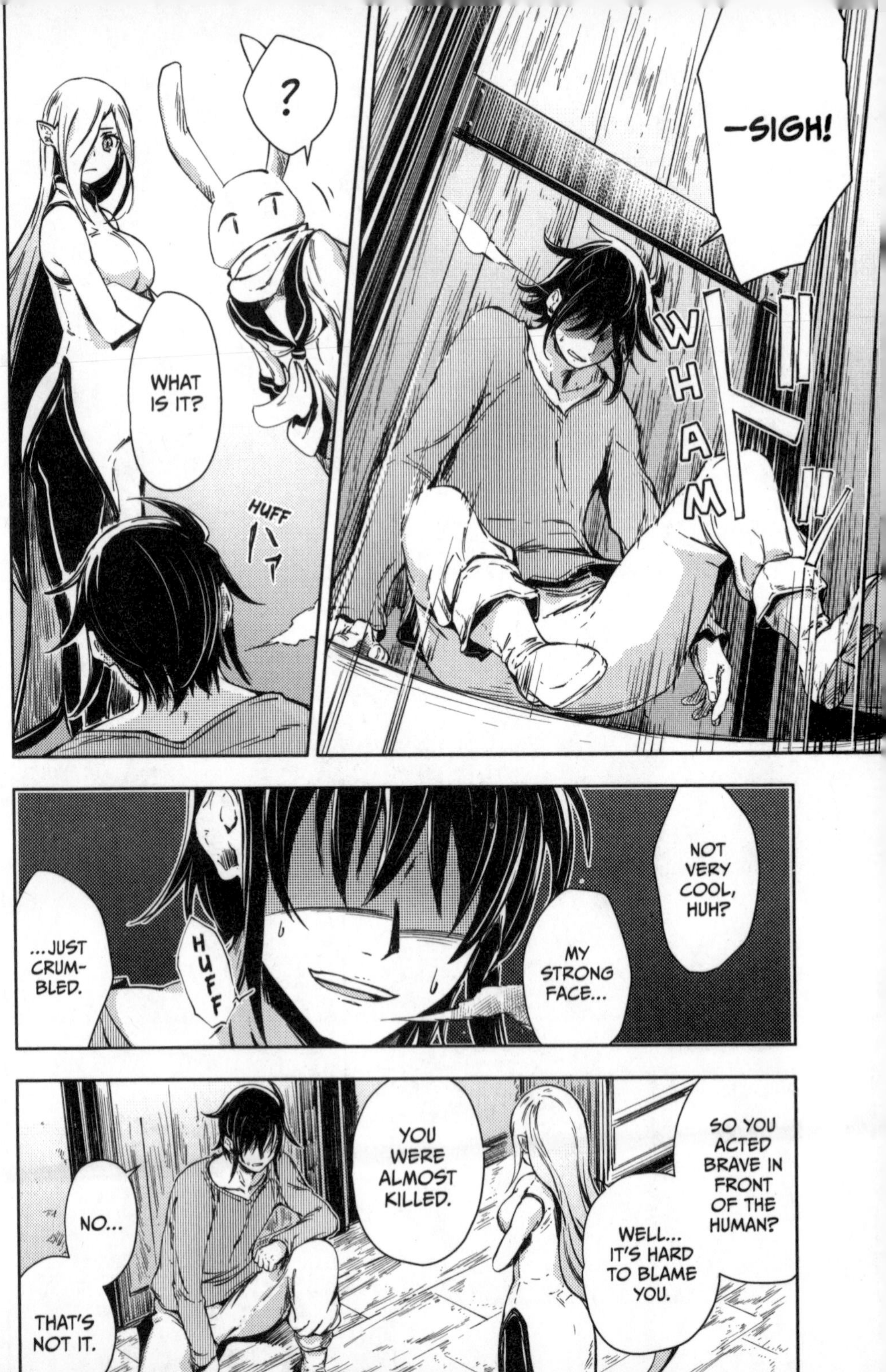
—SIGH!
WHAM!!
?
WHAT IS IT?
HUFF
NOT VERY COOL, HUH?
MY STRONG FACE...
HUFF
...JUST CRUMBLED.
SO YOU ACTED BRAVE IN FRONT OF THE HUMAN?
WELL... IT'S HARD TO BLAME YOU.
YOU WERE ALMOST KILLED.
NO...
THAT'S NOT IT.

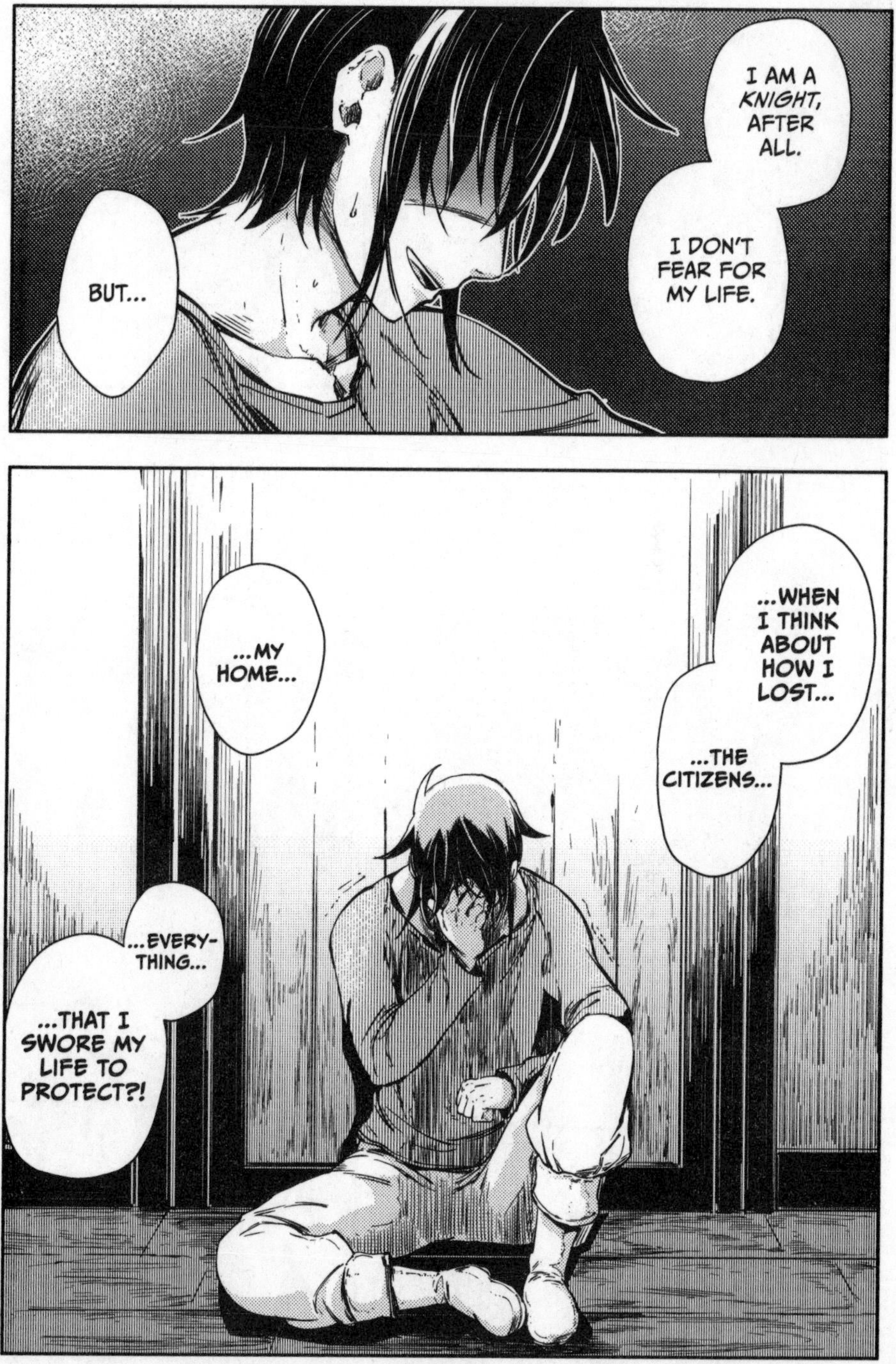
I AM A *KNIGHT*, AFTER ALL.
I DON'T FEAR FOR MY LIFE.
BUT...
...WHEN I THINK ABOUT HOW I LOST...
...THE CITIZENS...
...MY HOME...
...EVERY-THING...
...THAT I SWORE MY LIFE TO PROTECT?!

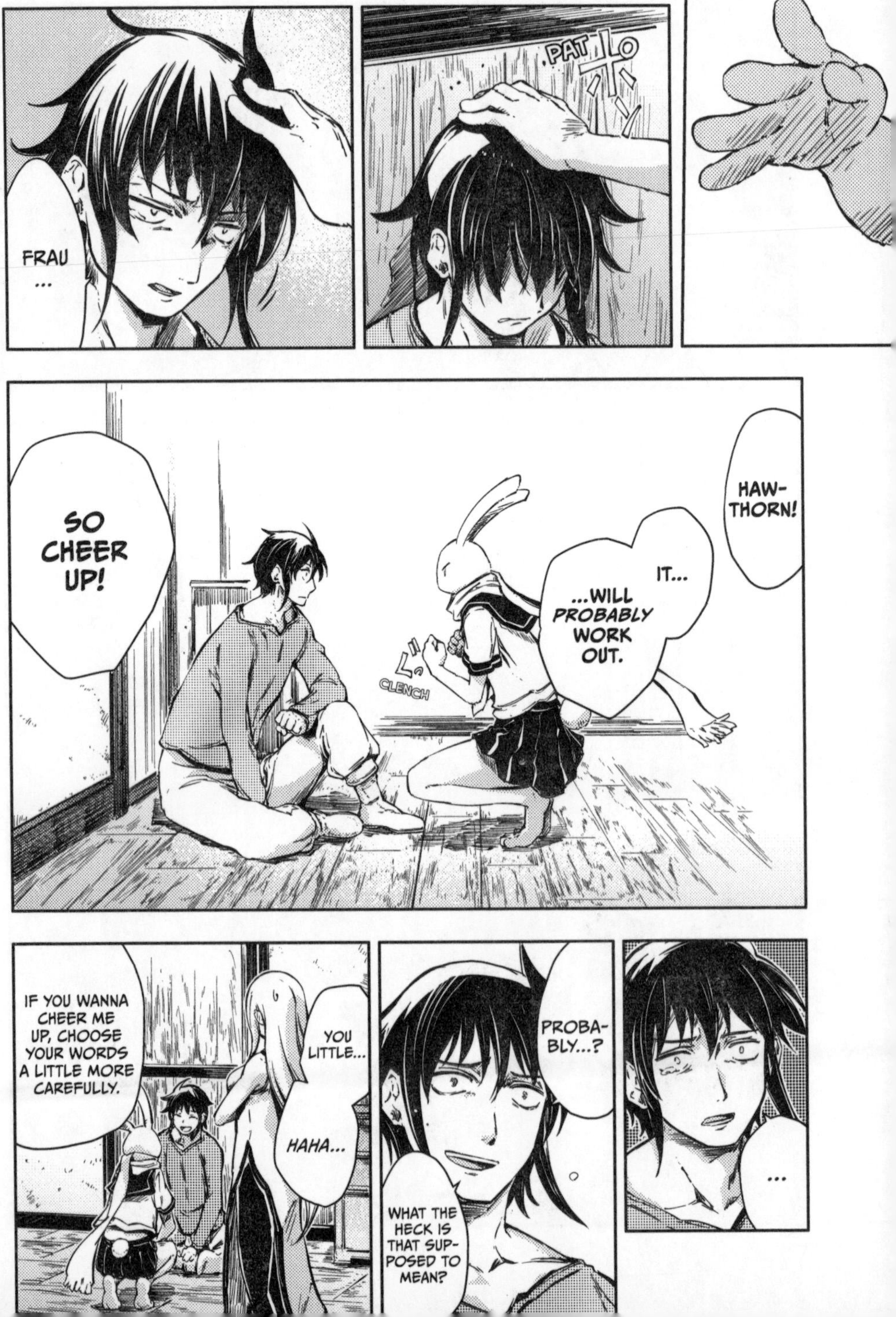
PAT
FRAU ...
HAW-THORN!
IT...
...WILL PROBABLY WORK OUT.
CLENCH
SO CHEER UP!
...
PROBA-BLY...?
WHAT THE HECK IS THAT SUP-POSED TO MEAN?
YOU LITTLE...
IF YOU WANNA CHEER ME UP, CHOOSE YOUR WORDS A LITTLE MORE CAREFULLY.
HAHA...

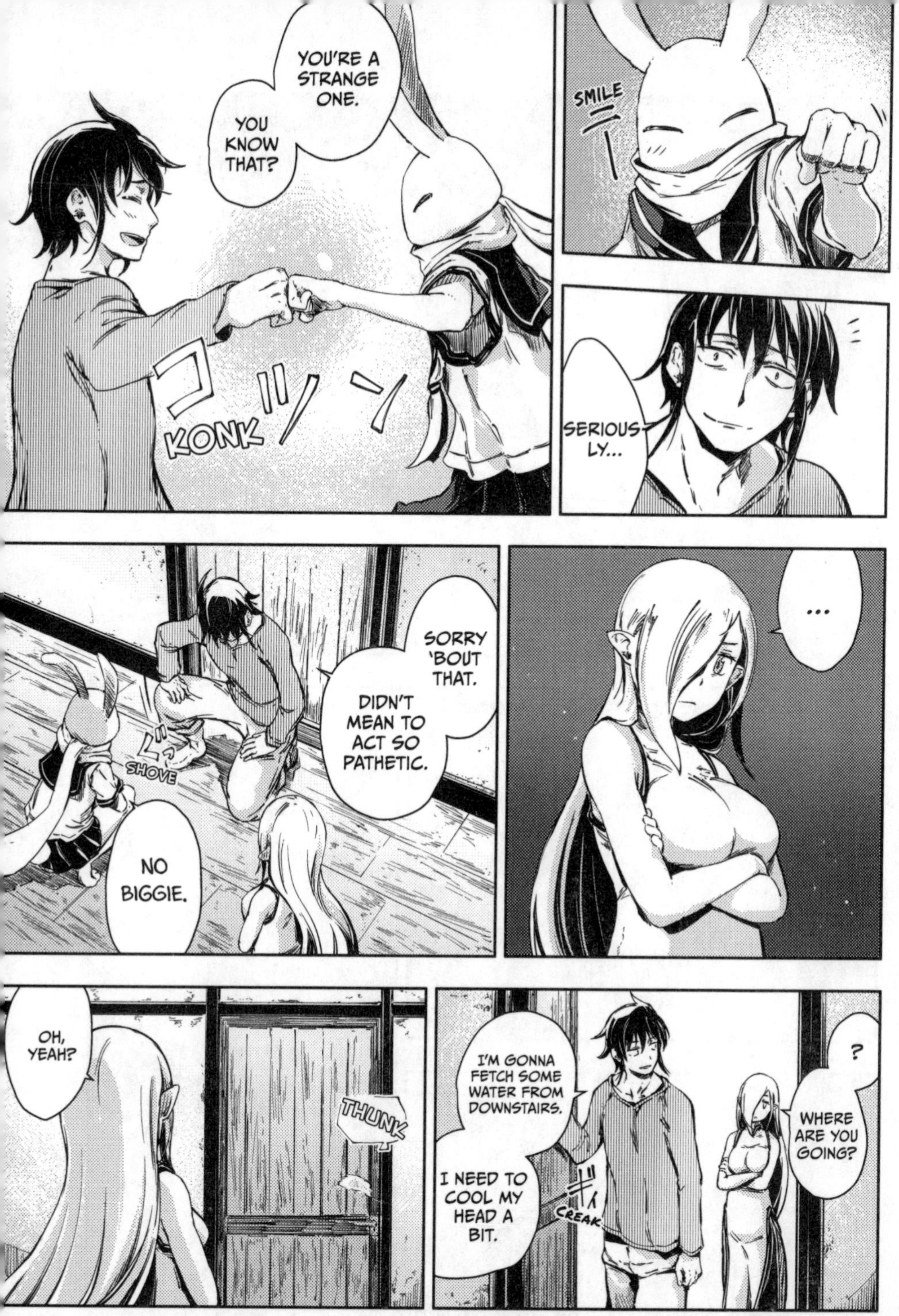
SMILE
SERIOUS-LY...
YOU'RE A STRANGE ONE.
YOU KNOW THAT?
KONK
...
SORRY 'BOUT THAT.
DIDN'T MEAN TO ACT SO PATHETIC.
SHOVE
NO BIGGIE.
?
WHERE ARE YOU GOING?
I'M GONNA FETCH SOME WATER FROM DOWNSTAIRS.
I NEED TO COOL MY HEAD A BIT.
CREAK
OH, YEAH?
THUNK

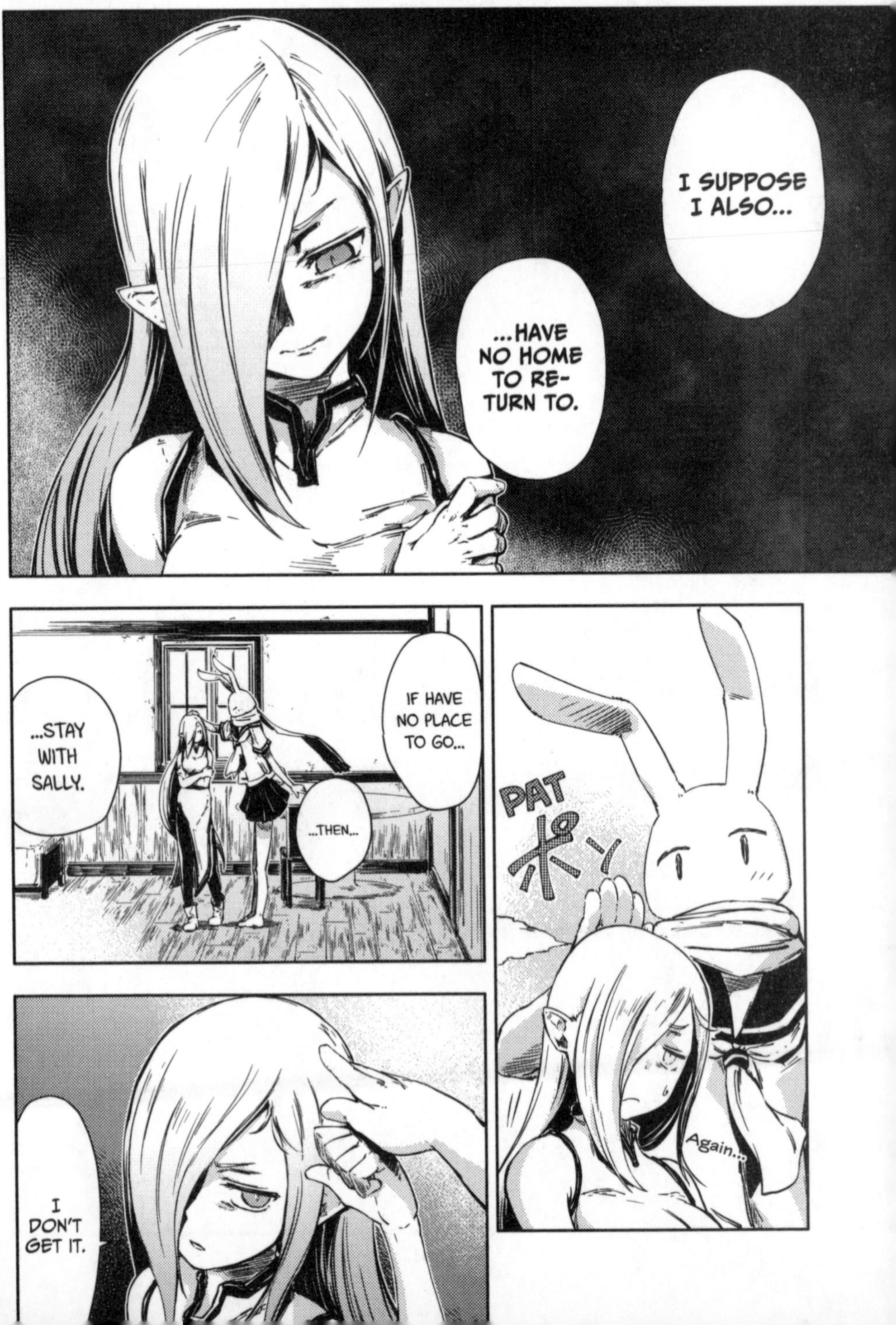
I SUPPOSE I ALSO...
...HAVE NO HOME TO RE-TURN TO.
PAT
ポン
Again...
IF HAVE NO PLACE TO GO...
...THEN...
...STAY WITH SALLY.
I DON'T GET IT.

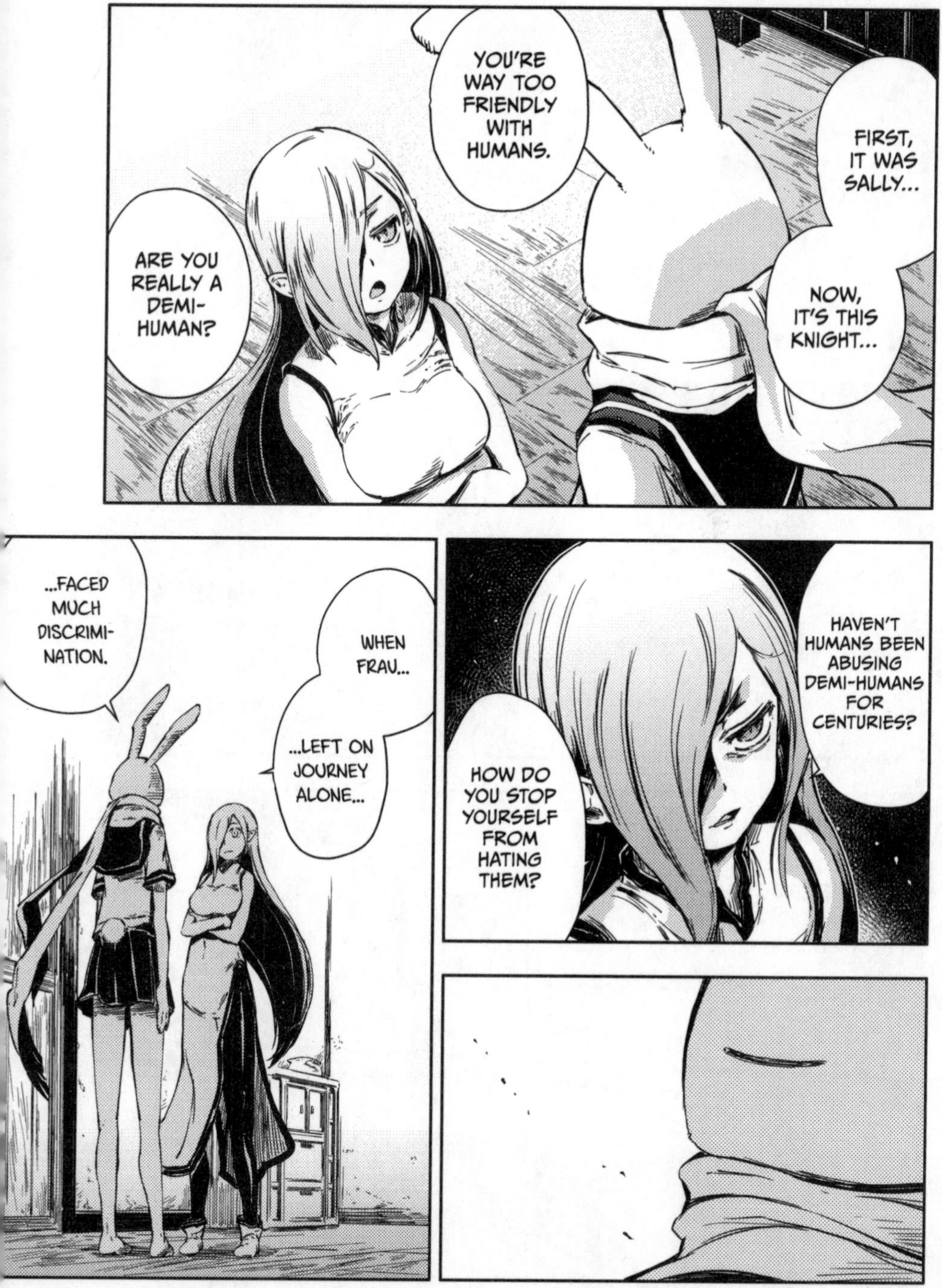
FIRST, IT WAS SALLY...
NOW, IT'S THIS KNIGHT...
YOU'RE WAY TOO FRIENDLY WITH HUMANS.
ARE YOU REALLY A DEMI-HUMAN?
HAVEN'T HUMANS BEEN ABUSING DEMI-HUMANS FOR CENTURIES?
HOW DO YOU STOP YOURSELF FROM HATING THEM?
WHEN FRAU...
...LEFT ON JOURNEY ALONE...
...FACED MUCH DISCRIMINATION.

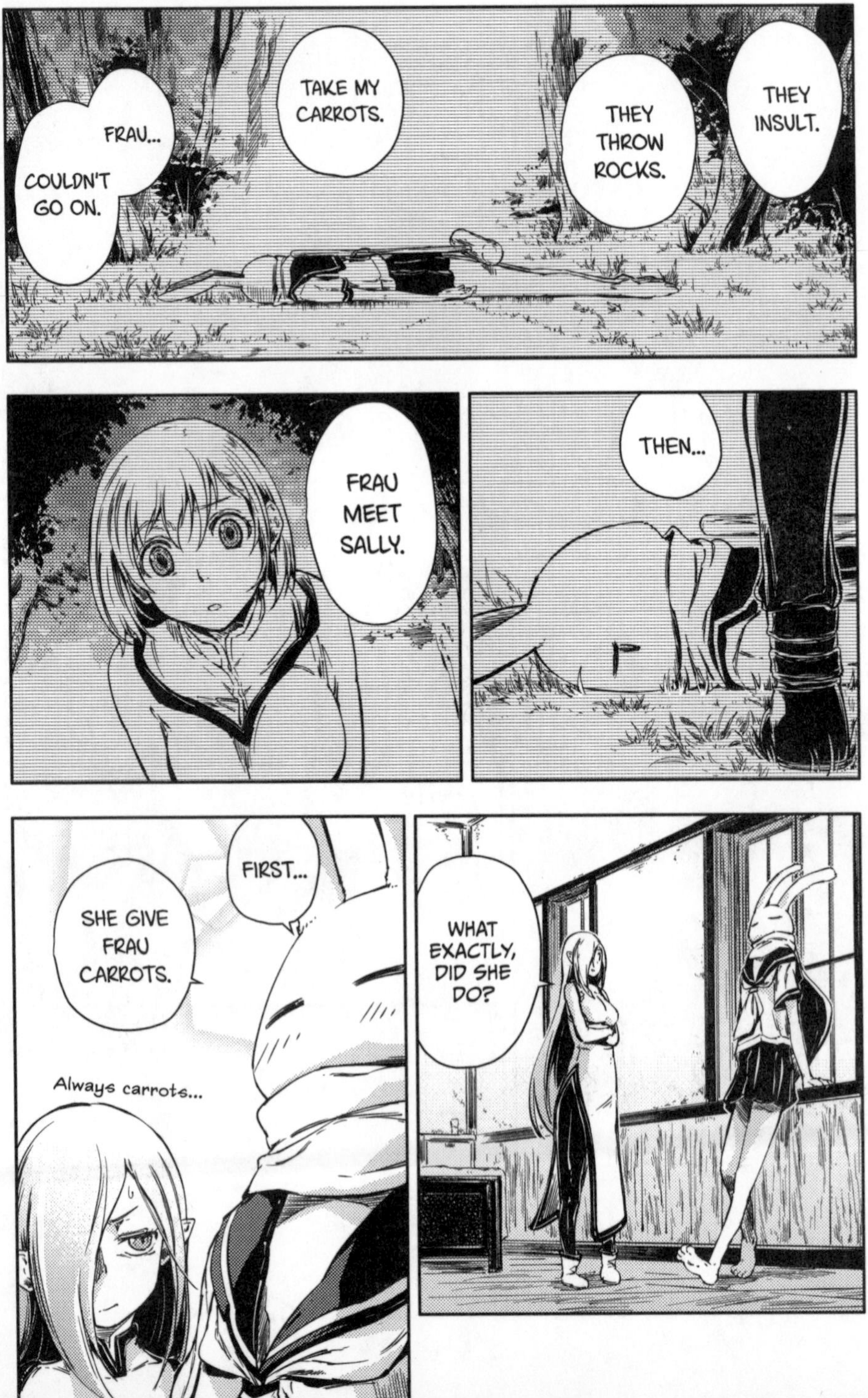
THEY INSULT.
THEY THROW ROCKS.
TAKE MY CARROTS.
FRAU... COULDN'T GO ON.
THEN...
FRAU MEET SALLY.
WHAT EXACTLY, DID SHE DO?
FIRST...
SHE GIVE FRAU CARROTS.
Always carrots...

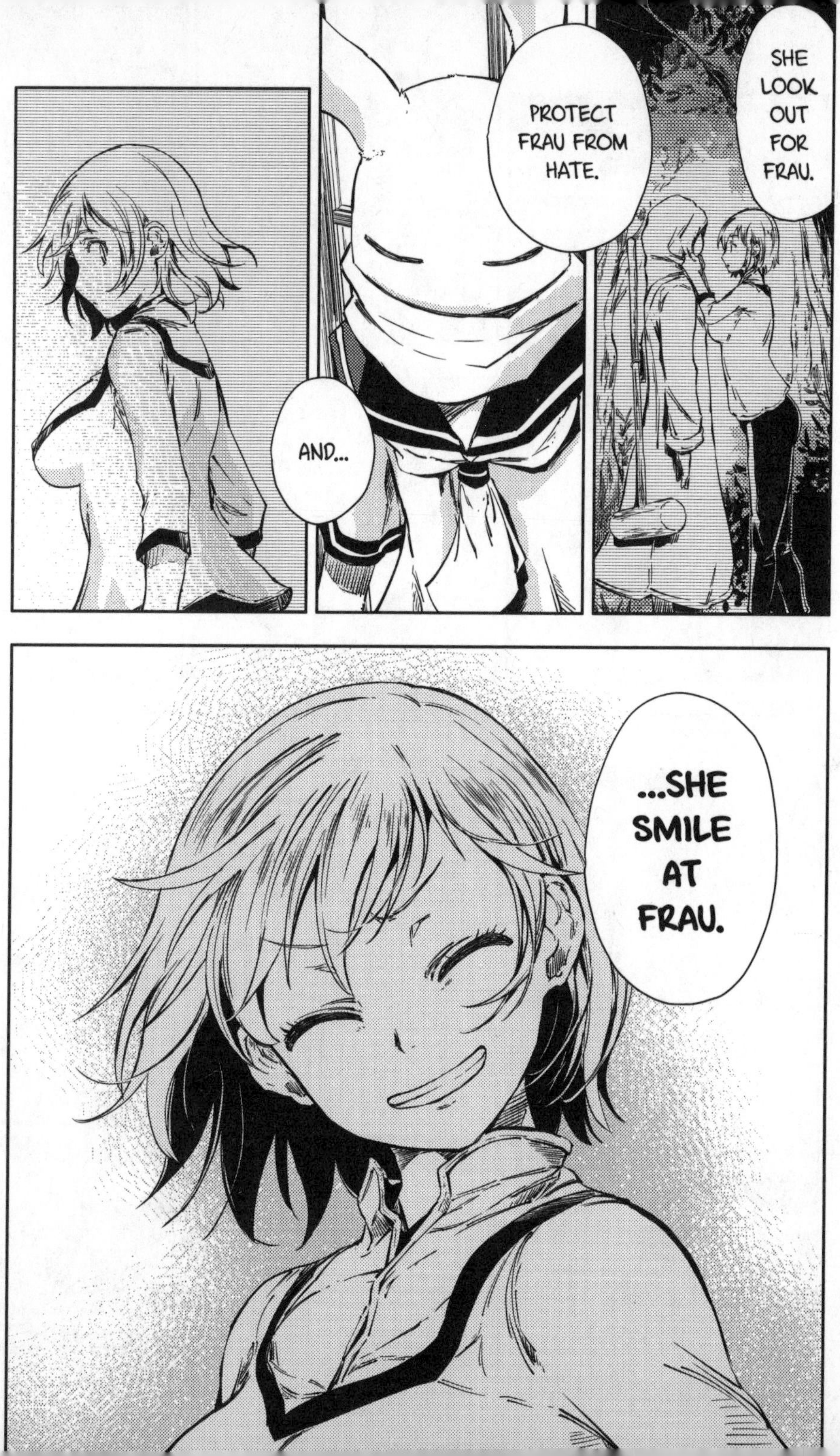
SHE LOOK OUT FOR FRAU.
PROTECT FRAU FROM HATE.
AND...
...SHE SMILE AT FRAU.

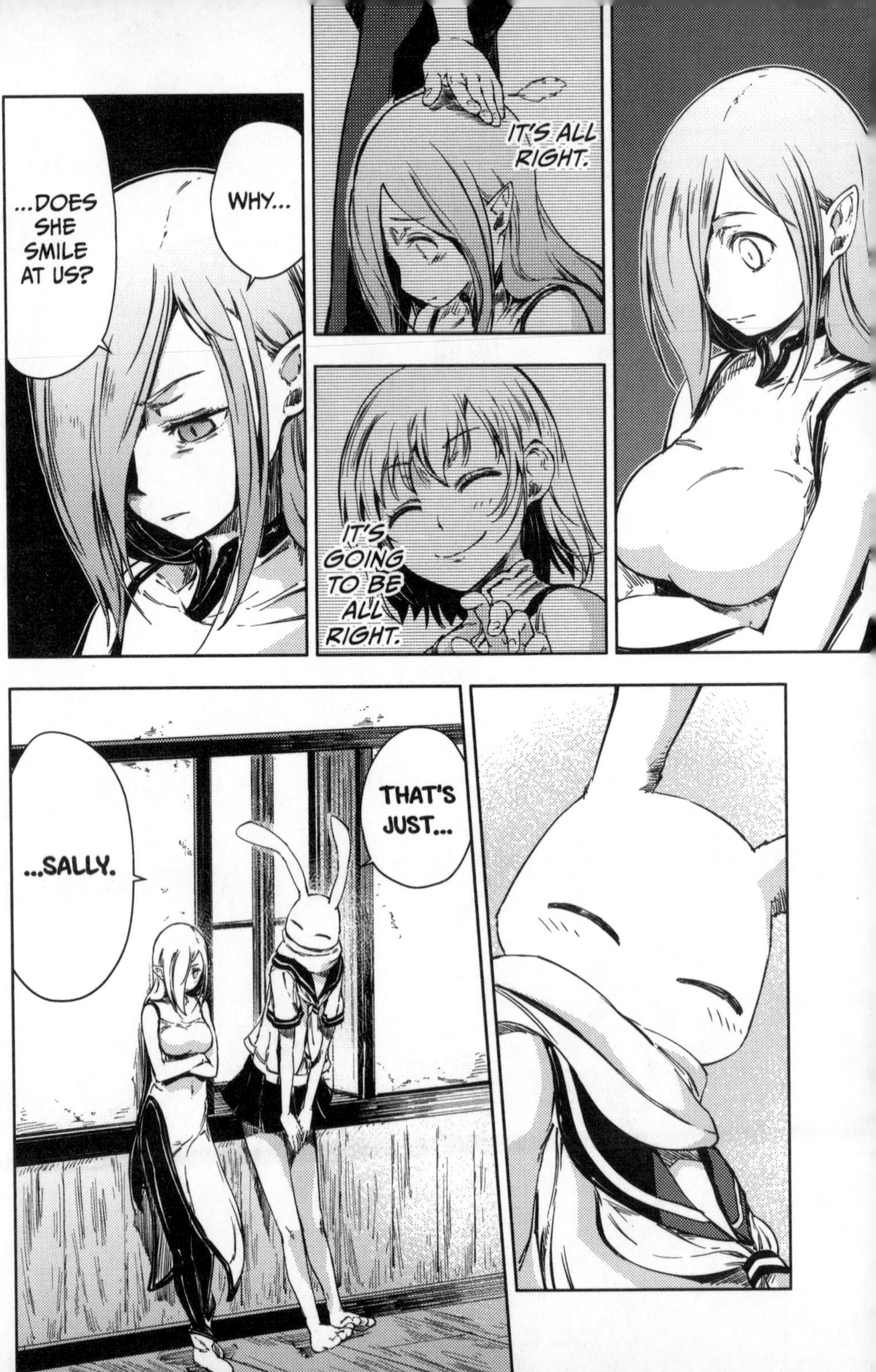
IT'S ALL RIGHT.
IT'S GOING TO BE ALL RIGHT.
WHY...
...DOES SHE SMILE AT US?
THAT'S JUST...
...SALLY.

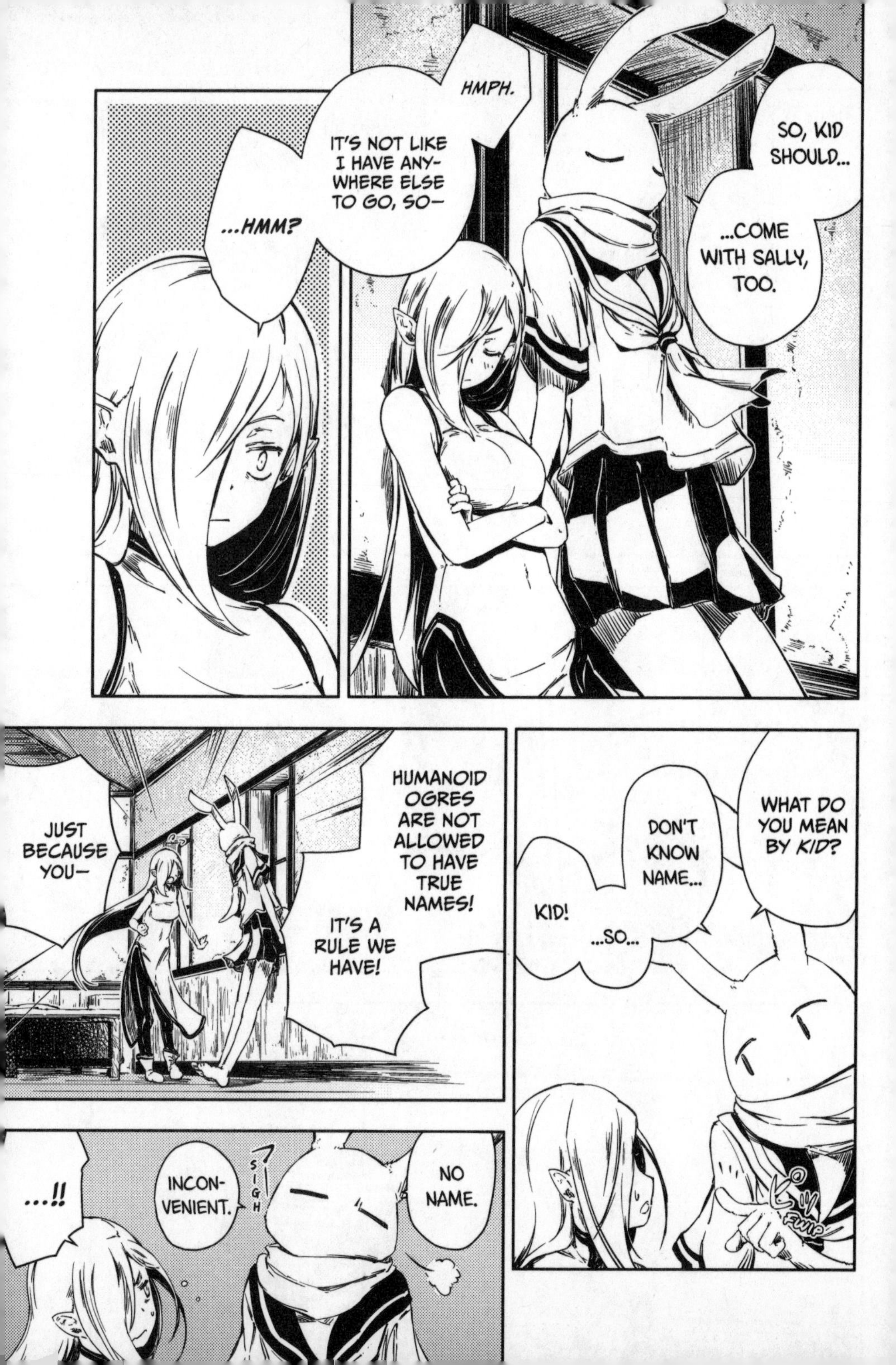
SO, KID SHOULD...
...COME WITH SALLY, TOO.
HMPH.
IT'S NOT LIKE I HAVE ANY-WHERE ELSE TO GO, SO—
...HMM?
WHAT DO YOU MEAN BY *KID*?
DON'T KNOW NAME...
...SO...
KID!
FWIP
HUMANOID OGRES ARE NOT ALLOWED TO HAVE TRUE NAMES!
IT'S A RULE WE HAVE!
JUST BECAUSE YOU—
NO NAME.
SIGH
INCON-VENIENT.
...!!

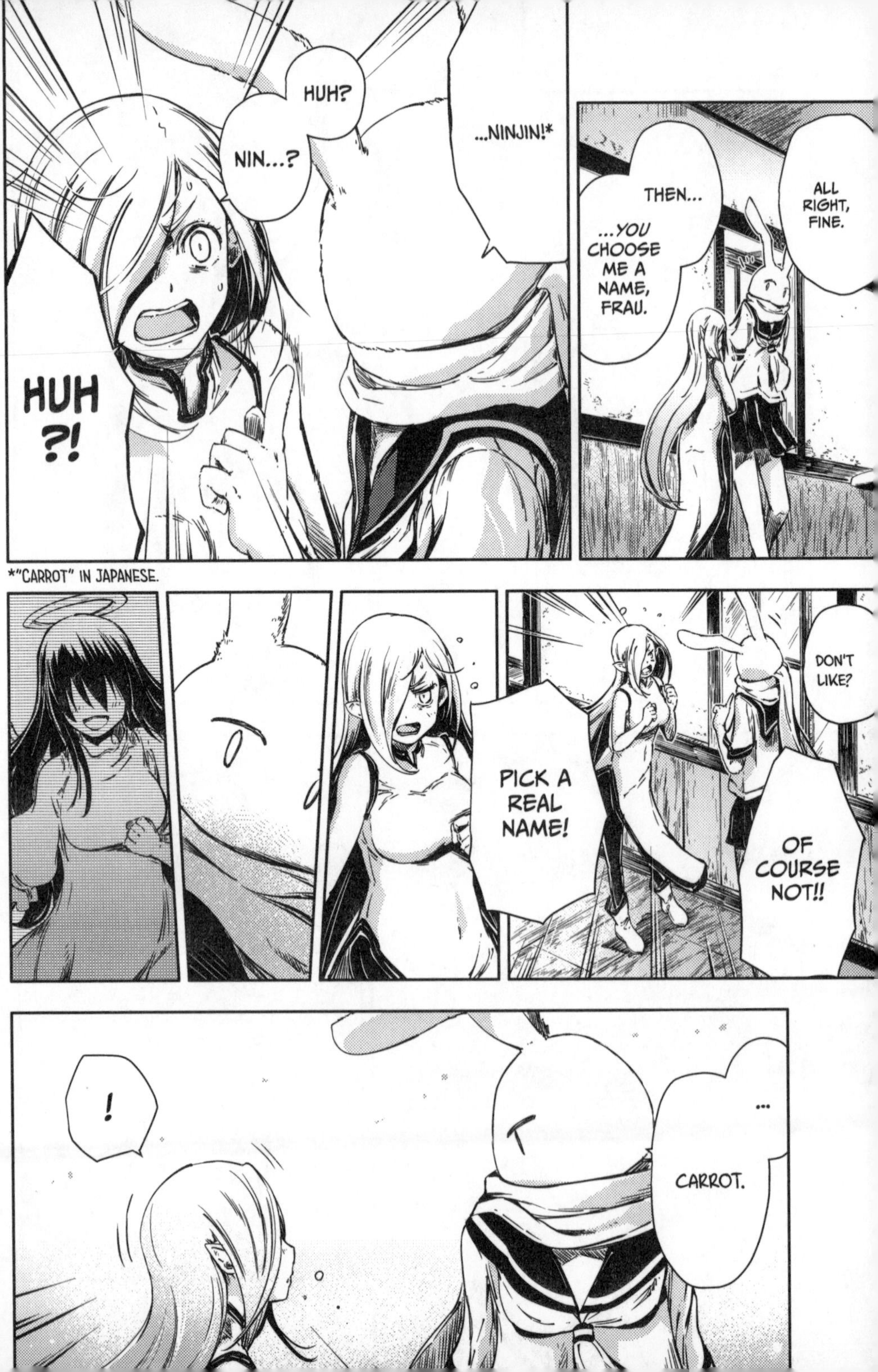

ALL RIGHT, FINE.
THEN...
...YOU CHOOSE ME A NAME, FRAU.
...NINJIN!*
HUH?
NIN...?
HUH ?!
DON'T LIKE?
OF COURSE NOT!!
PICK A REAL NAME!
...
CARROT.
!

*"CARROT" IN JAPANESE.

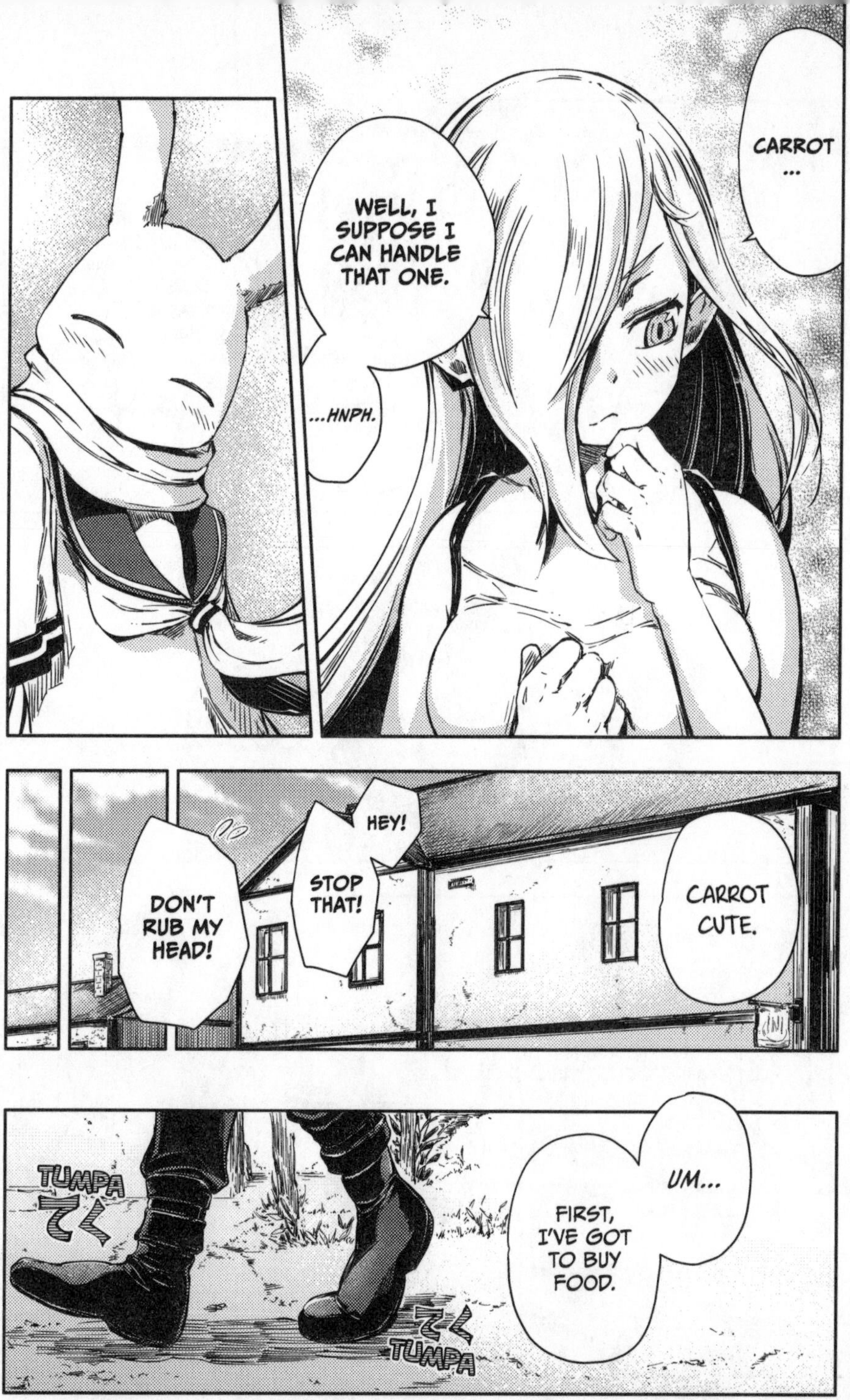
CARROT ...
WELL, I SUPPOSE I CAN HANDLE THAT ONE.
...HNPH.
CARROT CUTE.
HEY!
STOP THAT!
DON'T RUB MY HEAD!
UM...
FIRST, I'VE GOT TO BUY FOOD.
てく TUMPA
TUMPA てく

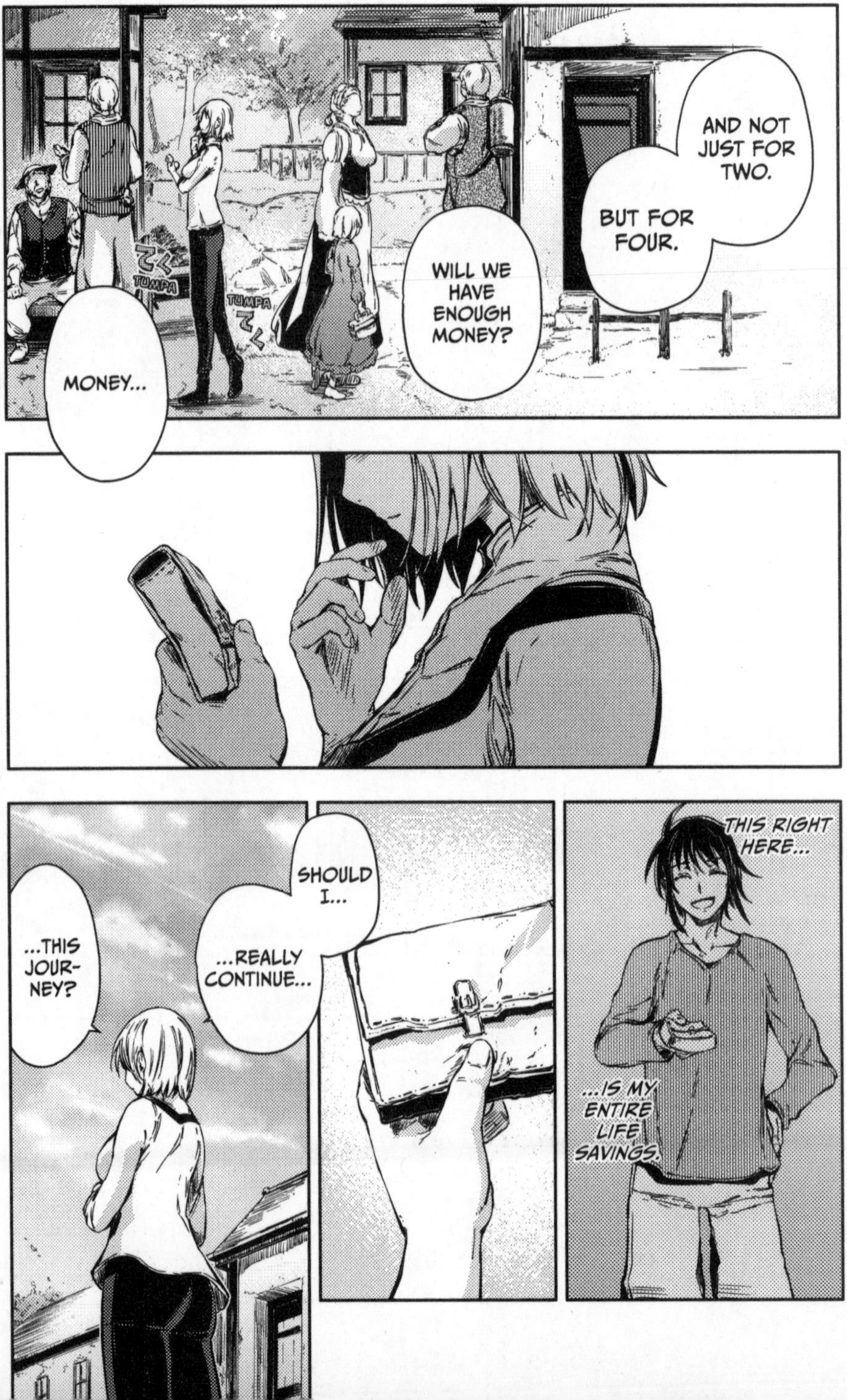
AND NOT JUST FOR TWO.
BUT FOR FOUR.
WILL WE HAVE ENOUGH MONEY?
TUMPA てく
てく TUMPA
MONEY...
THIS RIGHT HERE...
...IS MY ENTIRE LIFE SAVINGS.
SHOULD I...
...REALLY CONTINUE...
...THIS JOURNEY?

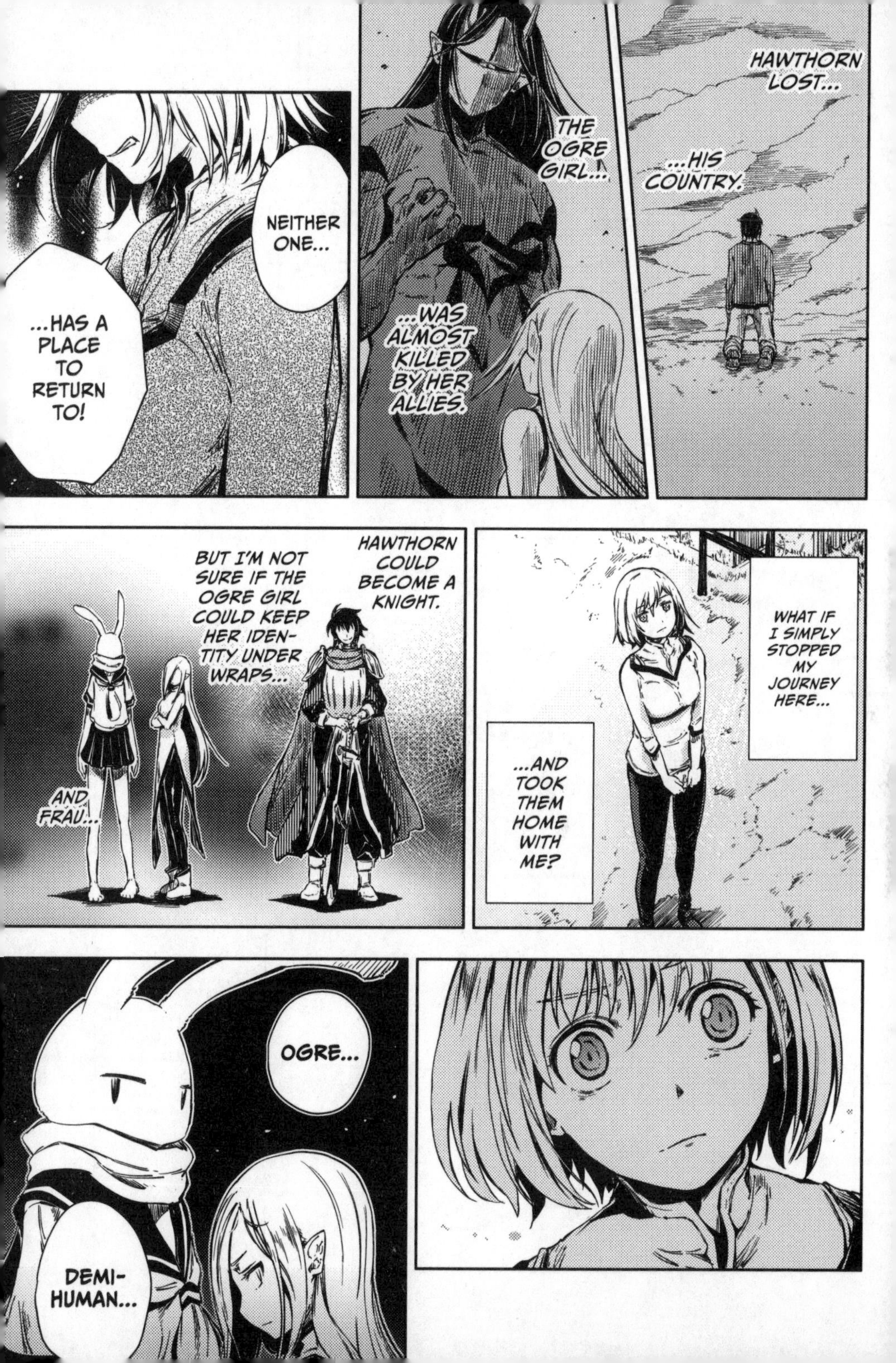
HAWTHORN LOST...
...HIS COUNTRY.
THE OGRE GIRL...
...WAS ALMOST KILLED BY HER ALLIES.
NEITHER ONE...
...HAS A PLACE TO RETURN TO!
WHAT IF I SIMPLY STOPPED MY JOURNEY HERE...
...AND TOOK THEM HOME WITH ME?
HAWTHORN COULD BECOME A KNIGHT.
BUT I'M NOT SURE IF THE OGRE GIRL COULD KEEP HER IDEN-TITY UNDER WRAPS...
AND FRAU...
OGRE...
DEMI-HUMAN...

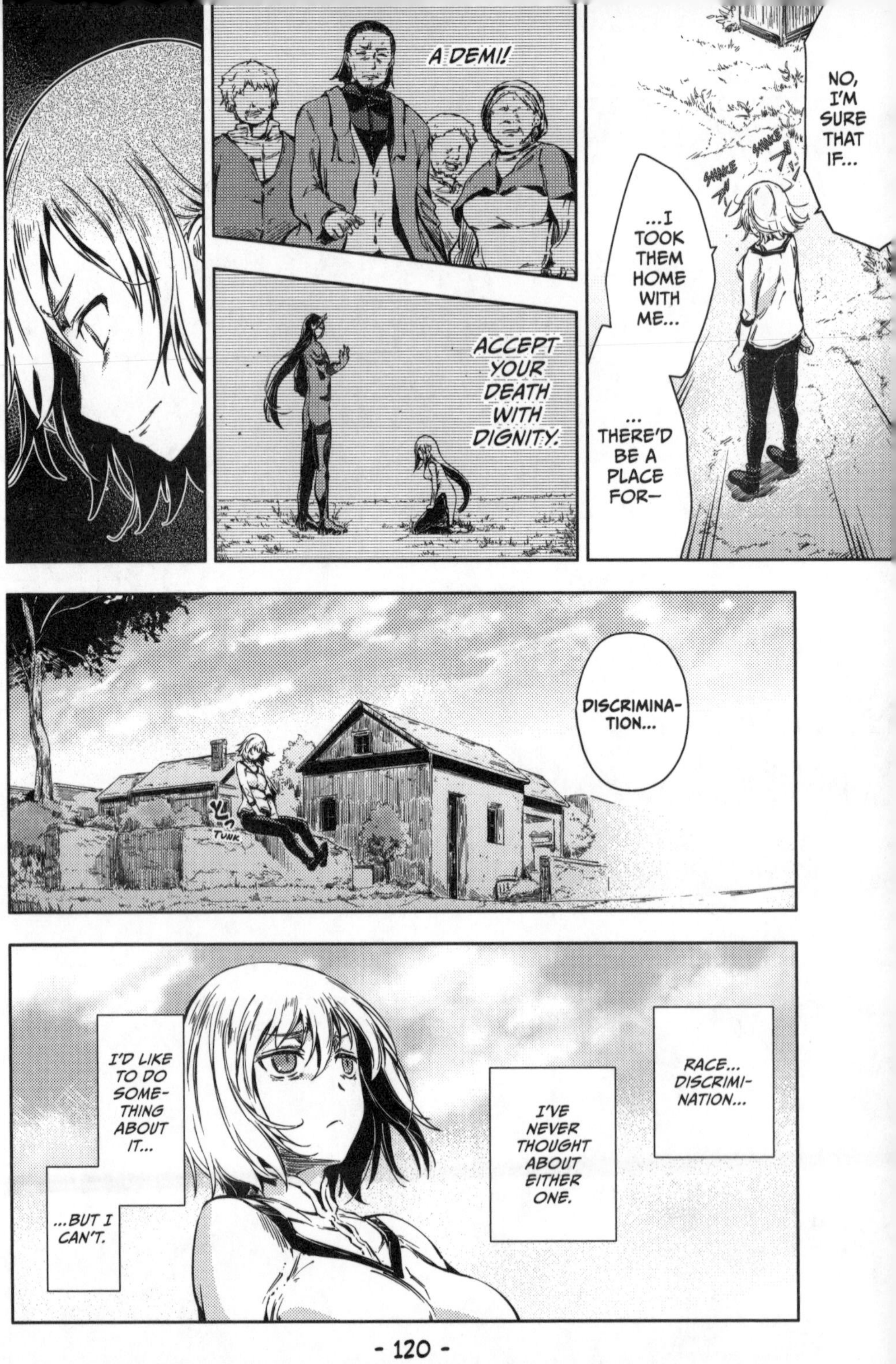
NO, I'M SURE THAT IF...
SHAKE
SHAKE
...I TOOK THEM HOME WITH ME...
...THERE'D BE A PLACE FOR—
A DEMI!
ACCEPT YOUR DEATH WITH DIGNITY.
DISCRIMINA-TION...
TUNK
RACE... DISCRIMI-NATION...
I'VE NEVER THOUGHT ABOUT EITHER ONE.
I'D LIKE TO DO SOME-THING ABOUT IT...
...BUT I CAN'T.

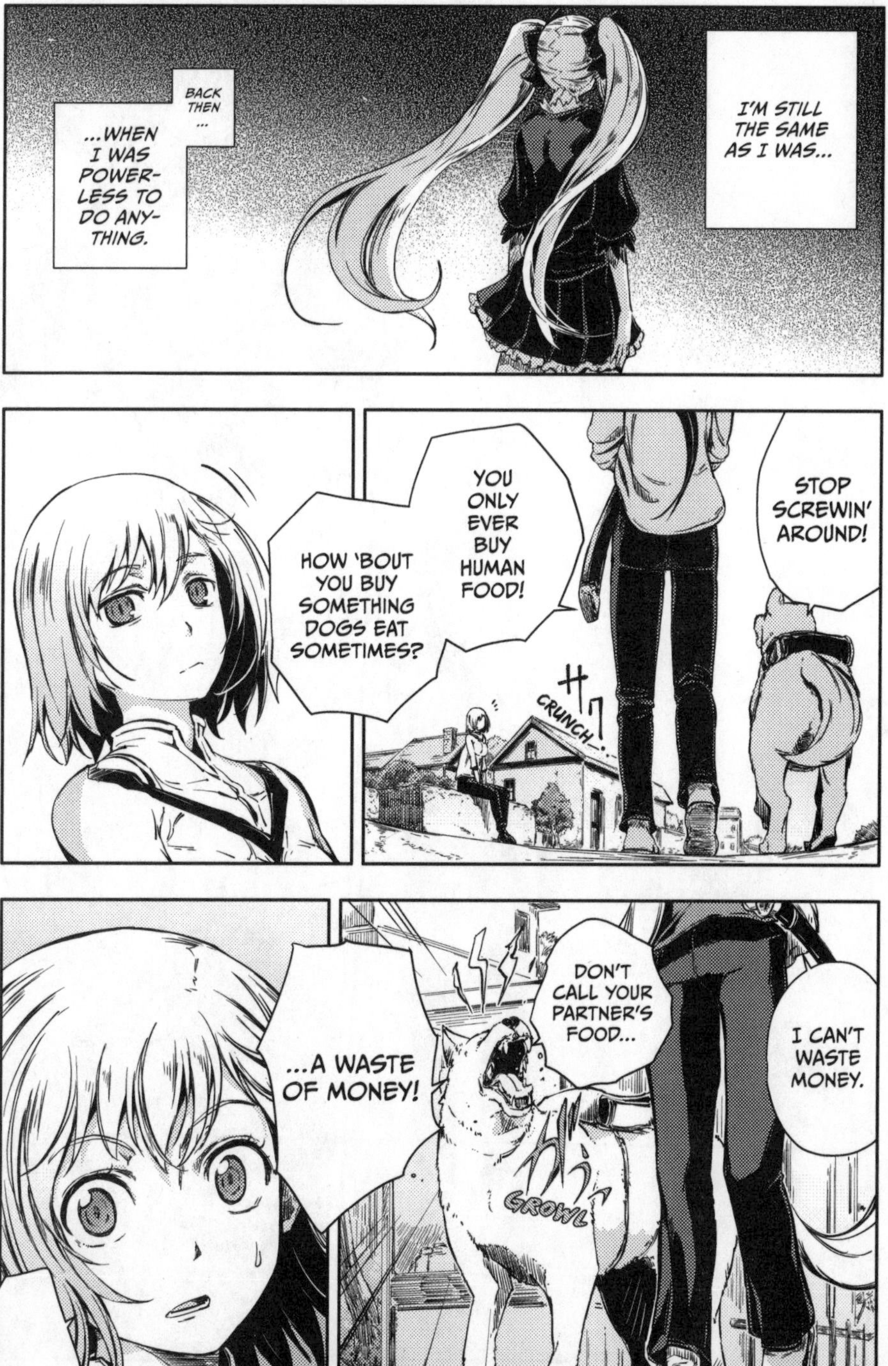
I'M STILL THE SAME AS I WAS...
BACK THEN...
...WHEN I WAS POWERLESS TO DO ANYTHING.
STOP SCREWIN' AROUND!
YOU ONLY EVER BUY HUMAN FOOD!
CRUNCH
HOW 'BOUT YOU BUY SOMETHING DOGS EAT SOMETIMES?
I CAN'T WASTE MONEY.
DON'T CALL YOUR PARTNER'S FOOD...
...A WASTE OF MONEY!
GROWL
MI...

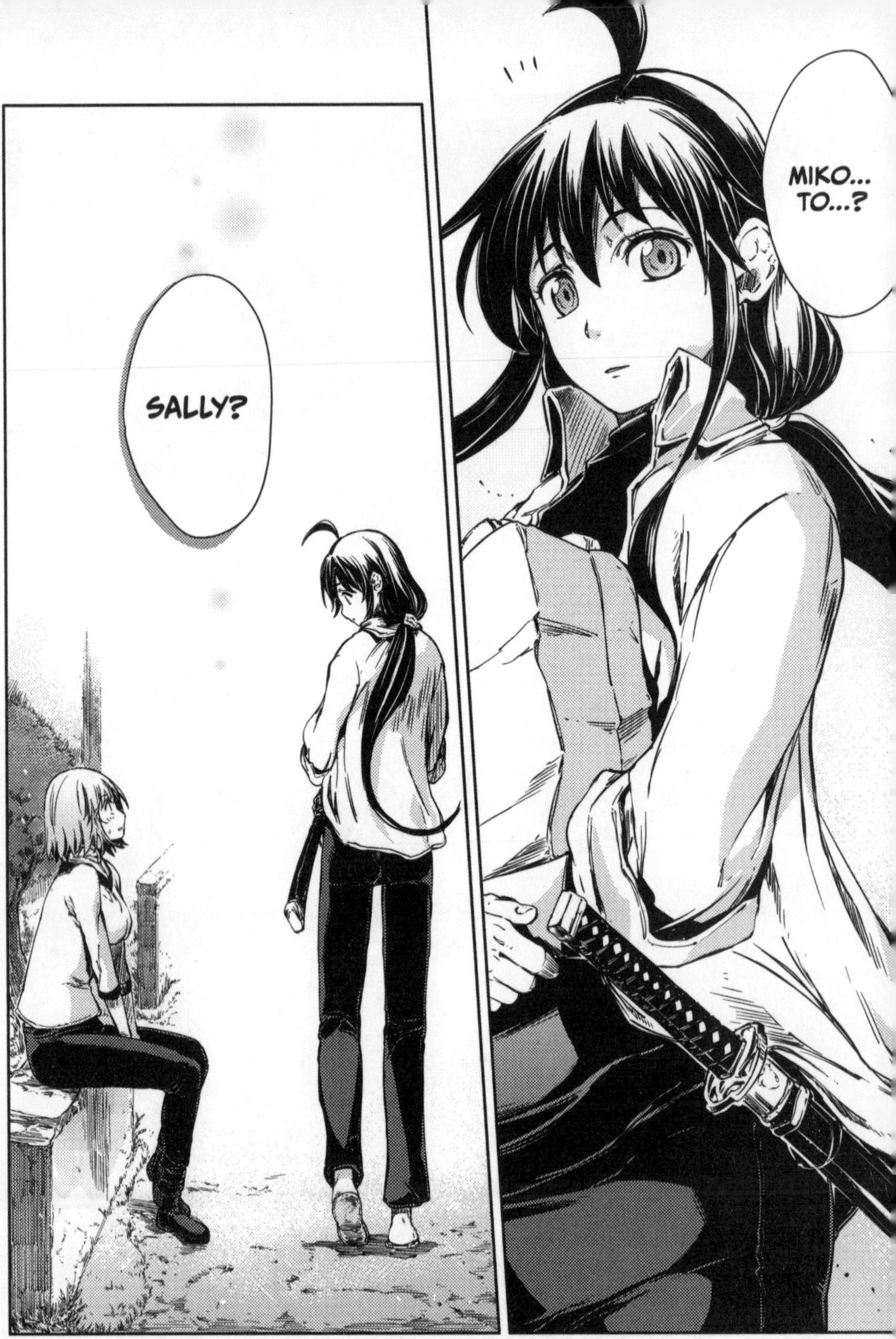
MIKO...
TO...?
SALLY?

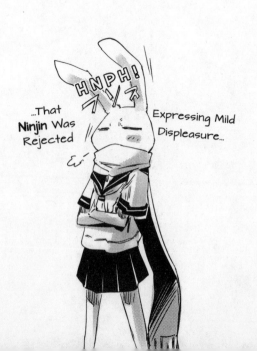

HNPH!
Expressing Mild Displeasure...
...That Ninjin Was Rejected

PEACH BOY RIVERSIDE

CHAPTER 7:
THE PEACH AND THE PEACH

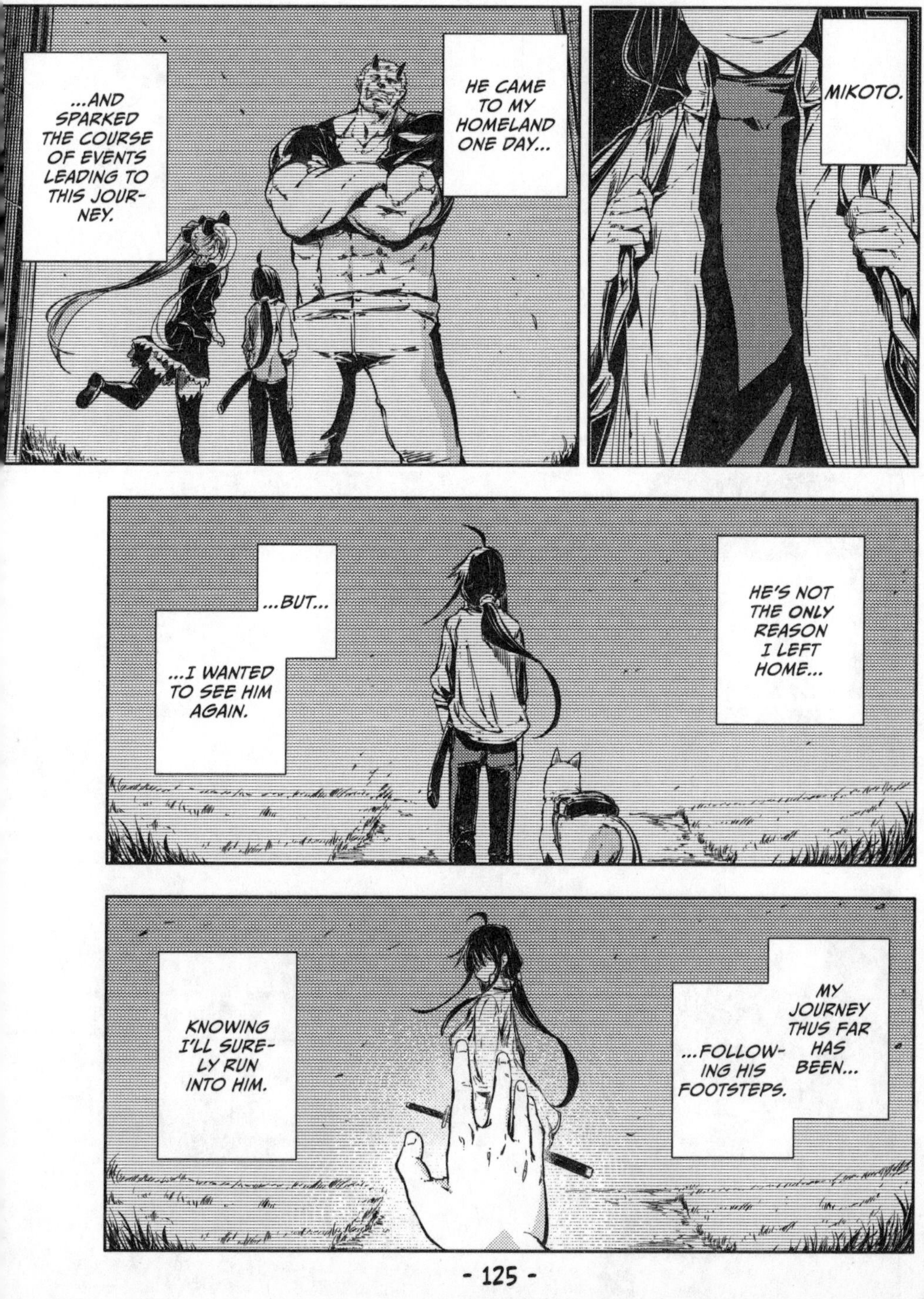
MIKOTO.
HE CAME TO MY HOMELAND ONE DAY...
...AND SPARKED THE COURSE OF EVENTS LEADING TO THIS JOURNEY.
HE'S NOT THE ONLY REASON I LEFT HOME...
...BUT...
...I WANTED TO SEE HIM AGAIN.
MY JOURNEY THUS FAR HAS BEEN...
...FOLLOWING HIS FOOTSTEPS.
KNOWING I'LL SURELY RUN INTO HIM.

CHAPTER 7:
THE PEACH AND THE PEACH

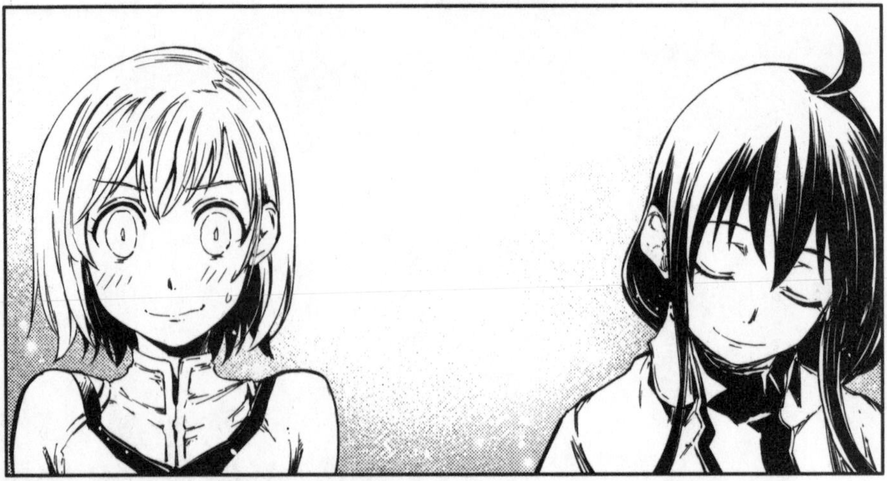

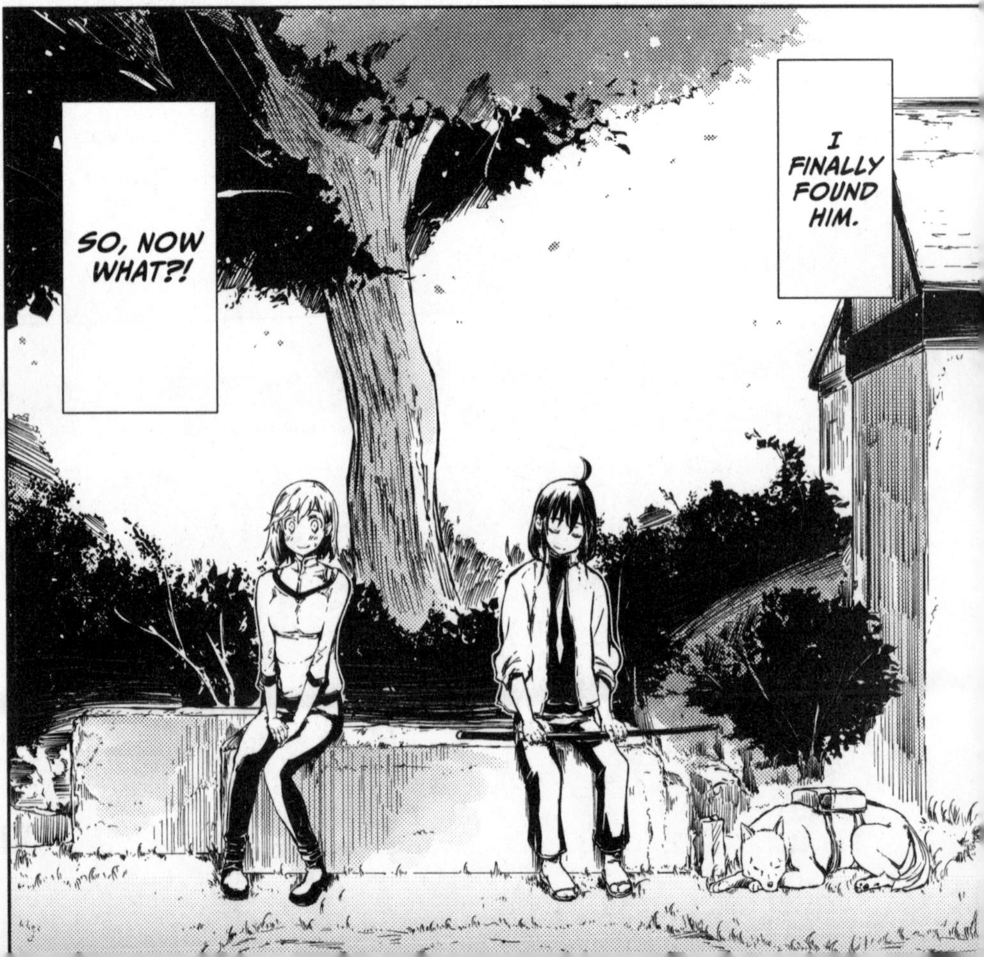
I FINALLY FOUND HIM.
SO, NOW WHAT?!

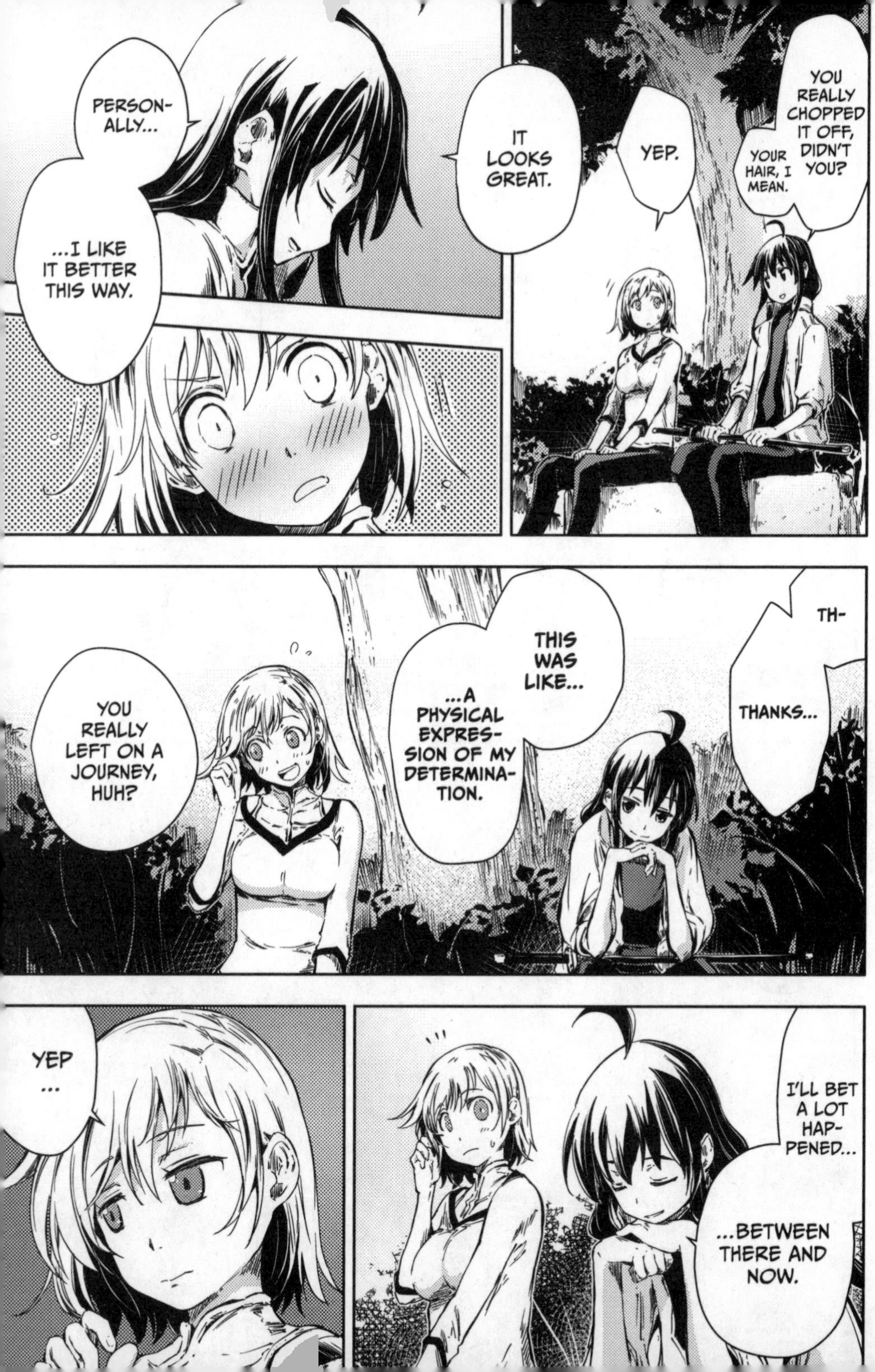
YOU REALLY CHOPPED IT OFF, DIDN'T YOU?
YOUR HAIR, I MEAN.
YEP.
IT LOOKS GREAT.
PERSON-ALLY...
...I LIKE IT BETTER THIS WAY.
TH-
THANKS...
THIS WAS LIKE...
...A PHYSICAL EXPRES-SION OF MY DETERMINA-TION.
YOU REALLY LEFT ON A JOURNEY, HUH?
I'LL BET A LOT HAP-PENED...
...BETWEEN THERE AND NOW.
YEP ...

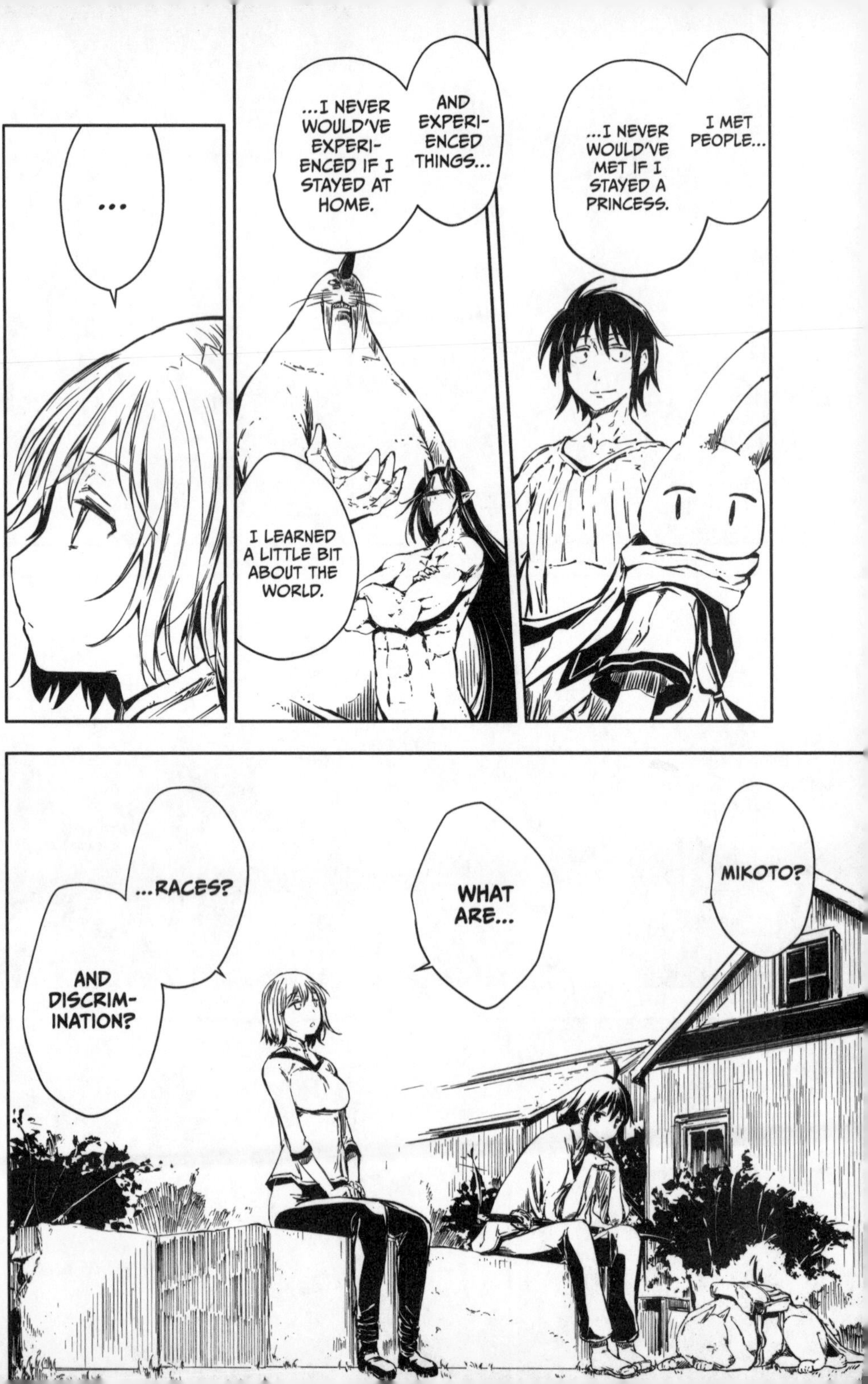
I MET PEOPLE...
...I NEVER WOULD'VE MET IF I STAYED A PRINCESS.
AND EXPERIENCED THINGS...
...I NEVER WOULD'VE EXPERIENCED IF I STAYED AT HOME.
I LEARNED A LITTLE BIT ABOUT THE WORLD.
...
MIKOTO?
WHAT ARE...
...RACES?
AND DISCRIMINATION?

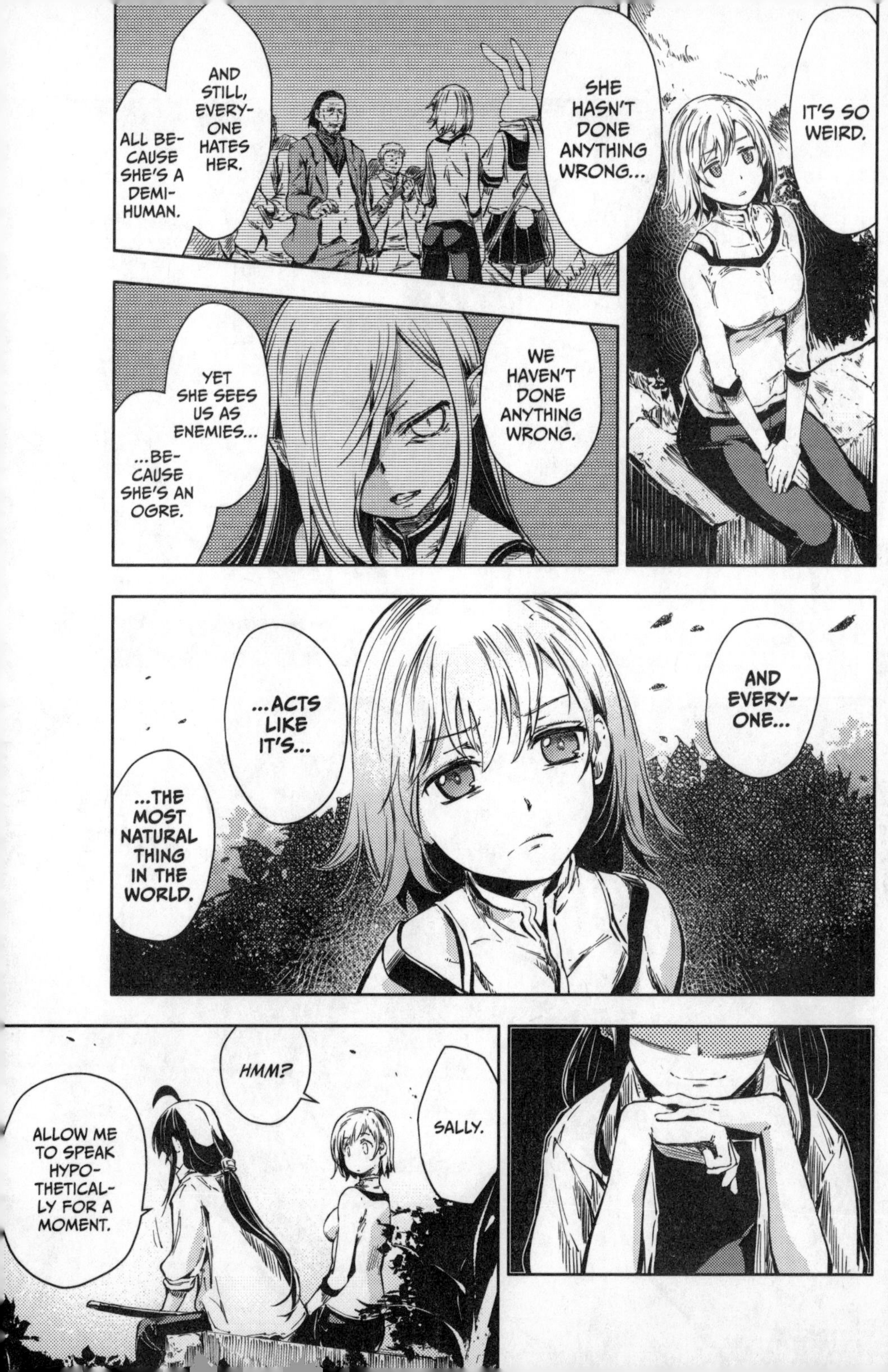
IT'S SO WEIRD.
SHE HASN'T DONE ANYTHING WRONG...
AND STILL, EVERYONE HATES HER.
ALL BECAUSE SHE'S A DEMI-HUMAN.
WE HAVEN'T DONE ANYTHING WRONG.
YET SHE SEES US AS ENEMIES...
...BECAUSE SHE'S AN OGRE.
AND EVERYONE...
...ACTS LIKE IT'S...
...THE MOST NATURAL THING IN THE WORLD.
SALLY.
HMM?
ALLOW ME TO SPEAK HYPOTHETICALLY FOR A MOMENT.

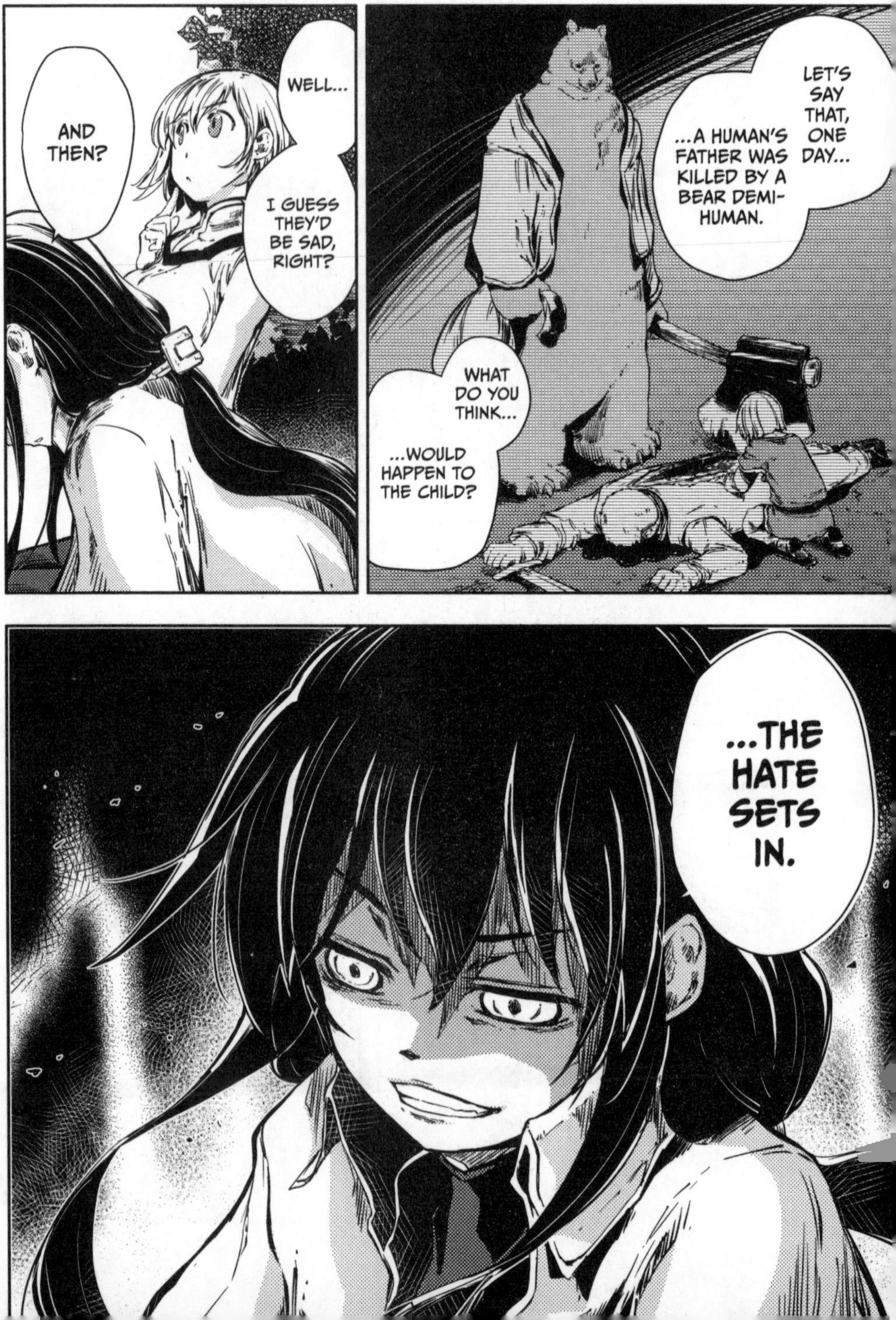
LET'S SAY THAT, ONE DAY...
...A HUMAN'S FATHER WAS KILLED BY A BEAR DEMI-HUMAN.
WHAT DO YOU THINK...
...WOULD HAPPEN TO THE CHILD?
WELL...
I GUESS THEY'D BE SAD, RIGHT?
AND THEN?
...THE HATE SETS IN.

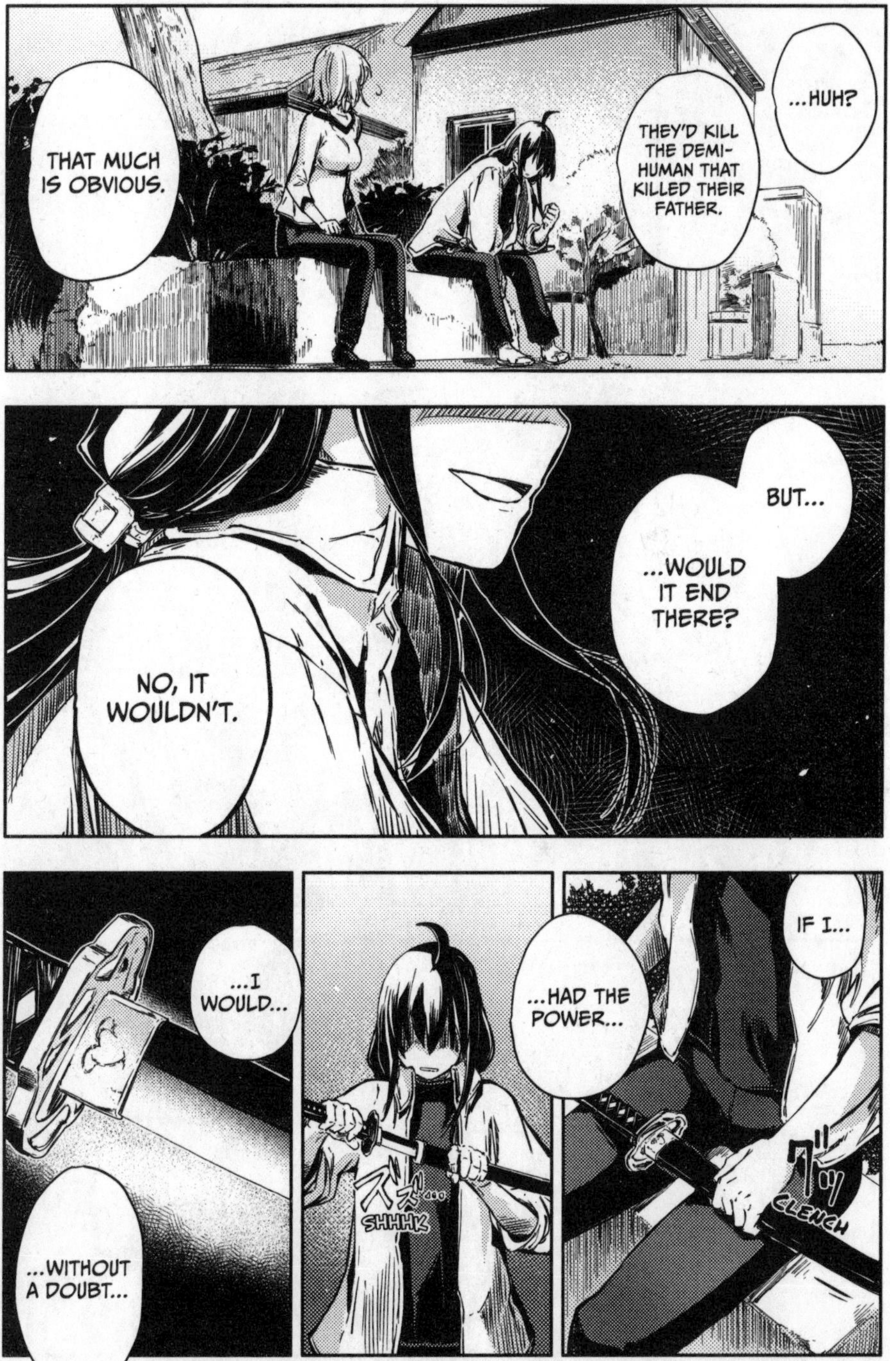
...HUH?
THEY'D KILL THE DEMI-HUMAN THAT KILLED THEIR FATHER.
THAT MUCH IS OBVIOUS.
BUT...
...WOULD IT END THERE?
NO, IT WOULDN'T.
IF I...
...HAD THE POWER...
CLENCH
SHHHK
...I WOULD...
...WITHOUT A DOUBT...

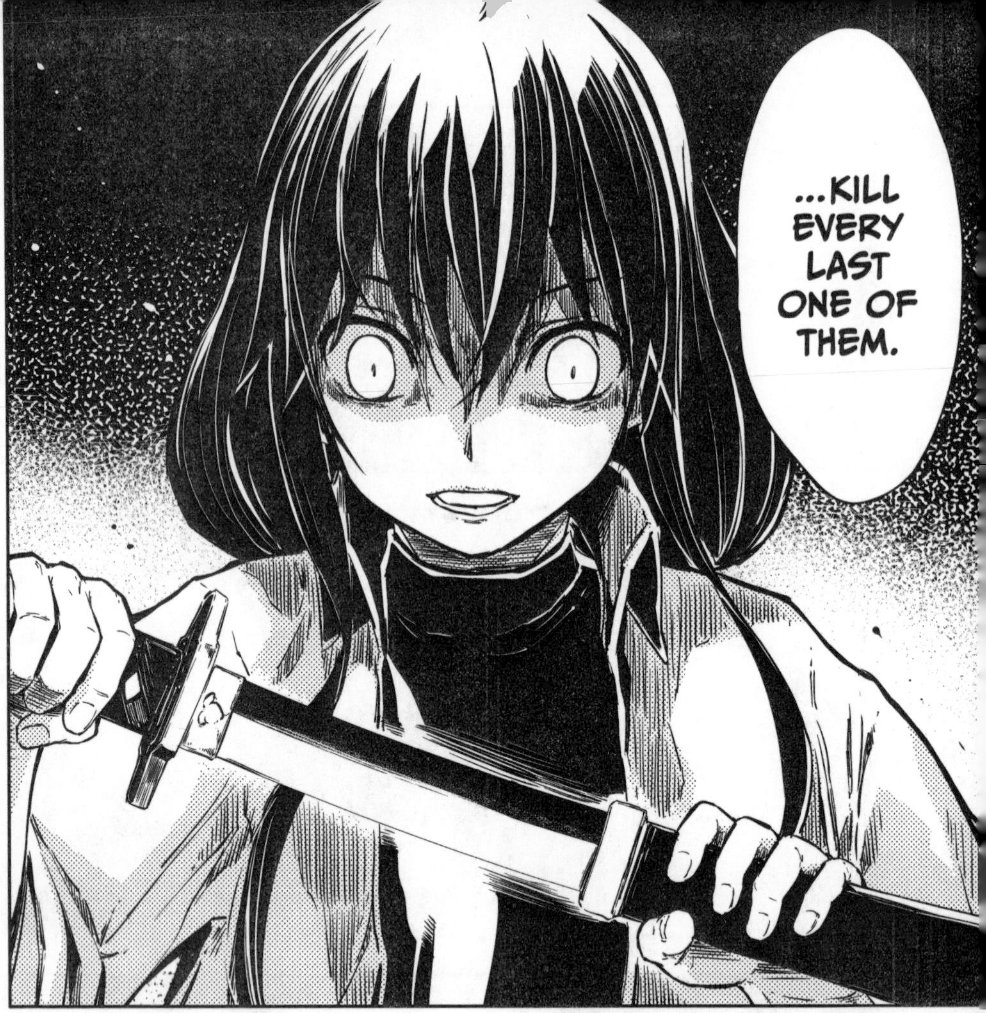
...KILL EVERY LAST ONE OF THEM.

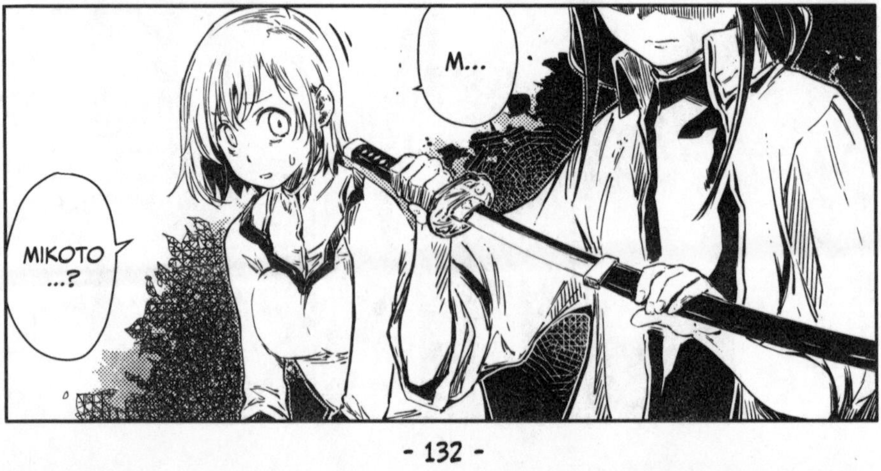
M...
MIKOTO ...?

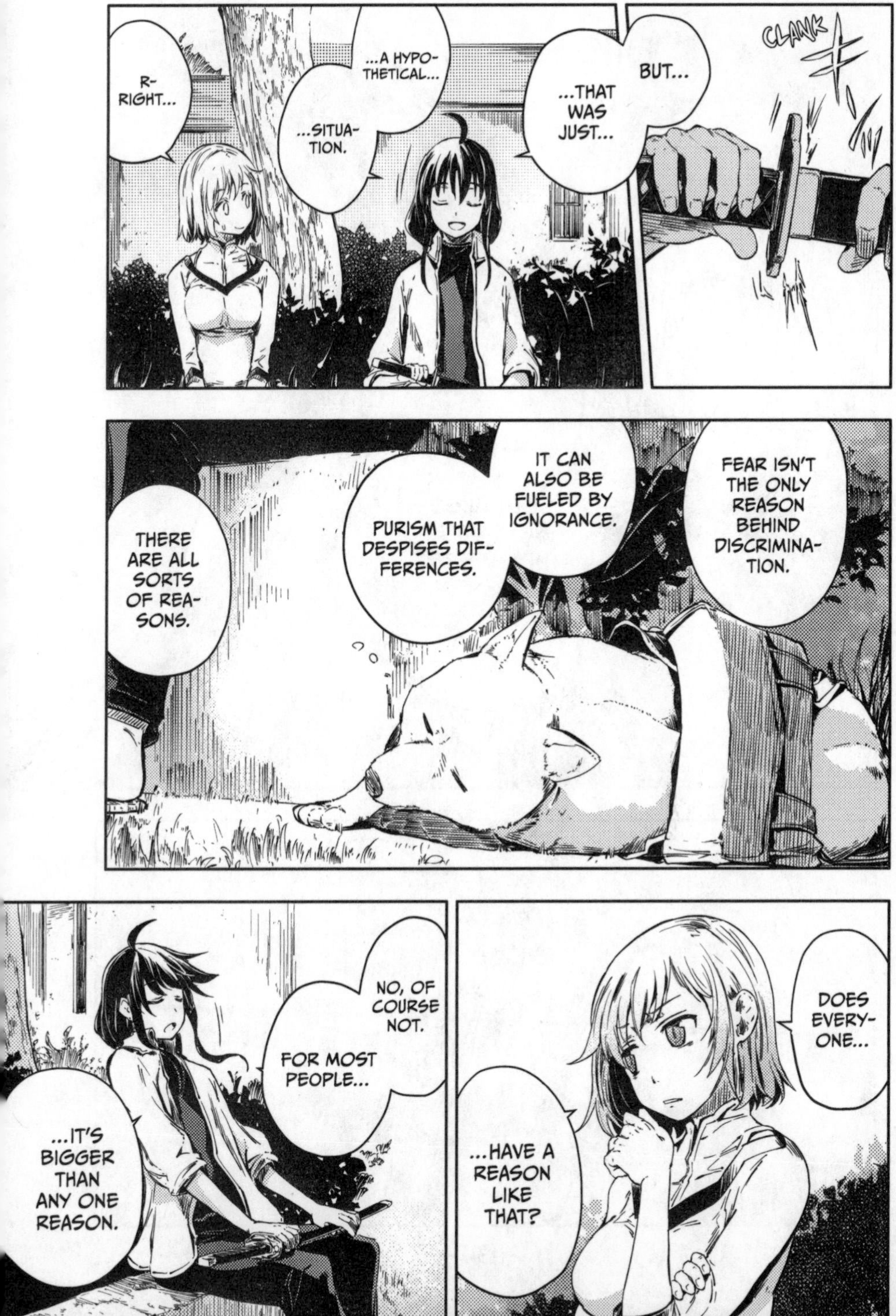
CLANK
BUT...
...THAT WAS JUST...
...A HYPOTHETICAL...
...SITUATION.
R-RIGHT...
FEAR ISN'T THE ONLY REASON BEHIND DISCRIMINATION.
IT CAN ALSO BE FUELED BY IGNORANCE.
PURISM THAT DESPISES DIFFERENCES.
THERE ARE ALL SORTS OF REASONS.
DOES EVERYONE...
...HAVE A REASON LIKE THAT?
NO, OF COURSE NOT.
FOR MOST PEOPLE...
...IT'S BIGGER THAN ANY ONE REASON.

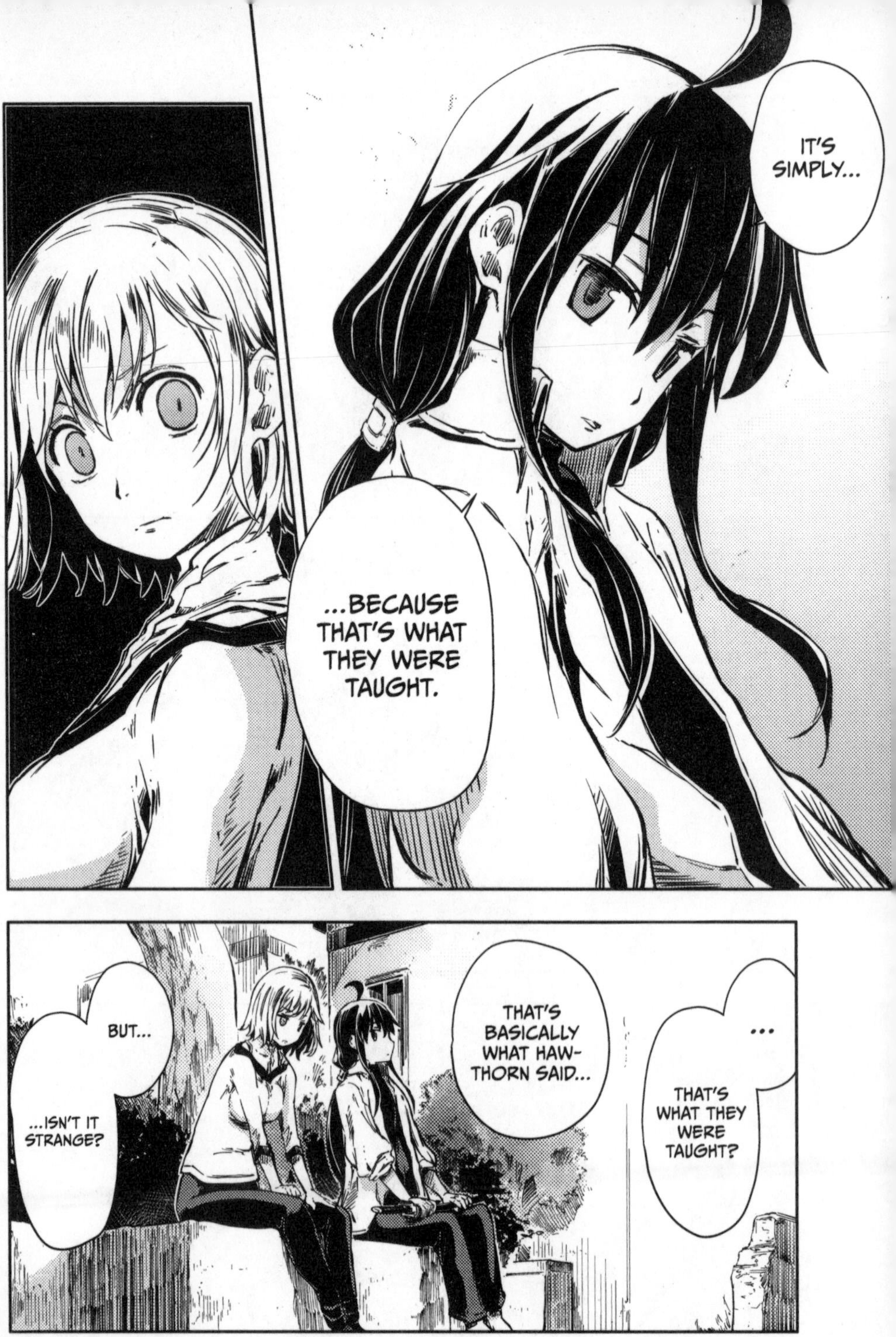
IT'S SIMPLY...
...BECAUSE THAT'S WHAT THEY WERE TAUGHT.
...
THAT'S WHAT THEY WERE TAUGHT?
THAT'S BASICALLY WHAT HAW- THORN SAID...
BUT...
...ISN'T IT STRANGE?

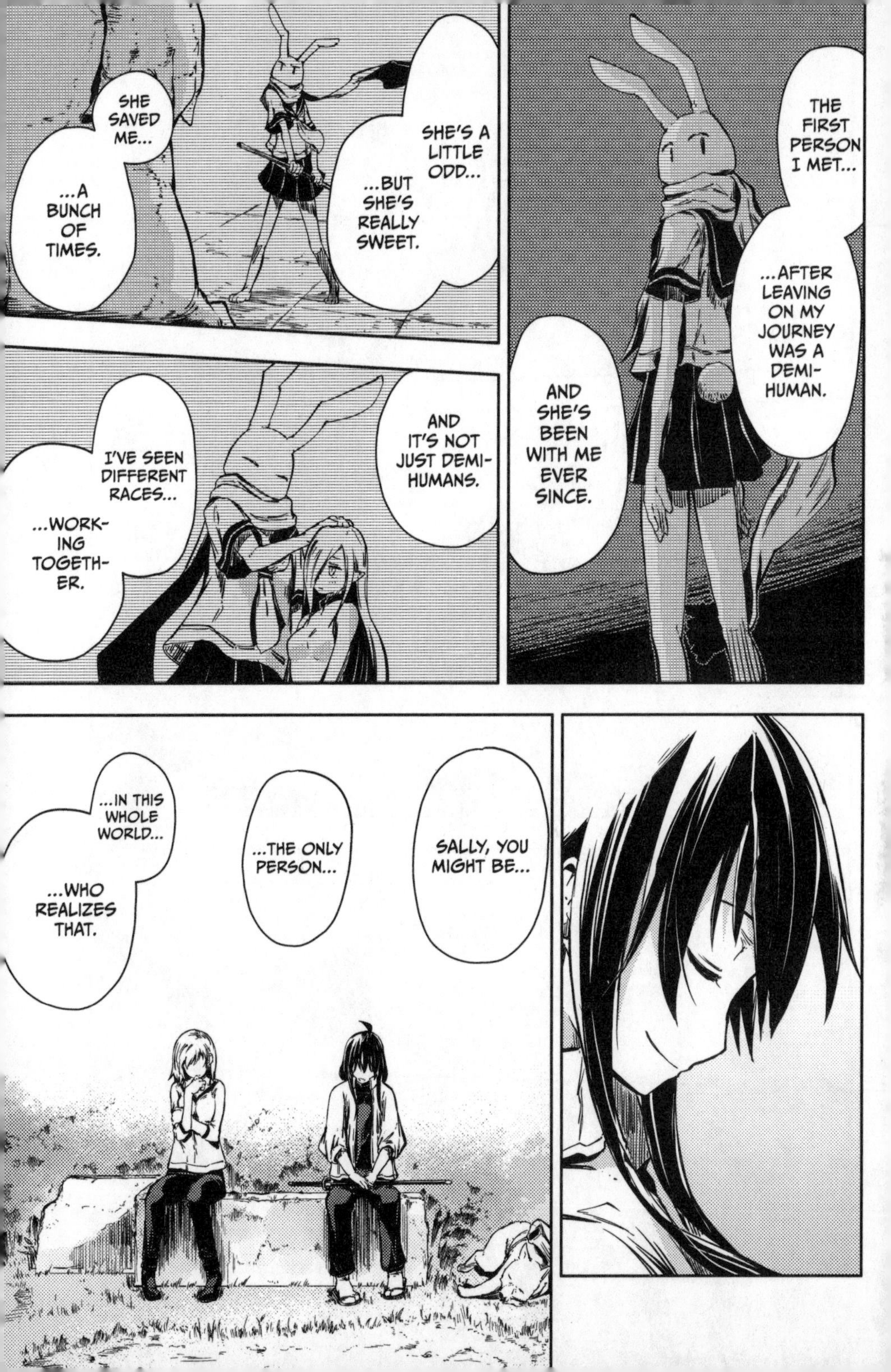
THE FIRST PERSON I MET...
...AFTER LEAVING ON MY JOURNEY WAS A DEMI-HUMAN.
AND SHE'S BEEN WITH ME EVER SINCE.
SHE'S A LITTLE ODD...
...BUT SHE'S REALLY SWEET.
SHE SAVED ME...
...A BUNCH OF TIMES.
AND IT'S NOT JUST DEMI-HUMANS.
I'VE SEEN DIFFERENT RACES...
...WORK-ING TOGETH-ER.
SALLY, YOU MIGHT BE...
...THE ONLY PERSON...
...IN THIS WHOLE WORLD...
...WHO REALIZES THAT.

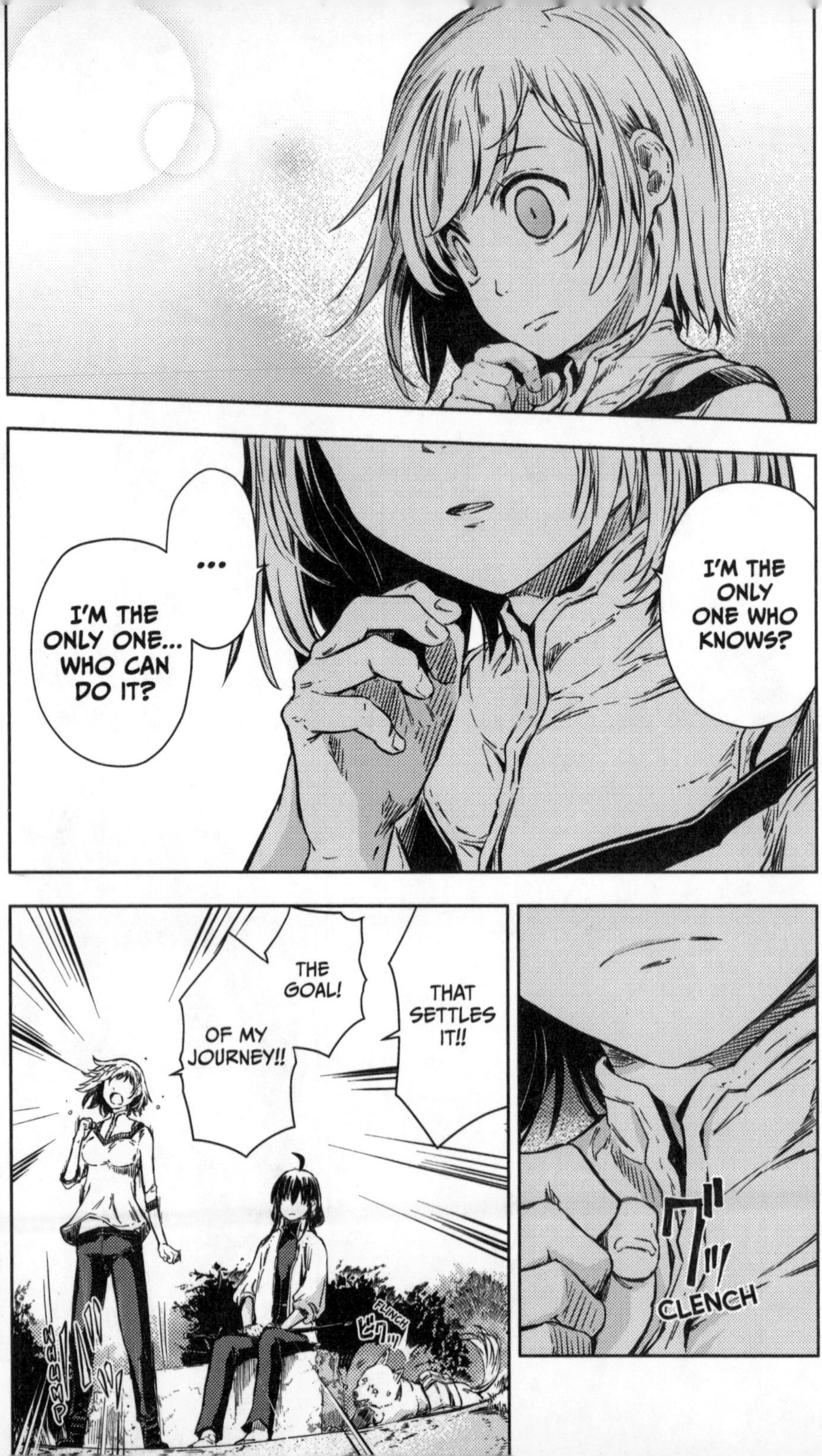
I'M THE ONLY ONE WHO KNOWS?
... I'M THE ONLY ONE... WHO CAN DO IT?
CLENCH
THAT SETTLES IT!!
THE GOAL! OF MY JOURNEY!!
WHUMP
FLINCH

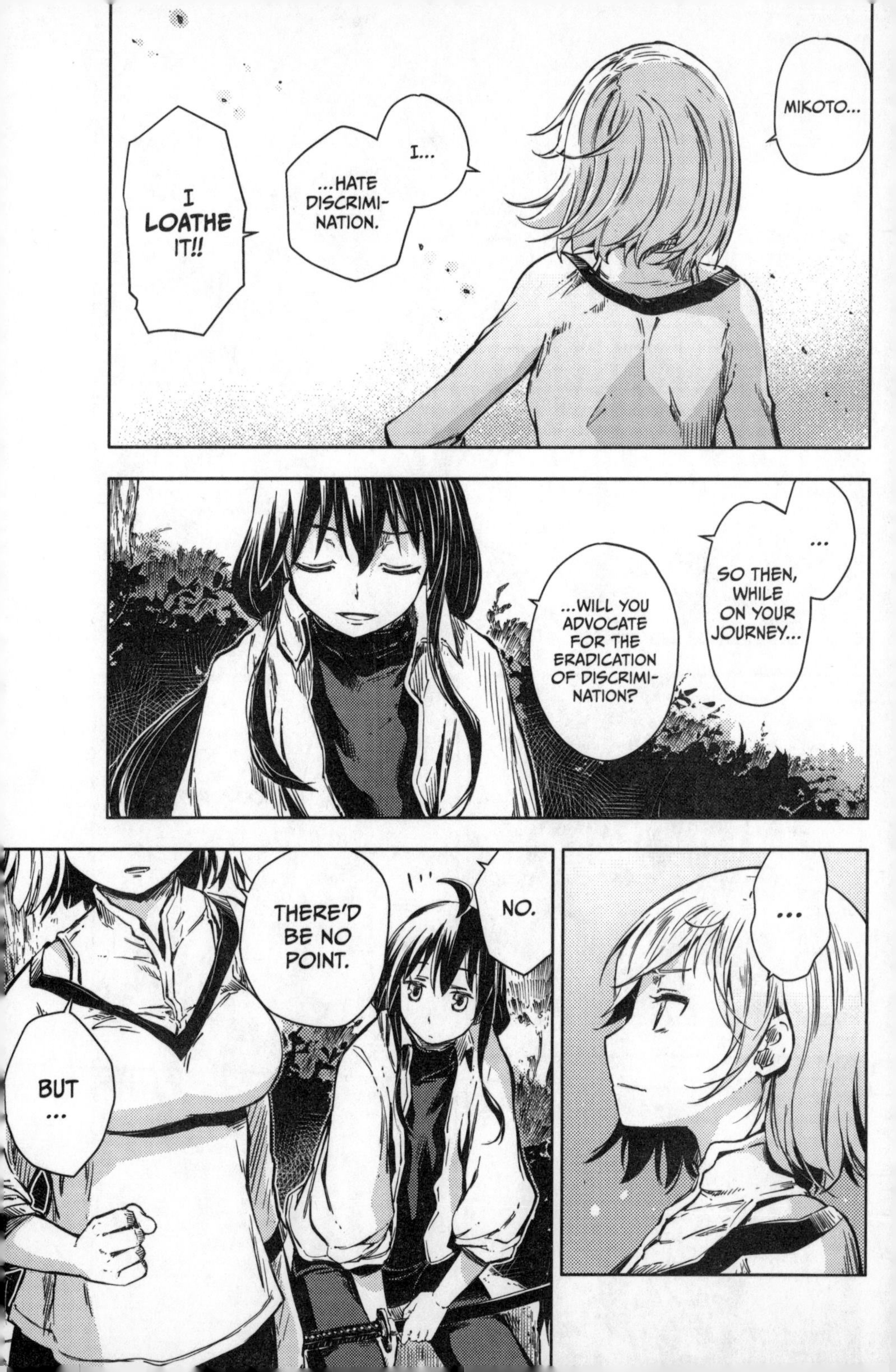
MIKOTO...
I...
...HATE DISCRIMI-NATION.
I LOATHE IT!!
...
SO THEN, WHILE ON YOUR JOURNEY...
...WILL YOU ADVOCATE FOR THE ERADICATION OF DISCRIMI-NATION?
...
NO.
THERE'D BE NO POINT.
BUT ...

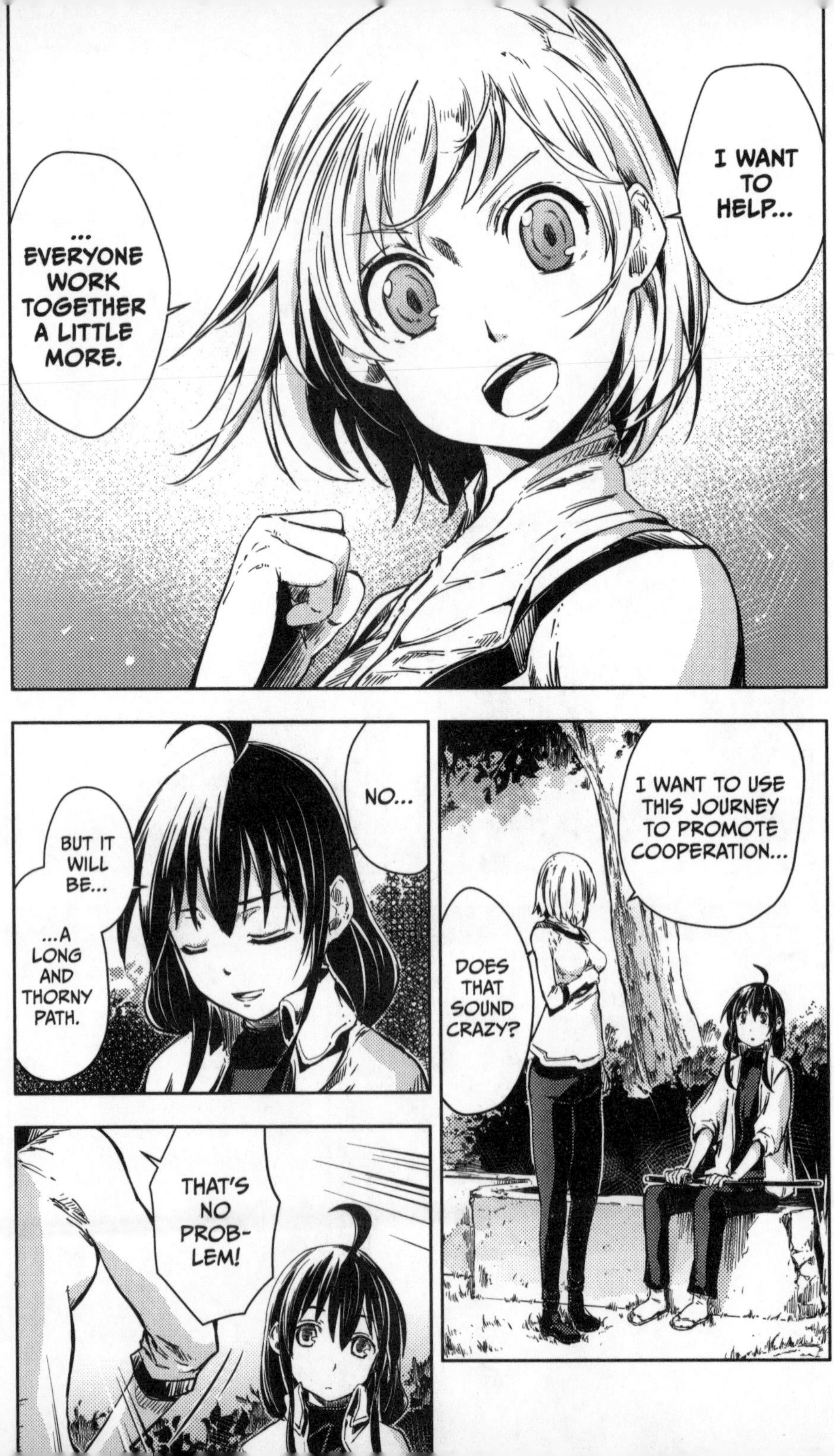
I WANT TO HELP...
... EVERYONE WORK TOGETHER A LITTLE MORE.
I WANT TO USE THIS JOURNEY TO PROMOTE COOPERATION...
DOES THAT SOUND CRAZY?
NO...
BUT IT WILL BE...
...A LONG AND THORNY PATH.
THAT'S NO PROB-LEM!

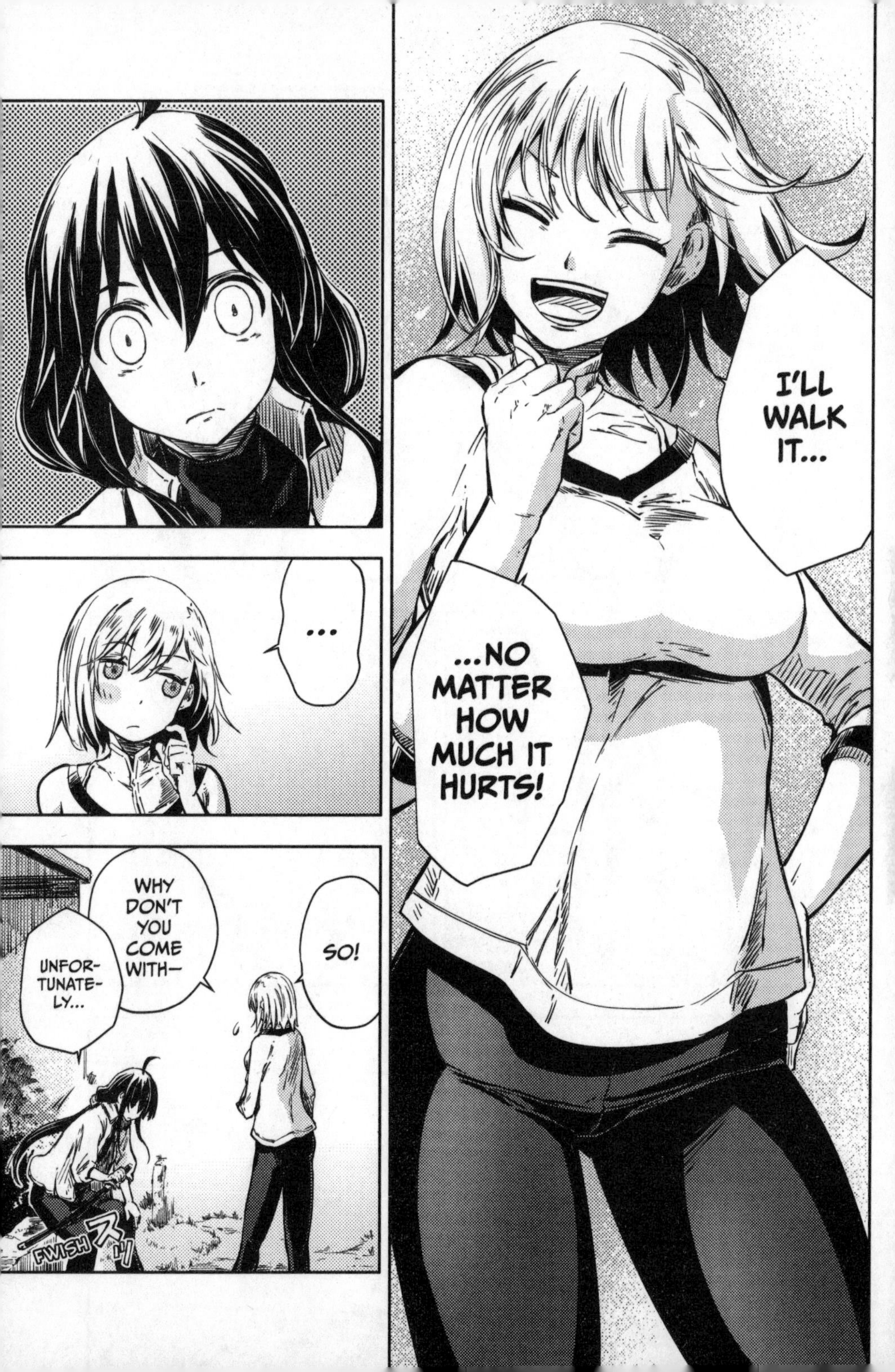
I'LL WALK IT...
...NO MATTER HOW MUCH IT HURTS!
...
SO!
WHY DON'T YOU COME WITH—
UNFORTUNATELY...
FWISH

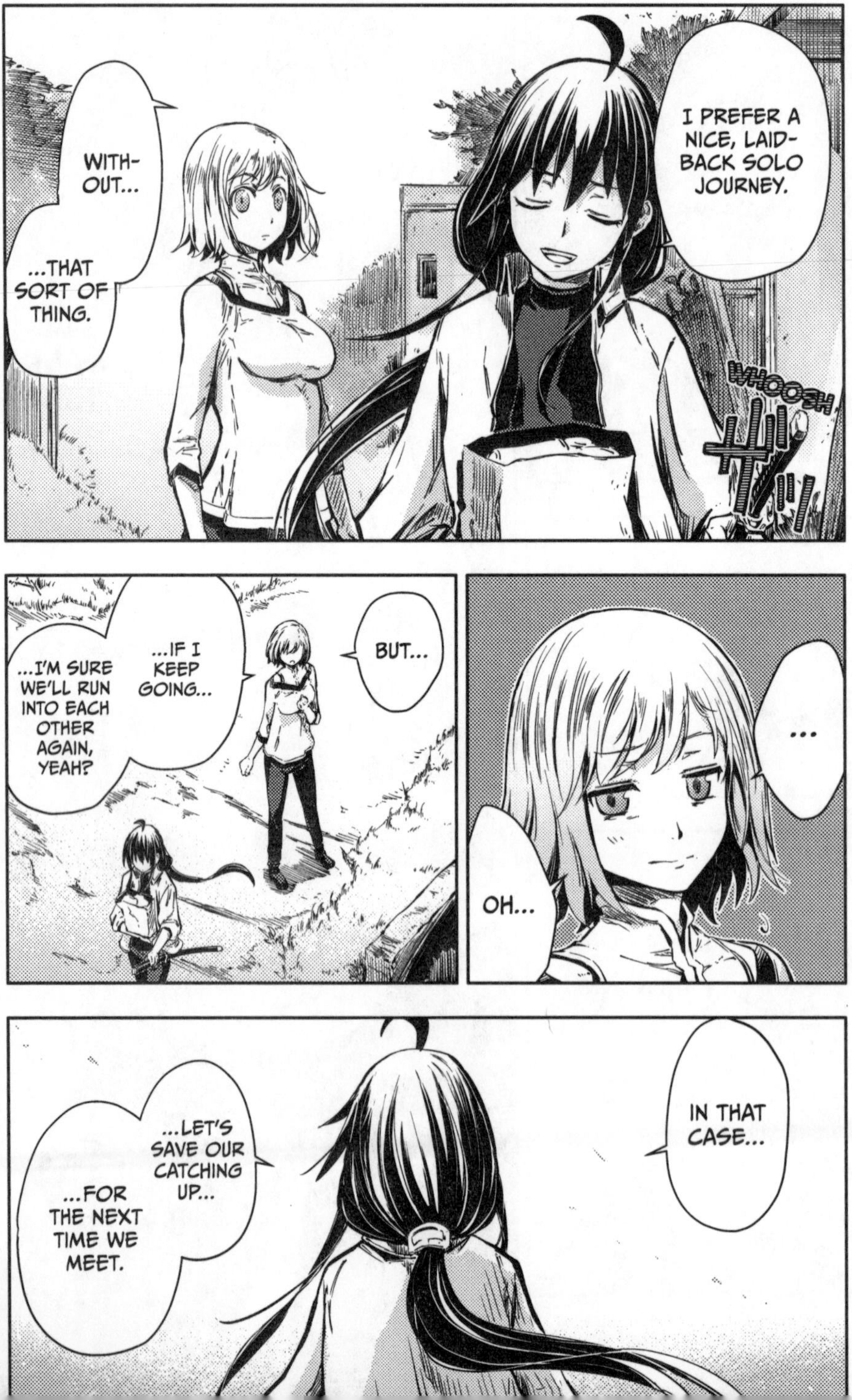
I PREFER A NICE, LAID-BACK SOLO JOURNEY.
WHOOSH
WITH-OUT...
...THAT SORT OF THING.
...
OH...
BUT...
...IF I KEEP GOING...
...I'M SURE WE'LL RUN INTO EACH OTHER AGAIN, YEAH?
IN THAT CASE...
...LET'S SAVE OUR CATCHING UP...
...FOR THE NEXT TIME WE MEET.

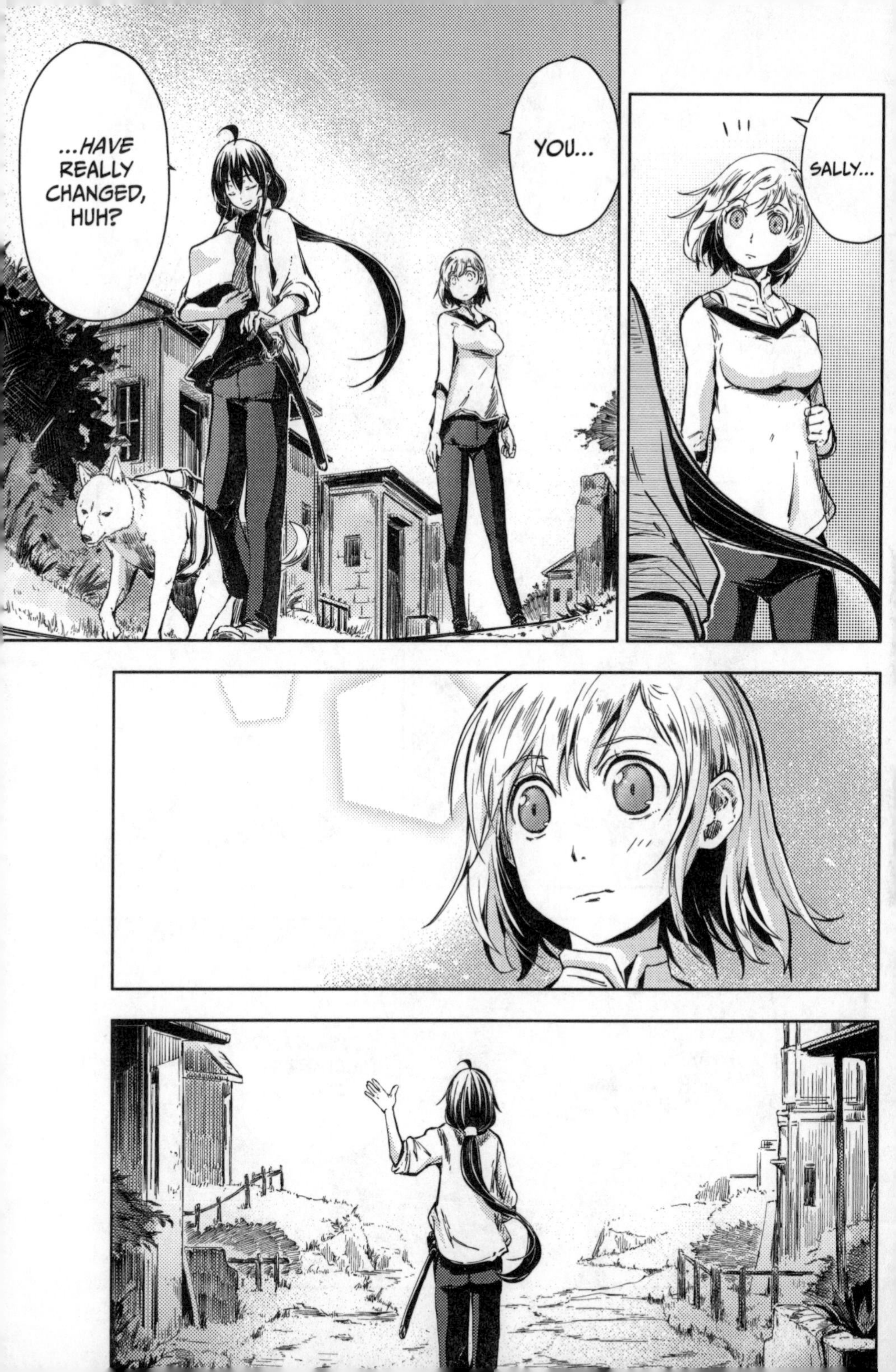
SALLY...
YOU...
...HAVE REALLY CHANGED, HUH?

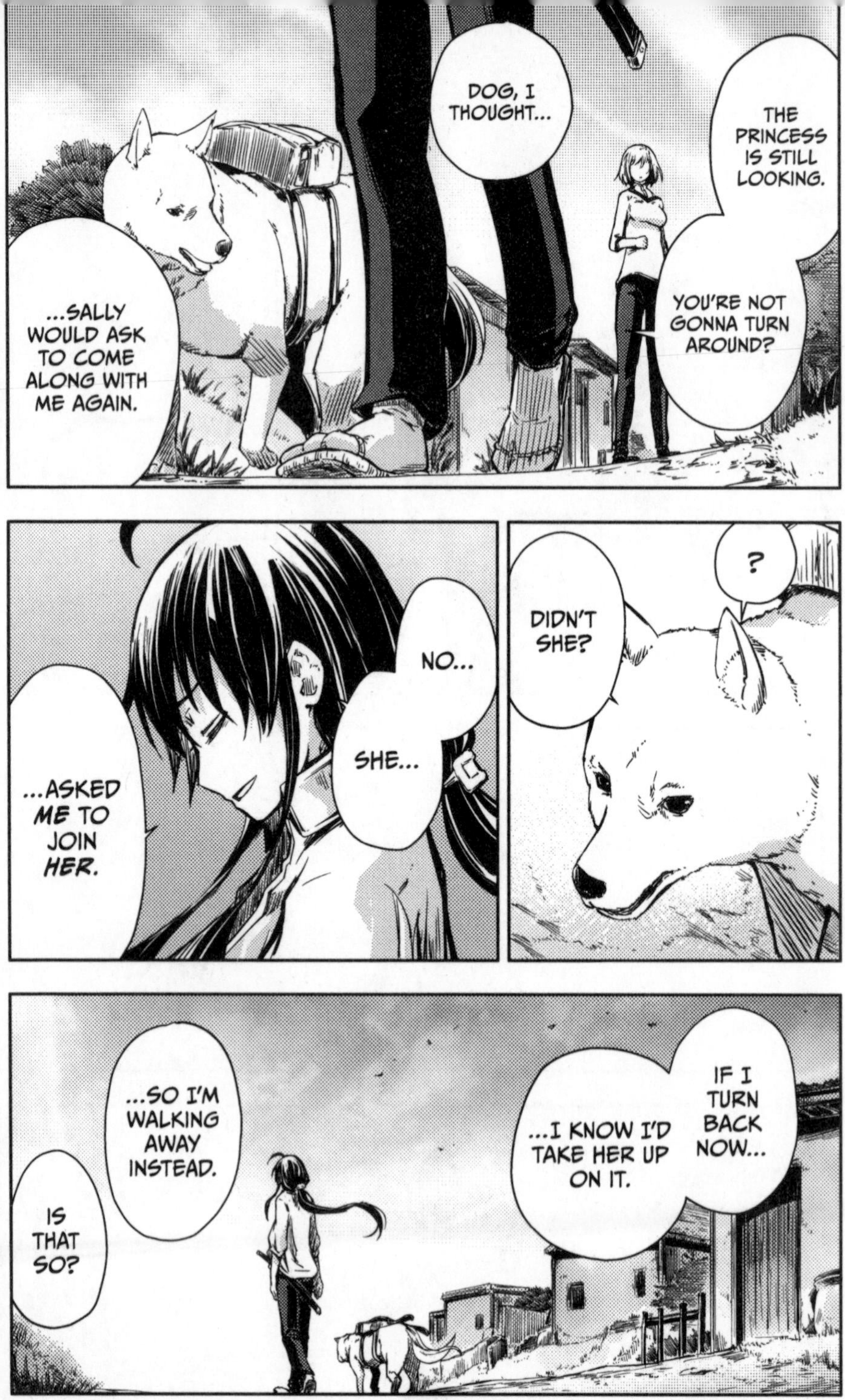
THE PRINCESS IS STILL LOOKING.
YOU'RE NOT GONNA TURN AROUND?
DOG, I THOUGHT...
...SALLY WOULD ASK TO COME ALONG WITH ME AGAIN.
?
DIDN'T SHE?
NO...
SHE...
...ASKED *ME* TO JOIN *HER*.
IF I TURN BACK NOW...
...I KNOW I'D TAKE HER UP ON IT.
...SO I'M WALKING AWAY INSTEAD.
IS THAT SO?

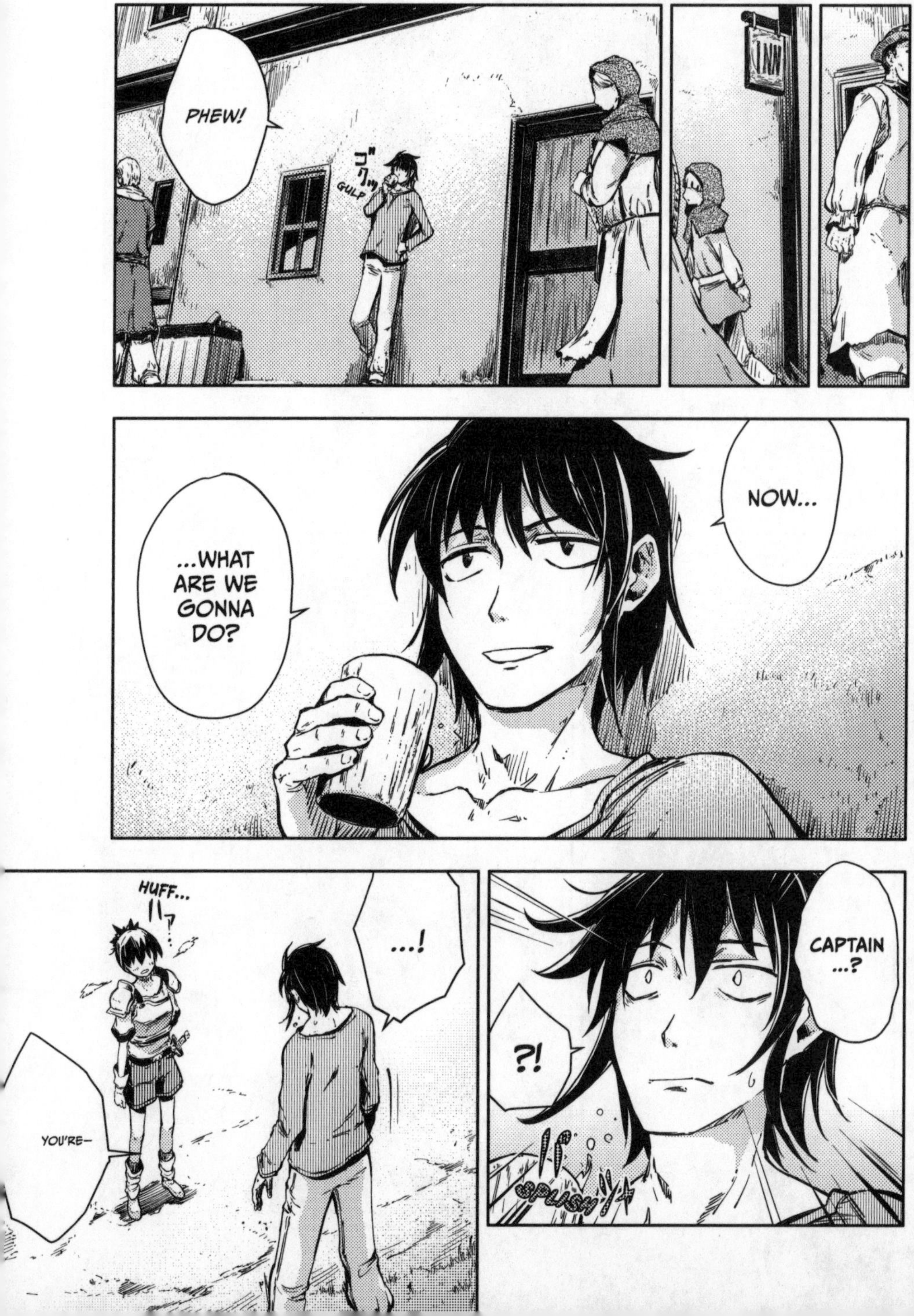
INN
PHEW!
ゴクッ
GULP
NOW...
...WHAT ARE WE GONNA DO?
CAPTAIN ...?
?!
SPLISH
...!
HUFF...
ハァ
YOU'RE—

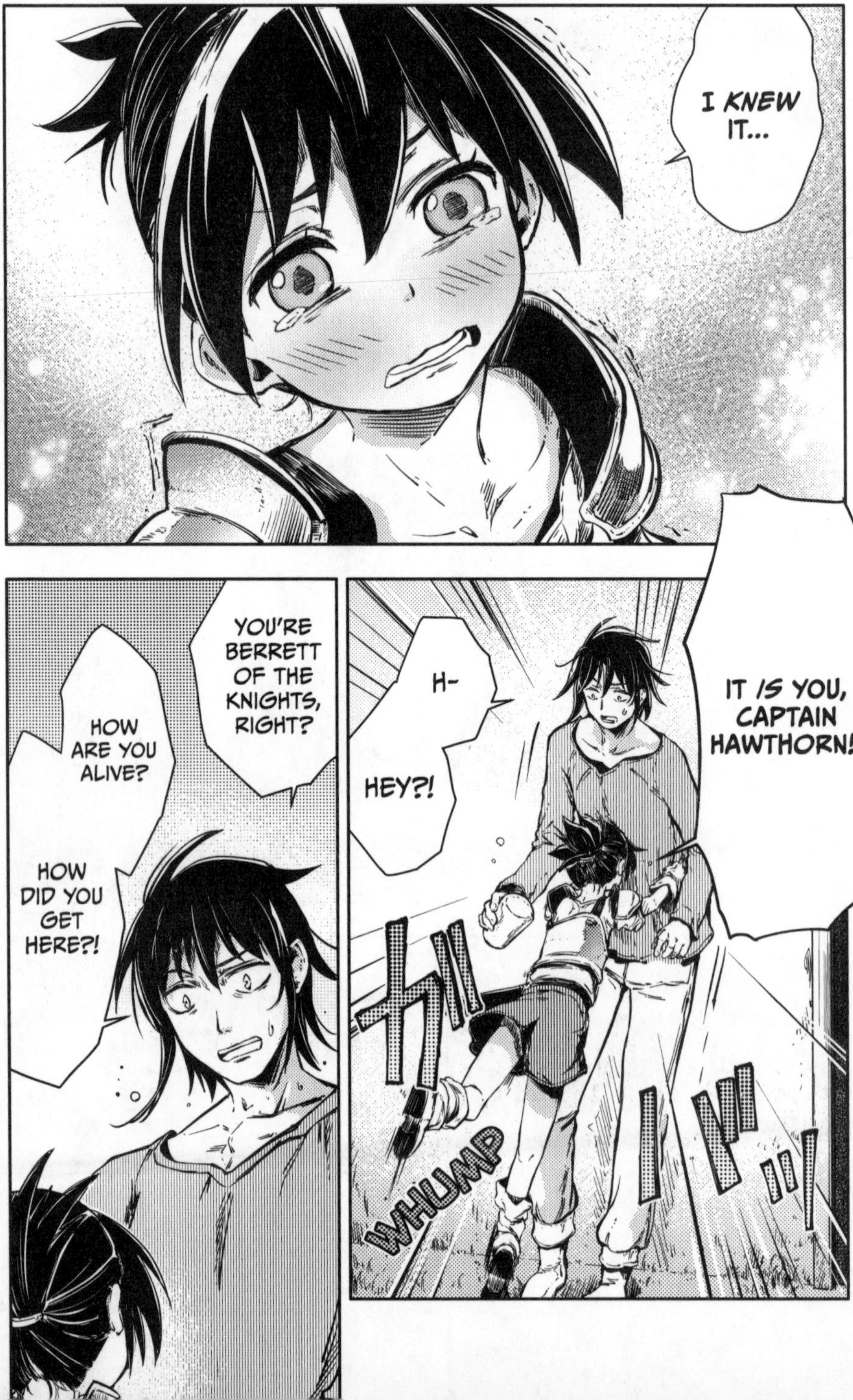
I KNEW IT...
IT IS YOU, CAPTAIN HAWTHORN!!
H-
HEY?!
WHUMP
YOU'RE BERRETT OF THE KNIGHTS, RIGHT?
HOW ARE YOU ALIVE?
HOW DID YOU GET HERE?!

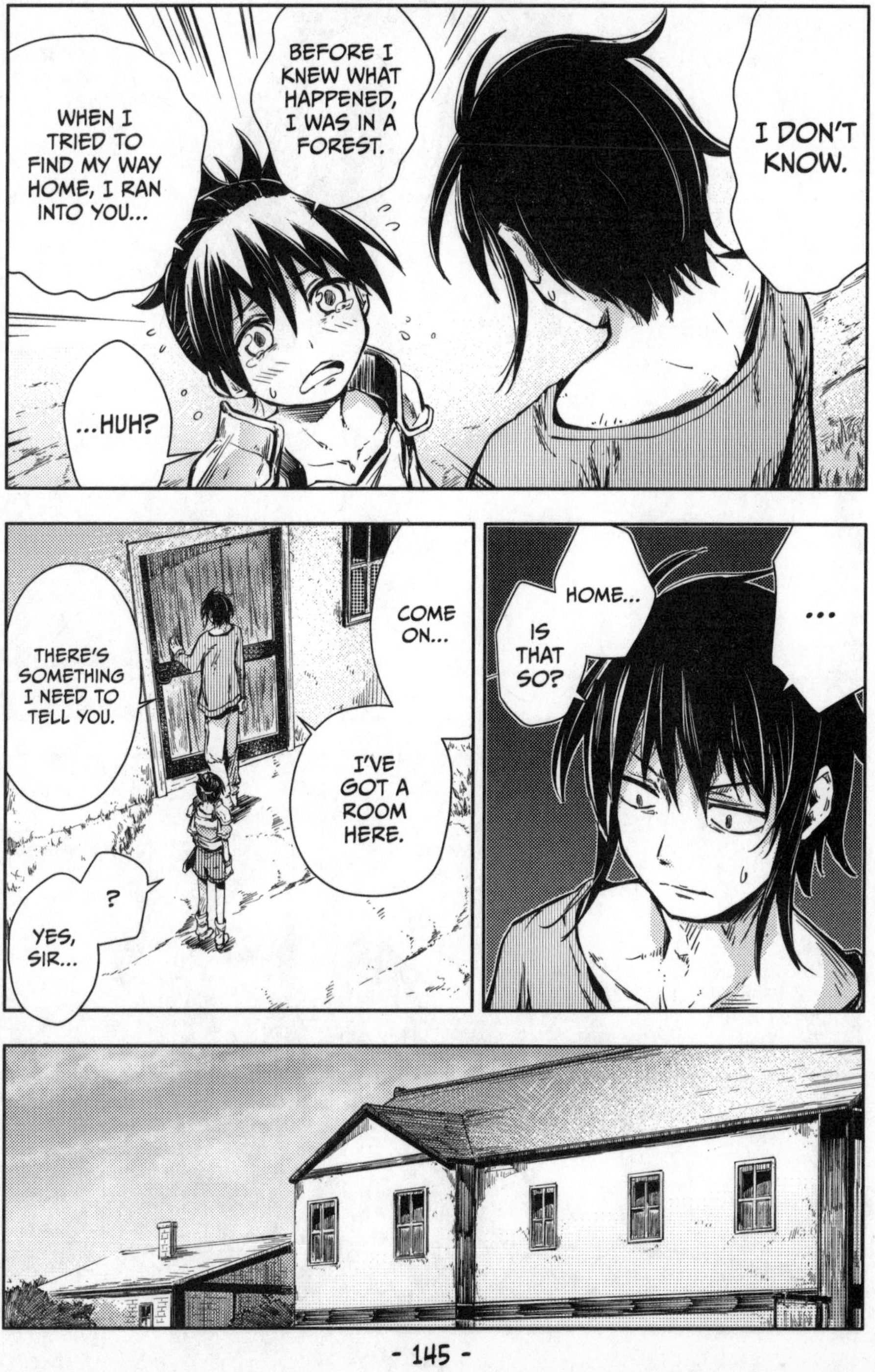
I DON'T KNOW.
BEFORE I KNEW WHAT HAPPENED, I WAS IN A FOREST.
WHEN I TRIED TO FIND MY WAY HOME, I RAN INTO YOU...
...HUH?
...
HOME...
IS THAT SO?
COME ON...
I'VE GOT A ROOM HERE.
THERE'S SOMETHING I NEED TO TELL YOU.
?
YES, SIR...

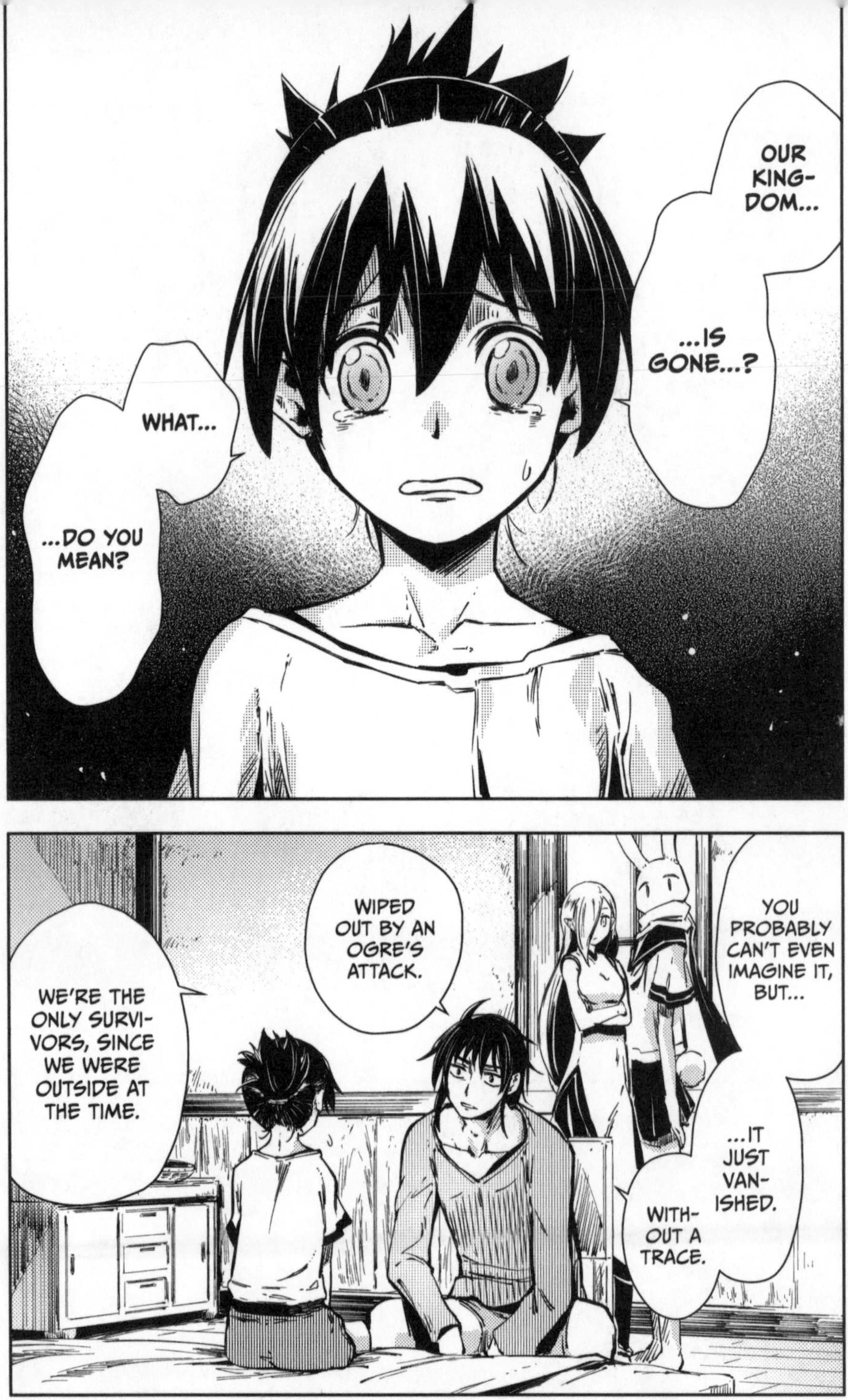
OUR KING-DOM...
...IS GONE...?
WHAT...
...DO YOU MEAN?
YOU PROBABLY CAN'T EVEN IMAGINE IT, BUT...
...IT JUST VAN-ISHED.
WITH-OUT A TRACE.
WIPED OUT BY AN OGRE'S ATTACK.
WE'RE THE ONLY SURVI-VORS, SINCE WE WERE OUTSIDE AT THE TIME.

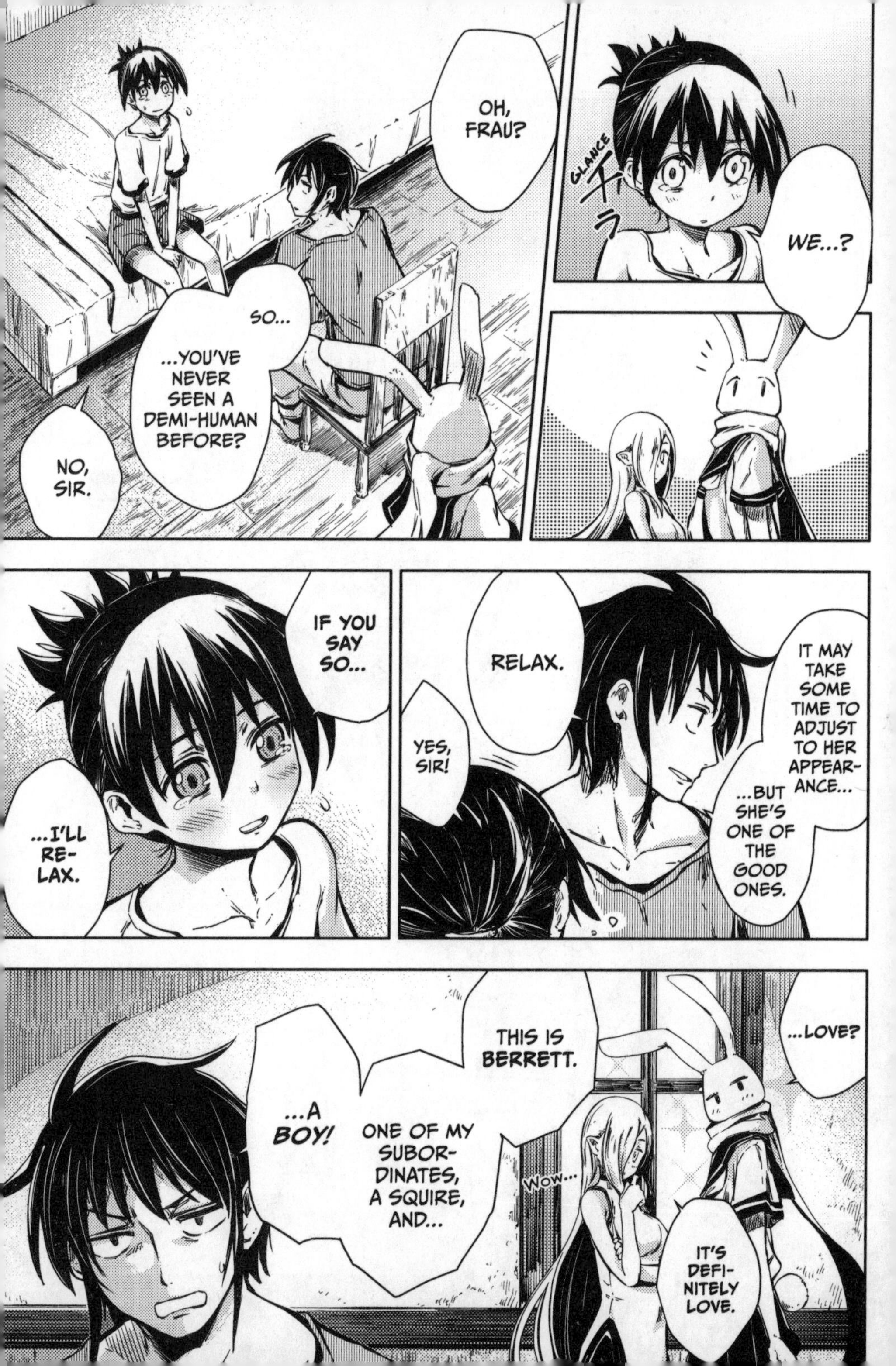
GLANCE
WE...?
OH, FRAU?
SO...
...YOU'VE NEVER SEEN A DEMI-HUMAN BEFORE?
NO, SIR.
RELAX.
IT MAY TAKE SOME TIME TO ADJUST TO HER APPEARANCE...
...BUT SHE'S ONE OF THE GOOD ONES.
YES, SIR!
IF YOU SAY SO...
...I'LL RELAX.
THIS IS BERRETT.
ONE OF MY SUBORDINATES, A SQUIRE, AND...
...A *BOY!*
Wow...
...LOVE?
IT'S DEFINITELY LOVE.

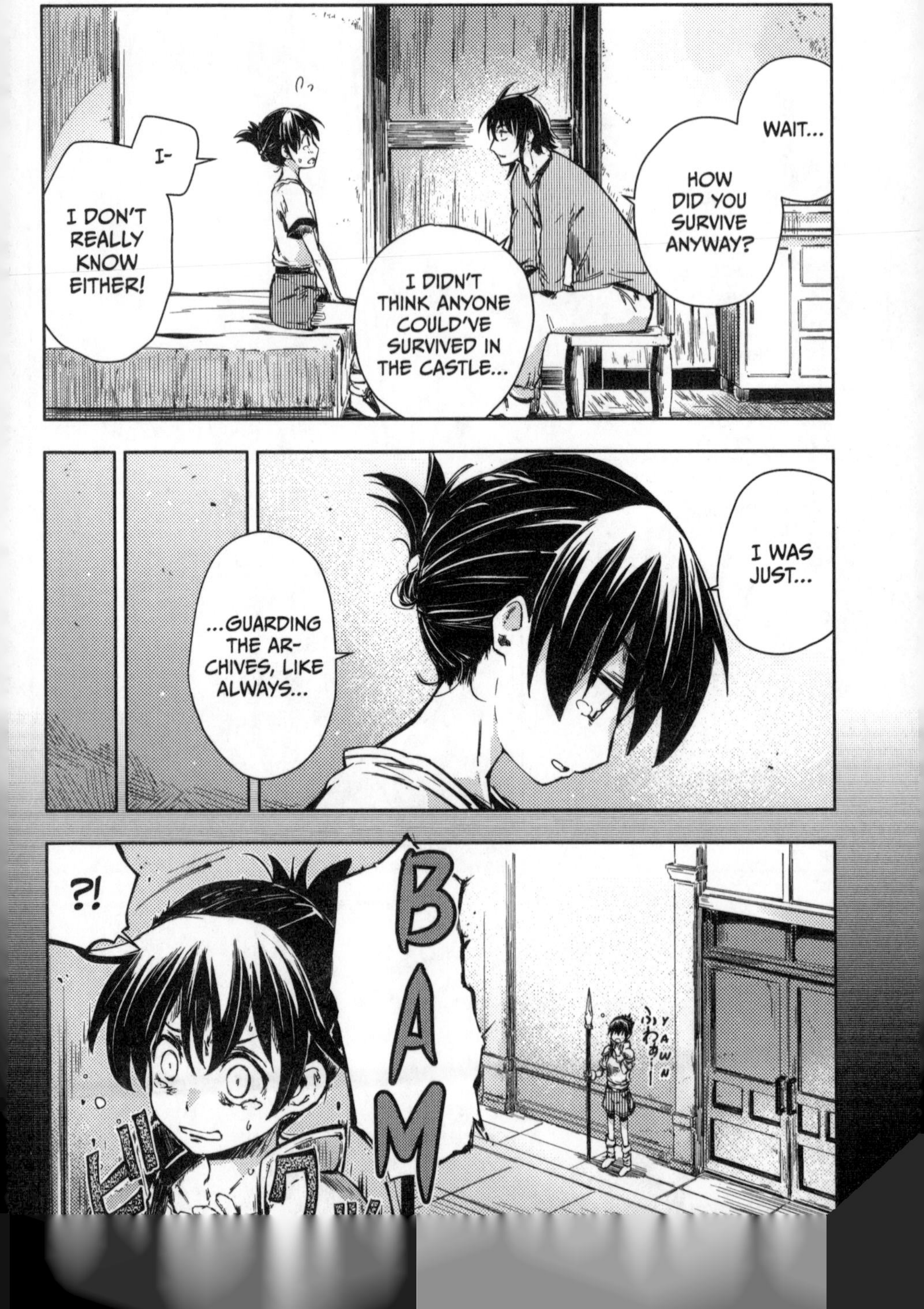
WAIT...
HOW DID YOU SURVIVE ANYWAY?
I DIDN'T THINK ANYONE COULD'VE SURVIVED IN THE CASTLE...
I-
I DON'T REALLY KNOW EITHER!
I WAS JUST...
...GUARDING THE ARCHIVES, LIKE ALWAYS...
YAWN
BAM
?!

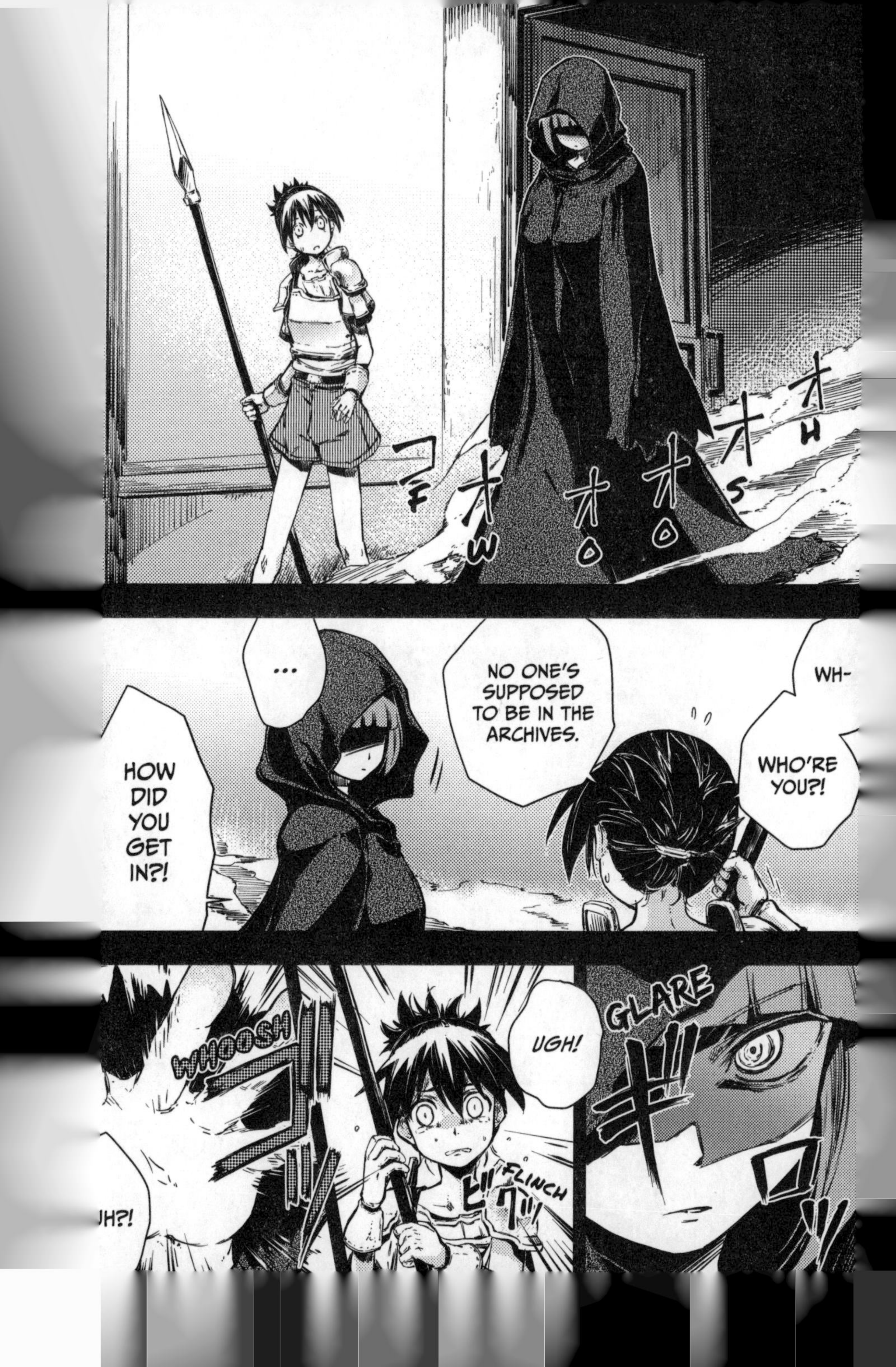
FWOOSH
WH-
WHO'RE YOU?!
NO ONE'S SUPPOSED TO BE IN THE ARCHIVES.
...
HOW DID YOU GET IN?!
GLARE
UGH!
FLINCH
WHOOSH
UH?!

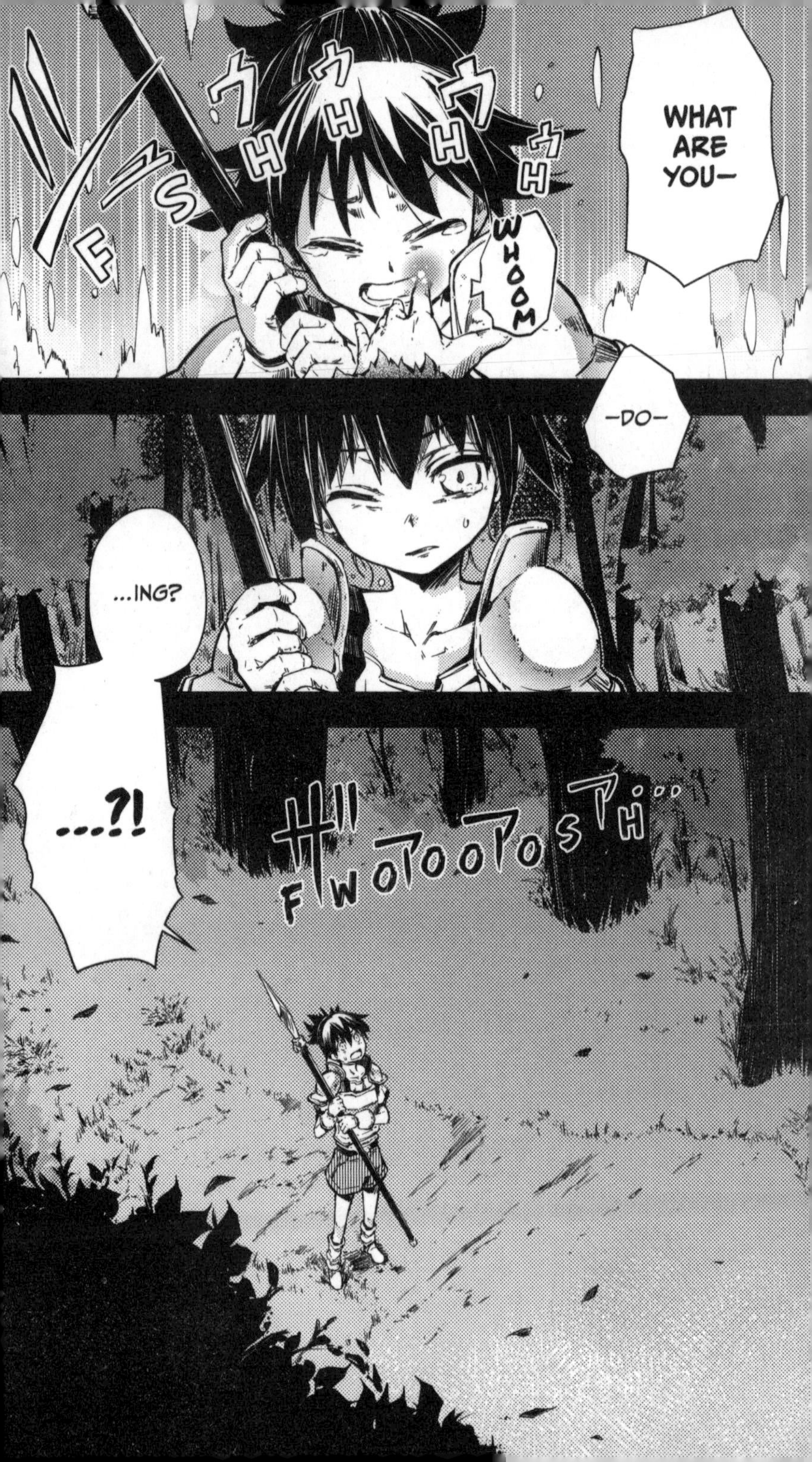

WHAT ARE YOU—
FSHHHH
WHOOM
—DO—
...ING?
...?!
FWOOOOSH

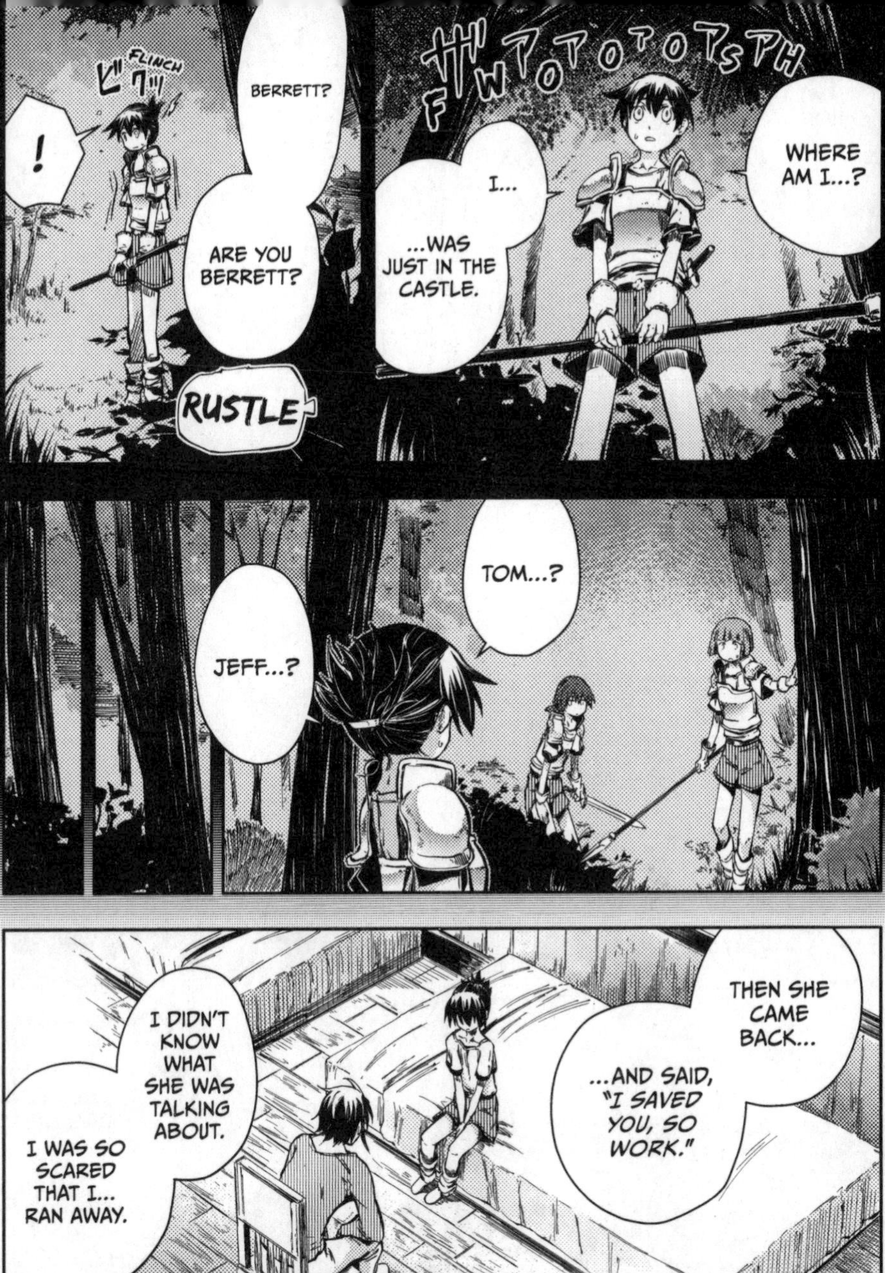
WHERE AM I...?
FWOOOSPH
I...
...WAS JUST IN THE CASTLE.
BERRETT?
ARE YOU BERRETT?
RUSTLE
FLINCH
!
TOM...?
JEFF...?
THEN SHE CAME BACK...
...AND SAID, "I SAVED YOU, SO WORK."
I DIDN'T KNOW WHAT SHE WAS TALKING ABOUT.
I WAS SO SCARED THAT I... RAN AWAY.

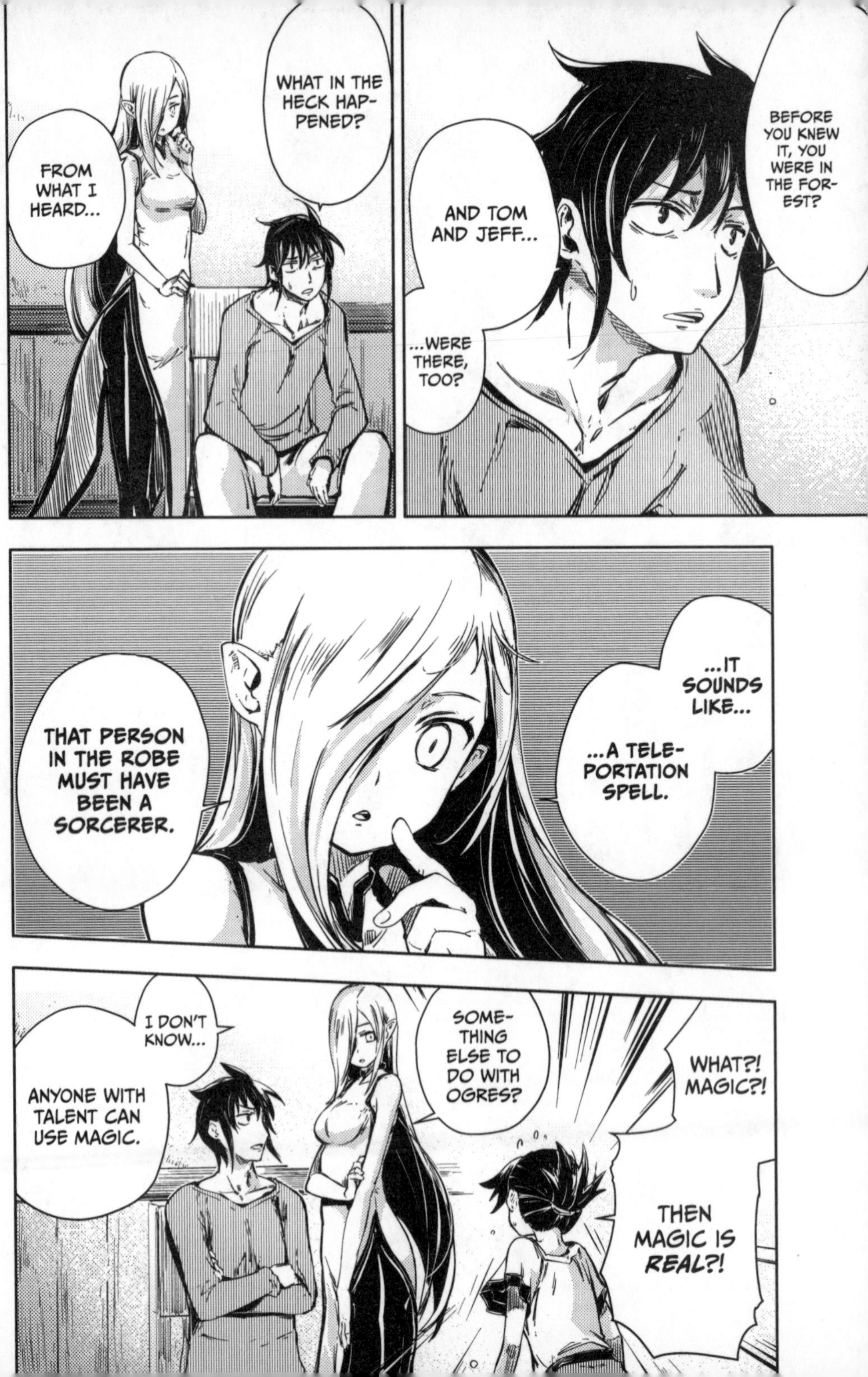
BEFORE YOU KNEW IT, YOU WERE IN THE FOREST?
AND TOM AND JEFF...
...WERE THERE, TOO?
WHAT IN THE HECK HAPPENED?
FROM WHAT I HEARD...
...IT SOUNDS LIKE...
...A TELEPORTATION SPELL.
THAT PERSON IN THE ROBE MUST HAVE BEEN A SORCERER.
WHAT?! MAGIC?!
THEN MAGIC IS *REAL*?!
SOMETHING ELSE TO DO WITH OGRES?
I DON'T KNOW...
ANYONE WITH TALENT CAN USE MAGIC.

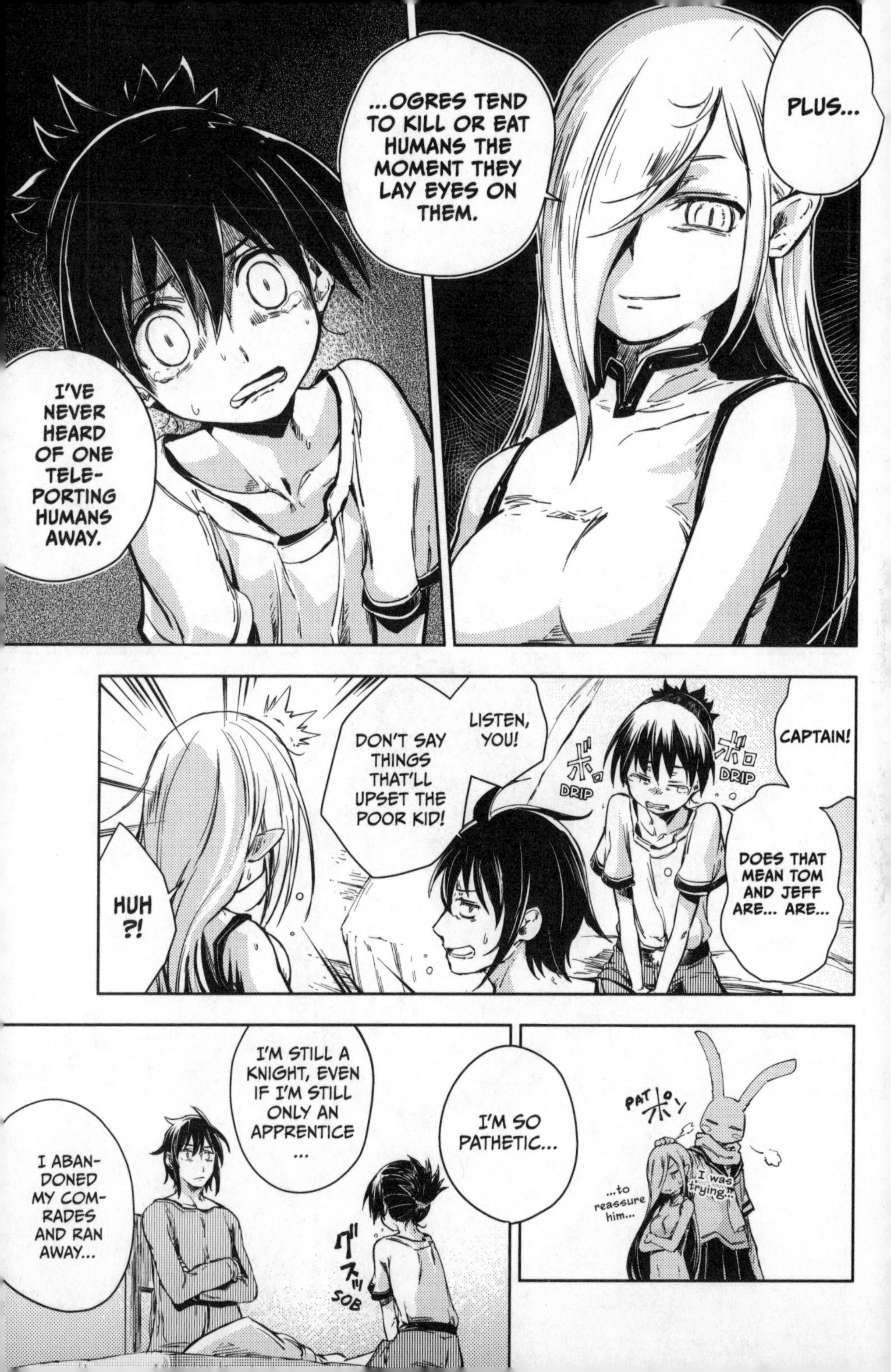
PLUS...
...OGRES TEND TO KILL OR EAT HUMANS THE MOMENT THEY LAY EYES ON THEM.
I'VE NEVER HEARD OF ONE TELE-PORTING HUMANS AWAY.
CAPTAIN!
DRIP
DRIP
DOES THAT MEAN TOM AND JEFF ARE... ARE...
LISTEN, YOU!
DON'T SAY THINGS THAT'LL UPSET THE POOR KID!
HUH?!
PAT
I was trying...
...to reassure him...
I'M SO PATHETIC...
I'M STILL A KNIGHT, EVEN IF I'M STILL ONLY AN APPRENTICE...
I ABAN-DONED MY COM-RADES AND RAN AWAY...
SOB

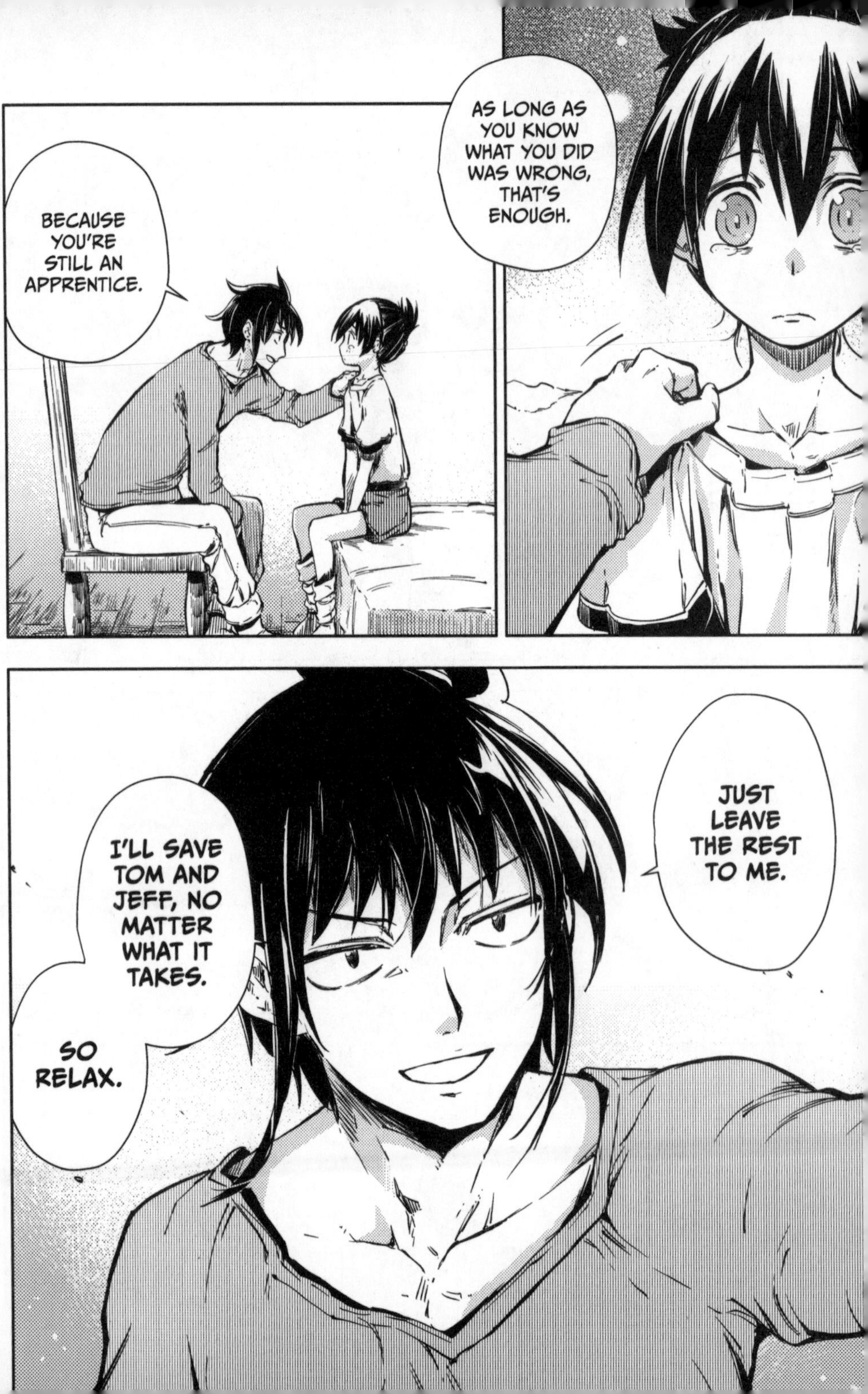
AS LONG AS YOU KNOW WHAT YOU DID WAS WRONG, THAT'S ENOUGH.
BECAUSE YOU'RE STILL AN APPRENTICE.
JUST LEAVE THE REST TO ME.
I'LL SAVE TOM AND JEFF, NO MATTER WHAT IT TAKES.
SO RELAX.

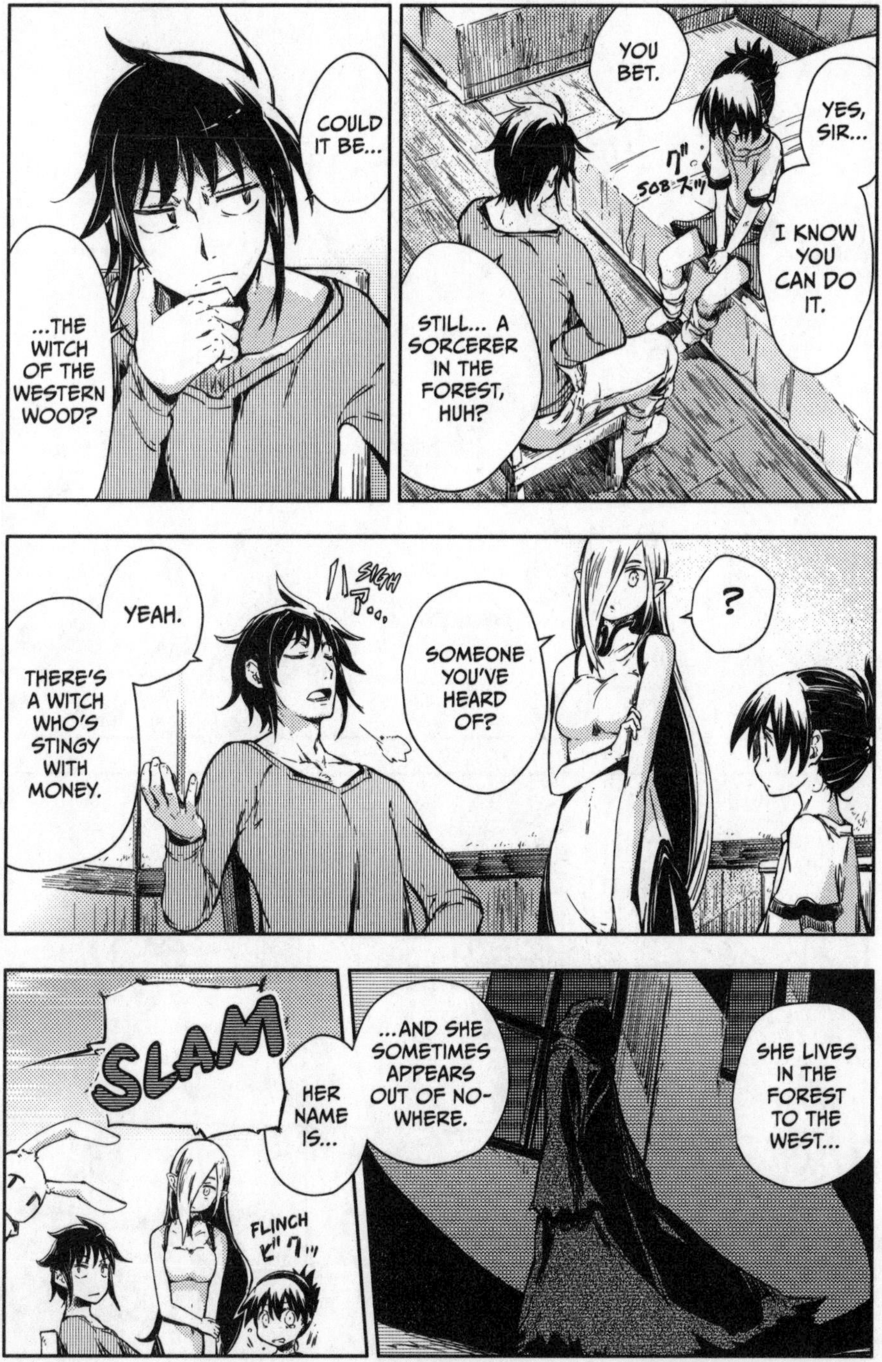
YOU BET.
YES, SIR...
SOB
I KNOW YOU CAN DO IT.
STILL... A SORCERER IN THE FOREST, HUH?
COULD IT BE...
...THE WITCH OF THE WESTERN WOOD?
?
SOMEONE YOU'VE HEARD OF?
SIGH
YEAH.
THERE'S A WITCH WHO'S STINGY WITH MONEY.
SHE LIVES IN THE FOREST TO THE WEST...
...AND SHE SOMETIMES APPEARS OUT OF NO-WHERE.
HER NAME IS...
SLAM
FLINCH

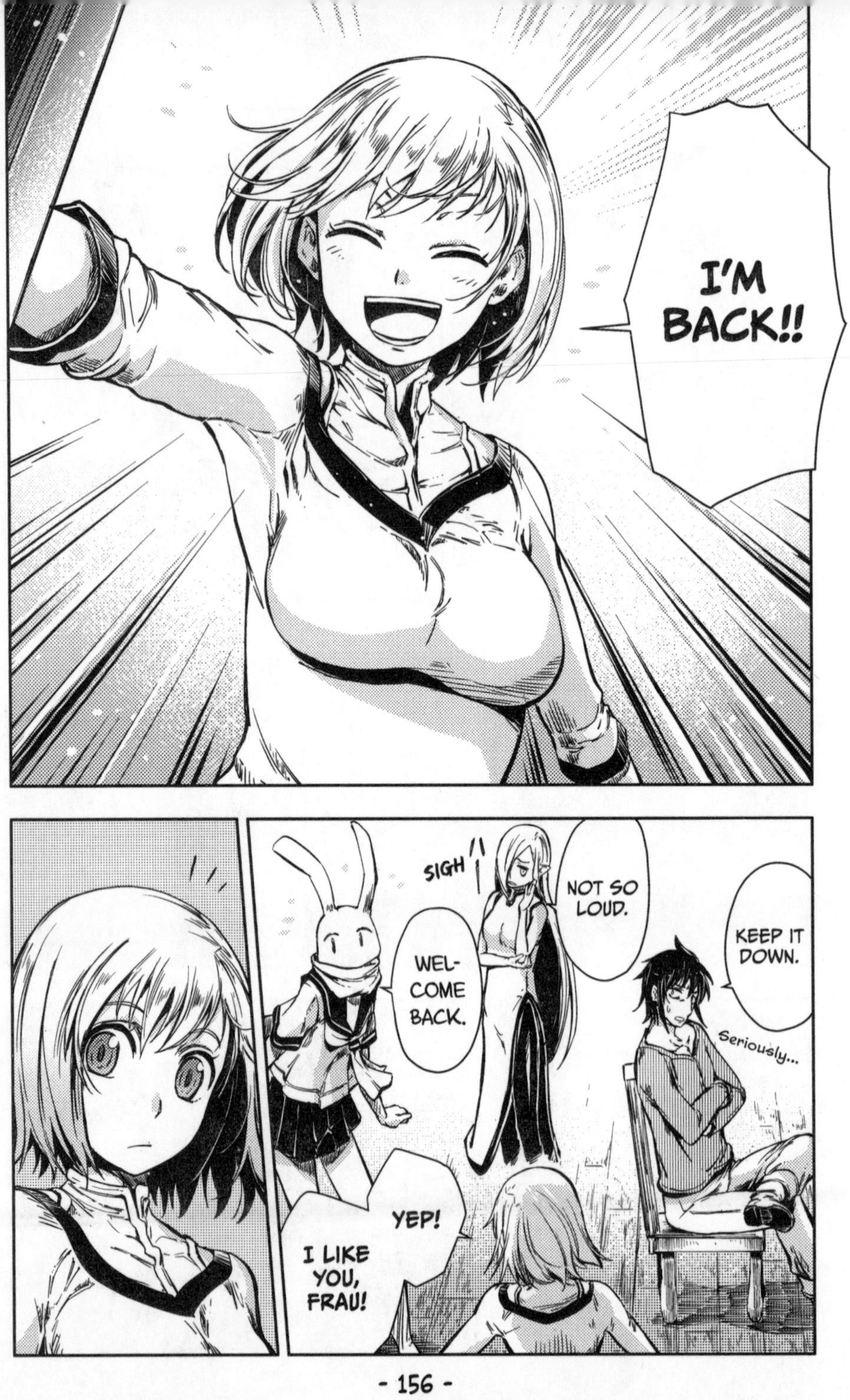
I'M BACK!!
KEEP IT DOWN.
Seriously...
NOT SO LOUD.
SIGH
WEL-COME BACK.
YEP!
I LIKE YOU, FRAU!

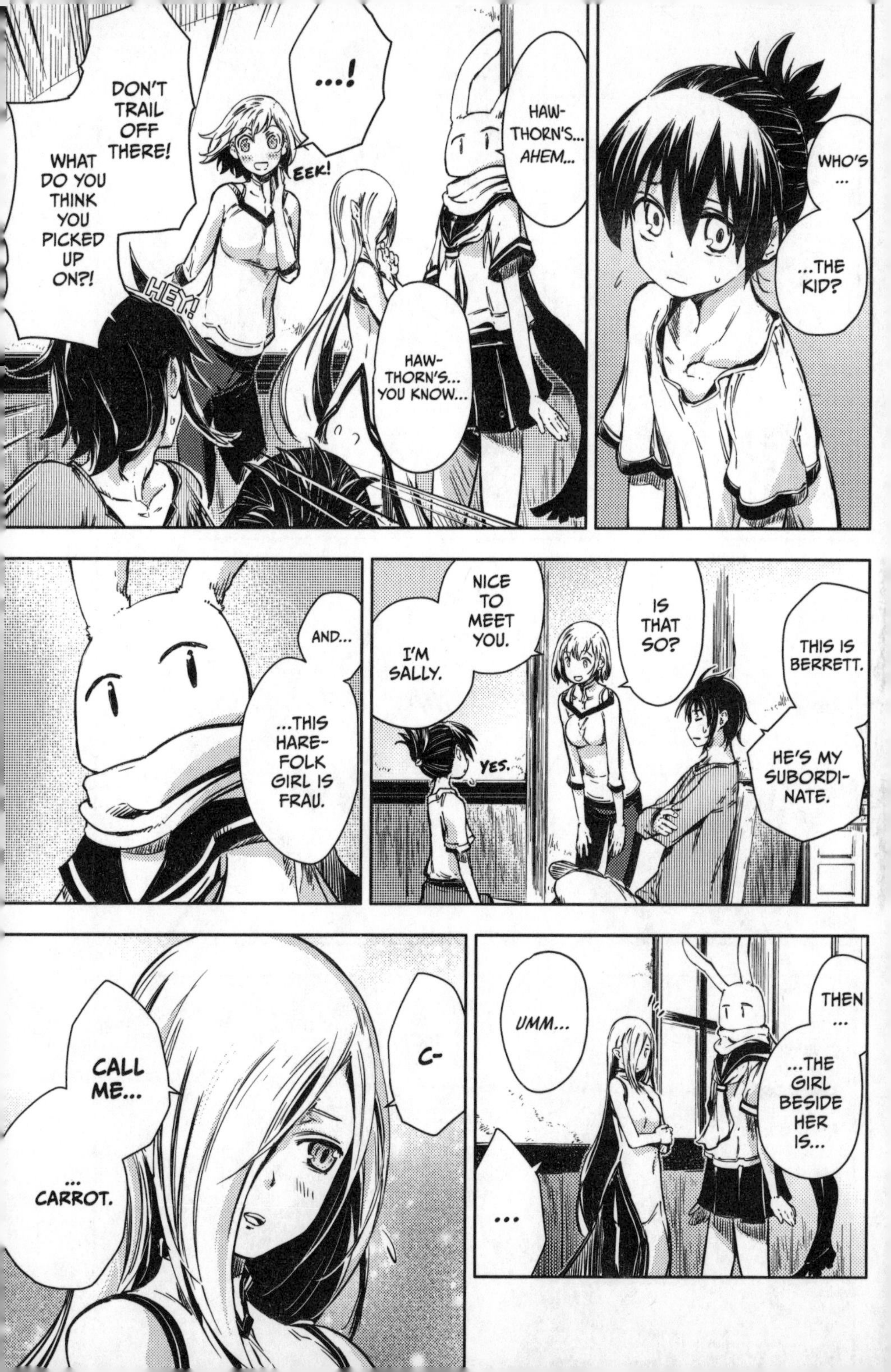
WHO'S ...
...THE KID?
HAW-THORN'S... AHEM...
...!
EEK!
DON'T TRAIL OFF THERE!
WHAT DO YOU THINK YOU PICKED UP ON?!
HEY!
HAW-THORN'S... YOU KNOW...
THIS IS BERRETT.
HE'S MY SUBORDI-NATE.
IS THAT SO?
NICE TO MEET YOU.
I'M SALLY.
YES.
AND...
...THIS HARE-FOLK GIRL IS FRAU.
THEN ...
...THE GIRL BESIDE HER IS...
UMM...
...
C-
CALL ME...
... CARROT.

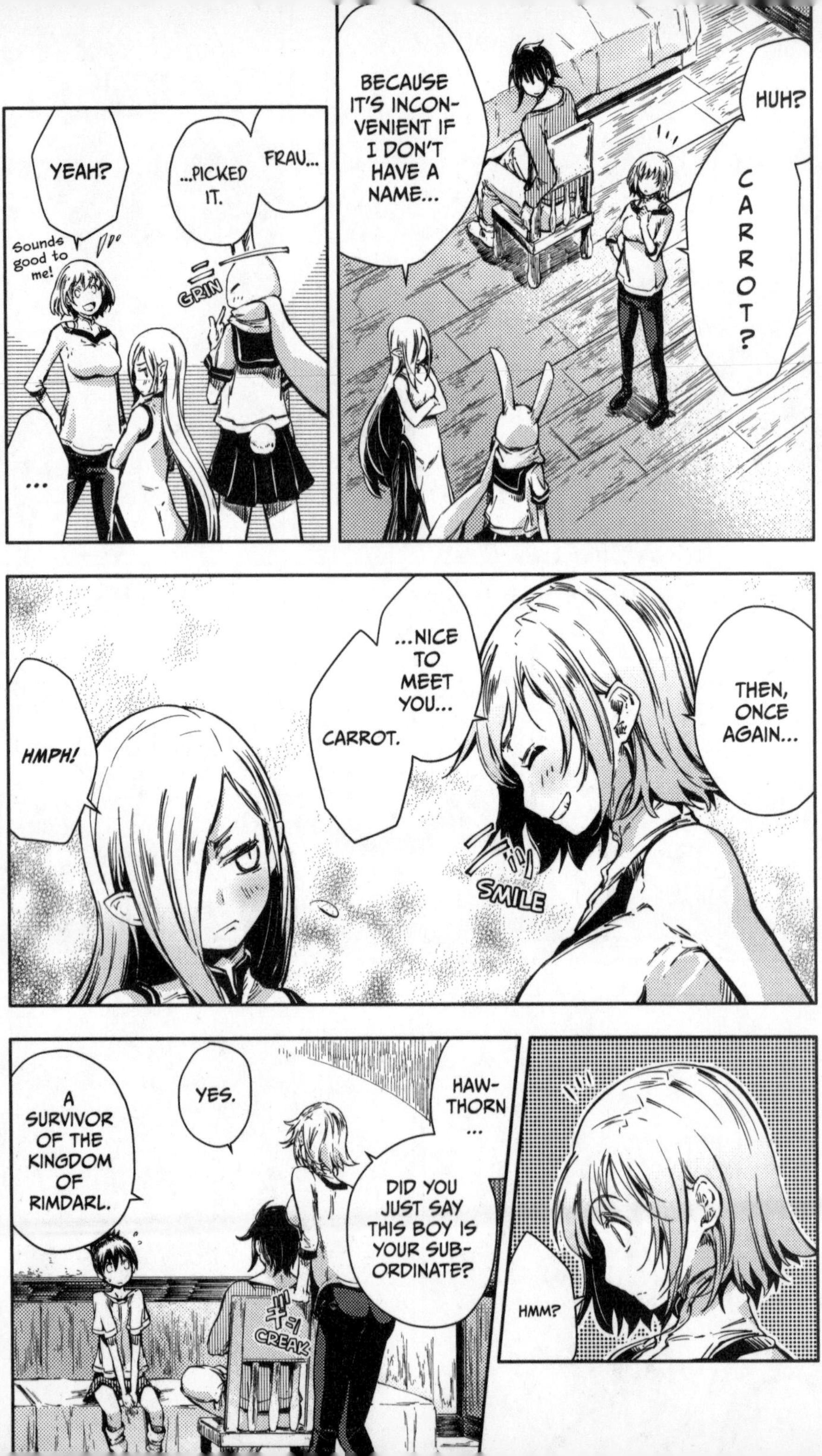
HUH?
CARROT?
BECAUSE IT'S INCONVENIENT IF I DON'T HAVE A NAME...
FRAU...
...PICKED IT.
GRIN
YEAH?
Sounds good to me!
...
THEN, ONCE AGAIN...
...NICE TO MEET YOU...
CARROT.
SMILE
HMPH!
HMM?
HAWTHORN...
DID YOU JUST SAY THIS BOY IS YOUR SUBORDINATE?
CREAK
YES.
A SURVIVOR OF THE KINGDOM OF RIMDARL.

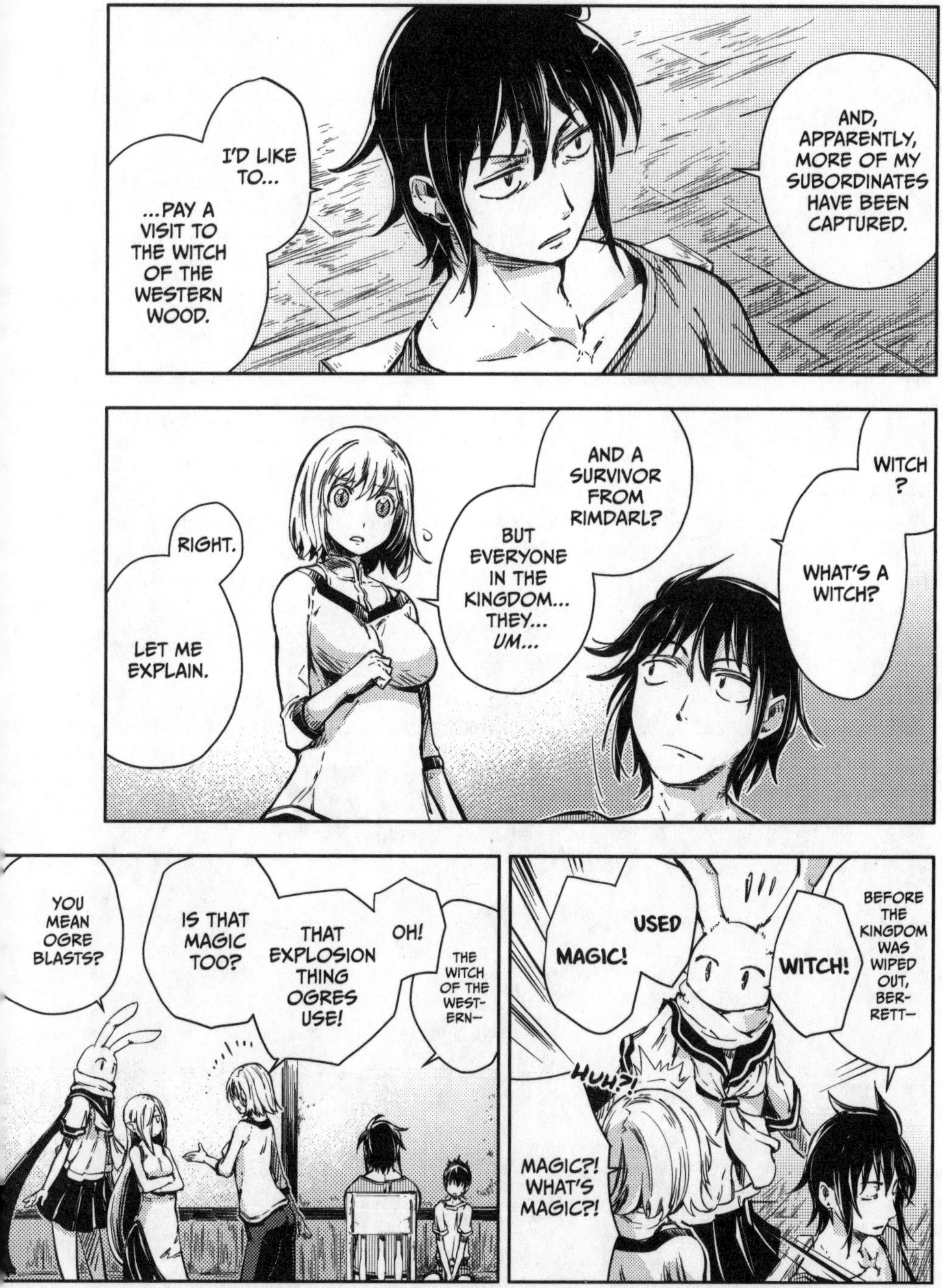
AND, APPARENTLY, MORE OF MY SUBORDINATES HAVE BEEN CAPTURED.
I'D LIKE TO...
...PAY A VISIT TO THE WITCH OF THE WESTERN WOOD.
WITCH?
WHAT'S A WITCH?
AND A SURVIVOR FROM RIMDARL?
BUT EVERYONE IN THE KINGDOM... THEY... UM...
RIGHT.
LET ME EXPLAIN.
BEFORE THE KINGDOM WAS WIPED OUT, BER-RETT—
WITCH!
USED
MAGIC!
HUH?!
MAGIC?! WHAT'S MAGIC?!
THE WITCH OF THE WEST-ERN—
OH!
THAT EXPLOSION THING OGRES USE!
IS THAT MAGIC TOO?
YOU MEAN OGRE BLASTS?

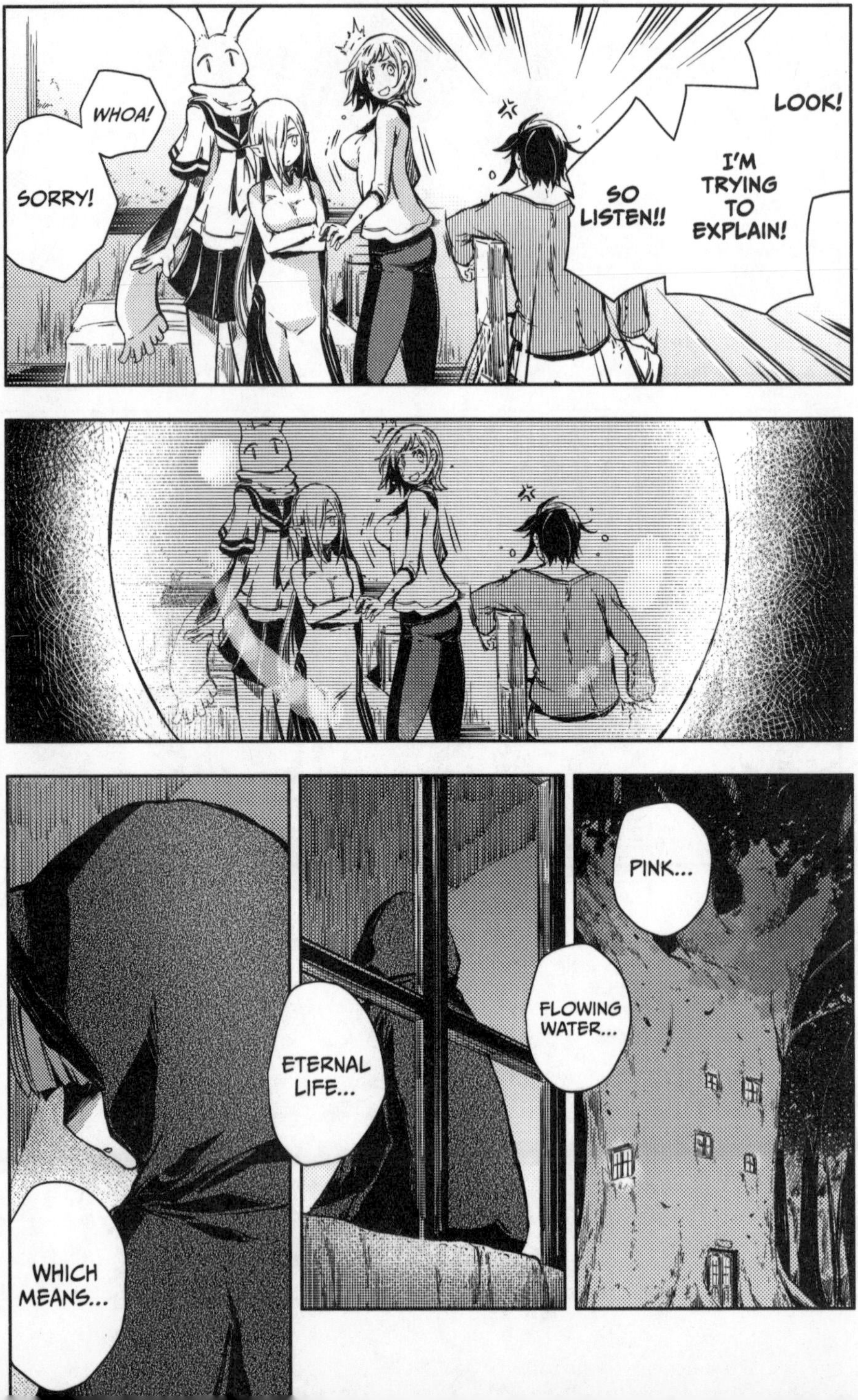
LOOK!
I'M TRYING TO EXPLAIN!
SO LISTEN!!
WHOA!
SORRY!
PINK...
FLOWING WATER...
ETERNAL LIFE...
WHICH MEANS...

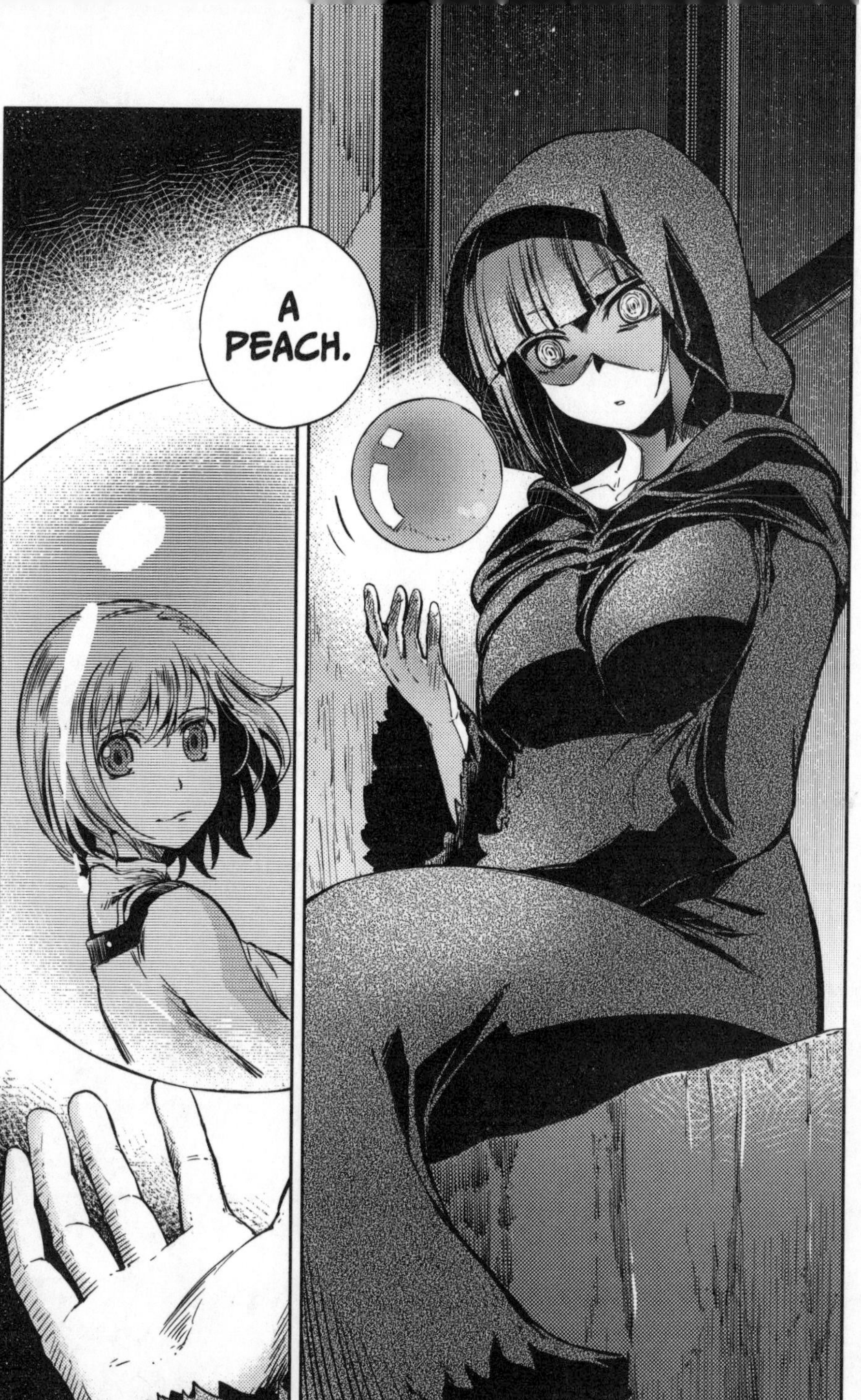
A PEACH.

CONTINUED IN VOLUME 3

PEACH BOY RIVERSIDE

See
you...

...next
time.

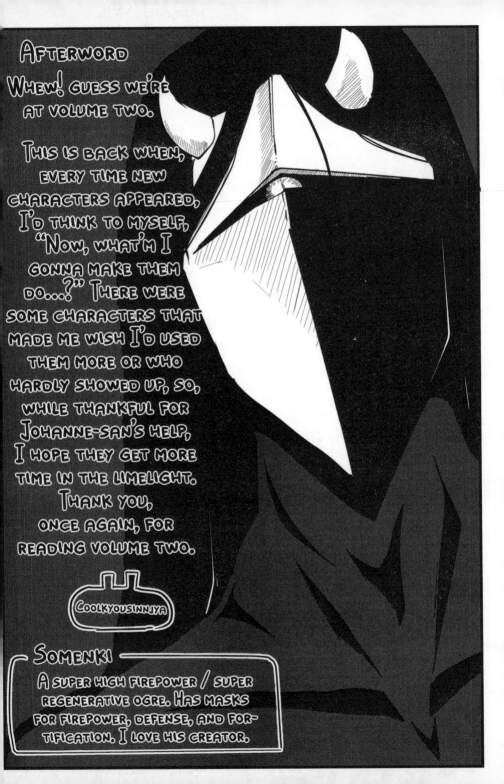

AFTERWORD

WHEW! GUESS WE'RE AT VOLUME TWO.

THIS IS BACK WHEN, EVERY TIME NEW CHARACTERS APPEARED, I'D THINK TO MYSELF, "NOW, WHAT'M I GONNA MAKE THEM DO...?" THERE WERE SOME CHARACTERS THAT MADE ME WISH I'D USED THEM MORE OR WHO HARDLY SHOWED UP, SO, WHILE THANKFUL FOR JOHANNE-SAN'S HELP, I HOPE THEY GET MORE TIME IN THE LIMELIGHT. THANK YOU, ONCE AGAIN, FOR READING VOLUME TWO.

COOLKYOUSINNJYA

SOMENKI

A SUPER HIGH FIREPOWER / SUPER REGENERATIVE OGRE. HAS MASKS FOR FIREPOWER, DEFENSE, AND FORTIFICATION. I LOVE HIS CREATOR.

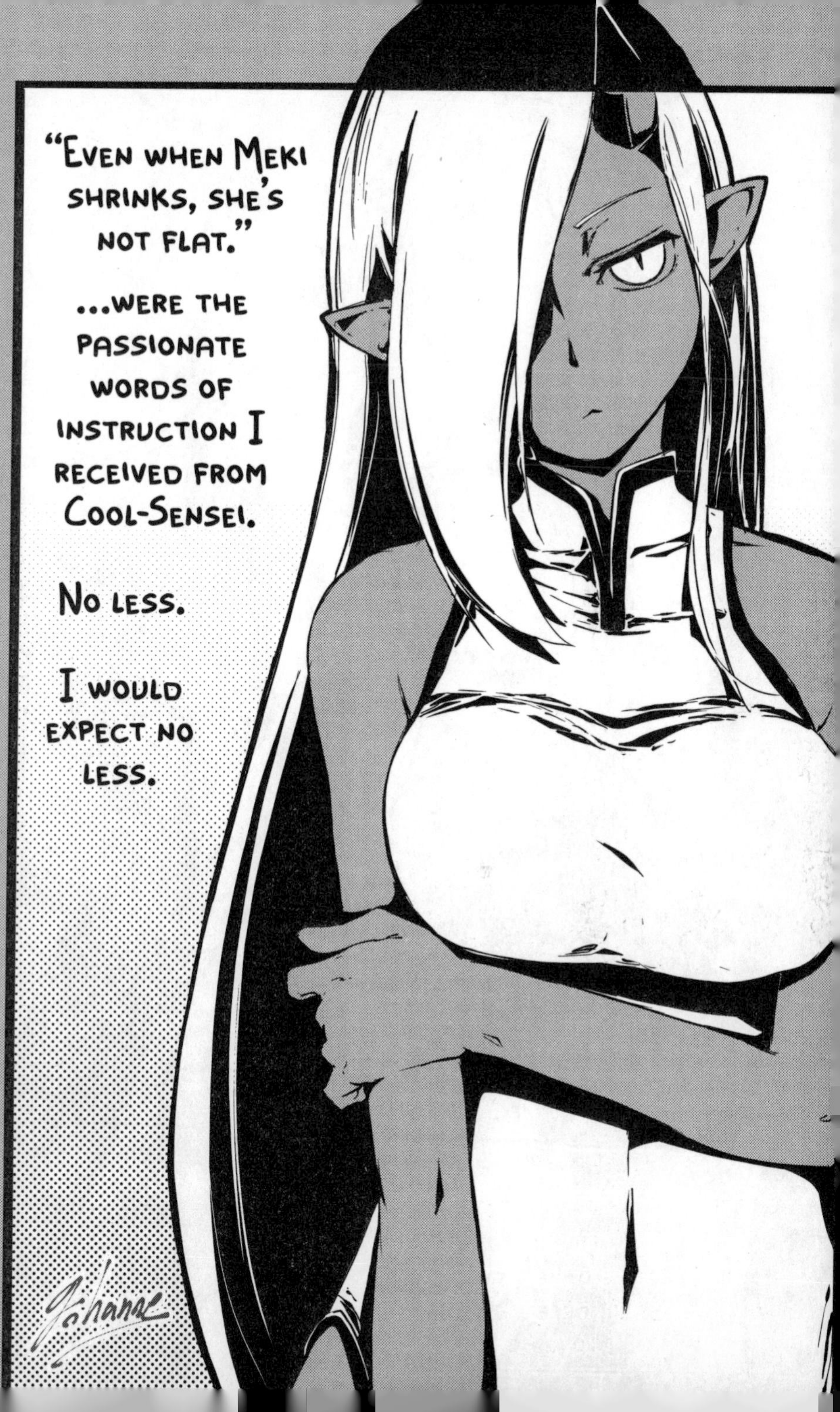
"Even when Meki shrinks, she's not flat."
...were the passionate words of instruction I received from Cool-Sensei.
No less.
I would expect no less.

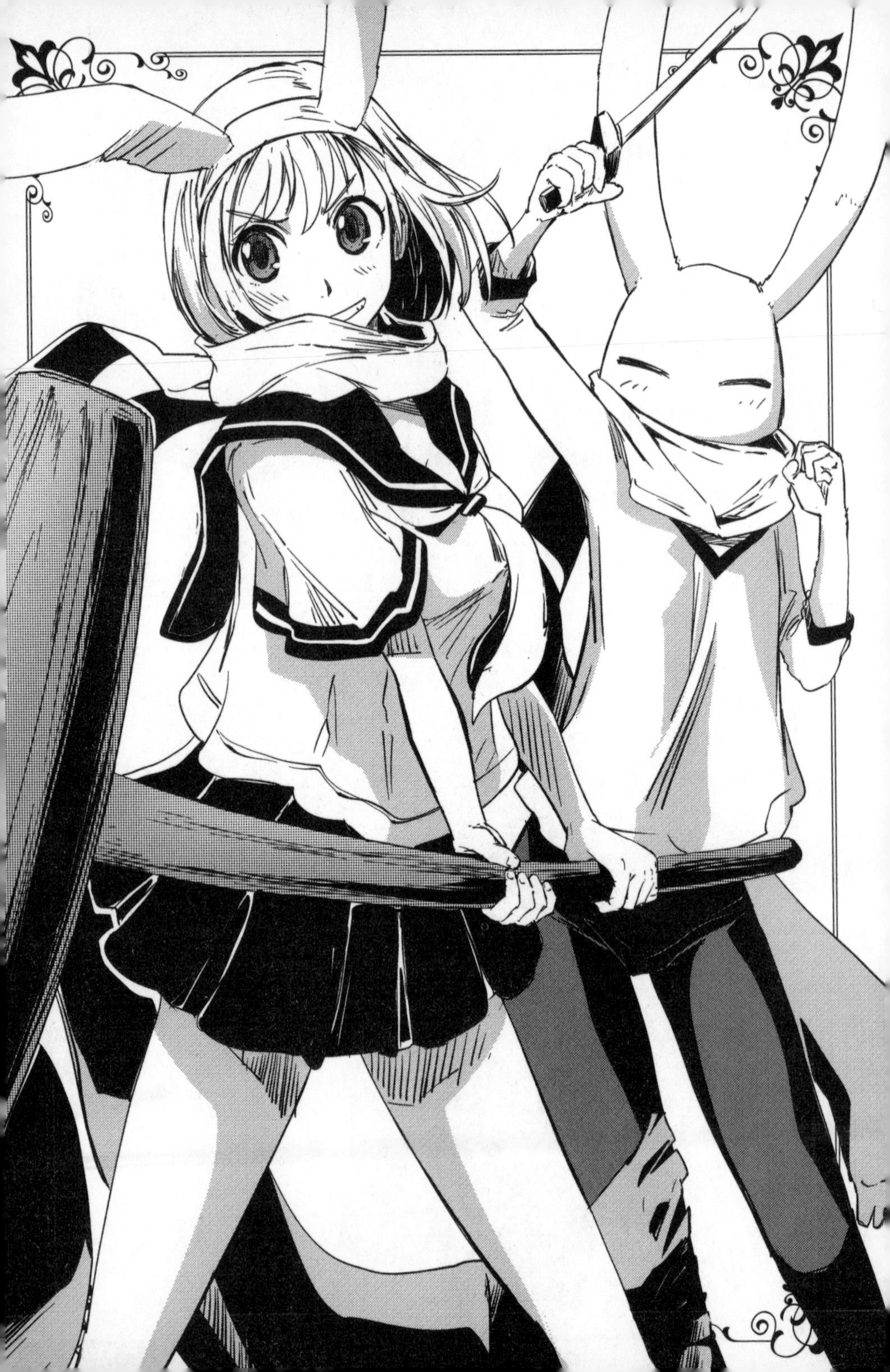

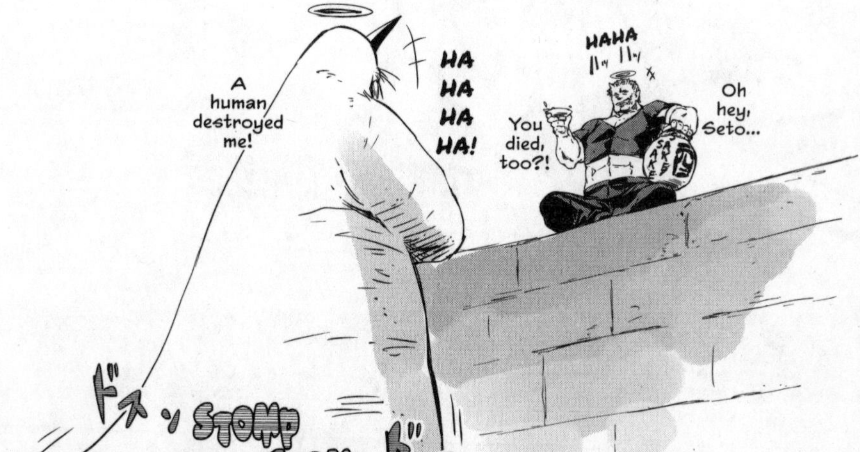
Oh hey, Seto...
HAHA ハッハッ
You died, too?!
HA HA HA HA!
A human destroyed me!
ドスッ STOMP
STOMP ドスッ

The boys are back, in 400-page hardcovers that are as pretty and badass as they are!

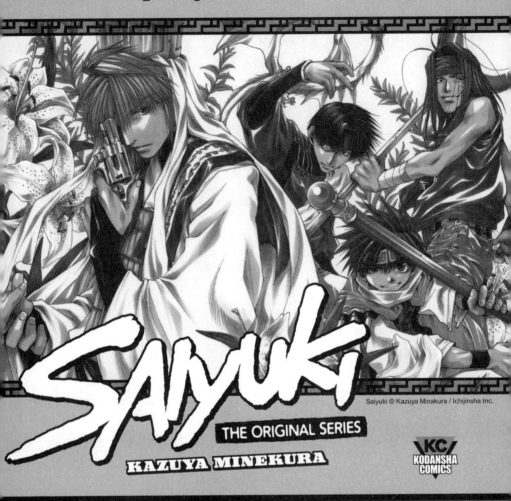

Saiyuki © Kazuya Minakura / Ichijinsha Inc.

SAIYUKI
THE ORIGINAL SERIES
KAZUYA MINEKURA

KC KODANSHA COMICS

"AN EDGY COMIC LOOK AT AN ANCIENT CHINESE TALE." —YALSA

Genjo Sanzo is a Buddhist priest in the city of Togenkyo, which is being ravaged by yokai spirits that have fallen out of balance with the natural order. His superiors send him on a journey far to the west to discover why this is happening and how to stop it. His companions are three yokai with human souls. But this is no day trip — the four will encounter many discoveries and horrors on the way.

FEATURES NEW TRANSLATION, COLOR PAGES, AND BEAUTIFUL WRAPAROUND COVER ART!

Knight of the ICE ©Yayoi Ogawa/Kodansha Ltd.

Yayoi Ogawa

SKATING THRILLS AND ICY CHILLS WITH THIS NEW TINGLY ROMANCE SERIES!

A rom-com on ice, perfect for fans of *Princess Jellyfish* and *Wotakoi*. Kokoro is the talk of the figure-skating world, winning trophies and hearts. But little do they know... he's actually a huge nerd! From the beloved creator of *You're My Pet* (*Tramps Like Us*).

Chitose is a serious young woman, working for the health magazine *SASSO*. Or at least, she would be, if she wasn't constantly getting distracted by her childhood friend, international figure skating star Kokoro Kijinami! In the public eye and on the ice, Kokoro is a gallant, flawless knight, but behind his glittery costumes and breathtaking spins lies a secret: He's actually a hopelessly romantic otaku, who can only land his quad jumps when Chitose is on hand to recite a spell from his favorite magical girl anime!

KC
KODANSHA
COMICS

CUTE ANIMALS AND LIFE LESSONS, PERFECT FOR ASPIRING PET VETS OF ALL AGES!

Yuzu the Pet Vet © Mingo Ito / NIPPON COLUMBIA CO., LTD. / Kodansha Ltd

KODANSHA COMICS

YUZU THE PET VET

1

BY

MINGO ITO

In collaboration with

NIPPON COLUMBIA CO., LTD.

For an 11-year-old, Yuzu has a lot on her plate. When her mom gets sick and has to be hospitalized, Yuzu goes to live with her uncle who runs the local veterinary clinic. Yuzu's always been scared of animals, but she tries to help out. Through all the tough moments in her life, Yuzu realizes that she can help make things all right with a little help from her animal pals, peers, and kind grown-ups.

Every new patient is a furry friend in the making!

The adorable new odd-couple cat comedy manga from the creator of the beloved *Chi's Sweet Home*, in full color!

Praise for Chi's Sweet Home

"Nearly impossible to turn away... a true all-ages title that anyone, young or old, cat lover or not, will enjoy. The stories will bring a smile to your face and warm your heart."

—School Library Journal

Sue & Tai-chan
Konami Kanata

Sue is an aging housecat who's looking forward to living out her life in peace... but her plans change when the mischievous black tomcat Tai-chan enters the picture! Hey! Sue never signed up to be a catsitter! *Sue & Tai-chan* is the latest from the reigning meow-narch of cute kitty comics, Konami Kanata.

KC KODANSHA COMICS

Young characters and steampunk setting, like *Howl's Moving Castle* and *Battle Angel Alita*

Beyond the Clouds © 2018 Nicke / Ki-oon

A boy with a talent for machines and a mysterious girl whose wings he's fixed will take you beyond the clouds! In the tradition of the high-flying, resonant adventure stories of Studio Ghibli comes a gorgeous tale about the longing of young hearts for adventure and friendship!

SAINT ☆ YOUNG MEN

A LONG AWAITED ARRIVAL IN PREMIUM 2-IN-1 HARDCOVER

After centuries of hard work, Jesus and Buddha take a break from their heavenly duties to relax among the people of Japan, and their adventures in this lighthearted buddy comedy are sure to bring mirth and merriment to all!

"Brilliant...the physical comedy and facial expressions will make you literally LOL."
—Sam Humphries
(host of *DC Daily*; writer, *Green Lanterns, Legendary Star-Lord*)

PERFECT WORLD

Rie Aruga

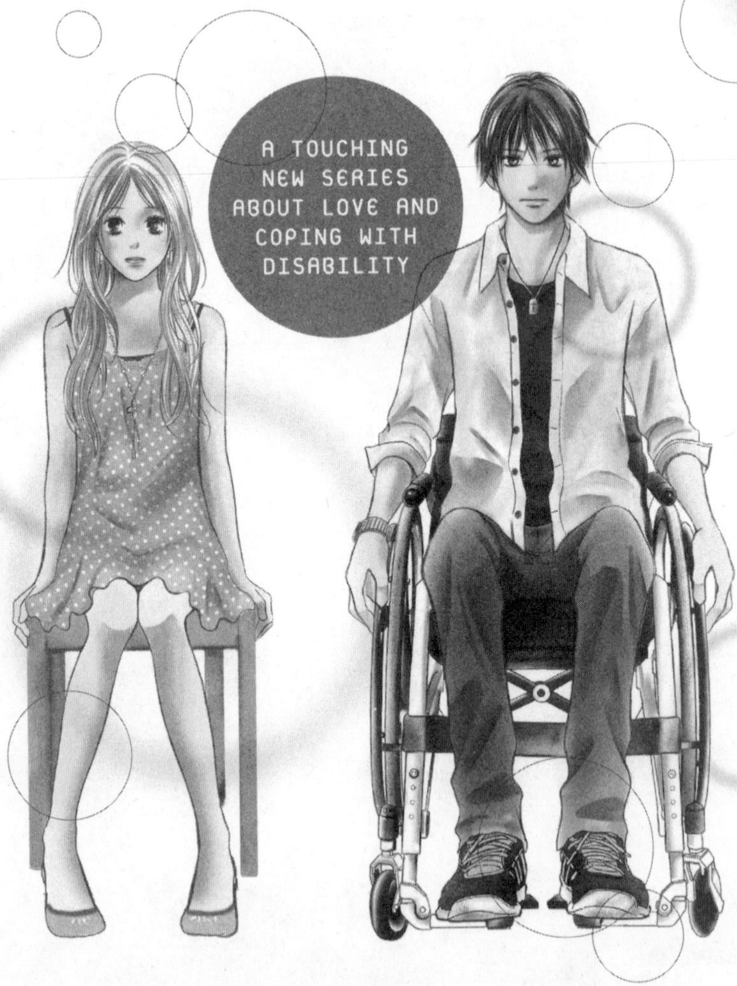
A TOUCHING NEW SERIES ABOUT LOVE AND COPING WITH DISABILITY

An office party reunites Tsugumi with her high school crush Itsuki. He's realized his dream of becoming an architect, but along the way, he experienced a spinal injury that put him in a wheelchair. Now Tsugumi's rekindled feelings will butt up against prejudices she never considered — and Itsuki will have to decide if he's ready to let someone into his heart...

"Depicts with great delicacy and courage the difficulties some with disabilities experience getting involved in romantic relationships... Rie Aruga refuses to romanticize, pushing her heroine to face the reality of disability. She invites her readers to the same tasks of empathy, knowledge and recognition."
—Slate.fr

"An important entry [in manga romance]... The emotional core of both plot and characters indicates thoughtfulness... [Aruga's] research is readily apparent in the text and artwork, making this feel like a real story."
—Anime News Network

KC KODANSHA COMICS

A SMART, NEW ROMANTIC COMEDY FOR FANS OF *SHORTCAKE CAKE* AND *TERRACE HOUSE!*

A romance manga starring high school girl Meeko, who learns to live on her own in a boarding house whose living room is home to the odd (but handsome) Matsunaga-san. She begins to adjust to her new life away from her parents, but Meeko soon learns that no matter how far away from home she is, she's still a young girl at heart — especially when she finds herself falling for Matsunaga-san.

A Kodansha Comics Trade Paperback Original
Peach Boy Riverside 2 copyright © 2016 Coolkyousinnjya/Johanne
English translation copyright © 2021 Coolkyousinnjya/Johanne

Published in the United States by Kodansha Comics, an imprint of Kodansha USA Publishing, LLC, New York.

Publication rights for this English edition arranged through Kodansha Ltd., Tokyo.

First published in Japan in 2016 by Kodansha Ltd., Tokyo.

ISBN 978-1-64651-340-6

Original cover design by Tadashi Hisamochi (hive&co.,ltd.)

Printed in the United States of America.

www.kodansha.us

1st Printing
Translation: Steven LeCroy
Lettering: Andrew Copeland
Additional Lettering: Belynda Ungurath
Editing: Michal Zuckerman
YKS Services LLC/SKY Japan, Inc.
Kodansha Comics edition cover design by Adam Del Re

Publisher: Kiichiro Sugawara

Director of publishing services: Ben Applegate
Associate director of operations: Stephen Pakula
Publishing services managing editors: Madison Salters, Alanna Ruse
Production managers: Emi Lotto, Angela Zurlo
Logo and character art ©Kodansha USA Publishing, LLC